Getting Ghost

Getting Ghost

Two Young Lives and the Struggle
for the Soul of an American City

LUKE BERGMANN

THE NEW PRESS

NEW YORK
LONDON

Requests for permission to reproduce selections from this book should be mailed to:
Permissions Department, The New Press,
38 Greene Street, New York, NY 10013.

Published in the United States by The New Press, New York, 2008
Distributed by W. W. Norton & Company, Inc., New York

LIBRARY OF CONGRESS CATALOGING-IN-PUBLICATION DATA
Bergmann, Luke.
Getting ghost : two young lives and the struggle for the soul of an American city /
Luke Bergmann.
p.   cm.
Includes bibliographical references and index.
ISBN 978-1-59558-139-6 (hc.)
1. Juvenile delinquents—Michigan—Detroit.   2. Drug
dealers—Michigan—Detroit.   3. African Americans—Michigan—Detroit.
4. Detroit (Mich.)—Race relations.   I. Title.
HV9106.D48B47   2008
364.3609774'34—dc22   2008025065

The New Press was established in 1990 as a not-for-profit alternative to the large,
commercial publishing houses currently dominating the book publishing industry.
The New Press operates in the public interest rather than for private gain, and
is committed to publishing, in innovative ways, works of educational, cultural,
and community value that are often deemed insufficiently profitable.

www.thenewpress.com

Composition by NK Graphics
This book was set in Fairfield
Map on page xi by Rob Carmichael

Printed in the United States of America

2   4   6   8   10   9   7   5   3   1

In Loving Memory of Ron Gu's

Contents

Acknowledgments
ix

Dramatis Personae
xiii

Chapter 1: Introduction
1

PART I: STOLEN STREETS AND PROMISED LANDS

Chapter 2: Detroit Revisited, Revisionist History
33

Chapter 3: Renewal, Relocation, and Riot
43

Chapter 4: Called by a Holy Name
59

PART II: DREAMHOUSE

Chapter 5: Families and Fortunes, Spots and Homes
79

Chapter 6: The Thickness of Blood
111

PART III: TIME MACHINERY

Chapter 7: Playgrounds and Punishment
147

Chapter 8: Across the Street
173

PART IV: OWNERS, OCCUPANTS, AND OUTCASTS

Chapter 9: Neighborhood Watching
197

Chapter 10: Of Hot Dogs and Heroin
223

Chapter 11: Being Seen
258

Notes
285

Index
307

Acknowledgments

Over the past several years, as my own personal life has gone through a significant transformation—culminating with the birth of my beautiful son, Esai—the stories and lives in *Getting Ghost* have been constant companions. Many of the central "characters" in the book, whose names I've changed, will probably be the most eager readers of this narrative. It is to these folks, of course, that I owe the greatest debts of gratitude. This text is woven out of their experiences and lives. And for their willingness to bring me into the most intimate corners of their world, for their courage, respect, friendship, and faith, I am so grateful.

This book began a number of years ago as a doctoral dissertation in the Department of Anthropology and the School of Social Work at the University of Michigan, and many people at Michigan helped me along the way. Tom Fricke, in whom I discovered a shared obsession with James Agee, encouraged me to work beyond the disciplinary conventions I'd been trained to observe. Beth Reed, Rosemary Sarri, Carol Boyd, and Bill Birdsall were all guardian angels for me while I was living in Detroit. Janet Finn, Alford Young Jr., and Fernando Coronil helped me get my head straight at various points. And for their support, encouragement, and kindness about my fledgling efforts to do this work, I want to thank John Ramsburgh, Jeffrey Shook, Alex Ralph, Sebastian Matthews, Greg Harris, James Reische, and Sarah Munro. Skip Rappaport was also in my mind and heart as I was working on *Getting Ghost*. I hope it does not disappoint him.

At the University of California at San Francisco and Berkeley, I have benefited from the advice and guidance of Philippe Bourgois, Deborah Gordon, Paul Rabinow, Jeff Schonberg, Kelly Knight, Nick Bartlett, and Laura Schmidt.

Irene Skolnick believed in this book from the get-go and secured the perfect home for it. I feel so fortunate that The New Press exists. Andy Hsiao got support for the manuscript at The New Press, and Furaha Norton has been heroic in making it a clearer, better told story. Needless to say, I bear full responsibility for any of the text's shortcomings.

This work could not have been completed without financial support from the University of Michigan Substance Abuse Research Center, the Rackham School of Graduate Studies and the Advanced Study Center at the University of Michigan, the Agency for Healthcare Research and Quality, the Institute for Health Policy Studies at the University of California at San Francisco, and the Prevention Research Center and UC Berkeley School of Public Health. I am grateful to all.

For my family, this project has shadowed me like a second life. All six of my wonderful sisters have lent their sympathetic ears and helped me to stay centered. Andrea Sankar has been an important source of intellectual and logistical help. Aunt Renee McCoy took me in and continues to inspire me. Taya Nelson picked me up when I was falling apart on many occasions and has consistently steered me toward deeper explorations of the emotional dimensions of this work. Eric Nelson has enriched this project with good humor and warm support. Frithjof Bergmann has been, for many years now, my closest and most valuable intellectual ally. Jessie Flynn was accommodating and loving throughout the many years that I spent in and around Detroit. And finally, Rosemary Polanco has been a pitch-perfect editor, brutally honest sounding board, and incredible mother to our lively son as the book has gone through its final trimester. It is so rare that any of us find someone whose opinion and judgment we implicitly trust. I am lucky indeed.

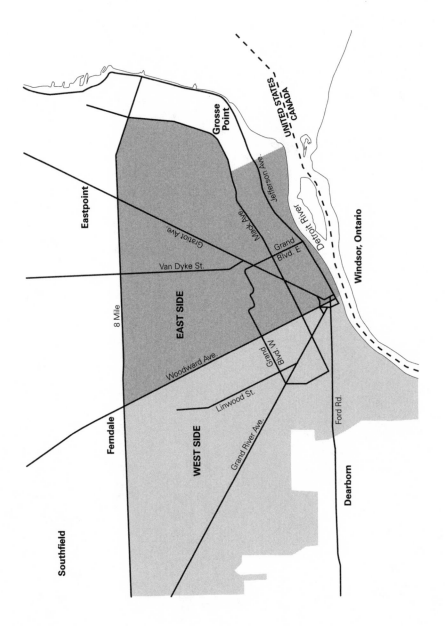

Dramatis Personae

EAST SIDE

Dude Freeman, Family, and Friends

Dude Freeman	16-year-old East Sider

Ruby	Mother
Forrester	Older brother
Felicity	Older sister
Evelyn (Evie)	Older sister
Elvin	Evie's twin
May	Oldest sister
Lydia	Paternal aunt
Marvin	Father

Dude's Friends

Billy
Chewie
Treb
Aisha
Janet
Walker

Detention Facility

Cedric Mann
Branford Wilson
Fredrick Nelson
Bosworth
Raul
Willis Harrison
Justin
Bernardo
Ms. Bailey
Mr. Mallard

WEST SIDE

Rodney Phelps, Family, and Friends

Rodney Phelps	19-year-old West Sider
Maria	Mother
Antonio	Younger brother
Julie	Older sister
Princess	Older sister
Annie	Girlfriend

The Dexter Boys

Sheed
Kilo
Loc
Hector
Shell
Ebo
Oscar
Timmy Mason
Rabbit
Jeremiah
Z
Dante
Marley

Coney Island

Larry
Mikey
Polly
Patty

Household on Pingree

Esther
Juwan
Benjamin
Dwayne

Getting Ghost

1

Introduction

Many die too late, and a few die too early.
The doctrine still sounds strange: "Die at the right time!"
     —Friedrich Nietzsche, *Also Sprach Zarathustra*

BIFF: He had the wrong dreams. All, all, wrong.
HAPPY: Don't say that!
BIFF: He never knew who he was.
CHARLEY: Nobody dast blame this man. . . . Nobody dast blame this man.
A salesman is got to dream, boy. It comes with the territory.
     —Arthur Miller, *Death of a Salesman*

Having escaped the fires, they trudged in tattered, soot-stained clothing toward a busy street where they might find help. Somewhere, a keen-eyed photographer for the *Detroit Free Press* captured the young black family, the morning after the first day of rioting in the city, as they walked with their few salvaged belongings underneath a row of smoldering brick chimneys, which shot through the collapsed houses around them.

 Though the riots of summer 1967 spread from one corner of Detroit's interior to the other, consuming building after building on the East and West Sides, and up and down some of the city's most bustling streets, the houses shown burning in the *Free Press* photograph, just off Linwood Street between Pingree and Blaine, represent the center of what would be the city's most devastating residential damage. Nearly the entire square block burned down after wind-borne embers from a nearby business landed on the roofs of several houses.

Over thirty years later, when I moved into the bottom floor of a two-family flat on Pingree, in one of the spared homes across the street from what had been this residential conflagration, the chimneys were long since toppled and cleared away, and a city park had been made of the vacant field left by the fire. Now, when I stood on the worn oak floor in my room and looked out the window, I could see chain-link softball backstops facing each other from the corners of the park and a wavy asphalt basketball court that had been built off to the side.

But despite the transformation of the razed block into a minimally functional playground, the neighborhood wore most of the changes of the previous half-century like a raised scar. The Linwood and Dexter area, on the near northwest side of the city, blocks away from the former headquarters of General Motors and the old Motown studios, was typical of Detroit in that its disjunctive history was plainly evident to the naked eye. The neighborhood's conversion from a middle-class Jewish enclave lined with delis and other shops into a symbol of the late-century urban crisis—vacant lots, abandoned houses, closed storefronts, and exclusively African American residents—had been less gradual than punctuated by episodes of extraordinarily rapid demographic, infrastructural, and institutional change. Even relatively young people in the neighborhood, none of whom had lived through the postwar transformation of the city, could recognize and would acknowledge this historical discontinuity. They knew that something cataclysmic had happened in their city. And they understood that Detroit had become an emblem of both the promise and disappointment of recent U.S. history—at the cutting edge of this country's successes and failures—and a cautionary tale in which they might figure as important players. More than this, young people in our neighborhood felt that dramatic shifts were still afoot, that with big developments downtown the city was tilting toward change again.

As the city around them was changing, young men and boys on the street where I was living were themselves elusive subjects, always "getting ghost" they would say, as they floated in and out of the drug trade and weaved their way through lives of economic enterprise and circumscribed opportunity. As young drug dealers strive to find ways toward "legal" jobs and straight lives, getting ghost is a rich metaphor—for leaving a scene, for quitting the trade, and for their own mortality. Despite their occasional bravado, all of the young people on the block were hoping to avoid the early and ignominious deaths of so many young black street salesmen—common but still extraordinary in Detroit's poor neighborhoods, which are populated both with the old ghosts of those who left long ago and the young ghosts of those more recently lost.

I was there among the ghosts of Detroit, sometimes seeing them, often being mistaken for one, trying to understand and write about the Motor City in the postindustrial age and the lives of young street drug dealers there with whom I lived, worked, and moved. And the more I learned, the more I knew that I would need to listen to the haunting voices of Detroit's past. For nothing more clearly illuminates and animates the social and symbolic significance of drug dealing on the streets of Detroit than the fiery, deadly, mortifying, and exultant history of the city's racial and class politics.

In matters of public policy and opinion, with startling and historically unprecedented rates of incarceration and undiminished social inequality, neither guilt-ridden apologists nor the admonishing bootstrappers currently holding forth are doing enough to help us understand the complex lives and self-reflective perceptions of young African Americans in our most destitute and devastated urban centers.

In a context shaped by the historical struggle over and for the soul of Detroit, I have tried to document something beyond the social mechanics of petty drug dealing in urban America, to look beyond the ordering or disordering *function* of drug dealing in black neighborhoods, or the moral liabilities and threatened masculinities that it is presumed to represent. *Getting Ghost*, rather, is about how the drug trade and the legacies of the city's postwar history become interwoven with the always emerging identities of young people in Detroit. It is about how the drug trade shapes the meanings that they ascribe to the lives and deaths in their midst, and the basic spaces that constitute their experience: their homes, their neighborhoods, and their city.

Shooting, Strolling, Rolling

On a late summer evening in the year 2000, I joined several boys from the block on Pingree, standing with them in a loose gathering against the chest-high fence surrounding the park. As on many nights during the warm months of the year, they were shooting dice against the street curb for small bills. I stood behind Juwan, a nineteen-year-old who lived in a room directly above mine in a house just a few yards down the block.[1] He crouched at the center of the oval congregation and announced his intention to roll: "7, 11, baby! No 68s." Both the confident and more dubious members of the group dropped dollar bills on the ground with a kind of conspicuous disregard, until there was a deep pile on the street. Juwan shook and blew the dice in his loosely clenched fist and tossed them against the curb, snapping hard like he was striking a flint. Nothing. He lunged over them and swept his arm around, gathering the green plastic cubes in a single motion. They clicked against one another like marbles in a child's pocket. He threw again and again without winning or losing, as the others fidgeted and second-guessed, pulling up and putting down bills, always against round objections, with the waning and waxing of their uncertainty.

Finally, Juwan hit seven. The dice had scarcely come to a rest when the various bets on the ground had been collected. Juwan was $15 richer and ready to quit. He was supposed to go home to his two-year-old daughter and her mother, who had just returned from a class at a local junior college and was in no mood for dealing with the block craps game. Several minutes before, she had leaned out of a small square window on the second floor of the house, yelling up the street for him to come and help get dinner ready.

Before heading home, though, Juwan walked up toward the liquor store on the corner of Pingree and Linwood. The store is in a looming cinder block structure, painted bright white, with red and blue stripes wrapping around it like a birthday bow. It sits adjacent to the New Bethel Baptist Church, a gravitational center of civil rights activity during the 1960s, the site of a policeman's murder in 1963, and the place where Aretha Franklin first took the stage. There is a day care center across Pingree and an ice cream shop down the street. And the Shrine of the Black Madonna, another hub of political activity during the civil rights era, is just a few blocks to the south, near Grand Boulevard. Yet for most of its length through the near north side of the city, between Davison Avenue and Grand Boulevard, Linwood is block after block of empty, boarded storefronts; collapsed, charcoaled structures; and vacant lots.

Through the liquor store's double doors, a crowd of black customers waited in the aisles with bottles of beer and paper lottery numbers, loaves of bread, cans of beans, and cartons of milk to pay at the glass partition that spans the width of the store, sealing the owners and customers off from one another. Under fluorescent light, the Iraqi proprietors, the only nonblack fixtures in the neighborhood (besides me), looked past their own reflections in the glass. Juwan was there to pick up a Swisher Sweet, so he could roll a blunt for his girlfriend when he got home. In the vestibule, between two sets of glass double doors, a heroin addict leaning against the wall seemed to brighten with optimism as Juwan walked through. When he saw me he nodded and clicked his tongue with a polite, almost formal smile, and then looked out the door after us, as if he thought we were being followed. I was used to the inevitable, suspicious, sidelong glances that I'd get when walking around the neighborhood, even though many people there knew me by name. Though I tried to dress inconspicuously, with my jeans baggy and low and my shirts pressed and large, and though I kept my head shaved and hidden beneath a baseball cap a good deal of the time, being white in black Detroit gave me a visceral, stomach-churning sense for the intensity of racial politics in the daily lives of black Detroiters. This was especially true in the case of older folks, who were the only people ever to treat me with explicit hostility while I lived in Detroit. Even when driving around, I could feel the hot, worried stares of people in the neighborhood. "You got anything for me?" the addict asked Juwan. "I can get you, dog," said Juwan gently, without looking at him. "Oh, that's great," he blurted. " 'Cuz, you know, I was trying to get something this morning. And I couldn't find you; I couldn't find anybody out here. So I was glad when I seen you coming through." "Alright," said Juwan, trying to quiet the man's spasmodic expressions of gratitude. When we left, Juwan's customer followed us out the door and down Pingree, until Juwan reached into his pocket and pulled out a small paper pack of heroin and handed it to him, in exchange for $10. Juwan said that he was glad to have gotten rid of his last pack. He'd almost forgotten it was there.

We continued down the street, passing about five houses and one vacant lot, and then loped up the stairs of the oblong two-family flat and went inside. Juwan followed me into the downstairs apartment, where his Aunt Esther had left a tray of barbecued meat for her nephews. With no children of her own, but two younger sisters, Esther is the matriarch of the family. An ordained minister and successful public health official for the city, she was a guardian angel of sorts for her youngest sister's kids, all of whom lived in the upstairs flat with their mother.

The house had been bequeathed to all three sisters by their parents, and most of the first floor had been left exactly as Esther's mother had decorated it many years earlier. The walls were painted in dark colors—maroons and greens—and were covered high and low with ornately framed paintings, prints, and old photographs from disparate eras and aesthetic sensibilities. Antique furniture and old clocks were piled up against the walls and seemed to defy gravity as they leaned out into the living and dining rooms. Aged copies of the Virginia Park newsletter, with articles written in the early 1970s about efforts to rehabilitate the neighborhood in the wake of the riots, were stacked on bureaus and bookshelves.

At the dining room table downstairs, several kids from the block sat around a Monopoly board and distributed slips of colorful play money. They were drinking beer and smoking cigarettes. Juwan sat down in an empty chair and demanded that he be dealt into the game. "Who's runnin' the bank?" he growled, with his elbows on the table. They were dropping $50, $100, and $500 bills, in orange, pink, and green; moving houses; passing go; and going to jail. The rapper DMX barked in the background.

A couple of hours later we could hear yelling upstairs. Juwan's mother, who weighed close to three hundred pounds and never had a difficult time being heard, was screaming at someone. And then we heard the muted thunder of multiple sets of feet across the length of the upstairs apartment. Dust sprinkled down from the ceiling as Juwan's mother's voice grew louder, and echoed into the stairwell toward the front of the house. Then, like the roll of a kettledrum, we could hear one set of feet tumbling down the staircase. Benjamin, her second-youngest son—twelve at the time—burst wide-eyed through the front door of Esther's flat. He looked behind him and rushed past us with his arms flailing, scattering Monopoly money on to the floor. He disappeared toward his Aunt Esther's room at the back of the first-floor apartment, with his mouth open, gasping for breath.

Benjamin's mother had caught him with a small, cloudy, crumpled baggie with several crack rocks inside, which he had been cavalierly tossing from hand to hand, trying to impress a couple of his older female cousins upstairs. Now, having escaped her clutches, he sought refuge with his auntie. But a few moments later, Benjamin came running through the dining room again, this time followed by Esther, who carried a looped belt in her right hand; her intense, angry eyes bulged from under her brow. "Oh, you can run, boy!" she yelled after him, as he slammed the front door and darted outside, only forestalling the punishment that would inevitably come.

While everyone supposed that Juwan was dealing drugs on the block, Benjamin was so young. His voice was still high, and his face was smooth and chubby; he would collect stray dogs from the neighborhood and bring them home, begging his mother and auntie to keep them, then crying when he'd have to let them go. That he might be embroiled in the neighborhood drug trade startled the elder women in the household.

But the crashing, stomping weight of his mother's response, and Esther's soon to follow, had other origins as well. Their ferocious reactions to Benjamin's transgression grew out of a deep reservoir of confusion and sorrow in which the whole family had been caught since the brutal murder of another of Esther's nephews the previous fall.

Last Fall, a Suit, and a Sermon

Esther's oldest nephew, Dwayne, had been a bit player in a small but lucrative neighborhood weed ring; he sold marijuana out of his upstairs apartment in a house immediately behind our place on Pingree. On the morning after Thanksgiving a young man broke into the house. The intruder found Dwayne in the stairwell leading up to his flat, and shot him nine times as Dwayne's body fell and slid to the bottom landing. Dwayne was twenty-two when he died.

Three days later, on the morning of his funeral, the autumn sun shone through the tops of the buildings on Linwood, casting a sepia light over the New Bethel Baptist Church.

As were so many in the neighborhood and throughout Detroit, this was a young person's funeral, and the mourners looked like lost children as they congregated in clusters outside and stood somberly in the antechamber of the church. Most of the young guys wore gaudy gold-framed, tinted glasses and were lavishly dressed in colorful leather jackets over their starched white shirt collars and pressed black pants. Juwan was in a circular gathering with his brothers and others from the neighborhood, leaning against their Aunt Esther's black truck. They were crying, some with their heads bowed, wiping their eyes with the backs of their hands. They passed a bottle of Hennessey Cognac, pouring some on to the ground to honor Dwayne and others whom they had lost.

Esther circulated among those on the street in front, gently assembling Dwayne's extended family into a long line starting at the wide front doors of the church. As the procession disappeared into the building, friends filed in behind and settled into the arcing pews, which descended toward the altar at the far end of the cavernous space. Inside, the church was decorated sparingly, with big simple banners on the back walls announcing the commencement of various fund-raising programs—"Bucks for Jesus." In front of the altar, Dwayne's body lay in an open casket, with a bright stage light shining into the pillowy white lining of the casket's propped open top.

Soon a line of mourners began to file from left to right in front of his body. Some cried quietly while they strode past, holding a clenched fist under their noses. Others were overcome, writhing and swaying as they stopped to look, heads hanging over, into the illuminated box. Several crumpled into the pews or on to the floor in front of Dwayne. White-clad nurses rushed to them, wrapping arms around their backs and pulling out handkerchiefs for mopping up their tears and wiping their running noses.

The cathedral ceiling swallowed up the sobs of the women, as if they were moaning into water. But the deep voices of the men carried differently. Dwayne's father hadn't known his son well. He and Esther's sister had split up many years earlier, and he had long ago left Detroit. While others circled past the casket, Dwayne's father sat toward the back of the church in a dark blue denim suit, his face hidden under a white riding cap. He was leaning forward, with his arms in his lap. As the assembled continued their grim parade, Dwayne's mother walked up the long aisle between the pews and stopped at the row where Dwayne's father sat. She reached across people sitting to his left and pulled at his arm. "Come down," she said, her voice loving but firm, like an older sibling's. "Come down." He didn't move, initially, but eventually was pulled to his feet by those on either side of him. She held him under the arm, and they shuffled slowly down the aisle.

When they reached the body, Dwayne's father's knees seemed to buckle and he released a deep wailing cry that careened off the far walls of the church. He moaned as he lay his head on and embraced the closed half of the casket, holding his body to it as if it were floating debris, to save himself from drowning in an open ocean. "My little baby! My baby boy!" He rested there, with his face folded against the gleaming varnished wood, on the edge of the circle of light beaming down from the rafters. The others, now done filing past and back in their seats, had fallen into stunned silence and only began to murmur again as Dwayne's father was led back toward his seat.

Afterward, with his cries still ringing in the room, the formality of the service passed with the warm but indifferent hum of a distant train. There were a few short readings given by young cousins of Dwayne's and a wobbly plea from the presiding clergyman for the young men in attendance not to seek vengeance for his death. When it was over, those at the service walked into the low noon light and scattered toward their cars.

Juwan wasn't talking; he nodded miserably as people swung their arms around him and squeezed his shoulders. I put my hand on his back as I was leaving and told him I'd see him later, but he didn't turn around.

I hugged Esther before getting in my car and driving back downtown toward the juvenile detention facility where I had been spending most days for the previous few months. Once inside, past the sheriffs in front, then the metal detectors and buzzing steel doors, I walked along the main corridor of the facility. Branching off the long hallway are doors to all the residential units, divided by stretches of brightly lit classrooms where detained kids would spend midday hours. The walls dividing the classrooms from the hallway are of reinforced glass, so that guards pacing up and down the length of the facility can easily monitor the youths. Still dressed in my funereal black suit and tie, I was looking for Rodney Phelps, a seventeen-year-old kid who was locked up and awaiting trial for the shooting of someone on a busy corner in the Dexter-Linwood neighborhood, not far from where I lived. Even among the many young faces growing out of identical black, gray, and blue jumpsuits, it was usually easy for me to spot Rodney, with his long straight cornrowed braids, light skin, freckled face, and high forehead. Though the chairs in the rooms were always arranged in rows, Rodney would customarily pull his seat out of formation and lean it against the wall, usually behind the instructor's desk, facing the other kids in the room and allowing him to look back through the panoptic classroom glass.

When he saw me walk in front of his classroom, Rodney burst out laughing. I couldn't hear him squealing, but I could see him flail back hilariously. I put my arms up in the air to acknowledge the sartorial ridicule and then walked by the room, making like I wouldn't tolerate the derision.

In the next room I saw Dude Freeman, who not long before had been locked up for possession of a concealed weapon. About five feet, four inches tall, he stood next to the glass and looked into the hallway, cupping his hands over his eyes to eliminate the reflection. This was his seventh incarceration in the juvenile detention facility, but the first for a serious crime. As he explained to me, he had been riding in a truck with several other friends and a couple of handguns, and they had been pulled over. He tried to run, he said, but was caught by the Detroit police not far from the East Side house where he spent most of his time selling dope. I had met him the day of his most recent arrival, while he was sitting alone on one of the rubber couches in his unit.

While Rodney was the life of the proverbial party on his unit, bright and noisy in a way that seemed reminiscent of his West Side neighborhood, Dude was, at this stage at least, taciturn and reclusive—a quiet kid from the East Side. When he and I first talked, he was reflective about his circumstances, already possessed of a kind of convict's wisdom. His oldest brother was in a maximum-security prison in the remote reaches of northern Michigan, convicted of murder—though Dude insisted he was innocent—and sentenced to life behind bars. Another older brother had been in and out of prison for several years. Meanwhile, Dude's mother had been struggling to mount an appeal against his brother's conviction, but needed dialysis three times a week for her kidney disease and so was having difficulty getting much done. In any case, she was losing faith in the possibility that the judicial system might ever address its error—no matter what she did.

Dude was more than a little cynical about the criminal justice system. But he was philosophical about his and his family's troubles. "Life ain't all peaches and Kool-Aid," he told me. Dude looked forward to beating the concealed weapon case, or winding up with a light probationary sentence— about which he seemed pretty confident—and getting back home. He realized that it was too much for his mother to deal with the stress of his being locked up, with everything else that she was facing, and he wanted to start making money again to help with the household expenses. "Ain't nothing free in this world," he would often say.

Dude said that he didn't care about what the staff at the detention facility or other kids there thought about him, as long as they left him alone. He stood by himself now, and nodded slightly and slowly toward me, stepping back away from the classroom window and pulling his hands off the glass, pointing at my black suit and smirking. "Come talk to me later," he mouthed through the glass.

Willis Harrison, a huge fifteen-year-old with a booming, resonant voice, opened the door to the other classroom and said, "Hey Luuuuuke, what's going on man? You all in black!" I walked up and slapped his outstretched hand. Rodney skipped across the room toward the door. "So what's up man, why you dressed like that? What kind of material is that? . . . How long has it been since you've worn that suit . . . two years? . . . Man, we got to get you some clothes." I told him that I was just returning from the funeral of a friend of mine, on Linwood. Rodney didn't ask who had died, but grabbed the lapel of my old black jacket and considered it disapprovingly. His brow furrowed over his almond eyes, and he smiled sharply. "You wore this in my neighborhood?" "Yeah, man," I answered. Rodney doubled over and whooped with delight, bobbing his head and waving his hand to an imaginary beat. "Who did you see out there? Did you see a dark-skinned cat with a big white winter jacket on?" I said that I might have. "That's my man Sheed! What was he doing out there?" he asked me. "Just walking," I said, not quite sure that I had seen him. "Ohhh, he's just out there like he don't give a fuck! That's my man! My man. . . . Damn, nigga, you was right in the hood!"

One of the detention facility guards, in her gray military uniform and incongruous black tennis shoes, yelled from down the hall that we'd better step through the classroom door or risk getting into trouble. Inside, the facility's volunteer chaplain was sitting on the teacher's desk at the head of the room, and in a voice like a trumpet he bellowed for us to come in and join the flock. "Never too crowded to hear the Lord's word," he sang. "There's always room with God, if you want to sit with him." The chaplain smiled mischievously. Rodney walked in just in front of me and leaned his chair back against the wall. I sat at a desk in the row beside him.

The chaplain, a short but hulking man who had been a professional boxer, firefighter, and actor, acknowledged me with a smile and wink, and then began a kind of Socratic sermon.

"What's your favorite part of the Bible? Do you have a favorite part?" he asked. There was no discernible answer from the kids in the room. "What does the Bible teach you?" he added.

"About God, about where to go, what to do," several voices answered haltingly. "Then why are we all in here?" others asked.

"We made the wrong choices?" a soft voice proposed.

"That's right! You were all disobedient," answered the chaplain with a burst of enthusiasm. "And so you need to figure out how to make it right with the Lord. What if the world was going to end in an hour and a half? What would you do?" The chaplain peered into the eyes of his captive parishioners.

"I would go have fun," someone whispered behind me.

"Yeah, I would get blowed, man."

More audibly, "I would pray. . . . I would ask forgiveness."

"And would he forgive you?"

"Well, if you sincere, then he's going to forgive you, for sure."

"Why?" persisted the chaplain.

"'Cause, he's always forgiving you." A short inmate, dressed in a blue jump-suit typically worn by the smaller kids at the facility, said, "We children anyway, so we need to be forgiven. 'Cause it says in the Bible that he will forgive us."

A skinny inmate with dark black skin interrupted: "Hey, is smoking weed a sin?" Rodney rolled his eyes and smiled out of the side of his mouth. The chaplain responded: "Let me ask you then, when you smoke weed, can you think straight?"

The boys in the room looked at each other and seemed to want to announce, "Yes." The chaplain continued.

"It takes away from what God gave you; anything that takes away from what God gave you is definitely a sin, right?"

Rodney let the front legs of his chair fall to the ground with a hammering thud and giggled.

"But God gave us weed! For real!"

He laughed and shrugged, happy with his irrefutable logic. The chaplain shook his head and smiled.

"I mean, you guys are funny. You're going to justify doing whatever you want to do. If you looked at me funny, and I shot you for it, I could justify it. But God's not going to buy it. 'Cause nobody knows exactly when they're going to die. If they did, then everybody would go to heaven. Some of you are going to barely get in. By the skin of your teeth. No, sir, you don't want to die at the wrong time, 'cuz then there won't be no hope for you. I mean, my man right here," he said, gesturing toward me. "He just this morning been to a funeral. You think, last week, your friend thought he was going to be at his own funeral today?" I shook my head.

"None of the young people dying out here know it's going to happen." The chaplain paused and shook his shoulders.

"Lemmie ask y'all something: How many of you have been to a wedding?"

Not a single person among the thirty or so kids in the room raised his hand.

"Hmmph," grunted the chaplain. "Now, how many of you have been to a funeral?"

He was rewarded with the anticipated response, as all the kids in the room simultaneously lifted their arms in the air and rotated their heads to see the others.

"*That's* what our communities are facing. Young people see so many people dying all the time. And how many of the young people who die in our communities are ready to die? How many are really right with God?"

From his vantage against the wall, Rodney looked around the room at the others, seeming dubiously to check them off one by one.

Detroit, Divisions, and Dealers

When I set out to begin research for this book, I didn't think that I would spend so much time talking and thinking about drug dealing. After establishing an unpaid internship for myself at the juvenile detention facility—which allowed me virtually free movement through the highly restricted institution—I had planned to write a book about the nature of "community reintegration" among youths who had spent time locked up downtown. This would have been a more conventional topic for social scientific research, and probably a more logistically easy undertaking than that which the present book reflects. But telling the stories of young people in Detroit through that institutional frame would have resisted and ultimately twisted their narratives and orientations to the world.

For among the young people locked up in downtown Detroit with whom I spent time, the most important social institution—the locus for their senses of identity, politics, and promise in the world—was the street drug trade. As they would describe it in the detention facility, drug dealing governed the seasonal cycles of their lives and taught them about the nature and power of the state, capitalism, and family. It shaped their senses for the shifting distinction between childhood and adulthood, the length of a natural life, and a timely death.

My interest, in any case, was never simply in matters of institutional politics or community resources. Rather, I imagined people in the juvenile and criminal justice systems, who are some of the most vulnerable residents of Detroit, as unwitting canaries deep within the mines of the city's wild and profound social transformation. In order to understand what was happening in Detroit, we would need to understand their experiences; and in order to understand poor young people there, we would need to understand the broader historical and social forces shaping the city.

Motor City: The Latest Model!

In the 1970s and early 1980s, when I was growing up in Ann Arbor (a short drive but a world away from Detroit), the Motor City seemed to me both mysterious and foreboding. I was, after all, just a kid from a college town that still fiercely guards itself against the construction of tall buildings. I knew Detroit then from two deeply discordant sets of experiences. My step-mother's parents were both lifelong Detroiters—friendly, wide-smiling white Midwesterners with sturdy accents that matched the city's flat topography. Both had suffered through the Depression as children and prospered in postwar Detroit's real estate market. The child of immigrants, my step-mother's dad was a dues-paying member of the Detroit Economic Club, a bastion of white economic power and culture in this otherwise African American city. His wife was from one of the oldest and, before being finan-cially wiped out in the stock market crash, most prosperous families in De-troit. They lived together in a stately home in the precious "Indian Village" enclave, several square blocks of impressive old houses and mansions that now have national historical designation and that have been largely pro-tected from the blight in the immediately surrounding neighborhoods. My stepmother's parents always drove a new, leased General Motors car, and I remember sitting in the back, thrilled by the luxurious plush interior and driven to distraction by the silver buttons that moved the windows up and down. This was Detroit.

But from the vantage of the roomy backseats in their big cars, even to the temporally shortsighted eyes of a small child, their lives in Detroit were from another era. Talk at their house, around the holidays and summer gather-ings, was often of what had gone wrong in the city, or of how dark-skinned people from outside the Village were skulking around, thieving and hopeless.

Meanwhile, my father, a restless professor at the University of Michigan, was making frequent trips into the city to work with laid off and usually des-perate autoworkers at the height of the early 1980s' auto industry crisis in Michigan, when cities like Detroit and Flint were hemorrhaging people and revenues. Tagging along with him, it already seemed to me that Detroit was dead. Its failure was permanent. It had claimed a much-ballyhooed "renaissance" ten years before, but came out of it stillborn. Now, when I visited, all I could do was look around its carcass and wonder, like people must when they visit an Incan ruin, how something so massive and inexorable could have come to such a sudden end.

Twenty years later, I returned to the scene where these early childhood impressions were formed. But when I moved back to Detroit, around the turn of the new millennium, the city was just entering a new period of attempted redevelopment; a *post*industrial, *post*urban renewal, twenty-first-century repackaging. In some ways this was part of a national trend. Beleaguered cities across the country had been working to make and sell themselves anew for the previous couple of decades.[2] Some of these places, like Cleveland and Pittsburgh, are also cities along the rust belt's buckle, and at various points have been the butts of all kinds of cheeky and macabre dystopian humor: of Cleveland, "Anyone who falls into the Cuyahoga does not drown. . . . He decays"; or less cleverly of Detroit, "'Murder city' . . . where the weak are killed . . . and eaten."

Yet the emphasis in the most recent wave of urban revitalization has been a far cry from the modernist projects of the postwar era, which forcibly moved people into carefully surveilled spaces, managing citizens as if they were movable cogs in a machine (or on an assembly line), still with an eye toward how they might be productive in (and for) the chugging Fordist economy.[3] Nor have the recent changes in Detroit simply been gentrification writ large, the movement of populations from one neighborhood to another, or the revanchist claiming of space around a global center of capital circulation in the new information economy, on the order that might be evident in San Francisco, Los Angeles, New York, São Paulo, or London.[4]

The most recent "revitalization" in Detroit is a different and maybe even more insidious beast. We have at this point heard plenty about the emergence of the "neoliberal citizen," the imagined subject of a body politic that is woven through with familiar consumer-cultural and corporate interests, motivations, and sensibilities. But the dreamed-about beneficiaries of Detroit's most recent attempted revitalization might better be described as "shareholder citizens." For in many ways, current efforts to remake Detroit are particularly reminiscent of efforts to "cure" unhealthy corporate behemoths, where the well-being of workers is sacrificed for the sake of corporate shareholders. Likewise, this revitalization effort seems in some ways less about making infrastructural, cultural, or political changes in the city for the obvious benefit of its resident workers, the people who call it home, than about increasing its market value to interests that have a greater stake in its profitability and "brandability." So even as the city finally makes its once beautiful riverfront more accessible to pedestrians, as tourists are bused in from out of town to pull slot machine levers at enormous new casino hotels, and as sports stadiums in the downtown area thrive, the majority of Detroit's African American residents will neither enjoy nor even indirectly benefit from such developments.

In fact, as the city's shareholders continue to plot and motivate Detroit's salvation, many African American residents are increasingly worried that, in some form or another, they will be handed residential pink slips, losing their place in and control over the quintessentially black U.S. metropolis. Of course, and in spite of the fact that countless politically ambitious corporate executives tout their experience "running things," human sociopolitical communities are not like corporations. As this book goes to press, more hotels are on the cusp of opening downtown, and yet the most recent news from Detroit to hit the national airwaves is that it has once again been designated "The Most Dangerous City in America."[5]

Schooled in Race: Identity Politics in Metro Detroit

Readers may be surprised to discover that, although my work focuses on the lives of school-age adolescents in Detroit, schools play only a minimal role in this book. This isn't out of willful neglect, but rather reflects the important fact that most of the kids with whom I was spending time (as with many others in the drug trade) had only minimal interaction with formal schooling past the eighth grade. Rodney had gotten kicked out of Northwestern High School on Detroit's West Side when he was only fourteen, after getting into fights with other kids there. Before being locked up most recently, he would occasionally sneak into the school to see old friends. But as with many other school-age youths in his neighborhood, school wasn't a meaningful institution in his life. Meanwhile, though Dude hadn't gotten kicked out of school, he attended only rarely. Early on he had been tracked into the special education program at Osborne High, in the northeast corner of the city. He would talk about the other kids there with a mix of morbid curiosity and comic relief: "They got me in there with a bunch of retarded kids, droolin' on the desks and shit!"

While I don't mean to suggest that the state of the Detroit Public Schools system is a *cause* for the great numbers of young people selling illegal narcotics in Detroit (as there are plenty of kids who are doing well in school *and* selling drugs), it is likely that problems with the public schools have some sort of mutually reinforcing relationship with Detroit's drug trade. The school system in Detroit is in financial ruin. The district faced a $78 million deficit for the year 2004, and its budget shortfalls have continued to increase. In May 2006, the Detroit School Board voted to borrow $200 million to cover its cash flow obligations. This debt was added to the $3 billion that the district already owed on various bonds, and things will likely continue sliding downward. Meanwhile, performance and graduation rates are dismally low. According to some estimates, approximately 75 percent of black males once enrolled in Detroit's public schools drop out before graduating.[6] The schools are violent, ugly, and heavily policed.[7] After a teacher strike in 2006 and in spite of an array of extravagant student incentives, including free iPods and televisions, the district lost over 25,000 students in the 2006–7 academic year. As a result, the Detroit Public Schools system plans to close almost one hundred schools by 2009.[8]

At the same time, service-providing institutions in the city, which might offer alternatives to some young drug dealers, are structurally disengaged from the struggles of youths there. Most of what we would call "prevention programs" in the city, of which there is hardly an abundance, are in various ways institutionally attached to the school system. And with so many young people out of school, these programs do not reach those most in need of them. For kids who have dropped out of school or who have been forced out through the expansion of "zero-tolerance" policies, the most frequent avenue into social service aid is through the juvenile justice system, which offers a number of "aftercare" programs, most in the form of some sort of intensive probation. These programs have their own foibles, however, and even when extraordinarily equitable are frequently unsuccessful.[9] Most of the young people about whom I write here have dropped out of or are only marginally engaged with school, and almost all are moving in and out of the justice system.

Indeed, the beleaguered school system in Detroit might be taken as both a representation of and central fulcrum in the dynamic relationship between the African American community and the city of Detroit. In a city with an African American population that consistently hovers between 80 and

85 percent, and where many of the white residents are elderly or, if they have young children, tend to send them to private schools, it's not surprising that Detroit's public schools are overwhelmingly African American.[10] But more significantly, for many residents of Detroit, the public schools have come to represent everything that is wrong with the city and its governance: the historical absence of a consistent tax base (the loss of nearly two-thirds of the city's population over the last fifty years), administrative ineptitude, and municipal corruption. The public schools in Detroit are institutional embodiments of years of "urban crisis" in the city. And among public agencies, the school system is the institutional apparatus that most strongly marks a distinction between Detroit's difficulties and the relative desirability of the many surrounding suburbs. While recent efforts at urban renewal in the central business district represent potential points of tourist interest in the city, it is clear that even families with such a preference will not move back to Detroit until the school system is improved.[11]

Yet for all the ridicule that the city suffers for the condition of its public schools, the civic leadership in Detroit is fiercely defensive of its tenuous control over the city's school system. Between 1999 and 2005, with the passage of what was colloquially called "the school-takeover law," members of a board who were jointly elected by the state governor and the mayor of Detroit displaced the popularly elected school board and assumed control over the school system. Throughout the city, among residents as well as community and political leaders, there were concerns about the intrusion of the state into the city's business. This culminated in 2004, as the designated takeover period was coming to a close and questions about it being extended were hovering. On one side was a group of pedagogical pragmatists who felt that state oversight was the only way that kids would have access to a decent education. This group was highly suspicious of the possible political motivations of city officials. As they opined in a *Free Press* editorial, "[The city] can argue that Detroit must hold on to every inch of political power it possibly can. What has that got to do with teaching kids how to read and perform basic math?"[12]

On the other side were people who felt that the state was encroaching into Detroit's domain over its own business. Some activist factions in the city saw in this struggle an expansive web of political ramifications. In another *Free Press* article, Helen Moore, a member of an emergent organization called the Keep the Vote, No Takeover Coalition, suggested that the state wanted to keep school board elections off the upcoming ballot in order to discourage Detroit voters from going to the polls. "This is a betrayal of our right to vote in November. . . . The main issue is that [state officials] want to make sure that Detroiters don't turn out en masse for the presidential election."[13] At the core of suspicions such as this was a deep sense of conflict among most Detroiters involving, on the one hand, their identification with the city—their sense of political self-determination and citizenship—and, on the other, a deep fear that their city—even with all of its afflictions and abandonment—might easily be taken from them. Indeed, it is precisely the tension characterizing the struggle over public schools—between a sense of domain and alienation, ownership and disenfranchisement—that describes the larger situation of the black community in Detroit and that undergirds the stories that unfold in this book.

Where one might suggest that new urban centers in the global economy are cities without history (think of Dubai), just the opposite might be more true of Detroit, where the city's *possession* of history seems often on the edge of confusion with its *being* history. The divisions that percolated through Detroit's explosive expansion during the early twentieth century and became entrenched through that century's latter half are stubborn. And even recent change in Detroit is understood through terms that emerged during the postwar era.[14] Detroit is usually talked about in terms of social dynamics that feel like remnants of a bygone era and that are particularly binary— between blacks and whites, labor and management, the period of manufacturing expansion and the subsequent rise of a service economy, and, most pointedly and emblematically, the city and the surrounding suburbs.

Detroit is consistently the most segregated major metropolitan center in the country; it is a place where blacks have a firm grip on municipal political power, but for whom there is still a pervasive and foreboding sense of social and economic disenfranchisement. The controversy surrounding control over the school system would suggest as much. And while some of this grows immediately out of tensions between the city and the state's bureaucracies, it much more significantly revolves around senses of discordant interest between city and suburb. This division is Detroit's most abiding characteristic, and implies an alliance of the edge cities surrounding Detroit with both large corporations and nonblack-owned small businesses in the city. Meanwhile, African American residents, who are largely excluded from these institutions and communities, often feel vulnerable to their strategies for expansion and exploitation.

Though always ideological, claims to community ownership and battles against social disenfranchisement in Detroit usually have been negotiated through struggles over access to and dominion over the physical geography of the city. Throughout periods of explosive growth, "racial covenants," and protracted white flight, social struggle in Detroit has been over and for space. With the most recent push for revitalization in downtown Detroit and multiple market-price housing developments creeping out from the central business district, Detroit's African American residents are uncertain about the future of their city and their place within it.

The drug trade itself is peculiarly situated with respect to the spatial dimensions of tensions over ownership and belonging, for the drug trade tends to develop around places where ownership and belonging are contested most fiercely. Drug dealing flourishes in spaces that are visible but also invisible, institutionalized but also transient, those that might be subject to sudden or continual redefinition and reconfiguration. In Detroit, such spaces emerge around abandoned houses, in the midst of fluid traffic through legitimate businesses, in unbounded public places—on sidewalks and street corners—spaces defined by movement, routes between one house and another, or between houses and liquor stores. Young dope hustlers are always striving to claim ownership of spaces that are effective and secure, but that are simultaneously impossible to map, invisible, and mutable.

The Changing Game

Detroit has a prominent and notorious place in the history of young people as street dealers. Drug dealing became widely practiced among adolescent boys in Detroit during the late 1970s and early 1980s, when a drug gang called Young Boys Incorporated (YBI) gained control of the heroin market there. A few young men organized YBI on the grounds of an elementary school on Detroit's West Side. Among these was a scrappy up-and-comer named Milton "Butch" Jones, who had not long before been released from prison after serving a three-year sentence for manslaughter. Within a year, Jones ascended to the top position in the organization. Not long afterward he established a rigid, coded organizational structure and system of distribution, which included the innovative use of children as runners along with street dealers who would report directly to older captains and lieutenants in the organization.[15]

Since the glory days of YBI, the local drug trade has fundamentally transformed. Over the last couple of decades, and consistent with trends in many other cities, youth gang membership in Detroit has been both declining and becoming more flexible, especially among African Americans. In fact, among young people in Detroit, gang participation and involvement in the drug trade are usually described as explicitly alternative and even mutually exclusive possibilities. Young people in the drug trade will say, "If you're making money dealing drugs, why would you want to mess around with gang stuff; it's for kids."[16]

Even as the crack epidemic of the 1980s and early 1990s has waned and fewer young people are doing hard drugs in the city, illegal narcotics still float through Detroit's streets like dandelion seeds.[17] This has something to do with the fact that the interior sectors of the city are drug market destinations for people who often live many miles away. Probably over half of the crack and heroin customers whom I saw and interacted with while I was living in Detroit were from the suburbs, including, and by bizarre and shocking coincidence, old colleagues and acquaintances of mine from my undergraduate days in Ann Arbor.

Currently, trajectories of drug distribution and exchange are diffuse and fluid, changing from day to day as the surrounding circumstances, such as supply and demand, and the various inclinations of those involved, shift. There are few overarching institutional structures in Detroit's contemporary drug trade. And communities of dealers, even those possessed of a fixed organizational or institutional identity (like an affiliation with a neighborhood), are best described as "spontaneous," reflecting the frequent and haphazard movement of individuals in and out of the drug trade. With opportunities so prevalent, and the institutional or structural obligations for inclusion so minimal, involvement in drug dealing has become casual, and being "in the dope game" has become, under these circumstances, a mundane fact of life for thousands of young people in Detroit.

Not surprisingly, this has far-reaching implications for the social significance and impact of street-level drug dealing in Detroit. The fluidity and mutability of the drug trade and legal economy, their unremarkable overlap and divergence, point to the steady involvement of broader community processes and family dynamics in drug dealing. The drug trade is not an isolated subcultural phenomenon that can be parsed from other institutions or cultural factors that bear on the lives of those involved—such as family, church, peer groups, school, and the juvenile and criminal justice systems. As I demonstrate, each of these institutions is deeply intertwined with young African American drug sellers, and the structures and spaces defined by the drug trade.

Souls at Stake: Young Black Lives in Detroit

In popular culture, and too much social science, the black community is subject to crude sociological divisions that have all kinds of economic indexes, but that are, more significantly, imagined to articulate some sort of deep cultural (and moral) fault line. This vulgar bifurcation has long historical roots and salient recent emblems, from the "field" and the "house," to Martin and Malcolm, to Dr. Huxtable and Dr. Dre. As various black middle classes have established themselves across the country, the "problem" of the "marginalized," "disaffected" underclass has come into ever-clearer focus. There are two black communities, trumpet the alarms, and one of them is in perpetual crisis. While the establishment of a growing black middle class reflects a story of the graceful beating of long odds—blacks in politics, academics, and big business, living in leafy suburbs, watching Oprah, and coveting the tasteful life she peddles—the other black community, so we hear, is being left behind, or more dangerously, willfully *doesn't want* to come along for the ride to the promised land. According to the prevailing wisdom, these people, mostly young men it seems, either face structural barriers to cultivating "mainstream" cultural sensibilities or, alternatively, understand the advantages of good education—can dissect the politics of symbolic capital in their country and among their "innocent countrymen"—but still reject it; they've seen a piece of the American pie and they'd prefer something else.[18] While marginalization from mainstream *resources* is a terrible artifact of postindustrial capitalism, it is the specter of the *cultural* marginalization of a discrete sector of the black population that seems most frightening to even the most determined progressive interventionists.[19]

In the social imaginary, young drug dealers in urban environments may be the emblems of this intractable, marginalized, subset of the black community. Young black men in the dope game, especially, are typically represented as inured to deadly violence and death itself, for its frequency and ubiquity in

America's inner cities. And with rooms of children sharing accounts of funerals they've attended, the prevalence of seemingly untimely deaths among poor blacks in Detroit is undeniable. Young people in poor, drug-infested neighborhoods in Detroit inhabit spaces that are, in some obvious ways, marginalized, and the trope of the "margin" might easily be taken both to describe and explain their circumstances. These places are bereft of many basic resources, are high in violent crime, and can indeed seem deeply disconnected from their suburban surroundings, some of which include among the most wealthy neighborhoods, townships, and counties in the world.[20]

But for all the profound social injustices that are at this point built into the country's poorest urban neighborhoods, projecting onto the inhabitants of these spaces an antagonistic "culture of the street" doesn't make much sense. Poor young black men are not simple, static subjects or members of a bounded subcultural element. They are not driven only by threats to their dignity or compulsions to salvage their manhood in the face of an emasculating service economy. Though they have nearly become archetypal figures in writing about urban America, and are thought of as stable fixtures in the economies and social orders of urban neighborhoods in the United States, the identities of young black drug dealers in Detroit are as complex and fluid as any "postcolonial" or "transnational" subject. Indeed, stories that tie together the coalescing of one identity around and through multiple cultures and politics, communities or nations, for all their exotic romance, are appealing (in fiction, film, and social science) precisely because so many people are now living at the blurred boundaries, and moving across borders between, points of political power and dispossession. In Detroit, in fact, young black drug dealers are not only crossing and fusing social divisions; they are also always managing their own representation. They understand that they and their stories are hot commodities, and that they are both exploited for and might themselves exploit their own symbolic power in U.S. life.

Detroit has been famously described as America's only "third-world city," surrounded by growing centers of postindustrial capital accumulation, where cultural, political, racial, and class divisions are cartoonishly categorical.[21] In the physically and culturally divided spaces of Detroit, it is exactly through a sensitivity to what the literary critic Homi Bhabha calls the *interstices* of culture and capital that young African American drug dealers need to be considered.[22]

One of the primary aims of this book, then, is to explore how the drug trade signals, opens, and moves across ruptures in established boundaries, divisions, and points of tension that are remnants of Detroit's postwar era. These remnants form the categories through which the city is most commonly understood by both its residents and scholars of its history and contemporary social scene. *Getting Ghost* explores how young African American men associate the drug trade with the transgression, mediation, and in some cases possible surmounting of divisions and acrimonies that now characterize the Motor City. These divisions include distinctions between white and black, the impoverished and the wealthy, ownership and occupancy, and city and suburb. Such distinctions are drawn into the intimate social landscape of the city and become inscribed into the habitual rhythms of its residents as they move through its built spaces—like liquor stores divided by bulletproof glass—which are always already laden with racial and class significance. Involvement in the drug trade can be a means for young people to imagine and create social spaces and identities that foil tectonic social pressures that are pervasive in the African American community (and Detroit generally); that traverse racial, economic, and cultural divides; and that lie somewhere between ownership and occupancy, where young people's statuses as outcasts are recast as something new.[23]

Many of the daily practices that configure space and give it meaning are quiet and subtle, like the delicate interactions of black customers and white or Middle Eastern store owners in local retail shops, or gatherings of neighborhood kids taking refuge around Monopoly boards in comfortable living rooms. But the deadly violence that rips through these spaces, sometimes killing young people as they stand on corners, walk up the steps toward their homes, or drive through their neighborhoods, has its own power as a fact of social life in Detroit. Such violence might mean many things to those in its path of influence. It may be seen simultaneously as both accident and fate, and it can both alienate young people from and more deeply connect them to the places they live, shifting the terms of their belonging, repulsing them at the same time that it draws them close.

As their lives and stories brushed against one another in the detention facility and then headed toward different sides of the city, Dude and Rodney found both great promise and tired despair in the drug trade. And as each puzzled over how and in what direction to steer their lives, lethal violence would redraw the maps of their experience.

Brother Love, a Long Life, and a Purpose

After his sermon in the juvenile detention facility had ended and most of the kids in the room had fallen into conversation, the chaplain gathered his things into his black rectangular briefcase and then sat facing Rodney, who was still leaning his chair against the wall. Many of the staff at the facility took a sort of special interest in Rodney. This had something to do with his age—he was older than most of the other inmates—and the fact that he had been in the facility for longer than many, as the charges against him were more serious. Armed with such experience, Rodney developed a preternatural ability to bob and weave gracefully and playfully through the tricky politics of incarceration. His capacity both to defer to and rebuke authority in the same gesture seemed especially captivating to his keepers in detention and won their respect more than prescribed docility might have. Because of this they would afford him latitudes that other kids didn't enjoy and would sit with him in conversation for their own pleasure. In these moments, Rodney's impishness would often give way to a deep and quiet seriousness. His big dark eyes would soften, and his hands would lie still. The chaplain seemed no more immune to Rodney's charm than the others.[24]

"How you doing, my man?" the chaplain asked him. Rodney said that he was doing really well, that he felt confident that he was going to be released soon.

"I don't know about all these other cats in here, but my charges ain't petty. Anyways, if they go on the evidence, I'm gonna beat this." The chaplain seemed to nod and frown simultaneously.

"You know, I just seen my own nephew in here today," he said, cocking his jaw to the side and seeming to fight a bad taste in his mouth. "I reached up and pulled my collar out of my shirt, so that he wouldn't have to be beaten by a man of the cloth." The chaplain laughed with explosive enthusiasm. "You know how it is with family," he said.

Rodney laughed. "Oh, I know. You want to protect them. But sometimes you gotta hurt them." The chaplain and Rodney giggled.

"That's how it is for parents," offered the chaplain.

"Yup," said Rodney, suddenly a little less enthusiastic. He wasn't usually eager to talk about either of his parents.

Rodney's father had been incarcerated in Ohio, sentenced to a ninety-nine-year prison term for a crime that had been committed the year that Rodney was born. Rodney had never met him. Before being locked up, Rodney had been living with his mother, Maria, and his younger brother, Antonio, in a formerly abandoned house that his mother's boyfriend had found and helped them move into. Maria was fiercely defensive of Rodney and imagined that his circumstances were born of some sort of profound metaphysical injustice or imbalanced accrual of wickedness. When visiting him at the detention facility, Maria would read to Rodney in a deep, smoke-worn voice from a small copy of the Bible (which she always seemed to carry) and implore him to trust that God would eventually balance the profane scales of justice in Detroit. She hated the city and was desperate to leave. Rodney always treated his mother's exhortations with a degree of chagrin and hesitation.

But he was eager to talk about his siblings—two sisters and Antonio—and quickly turned the conversation to them. "You know, with your sister, you be wanting to protect them, but it's different with your brother. You be needing to always, you know, anybody mess with them and you got to wreck those niggas. That's that special brother love. And Tonio be so nutty, man! My mama said that he was checking out on the hooks the other day. They brought him home in the cuffs, and he waited until they took them off, and then he started getting real nutty, yelling and shit. . . . They got him this time for curfew.[25] That be happening all the time to him, and I can't say too much because I used to get a lot of tickets for that too. You know, I got all this concern, but there's not much I can say."

"That brother love is some serious stuff," agreed the chaplain.

The young African American teacher in whose classroom we sat would run an irreverent show. He kept a stereo in the corner, and when the chaplain's sermon was done, he turned the thumping music back on, and with heads rocking, conversation broke out all over the room. As the chaplain got up to leave, Rodney and I entered the fray of an adjacent discussion. A couple of other inmates were talking about a friend of theirs from high school—an accomplished athlete with a bright future who had dropped out of the scene and was doing fifteen to twenty years for trafficking drugs. A kid with glasses reported that he had heard the guy got caught making a deal on his cell phone. "He played it like a fool, though, man. He on the phone with his man, saying, 'Gimme 4 keys, hard. . . .' Man, why would he dog his own man like that? He end up just doggin' himself." A corpulent facility guard who was sleepily slumped against the wall said, "Man, I just don't know. You can make a lot of money quick, but how long you gonna live?" He looked at us with his arms outstretched, his tone not exactly rhetorical but certainly pointed. "How long you think you gonna be able to do that?" he asked. "'Til you're twenty or thirty? 'Til you're thirty-five?" The bespectacled kid was defiant: "I know someone who's thirty-eight and still does it!" The guard mocked him. "Ooooo, thirty-eight. You think that's a long life?" The admonished youngster fell silent.

Rodney often found himself at the center of conversations about the drug trade in the detention facility. It was a sort of frequent performance in which the young detainees would regularly engage, subjected as they were to the disciplinary strategies of the facility, sitting in their canvas jumpsuits with the name of the institution stenciled on their backs, bereft of their street identities and prohibited from explicit displays of neighborhood or gang affiliation.[26]

"I'll live way past thirty-eight," said Rodney, with a typical bob of his head and sideways smile. "Man, this drug shit ain't hard. You just have to know what to do. That's the first thing I told this cat," he said, glancing toward me and tapping my arm with the back of his hand. "This ain't hard. It's all just common sense. You just getting stuff and selling stuff. And you just got to lay low and be careful doing it. These other cats just don't know what's going on." Undaunted by the fact that I had just returned from the funeral of a young man shot down in his neighborhood, Rodney insisted, "I'm gonna live a long ass time. Come up out of the game. You'll see; you'll see." Rodney giggled and bobbed his head again.

When the chaplain left, I followed him out, leaving Rodney still holding forth, and went into the classroom next door to check in again with Dude. He was sitting alone in a corner of the room while others talked among themselves. Dude crouched low over a piece of paper, on which he was working studiously to answer a letter from his oldest brother. He printed each word with great deliberation and commitment, moving slowly down the page, spelling everything phonetically. He leaned back when I sat down next to him and gestured toward me. "Kick it with me, Luke. For real, kick it with me," he said, expectantly. I asked him how he liked my suit. "You look alright," he said, and mentioned that he hadn't had clothes to wear in any of his court hearings. He read me some of the letter that he was writing, in which he was assuring his brother, who would be in prison for the rest of his life, that he didn't need to worry about their mother. Dude would look after her when he got out of the juvenile detention facility and make sure that she would have money.

"Through my whole little lifetime, I've been going through some deep stuff, here and there," he said. "Growing up in a family that's just involved in selling drugs, that's just out there, wild." Dude's family was a sort of notorious fixture in the retail drug scene around Kercheval Avenue in southeast Detroit, one of the city's oldest and poorest neighborhoods. In addition to his two brothers, both of his older sisters had been deeply involved in the dope game at various points, and his recently deceased father, Marvin, had been dealing drugs from as early as Dude could remember. Even Dude's mother, he told me, had been selling prescription medication to make ends meet. Sitting across from me now, he seemed especially distraught about this, and shook his head in disgust.

"You know, I used to make promises to my mama. I used to make promises like, 'I ain't gonna never go to jail,' or 'I ain't going to never smoke no cigarettes.' And I don't smoke cigarettes, but shit, I started smoking *weed* instead. And it's like, know what I'm saying? I don't know why I didn't respect her like I should. Mama is my heart. That's my heart right there. I can't be a kid no more; I gotta be the man of the house when I get out. . . . I remember the first time they brought me to the youth home. Now your man's like twelve. Man, I was scared as a motherfucker. They put me on the big boys unit; everybody's like fifteen, sixteen, seventeen years old. Man, I went to court scared, 'cuz I'm telling them a whole bunch of lies about stealing this boy's bike and shit. But then I got out! I'm telling my boys on the outs, lying and stuff: 'Yeah, I was in there, I was telling niggas, "Don't look at me" and all this.' I thought it was cool, know what I'm saying?"

Dude, who had been staring off in another direction, looked at me intently: "But I'm sixteen now and it's like, 'Hell no, this shit ain't cool,' you know what I'm saying? Nothing about it's cool. Jail ain't fun. The youth home ain't fun; this ain't even jail, this just, this just kiddie camping, and it ain't nowhere near fun. So it's like man, I think reality done elbowed me right in the face. If I had a chance to do it all over again, to hop in that truck and ride over there, or to stay on that porch and sell some dope, man, I would have stayed on that porch and sold me some dope."

Dude's disquisition was now gaining momentum, and he spoke more quickly. "My life, man, I don't know. I used to ask myself, 'What's my purpose on this earth?' Ever since I was a young age, I been getting in trouble, coming into detention facilities. You know, that's the type of shit you hear on talk shows. Either 'your teen is this' or 'your teen is that.' But I look at myself like, man, I got a good head on my shoulders, and I don't use the motherfucker, know what I'm saying? And if I use it, I just use it to a certain extent," Dude explained.

"Sometimes I'm just like, man, what's my purpose on this earth? It's deep. I'm steady getting into trouble, I'm steady getting out of here, and then I go hit licks, know what I'm saying? And sell some dope and beat this guy for nothing, and shoot this gun for nothing. It's just like, damn, man, what's wrong with you? And then when you come in here, you don't want to be locked up, but then I have to think about it: Look at all the dirt you done did. All the shit you did. So how can I complain about being locked up?"

Dude folded the letter he had been writing into thirds, pressed the creases down several times, and tucked it into his jumpsuit.

"I guess it go back to that point again, like I'm saying . . . even when I was at home, I could be going to the store, getting me a double deuce of St. Ives, and I'll be thinking . . . God. God be in my head, know what I'm saying? Like I say, I can just have the pistol on me, God be in my head, know what I'm saying? Or I can be just, getting ready to shoot off the porch for no reason, God be in my head. And it go back to that point. What's my purpose on this earth? Is it to live 'til I'm about nineteen and get killed? Or go up to a penitentiary for the rest of my life? I'm telling you, I don't want to go up to no penitentiary. And I don't want to die."

PART I

Stolen Streets and Promised Lands

And ye came near unto me every one of you, and said, We will send men before us, and they shall search us out the land, and bring us word again by what way we must go up, and into what cities we shall come.

—Deuteronomy 1:22

2

Detroit Revisited, Revisionist History

In 2001, on the eve of its three hundredth birthday, Detroit's image makers—the captains of industry, service, and politics in the city—gave themselves an almost incomprehensibly strange task. Calling themselves the Detroit 300 Committee, their charge, assumed with smiling faces and a lighthearted self-congratulatory air, was to honor and celebrate a city that has become, perhaps more than any other in the United States, emblematic of postindustrial urban tragedy.[1]

In the relatively recent past, Detroit has undergone reimaginings similar to those undertaken by the Detroit 300 Committee. With the opening, in the late 1970s, of the riot-proof "Renaissance Center," a gathering of cylindrical glass skyscrapers that was to hold office and retail space in the deserted central business district along the Detroit River, the city proclaimed itself born anew. But over the twenty years that followed, the Renaissance Center and the accompanying rhetoric of rebirth had a negligible economic effect as well as a dispiriting social impact on the city. While functioning well as material for parody and overwrought cultural criticism, Detroit's willful renaissance in the 1970s and 1980s did little to attract investment or renewed interest.

Meanwhile, the marking of Detroit's 2001 tercentennial, with tours, tall ships, fireworks, and a new wave of business investment and influx of middle-class white residents on the horizon, was an altogether more complicated affair. The anniversary was, after all, presumably more than just a nod toward what Detroit might become, in the wildest hopes of the interests that would most benefit from it. It was also a formulation of what Detroit *was* and an opportunity to suggest a logic connecting Detroit's past with a future worthy of self-congratulation. The committee thus planned its tercentennial party so that it would elide the city's tragic history and point toward an unavoidably bright, fantastic future. Yet such a future for Detroit could only emerge through the reconfiguration of the city's past. Detroit would need to become something that it never was.

A pictorial time line produced by the Detroit 300 Committee (which was available on the tercentennial celebration Web site and as a paper brochure) was meant to mark significant milestones in Detroit's history. It begins with a bust of Antoine de la Mothe Cadillac (the eighteenth-century French founder of the city), and then moves to a print depicting the French and Indian Wars and the attack on Fort Detroit. It winds its way, in photographs and paintings with accompanying text, through the admission of the state of Michigan to the Union (1837), to the organization of the Republican Party, to the "heyday of the logging industry." It includes notations of the first car in Detroit (1896), the opening of Henry Ford's plant in Highland Park (1913), and the initial organization of the United Auto Workers and its successful effort to gain concessions from General Motors' management (1936 and 1937). The time line, of course, does not omit Detroit's heralded period as the "Arsenal of Democracy" during World War II, when Ford produced all the armed services' B-24 bombers at the Willow Run assembly plant west of Detroit. With the progression of U.S. involvement in the war, Sherman tanks came rolling out of factories owned by Chrysler. The gargantuan River Rouge plant, which had been producing all Ford and Mercury engines, began making army jeeps.

But the time line takes a curious turn here—or rather, skips a beat—to the present. Underneath a photograph of World War II–era B-24s lined up in an assembly hangar, the tercentennial committee gives us a view of the contemporary Detroit skyline, emphasizing the foreshortened, looming Renaissance Center. Aglow in orange sunlight and sparkling with illuminated office building windows, the city looks seemingly alive with hustle and bustle from the Canadian shoreline across the river. Under the heading "Detroit in the 21st Century" is a caption that reads, "Just looking at the downtown skyline is a reminder of the city's progress. The Renaissance Center marks the beginning of the city's rebirth into the new century." Indeed, looking at the city's skyline from across the wide berth of the Detroit River may furnish the best chimera of the city's progress. For the time line is a *nearly* effective effort to make the disappearance of sixty years of postwar history seem utterly natural. The reader is hardly encouraged to wonder, Did nothing happen between the end of World War II, Detroit's reign as the supposed Arsenal of Democracy, and the present?

Of course, if the logic of the time line guides readers' understanding, they may not be able to help asking, "*Rebirth* from what death?" While the tercentennial committee enthusiastically points to the imminence and inevitability of a rebirth, the morbid period that must have preceded this renewal is missing. Perhaps the most startling aspect of the omission of Detroit's postwar history is the absence of any acknowledgment that Detroit has become, by an overwhelming majority, an African American city. Looking at the tercentennial committee's brochure, one would have no idea that the city has a black cultural identity and was one of the most important centers of black political activity and power in the last decades of the twentieth century.[2]

As of this writing, the Detroit metro area is one of the most segregated in the nation. While the city is mostly black, the whites and ethnic minorities who *do* reside in Detroit themselves live in markedly segregated neighborhoods. Meanwhile, the suburbs (Southfield and Warren to the north; Dearborn, Melvindale, and Allen Park to the west; and Grosse Point, East Point, and St. Claire Shores to the East, to name just a few) have been the destinations for whites desperately fleeing the city over the last sixty years.

This has been a common postwar phenomenon across the nation, especially in northern industrial cities like Pittsburgh, Cleveland, Saint Louis, Chicago, and Newark. But the suburb/city divide, and its power as a racial and class signifier, is especially stark in Detroit. In the Detroit metro area, the suburbs are not configured as bedroom communities, where thousands of city employees sleep, only to return to work and play in the city center. In their current form, Detroit's suburbs are better described as edge cities, self-contained urban communities with their own civic and popular identities. The inhabitants of the Detroit metro suburbs do not imagine themselves living on the periphery of a dynamic urban center with which they closely associate. Indeed, many suburban dwellers seldom or ever venture across Detroit's clear boundaries.

Especially under the mayoral tenure and guidance of Coleman Young, who led Detroit for twenty years (1973–93), the city became identified as black *against* the white suburban edge cities surrounding it. Young was a big-city mayor cut of the same cloth as notorious mayors in Chicago, Boston, and New York—not necessarily corrupt, but certainly less a great manager than an overwhelming personality. Some in the Detroit press would refer to Young, Detroit's first black mayor, as the "last of the Irish Bosses."[3]

Young was elected only a few years after, and in a political climate shaped by, the city's 1967 riots. And in contrast to most other big-city mayors entering office at the tail end of the era of white flight and urban abandonment, Young was not interested in courting the suburbs or suburban interests. On the contrary, he seemed almost to cultivate hostility between city and suburb, and wasn't shy about naming the obvious significance of race in their distinction. According to most who remember him, Young's greatest achievement was the increase of black representation on the Detroit police force and in the upper echelons of city government. When asked why he was hiring so many blacks for key city positions, Young unapologetically told an inquiring reporter, "That means more at the TOP for blacks. . . . There ain't no shortage of blacks out there behind them garbage trucks!"[4] In a city that was becoming almost exclusively African American, he was the mayor of a black populace and represented the local black population's greatest aspirations for meaningful political empowerment. And since Young left office, African Americans have continued to hold Detroit's highest municipal offices. For many local residents, Detroit is, above all else, a rare bastion of black cultural and political power.

Where, we are left asking, does the city's pronounced racial identity fit into the history of Detroit conjured by the tercentennial committee? Or conversely, why does it not, within the internal logic of the time line, fit anywhere?

While strange, the tercentennial committee's formulation of Detroit's history, with its obfuscation of the history of race in Detroit, is instructively appropriate. For in its misplacement of Detroit's African American identity and legacy, in its removal of African Americans from Detroit's story, it reflects with an eerie pithiness the patterns of spatial displacement (and attendant economic disenfranchisement) around which African Americans have had to maneuver throughout long stretches of their history in the city.

One could make the case that the tercentennial celebration not only reflects these patterns but also in fact is reproducing them. In the last few years, General Motors has moved into the Renaissance Center and Compuware has built a new headquarters in the central business district. Three casinos have gone up as well as brand-new professional football and baseball stadiums. The construction of a huge new shopping district on Cadillac Square at the center of downtown has been progressing. On summer evenings, as crowds leave the baseball stadium, stragglers gather under the stars on a central green space where movies are screened during the summer months. In winter, hockey fans and children skate around on an ice rink built on the same ground.

Unequivocally and unabashedly, one of the major impetuses behind all these developments is to bring suburban (and likely white) people back to the city. And the tercentennial celebration might easily be seen as part of this effort. Mirroring the exclusion of African American subjects from this particular history of Detroit was their exclusion as an audience for it. Most of the celebrants of Detroit's three hundredth birthday were from the suburbs, many with familial pasts or former addresses within the city limits. It is toward these people that the discourse around the tercentennial anniversary was targeted; they made up the throngs crowding around the riverfront to watch the tall ships sail into town from Cleveland. But they were not just tourists. And they were more than pilgrims returning to a former home, gathering in ceremonious remembrance of a shared history. These people were summoned to this historical celebration as potential new, white, affluent residents. Contrary to Young's vision of Detroit as a black metropolis that does not rely on white suburban patronage, the tercentennial celebration imagines white suburban expats as central to Detroit's revitalization. The city's tercentennial celebration was more than an imagined past and future; it was the beginning of an activist reconfiguration of Detroit's population.

So were we to move the camera a bit closer, to seize it from the tercentennial committee and take it back from the Canadian shoreline, what would we see in contemporary Detroit?

With a wide-angle lens, we would find that the primary human-hewn geographic marker in Detroit is Woodward Avenue, which runs north and south along the center axis of the city, up from the Detroit River, through downtown and then Highland Park, and into the northern suburbs. Woodward divides the city into halves, designated as the East and West Sides, and for many residents of Detroit, allegiance to one or the other is a lifelong proposition. While both Dude (from the East) and Rodney (from the West) would frequently drive north to shop at the suburban malls or visit strip clubs or dance halls, for example, neither would happily cross from one side of Woodward to the other.

Panning to the east of Woodward, about a half-mile from its southern edge along the shore of the Detroit River, we would see Kercheval Street. Kercheval stretches eastward from the historic Mt. Elliot Cemetery through the southeast corner of the city and heads all the way into Grosse Pointe, a famously affluent suburb just beyond the city limit. The Kercheval area can nearly be taken as an emblem of the configuration of social space and capital in Detroit neighborhoods over the past fifty years, reflecting, like an archaeological site, waves of urban renewal, industrial development, contained and exclusive wealth, and crushing poverty.

At around its midpoint within the city, Kercheval is interrupted for several blocks by the sprawling and obtrusive Jefferson Avenue Chrysler plant. The relatively new (built in the late 1980s and early 1990s), blue-and-silver factory falls awkwardly across Kercheval—as if it had just descended from the sky. Further to the west, nearly equidistant from the Mt. Elliot Cemetery and the Chrysler plant, is an insulated community of well-tended and enormous old homes called Indian Village. One of only two small city neighborhoods occupied predominantly by affluent white people, Indian Village is named for several of the streets that run through it, such as Iroquois and Seminole, and is where some of Detroit's wealthiest citizens live, including the county prosecutor, several judges, and a host of doctors and lawyers. Surrounding this enclave on all sides, however, are some of the poorest, most run-down neighborhoods in Detroit. Most of Kercheval Street, once one of the major arteries for people moving between East Side residential districts and downtown, and a bustling commercial strip, is now almost completely desolate.

Zooming in closer, we might come to the intersection of Kercheval and Pennsylvania Street. Pennsylvania runs north and south across Kercheval and is now mostly demolished as well, with only a scattered handful of occupied houses dotting the unclaimed flowering lots and urban prairie land cleared years ago of blighted structures. Of course, despite its apparent desolation, there are still lots of people living in the neighborhood. Within the area's four census tracts, from Warren Avenue on the north to Jefferson Avenue on the south, there were 377 whites and 105 Native Americans counted in the 2000 census, dispersed among and in some cases within the households of nearly 14,000 African Americans.[5] Indeed, some residents have been in the area their entire lives and live in homes that were owned by their parents or grandparents. Many have a strong personal investment in their neighborhood.

Not too far from the intersection of Kercheval and Pennsylvania lives one of the neighborhood's least likely residents. Alberta Tinsley-Talabi has been a Detroit city councillor for fourteen years. She lives across the street from her sister and just a couple of blocks away from where Dude was arrested on the concealed weapon charge.

While most city council members live in exclusive enclaves within the city, often far away from their constituents in less affluent neighborhoods, Tinsley-Talabi takes refuge in the neighborhood that her parents moved into in 1948. When we talked in her cramped but impressive downtown office—on the thirteenth floor of the Coleman Young Municipal Building—she said that one significant advantage of living in this poor and notoriously crime-ridden neighborhood is that she doesn't have to worry about news reporters harassing her at home. With a burst of laughter, she told me, "Ain't nobody going to hang out over there for too long. You know, they [the reporters] chase my council colleagues around in their neighborhoods. I'm like, well, if they come over here, we'll know!" Continuing in a more grave tone, she said, "I have witnessed the complete destruction of that community. When I was young, there were a multitude of stores down Kercheval. I mean you had the Bank and Trust; you had at least three of those on Kercheval. You had an NBD [National Bank of Detroit] bank right there at McClellen and Kercheval. You had a fish market, Sam's fish market; you had an A&P right there, next to the alley; you had stores across the street, a five-and-ten-cent. I mean Kercheval was a primary artery. It really was. It's hard to believe that now. Now the only thing that remains is the liquor store. And it's the same in the residential areas. Whew!"

Detroit is now one of the poorest big cities in the country. One in three people there is living in poverty, and the mean income is several thousand dollars below the national average.[6] And many first-time visitors to the city, those who travel beyond the select areas favored by suburban day-trippers and sports fans, describe Detroit as like nothing they've ever seen before—

urban dilapidation on such a grand scale as to be fittingly termed "postapoc-alyptic." This is perhaps most dramatically evident in the many abandoned early-century skyscrapers that line the most famous, and formerly thriving, downtown streets: Woodward and Michigan avenues. The once grand high-rise rail station, with its ornate curtain wall falling to pieces, looks like a staged ruin from some century in the future. Yet the most devastating qual-ity of Detroit's urban blight is not in its most awe-inspiring vistas but rather in its sheer ubiquity, as neighborhood after neighborhood, from the far northwest to the deep southeastern corners of the city, are home to many blocks where property values have barely risen since the 1950s and aban-doned houses are an expected feature of the landscape.

None of this, of course, is prominent in the representations of Detroit of-fered by the Detroit 300 Committee. This might well suggest that Detroit's future will not include a public policy commitment to the equitable mainte-nance of old neighborhoods. But what does it suggest about the history of Detroit? We hear, in the celebratory gestures contrived by the committee, neither about the current pervasiveness of such neighborhoods in Detroit nor about the history of social struggle that created them—rife with political an-tagonisms, violent pitched battles, and massive demographic transformation.

In the Motor City, public debates about nearly every pressing social concern—moral, political, biological, and economic—have been waged through ques-tions about the habitation of and control over the city's flat geographic spaces. And ongoing struggles over racial, class-based, local, and national politics (among blacks, whites, and members of other ethnic communities, develop-ers and residents, city and neighborhood leaders) continue to unfold across the city's broad commercial thoroughfares and narrow residential streets. For all the spectacular public symbols of the history of social turmoil in De-troit, for all the unhealed scars torn into the city's infrastructure, the loci of contemporary social tension there, shaped by the accrual of history and mem-ory, are not crumbling skyscrapers or the sports palaces that rise from their ashes. Instead, they are the much more mundane small retail stores that populate the city's sprawling, dilapidated residential neighborhoods.

In Detroit, which is constituted of hundreds of square miles of suburban-like housing developments, small neighborhood businesses along the gridded commercial thoroughfares are unique public spaces. As they were founded mostly by groups of both white and Middle Eastern immigrants, they have

been set in especially stark juxtaposition to the rows of private houses and
postage stamp yards built for the massive influx of white autoworkers during
the first half of the twentieth century. Today, Detroit's small businesses are
where people of multiple racial and ethnic identities—blacks, whites, Arabs,
Chaldeans, and others—come into contact with one another most directly.
And small retail stores are the places around which public discussions about
race most frequently occur in the city.

But neighborhood shops are not simply utopian, pluralistic spaces, or
sources of an informal, uninstitutionalized public trust, as Jane Jacobs might
have us imagine.[7] Rather, because they occupy this important position in the
social landscape, small businesses become centers of *conflict* as well—
places where important social distinctions are negotiated, individual and
community identities are formed and reformed against one another, and social tensions are often heightened.[8]

The commercially zoned thoroughfares that begrid Detroit, running through
the city's residential neighborhoods, assume an almost generic consistency
for the ubiquity of closed storefronts, interrupted by hurried activity around
the few businesses and other establishments that are open. Most of the black
churches in black neighborhoods in Detroit are housed in either elaborately
appointed gothic buildings, abandoned by their now-suburban-dwelling white
Catholic parishioners, or squat, neoclassic concrete-and-stone bank buildings, which sit heavily on many corners of the city's poor neighborhoods—
no longer locales for depositing money, but perhaps especially good places to
pray for it. In addition to these churches, centers of activity along Detroit's
commercial strips include liquor stores, gas stations, and Coney Island
restaurants, a particular gustatory fetish of Detroiters, specializing in chili
dogs and cheap hamburgers.

The distribution of commercial space in Detroit's African American neighborhoods runs along clearly defined ethnic and racial lines. The city's gas
stations, which house small convenience food shops, are owned and run almost exclusively by Muslim Arab Americans, many of whom live in Dearborn, a suburb just to the west of the city. Most of the liquor stores are
owned and run by Chaldean Christians, most of whom have emigrated from
Iraq. Liquor stores double as neighborhood food marts and electronics outlets, offering prepackaged nonperishable staples and cell phone counters.
Coney Island restaurants, meanwhile, tend to be owned and operated by
members of Detroit's Albanian American community, which is both Catholic

and Muslim, and around fifty thousand strong throughout the metro Detroit area.

But African Americans are conspicuously absent from the small business community in their own neighborhoods in Detroit. And this isn't for a lack of interest in entrepreneurial work. On the contrary, African Americans are acutely aware of their exclusion from legitimate retail activity in Detroit.[9] Because of the predominant absence of blacks from the business community, young African Americans (especially those who are dealing drugs) often think and talk about the drug trade in opposition to legitimate retail operations. And such juxtapositions between legitimate and illegal commercial work become particularly poignant around their convergence in small retail spaces, where drug dealers hustle their goods alongside of, around, in front of, and in the interstices of legal commercial establishments.

In the following chapter, I trace a brief history of the configuration of urban space in Detroit with an eye toward its significance for and resonance among families and young people involved in the drug trade today. In telling about Detroit's past, I emphasize two defining phenomena in the city: urban renewal, begun in the early twentieth century and extending through the turn of the twenty-first, and the rioting of 1967. Both have shaped Detroit, and continue to shape sentiments among contemporary young drug dealers about business, home, and community. In chapter 4, I conclude this historical interlude by describing an episode of carnivalesque social confrontation among residents of Detroit's lower East Side. The confrontation is both staged and spontaneous, as these residents perform and articulate historically informed anxieties about race, class, and privilege through their concerns about the politics of small business and home ownership in Detroit.

3

Renewal, Relocation, and Riot

As the auto industry and then the World War II war machine boomed in Detroit, suburban-like housing developments spread out across the surrounding farmland with a speed and purpose rivaling even our present-day suburban sprawl. Through the first half of the twentieth century, neighborhood after neighborhood, each characterized by a different sort of architecture, with only slightly varying floor plans from house to house, was erected with dizzying efficiency. Much of the near-northwest section of the city, for example, is populated with square, two-story, four-bedroom, brick-faced houses, while most streets on the lower East Side surrounding Kercheval are lined with slat-sided rectangular houses and two-family flats. When they were built, most of these neighborhoods were associated with a particular factory or plant, where working residents would make a single-file commute in the morning and back in the evening.

Both Polish and German foreign-born residents of the city tended to settle in the Kercheval and Pennsylvania area. The neighborhood is near the stately and bepillared Deutzches Haus community center on Mack Avenue and is a short drive from the heart of the Polish community just north of Grand Boulevard. There were also many foreign-born Canadians in the neighborhood—families that had moved across the river to work in Detroit factories. Through the 1950s, Kercheval was one among many white, multiethnic, and working-class neighborhoods in the city.

Its transformation over the next decade was startling. By the early 1960s, along with most of Detroit, the area was almost exclusively African American.

Until around the commencement of World War I, most of Detroit's black population resided in a sixty-block area on the eastern edge of downtown, around Saint Antoine and Hastings streets. A long-established black community, the area was home to a thriving small business district. In addition to black-owned barbershops and other small stores, the area claimed some of the finest black-owned hotels, restaurants, clothing stores, and music clubs in the nation, many of which played host to celebrities of the Harlem Renaissance and luminaries in the national black community. Yet with a growing demand for cheap labor in Detroit and wildly growing myths of endless opportunity there among Southern blacks, the numbers of African Americans in Detroit would explode. Between 1920 and 1930, the total black population in the city increased from 40,838 to 120,066; by the outbreak of World War II a decade later, the black population would grow to nearly 150,000, around 10 percent of the city's total population. And while there were increasing numbers of small and isolated black enclaves in the city, particularly on the West Side, the great majority of blacks coming into the city from down South, especially the poorest among them, were moving into the black ghetto on the eastern edge of downtown.[1] Tongue-in-cheek, residents came to call the neighborhood Paradise Valley. This irony, though, was lost on many Southern blacks, who continued migrating to the city during the World War II industrial expansion.

Consequently, as black migration into Detroit continued, the lower East Side community became increasingly segregated. And while the small business district along Hastings bustled, with active church congregations as well as business and social organizations ensuring a rich civic scene, the area became more and more densely populated, and living conditions off the commercial strips deteriorated.[2]

There were multiple and convergent reasons for the housing shortage in the black community in Detroit in the 1940s and the consequent density and discomfort in Paradise Valley as well as the few other black enclaves in the city. Throughout Detroit, in both black and white neighborhoods, there wasn't sufficient new housing. The construction industry had slowed significantly since the Great Depression, and the new houses that were being built were too expensive for most people (of any race) to afford. And for African Americans who wanted to find housing outside the lower East Side ghetto, things were considerably more difficult. During the 1940s, blacks accounted for more than two-thirds of the population growth in Detroit, but the new housing available to them was appallingly insufficient. Of 186,000 housing units built in the Detroit metro area during the 1940s, only 1,500 were open to blacks.[3]

Inequality in the housing market in Detroit reflected a confluence of racially motivated neighborhood activism among many white Detroiters, opportunistic local bankers and real estate brokers, and the explicitly discriminatory policies of the federal government. Loan and mortgage eligibility in the city were determined through the use of "Residential Security Maps" and surveys, drawn up in a cooperative effort by the Federal Home Loan Bank board, local real estate brokers, and lenders.[4]

Through most of the 1940s, the ownership of property in many white neighborhoods was governed by "restrictive covenants" written into property deeds that prescribed the maintenance of "desirable residential characteristics," including the exclusion of certain religious, ethnic, and racial groups. And the Home Owners' Loan Corporation appraisers would assign the highest property values to white neighborhoods where African American inclusion was specifically prohibited. Even toward the late 1940s, when discriminatory racial covenants were being overturned in the courts, lending institutions and real estate brokers were still enmeshed in business networks that encouraged the exclusion of blacks from housing options in the city.[5]

Eventually, however, several processes contributed to the dispersion of African Americans out of the lower East Side ghetto. As the black population continued to grow and certain members of the black community on the lower East Side were able to consolidate more capital, middle-class blacks who had theretofore found themselves elite members of a ghettoized community began pushing with more force against old, discriminatory residential restrictions. But the most important factor associated with the movement of blacks through nearly all quarters of the city was the concurrent and consequent departure of whites, for whom the neighborhoods had initially been built. Perhaps the most widely recognized institutional dynamic in the flight of white residents from the city, and the transition of neighborhoods from white to black, involves a strategy employed by real estate brokers that came to be called "blockbusting."

While members of the Detroit Real Estate Board were not permitted to change the racial character of a neighborhood, many other brokers, both black and white, challenged this convention. As middle-class blacks began moving into neighborhoods, there was widespread fear among many whites of imminently falling property values.[6] Opportunistic brokers were able to stoke this fear by selling houses in white neighborhoods to black families or conspicuously parading black home buyers in white neighborhoods. Brokers would then often encourage concern among white residents by publicizing sales to blacks and even paying blacks to walk through neighborhoods distributing foreboding leaflets to whites.[7] With whites eager to leave such neighborhoods in order to salvage their equity in seemingly depreciating property, brokers were able to buy houses from them at significant markdowns and then sell the same houses back to African Americans, some of whom possessed copious capital but few housing options, at significant markups. Meanwhile, the major sources of employment for most whites, the automobile plants as well as the many supportive industries and factories in the city, had been steadily moving out to the suburbs, where the unions were much less well organized and where building restrictions and taxes were less constraining.

Yet shady real estate practices and bigoted or nervous property-owning whites were only part of a broader constellation of factors figuring in the eventual movement of African Americans through the far quarters of the city.

Urban Renewal and Busted Business

Through the twentieth century, most large-scale development projects in Detroit tended to exacerbate rather than alleviate conditions for the city's African American community. These projects were championed by city political leaders, garnered media attention, and inspired the strained voices of hope to proclaim that the city may be on the edge of recovery, or may become once again "world-class."[8] Most such developments have focused on the central business district, a geographically small area spreading about one mile in all directions from the intersection of Woodward and Jefferson avenues, along the Detroit River, and have been driven by their glitzy, high-profile marketing potential. Over the years, these have included Cobo Hall (a downtown convention center), the Joe Louis Arena (where the Red Wings play hockey), and the construction of countless cookie-cutter townhouses. More recently, in one of the most active periods of central business district development, a new baseball stadium (Comerica Park), a new football stadium (Ford Field), and three casinos have opened.[9] For many poor African

Americans, the recent wave of urban renewal has seemed more threatening than promising, portending the influx of new white residents, rising property taxes, and their own ultimate displacement.

Probably the most significant factor in the historical reconfiguration of the black community in Detroit, and the decimation of the oldest sections of black Detroit in particular, was the series of urban redevelopment and renewal programs that were first undertaken in the 1940s. Representing the interests of big business and reflecting the tight intermingling of corporate movers and political parties of the day, urban renewal and redevelopment plans and projects were often, according to some scholars, "thinly veiled experiments in a sort of social engineering through spatial rearrangement."[10]

The first and most vividly remembered of the projects to cut through black Detroit were the new freeways built in the late 1940s. Most egregiously, the Oakland-Hastings Freeway development, now known as the Chrysler Freeway, tore across the eastern edge of downtown, along Hastings Street, the central strip in Paradise Valley and the seat of the black business and civic community in Detroit.

While the African American population was fractured along class lines and was distributed in various enclaves throughout the city, this long-established district was critical to the entire black community's sense of history, stability, belonging, and community in Detroit. Both notorious and glorious, lined with the city's most prominent African American institutions—jazz clubs, restaurants, hotels, and other black-owned businesses—it is still in the public memory, a source of important cultural and civic identity for African Americans in the city.[11] Indeed, in the late 1940s and early 1950s, Detroit had more black-owned businesses than any other city in the nation.[12] And while many of the most successful black entrepreneurs in Detroit were living outside the lower East Side black neighborhood and had even developed business ties to the white community, black-owned businesses and surrounding institutions, such as the Saint Antoine YMCA near Hastings Street, were critical to the establishment and maintenance of a palpable black presence in Detroit business and civic life.[13]

Not long after Hastings Street was turned into rubble and replaced with a commutable throughway, the Lodge and Ford freeways cut through multiple black neighborhoods on the West Side.[14] Thousands of buildings, both residences and businesses, were moved and destroyed to accommodate freeway and highway construction. Black residents in Paradise Valley and other parts of the city, many of whom were renters and thus were offered no relocation assistance, faced the brunt of this construction storm.

Detroit's extensive residential renewal plan was perhaps an even more transparent exercise in the (re)engineering of racialized space in Detroit. The explicit motivation behind Detroit's postwar renewal program, a public-private partnership, was the removal of "slums" and the clearance of "blighted" areas to make way for the construction of middle-income housing that might revitalize the downtown economy.

Between the late 1940s and early 1970s, there were nearly thirty urban renewal projects commenced in various parts of the city. Several of the largest and most ambitious targeted the oldest black neighborhoods, east of Woodward and up along Gratiot Avenue, including sites at Lafayette Park, the Detroit Medical Center along the Chrysler Freeway, and Elmwood Park, on the northern edge of the Paradise Valley neighborhood. The most densely populated and dilapidated black neighborhoods, where absentee landlords had been keeping rents low by continually subdividing apartments and rooms, were replaced with towering, clean, high-rise apartments, civic institutions, and hospitals, and the former inhabitants were relocated to other neighborhoods, and some were eventually put into one of a few new public housing projects.

Of course, despite the attractive sheen of new architecture, none of this was easy for the thousands of people, most of them black, being forcibly moved by slum clearance. Because the city refused to build affordable or public housing that would be available before residents would have to move, and because the city left members of almost all households to find new accommodations without any governmental assistance, many had no place to go. Most of these people moved to areas immediately adjacent to their former neighborhoods, re-creating the same squalid, overcrowded conditions.

Ironically, the most deleterious aspect of postwar urban renewal programs may have been their lack of expediency. Between 1948 and 1971, out of the twenty-seven projects that were started, only four were completed. The redevelopment of the Elmwood Park and Detroit Medical Center areas on the East Side were first proposed as two parts of the "Detroit Plan," which was established by the administration of Mayor Edward Jeffries in 1949 and outlined the wholesale clearance and preparation of the lower East Side for private family housing.[15] Though first proposed in 1950, the renewal project did not begin until 1960. By that time, with rumors about the clearance of the area swirling around the neighborhood, property values plummeted, and the population had decreased by 30 percent. In areas slated for renewal, there was consistently little for the community to rally around, or around which to become organized and unified.[16] And the gradual removal of black residents from neighborhoods where they had an established and rich cultural history, and their redistribution into either under-available and segregated public housing or the constricted private housing market, contributed to the creation of residential spaces where there was a dramatically diminished sense of history, ownership, and civic identity. Residents in areas of urban renewal expressed intense sorrow at having to leave their communities. One reported that "it was a terrible feeling . . . a shock, like when you hear of a death."[17]

For small business owners, postwar urban renewal programs were no less disruptive. Of sixty-four businesses in the targeted Elmwood Park area, for example, over 50 percent were black-owned, and of these, almost all were local businesses like grocery stores, restaurants, barber shops, and retail stores that were dependent on walk-in traffic for most of their trade. In total, 69 percent of local businesses were unable to make the transition to new neighborhoods after being removed from their previous sites by urban renewal. Fifty-seven percent of black-owned businesses did not survive the relocation process, compared to 35 percent of white-owned businesses. Local businesses also suffered disproportionately to nonlocal businesses because of the multiple delays in and haphazard execution of the renewal process. As one local businessperson put it, "I was making more before the Urban Renewal Agency ever came in. I could see my customers slip away through the years. . . . There's four blocks across from me they've taken, but I'm stuck. No customers."[18]

The devastation of the small business community was not simply a difficulty for particular business owners; it was a hardship for black neighborhoods in general and contributed greatly to the plight of blacks in Detroit in the second half of the twentieth century. The relative dearth of small businesses owned by blacks and the absence of a sustained black cultural center have had untold but conceivably enormous significance for African Americans in the city. For the many problems associated with the old black neighborhood surrounding Hastings Street, the sort of business district that flourished there—a black business community serving black clientele—was a source of tremendous civic identity and public trust for African Americans in Detroit. And though there are certainly numerous black-owned businesses in the city today, many of them profitable and some achieving national and international recognition, the active participation of the black community in small, local businesses *within black neighborhoods* has never redeveloped to the same extent in Detroit.

Memories of Fire

While consistently struggling to stay afloat, several black-owned businesses on Kercheval, some of which had relocated from the Elmwood and Detroit Medical Center urban renewal areas, managed to stay open into the late 1960s.[19] Near the corners where McClellen, Pennsylvania, and Cadillac cross Kercheval Street were places with names like Edna's Variety Shop, the Exotic Style Room, Mack's Barber Shop, Jimmy's Records, and the LaChic Beauty Studio. These were interspersed among other white-, Arab-, and Chaldean-owned stores and businesses, including small grocery stores, hardware stores, and a multitude of various service stations and car garages. But in the late summer of 1967 these businesses would become, collectively, one of several epicenters of explosive violence, as the deadliest and most destructive riot of the civil rights era swept through Detroit.

On Sunday, July 23 at a little before four in the morning, members of the vice squad raided an after-hours drinking spot, or "blind pig," in an apartment on the second floor of a building at the corner of Twelfth and Clairmount, northwest of downtown. The drinking club was one of many along Twelfth Street, the central commercial strip in a neighborhood that had become almost entirely African American over the preceding decade. Officers from the Tenth Precinct had been casing the establishment for several months and had raided twice before, making several arrests each time. But the apartment was especially crowded on this evening—with eighty-five people celebrating the recent return from Vietnam of a member of the community—and things quickly got out of hand.

With all the usual nighttime activity on Twelfth, and the commotion caused by the crowd from the blind pig, it wasn't long before a gathering of local people surrounded the police vans. A patrolman stationed at the entrance reported that he heard someone from the crowd shout, "Black Power. Don't let them take our people away; look what they are doing to our people. . . . I'm going to baptize this motherfucker with a beer bottle!"[20] According to police reports, bottles started flying and the crowd surged forward. Both police and people from the neighborhood reported hearing calls to riot as the crowd grew more restless and emboldened.

Once ignited, the rioting spread with ferocious speed. By Sunday afternoon, people had been looting and setting fires along stretches of Linwood, Dexter, and Fourteenth Street, all of which run parallel to Twelfth. And by late that evening, rioting had broken out on the East Side as well, first along Mack, near McClellen, and then down Connors and along Kercheval.

By summer 1967, the stretch of Kercheval around McClellen and Pennsylvania had become one of the most impoverished neighborhoods in the city, and was underserved by private social agencies. Characterized by antagonistic police-community relations, especially with respect to young people, the city's Commission on Community Relations in 1966 had designated the Kercheval-Pennsylvania area as one of twenty-eight neighborhoods in the city that were sites of potential racially motivated unrest. The Adult Community Movement for Equality and the Afro-American Unity Movement, community organizations that had consistently difficult relations with police, were headquartered on Kercheval, contributing to the volatility in the area.

But whatever the political backgrounds, racial composition, and motivation of the first rioters, and the politics behind the initial calls to riot, the clarity of these positions dissolved as the violence progressed. When Monday morning dawned, looting was reported to be "almost citywide." By then, many of the looters, who were increasingly youthful and even frequently white, hardly knew what was going on, only that they had an opportunity that surely wouldn't come around often. Jake Brown, a local minister who grew up in the Kercheval area and was seventeen at the time, told me: "I had been away for the first night, and I was coming back from Canada 'cuz my girlfriend had lived in Windsor. I got back here and I said, I'm going home and going to bed. You know, I didn't want to get into this. My dad came downstairs and he said, 'Boy, what you doing downstairs?' I could see that he had been out there, he was all ruffled up. . . . So he and some of his boys had broken into the store around the corner. He said, 'Boy, go out and get some of that meat.' 'OK, Dad, cool.' I got the OK from my father. So I went out there and I was on the wild then. You know, 'cuz Dad said it was alright. So we broke into the store across the street, went into old Fredericks up on Harper, broke that out, and took coats. And then when they started shooting at us, then it wasn't fun anymore."

By late in the day on July 24, members of the National Guard and federal paratroopers had joined the Detroit Police Department in efforts to squelch the riot. Between the three forces, there were over seventeen thousand federal, state, and local troops patrolling the streets. As the rioting continued, some black residents assumed positions on the tops of buildings or in other strategic spots, and began firing on armed troops and officers whose use of weapons was becoming increasingly unregulated. From midmorning to midnight on July 23, there were nearly fifty reports of sniper fire filed with the police. And as increasing numbers of stores were looted of all their goods, fires were set, spreading from store to store and, in a few cases (such as the block where I lived on Pingree), to residential blocks. There were 1,617 alarms in fire stations during the rioting period (and doubtless many fires that did not signal alarms) spread over 132 separate streets. As historian Sidney Fine summarizes, "The damaged or destroyed Detroit establishments, nearly all of them looted, included 611 supermarkets, food and grocery stores; 537 cleaners and laundries; 326 clothing, department and fur stores; 285 liquor stores, bars and lounges; 240 drugstores; and 198 furniture stores."[21]

While looting became less discriminate as the rioting progressed, with both blacks and whites taking things from stores owned by black, white, and ethnic merchants, most of the initial targets of property destruction and looting were businesses in the area owned by nonblacks. And any black shop owners who could get to their stores took to spray painting "soul brother" in their front windows or posting equivalent signs to ward off rioters. Carl Perry, one of the first African American merchants on Twelfth Street, managed to keep looters out of his photography studio and his ice cream parlor up the street with such signs. A *Michigan Chronicle* reporter interviewed Perry as he prepared them: "'These are just in case the first ones weren't big enough,' said Perry, working fervently. 'One is for the dress shop down the street. A woman owns it and she's colored also.'"[22] Soon, some white and ethnic business owners were adorning their shops with "soul brother" signs as well, in a mostly vain effort to protect their storefronts.

Along Twelfth Street, Dexter, and Linwood, half of the nearly eighty Jewish-owned stores were destroyed by the end of the rioting. But the Iraqi

Chaldean community suffered the greatest losses. Fine reports that of 192 Chaldean-owned food stores located in black neighborhoods across the city, only "three or four . . . escaped the looters."[23]

By the time the rioting had calmed, on July 26, 43 people had been killed and 1,186 injured. As elsewhere in the city, the business district along Kercheval had been decimated. According to the Bresser's city directory, there were forty-four fewer open businesses along Kercheval in 1968 than there had been in 1967. Among the casualties during this precipitous decline were the Idle Hour Bar, the C & C Bike Shop, B & G Auto Parts, the B & B Market, and Renee's Hat and Wig in the vicinity of Kercheval and Pennsylvania. As the *Detroit Free Press* succinctly remarked in its July 25, 1967 edition, "Kercheval was burned and looted from Van Dyke east to Conner."[24] Owing to the riot fires, and of course a cascade of other liabilities that would develop later, the Kercheval business community has never recovered.

While the late 1960s violence that erupted in urban centers across the country was all somehow related to racial politics, historians and social scientists have disputed the extent to which race played a role in the Detroit riots of 1967.[25] A number have suggested that there should be a shift in emphasis from *race* to *poverty* in understanding what happened that summer. But we shouldn't be cavalier about teasing apart these important social dimensions. In the mid- and late 1960s, the black community in Detroit was suffering through the first wave of what would turn into a decades-long (and obviously still continuing) period of economic hardship. Through the 1950s and 1960s, the auto industry had steadily moved out of the city and into the less union-friendly suburbs, and many of the jobs at the remaining city plants were filled by workers who lived either in white districts of Detroit or outside the city limits. Even just twenty years earlier, when housing discrimination was especially bad, young black men could look forward with reasonable optimism to finding service employment at one of the auto plants or their subsidiary factories. But early in the 1960s, the job market for African Americans in the inner city had collapsed, and prospects, especially for young black men, were dismal. At the same time, with the civil rights movement gaining momentum in major metropolitan areas, young African Americans who felt marginalized by the established black middle class in Detroit were becoming increasingly politicized and well organized.[26]

Long-standing bad relations between members of the black community and the police in Detroit, perhaps more than anything else, set the stage for rioting in 1967. Summarizing a two-year evaluation of the Detroit Police Department in 1968, Burton Levy, head of the Community Relations Division of the state's Civil Rights Commission, wrote that "the police system recruits a significant number of bigots, reinforces the bigotry through the department's value system and socialization with older officers, and then takes the worst of the officers and puts them on duty in the ghetto, where the opportunity to act out the prejudice is always available." None of this was lost on blacks living in Detroit's impoverished neighborhoods. In 1965, the president of the Detroit National Association for the Advancement of Colored People (NAACP) summarized the black community's estimation of the police force with the following: "The Negroes in Detroit feel they are part of an occupied country. The Negroes have no rights which the police have to respect. It would appear that the average policeman looks upon the Negro as being a criminal type."[27]

Whatever their varied causes might have been, there are important disjunctures between what happened during the riots and how they are remembered. While the rioting was born of an obviously complex confluence of factors, it is primarily recalled as a *race* riot, and indeed, in many circles, a race "rebellion." Its legacy also still importantly informs current sentiments regarding and debates about, among other issues, the potential dangerousness and/or "lawlessness" of black youth in the city, the potency of black political action, and the political will of the black community generally.

On the tenth anniversary of the riots, the city's black newspaper, the *Michigan Chronicle*, published the reflections of a number of black civic leaders on the events of a decade earlier, including those of Mayor Young and Congressman John Conyers. The remarks of Lawrence Doss, the director of New Detroit Inc., were typical: "While the violence resulted in a tragic loss of life . . . and extensive property damage, it also woke people up to the problems of Detroit's minority and disadvantaged citizens. . . . Today, ten years after the civil rebellion, we . . . have reaffirmed our commitment to the coalition process."[28] Ten years later, on the twentieth anniversary of the outbreak of violence, the *Chronicle* published a multipage spread titled "Cause and Effect: Racism, Police Brutality Was the Cause, Riots and Rebellion Was the Effect." The increasingly frequent framing of the events as a rebellion or an "uprising" are as suggestive as anything of the political salience of the events in later years. A *Detroit Free Press* article reporting on a 1992 rally in observation of the riot's twenty-fifth anniversary illustrates this: "Talib Karim doesn't remember the Detroit riots of 1967. He hadn't been born yet. But Karim, a 22-year-old Howard University graduate who grew up in Highland Park, can feel the rage and despair of Detroit's rebellion. 'The same conditions that existed then exist now,' said Karim, who will begin law school at Howard this fall. 'Economic deprivation, lack of jobs, lack of political empowerment, lack of viable options. There's still rioting going on.'"[29]

In fact, from the first hurled epithet, the 1967 rioting has been widely understood as a milestone event in the civil rights movement. A 1997 flyer announcing a city march of "workers, youth, the poor, and members of the black community," protesting the allegedly racist practices of the Detroit Medical Center and organized by the Lomax Temple A.M.E. Zion Church, is typical in its formulation of the riot as a catalytic rebellion, going so far as to attribute the emergence of President Johnson's Great Society programs to the Detroit riot. It reads: "In 1967, Detroit's mass rebellion produced the Great Society Programs of the late 1960's and extended affirmative action."

This might be a stretch. But to the extent that the rioting is remembered as a rebellion, it is not remembered as a rebellion against a unified political front or a particular, coherent social institution. Thus, for long-term local Detroiters, the coherence of the rioting coalesces most vividly around the physical spaces where it unfolded and took its greatest toll: small businesses.

Karen Bennet grew up in her uncle's spacious single-family house on Pennsylvania Avenue, a half-block south of Kercheval, and was fifteen when the rioting broke out. Looking out the window of the same house now, at vast high-grass fields, she recalls, "The riot messed up all them businesses up there, the bank, the cleaners, all that. They were gone. But it didn't have nothing to do with the houses. I think after that people might have started leaving, one by one. I don't think they burned no houses down around here. It was just gradually. It was, like, one house would go. And then maybe two years later another house would go. And you know, two years after that another house would go. It wasn't like the riots come in and the neighborhood just gone. The neighborhood was still real beautiful then." Emerging from this and other similar recollections of area residents is a tale of two neighborhoods— where residential streets were unaffected by rioting, and business districts were decimated. Many residents and community leaders have developed subtle analyses of what has happened in Detroit over the last fifty years and see the origins of the city's decline in the convergence of many factors. The destruction of local business districts, however, is less ambiguously attributed to the outbreak of violence in late July of 1967.

Despite young Karim's assertion, there is clearly *not* rioting of the sort that prevailed in 1967 going on in contemporary Detroit. But while the sorts of struggle for space (and the many issues that struggles over space signal) in the city are different than thirty years earlier, the battlefield is still the same. Small businesses remain at the center of public debates about what is happening in Detroit. And small businesses and struggles over them are now invested with the gravity of their centrality to the riots, with the weight of a long history of racial tension and hostility, over urban renewal, economic disenfranchisement, civic insecurity, and political demoralization.

The Middle East Side

Members of the Christian Iraqi Chaldean community in the metro area are often at pains to remind people that they are not Muslim. Yet despite their efforts, most African Americans in the city tend to see the Muslim Arab and Chaldean communities as a single social entity, characterized by one feature: they own small retail businesses in black neighborhoods.[30]

From the first sizable waves of their immigration to metropolitan Detroit in the first half of the twentieth century, the Arab and Chaldean communities have been involved in the small business sector.[31] And as white store owners left their homes and businesses in the city from the 1950s on through the 1980s, Arab and Chaldean store ownership in African American neighborhoods continued to increase, as family networks brought more people into the fold and already-settled members of the community encouraged and facilitated extended family members' efforts to establish their own businesses.

There are a number of likely explanations for the relative dearth of small, black-owned retail businesses in Detroit's black neighborhoods. Some have suggested that African Americans migrating north for factory jobs were culturally disinclined toward entrepreneurial work.[32] Whether or not this may be the case, blacks who aspired to own small businesses were disenfranchised by misguided urban renewal programs and discouraged by the discriminatory lending practices of Detroit banks, which forced black entrepreneurs to seek capital from small, high-interest agencies or informal networks of friends and relatives.[33] But whatever the material causes for the configuration of business ownership in Detroit, many people in the black community there feel a distinct sense of outrage. They believe that they are economically marginalized and exploited, and many in the black community contend that Arabs and Chaldeans should shoulder at least part of the blame.

Within the past few years, several widely publicized incidences have provoked especially impassioned expressions of hostility, suspicion, and resentment of Arabs and Chaldeans among African Americans living in neighborhoods where Arab and Chaldean businesses predominate. In May 1999, a thirty-four-year-old black electrician named Kalvin Porter, who was driving with his five children in their family car, pulled into a Sunoco gas station at the corner of Mack and Gratiot avenues. Though there are conflicting versions of the ensuing events, most witnesses and reporters agree that there was a verbal altercation between Porter and the two Arab American clerks who were working behind the counter. Reports suggested that this likely resulted from one of the clerks saying something sexually provocative to Porter's twelve-year-old daughter. After only a few moments the altercation escalated, becoming a physical fight, and the two clerks, each armed with a tire iron, beat Porter to death.

There were multiple protests following the murder, during which black leaders and neighborhood groups voiced their intense exasperation with the state of African American and Arab American relations. Wendell Anthony, president of the Detroit chapter of the NAACP, said that the black community "cries out for justice for this family and for our community. . . . The African American community has too long been the victim of mistreatment and disrespect by some who operate and work in stores and gas stations in our neighborhood." At a meeting between Arab Americans and African Americans sponsored by the NAACP, community members decried the racist practices of the store owners and called for a boycott. "There's racism involved. There's prejudice involved. An eye for an eye, a tooth for a tooth. It's been going on for 400 years."[34] When a jury that included only one African American acquitted the clerks of any wrongdoing, the black community was again incensed, and more protests followed, forcing the gas station to close its doors and the owners to abandon the building. Years later, the gas station's windows were still boarded, and graffiti calling for the liberation of African Americans covered the walls.[35]

But small neighborhood businesses are not just a foil against which the African American community proclaims its indivisibility. To suppose that battle lines are drawn cleanly between store owners and neighborhood residents (or categorically "respectable" and categorically "street" neighborhood residents) would be to underestimate the complexity of neighborhood politics and of race and class identity in Detroit.[36] As during the rioting of 1967, and even harkening back to the demise of Hastings Street, small businesses are perhaps the most important fulcrums in complex debates both *between* and *among* African Americans, Arab Americans, and others about the nature of race relations, class conflict, and community in Detroit.

4

Called by a Holy Name

In front of the liquor store on the corner of Mack and Bewick, just north of Kercheval, stood an elderly black woman with long uncombed hair, which leaped from her head in willowy flames. She wasn't wearing a shred of clothing, except for a pair of plastic sandals that scraped on the concrete as she paced along the sidewalk. She held her long arms out in the spring afternoon sunlight. When cars passed on Mack and as kids walked home from school, she screamed for them to stop. "Hey, baby!" she yelled. "Where you going?" She stomped on the ground and flailed about in frustration, her breasts bouncing a beat behind. There were three young men leaning against a wall behind her, very likely there to sell drugs, and none seemed to take much notice. In the parking lot, where I was sitting in my car drinking juice and eating lunch, others went about their business. A middle-aged man was selling fake state identification cards and passports out of the car next to mine. Others had just rolled a blunt, and fragrant smoke was billowing out of their windows. All of this was typical of the area around the store on Mack and Bewick, which had become something of an underground bazaar and was a symbol of vice and neighborhood decrepitude throughout the city.

Local activists and vocal neighborhood leaders cringed at the store's notoriety. But it was especially troubling to Mack Alive, a well-organized community group that had made liquor stores on Mack its number-one enemy. Among grassroots neighborhood organizations in Detroit, Mack Alive enjoys a particularly influential membership. In addition to clergy and block-club captains, its ranks include city councillor Tinsley-Talabi and her sister Artena

Tinsley, a state representative who has also lived in the area. With permanent office space in a desirable building on Jefferson Avenue (on the edge of Indian Village) and several permanent staff, Mack Alive has power and influence that one rarely associates with neighborhood groups. According to one member, it is also focused on its mission: "Making Mack Avenue great again." In May 2000, to this end, Mack Alive mobilized to thwart the plans of a local Chaldean merchant who hoped to open a new convenience and liquor store on Mack Avenue, about a half-mile down the road from the bacchanal on Bewick, in an old theater building that had been sitting abandoned for the previous thirty years.[1]

Lou Nafso had already owned and run a small neighborhood grocery store on Mack for the previous couple of decades. The proposed new store, Lou's Motor City Marketplace, would be similar to his old grocery except in one respect: although he had sold only beer and wine before, Nafso planned to sell hard liquor at the new venture. In an effort to secure a license, he went door-to-door in the area surrounding the proposed site, just off Saint Jean Street on Mack, under shadows cast by the looming Jefferson Avenue Chrysler plant, and distributed a petition explaining his business and his intention to sell alcoholic products there. While everyone who was given a petition signed it, Mack Alive responded with alarmed concern. After voicing their opposition at a public hearing, during which the licensure went before the city government, members of the organization distributed a flyer around the East Side that read, "Community Alert! No More Liquor Stores!" The flyer said that the organization wanted "to inform the community that we are not in support of another liquor store on Mack Ave" and announced that there would be a "Zero Tolerance" rally in front of the proposed site.

The city approved the liquor license, but Mack Alive wasn't going to let the store open without pitching a public battle. I had heard about the rally from city councillor Tinsley-Talabi, who handed me a flyer as I was leaving her office after our conversation about the neighborhood. She encouraged me to come, telling me that they needed all the support they could get. I was only too glad to have an opportunity to witness the hullabaloo around the prospect of an additional liquor store in Detroit. I wanted to see firsthand how history, memory, and the social geography of the metro area were fueling outrage in the black community over the pecuniary interests of nonblack small business owners. According to their detractors on the East Side, such merchants sell liquor with impunity to vulnerable African Americans in Detroit neighborhoods; they are drug dealers with licenses to do their business—peddling "liquid crack," as one Mack Alive supporter suggested. Moreover, as on the corner of Mack and Bewick, such outlets are seen as magnets for other so-called disorderly behavior, including prostitution and street drug dealing. Indeed, gatherings of young black men leaning against liquor store walls are archetypal symbols of street drug markets. And for most residents of Detroit, the social significance of liquor stores is inextricably connected to the drug dealing that happens around them.

On this weekend afternoon, I figured, the black community would be taking a unified stand on two battlefronts: the substance abuse crisis in Detroit and the exclusion of African Americans from the small business community. What unfolded, however, was much different—and hardly a display of homogenous community solidarity.

Boot Dancing for Nafso

When I arrived on the corner of Mack and Beniteau streets, a little after one in the afternoon, things were just getting going. Mary Finch, the white-haired president of a local neighborhood block club, was standing across from the gutted Admiral Theater building that was to become Lou's Motor City Marketplace. It is a grand-looking facade of brick and limestone. The name of the theater and the date of its construction as the first movie palace on the East Side of the city are carved in ornate script above the central entrance. Finch was stationed next to a fold-up table, on which there were scattered stacks of flyers describing Mack Alive along with petitions to the Building and Safety Engineering Department to rescind the transfer of the liquor license. She and other people from Mack Alive were wearing green and yellow shirts with "Mack Alive" blazoned across the front, and there was a big banner that read "Mack Alive" strung between the table and the corner light post. She was holding a cobbled-together poster board sign that read, "Take it to *your* community." Others standing around her, or along the sidewalk, were holding or putting together other signs that stated, "No more liquor stores," "Take it home, Lou," and "Get it out, Louie." These stood out among the many mass-produced signs that Mack Alive protesters were bobbing up and down and waving in the air. "Denounce the 40 Ounce," they read, with a slash through a cartoon rendering of a 40-ounce bottle of beer.

"What they plan to give us is a bigger and better liquor store," Finch told me. "All of our kids are on drugs; they're having enough problems running around being right in the mind as it is. And the women are getting pregnant. And they don't know this, but the drugs are messing up their children. I think it's just degrading really, for them to think that what we needed was another liquor store. He promised to put flowers and stuff. He's been down there for twenty-three years and he's never put flowers down there, so why should anything change?"

As Finch was talking, a small commotion was brewing across the street. A short, wiry, African American man named Mike, who lived just around the corner from the Admiral Theater, was skittering up and down the sidewalk in front of the building, engaged in a yelling match with several of the Mack Alive demonstrators. When I got to the other side of the street, he was pleading with the youthful director of Mack Alive, Evelyn Wyche. A slight woman with oversize glasses and a background in real estate development, she had started marching back and forth on the sidewalk in front of the theater's entrance.

"Woman, you have criminals," Mike yelled. "Look, you have crack houses, everything! Go down to the city-county building, or go down to one of them and protest that!" Before he had finished, she screamed back in a powerful, high-pitched voice, "We have! We have! We went to the city-county building, we wrote letters, we done it all. What have you done? Thank you!"

"I'm out here doing something right now, OK!" he shouted, thrusting his arms out to his sides. "This man," he said, speaking of Nafso, "has been in the neighborhood for a long time. This man didn't leave here like every dog-gone body else." Pointing west, toward the infamously crime-troubled liquor store on Mack and Bewick, he told Wyche to "talk about the store down there if you want to protest!"

"We are! We talking about all of them. We have a campaign going on. All of them!" she responded.

By this time, a staff person with Mack Alive named Grover Pitts and several others had come across the street to join them. "So just because pimps and players want to stay in the community, that means it's right?" the tall, dark-skinned Pitts interjected. "Does that mean it's right?"

Mike answered: "Homeboy, look, you do not live across the street like I do." Pitts cut him off, and they lapsed into a heated back-and-forth argument. "Don't tell me nothing about where I do not live; it's still my community, my man."

"Go around here and live across the street from where I live," Mike shot back through choruses of "No More Liquor Stores, No More Liquor Stores!" coming from Wyche.

"It's still my community," said Pitts.

"Well, it's my community too," said Mike, "and I would really like to know, what is the big deal? What is the big deal about a liquor store? First of all, if you don't drink, you don't drink. You ain't got to buy no liquor."

Now, several others who were not affiliated with Mack Alive but lived in the immediate area had come around. A tall bald man named James said, "Thank you! Thank you! You guys don't even live around here!" And an obviously inebriated woman, standing by with a forty-ounce beer in a brown paper bag, yelled and pointed eastward, "They don't even live here. You live over there!"

Mike broke back in, "You all don't even live around here. You all live across the bridge!! You live across the bridge. This ain't even your neighborhood!" "The bridge" to which Mike referred is the stretch of Mack Avenue—just beyond Saint Jean to the east—that elevates over the late 1980s expansion of the Jefferson Avenue Chrysler plant, as if it were a natural feature of the landscape.

The drunk woman rasped, "Go home! Go home! Go back across the bridge!"

An elderly woman from Mack Alive, dressed in a conservative business suit under her green T-shirt, pointed at the woman with the bottle of beer. "That's why we don't need no more liquor stores," she said. "Because of that. Your brain is all burned out. You're sick, lady. You're sick. You're a poor excuse for a black woman." Turning to Mike, she said, "And you're a poor excuse for a black man."

Mike looked genuinely taken aback. "Well, you shouldn't say that. Excuse me, look, excuse me," he said, catching his breath. "Look, Miss, I don't want you to be upset with me, OK, but there's one thing y'all don't understand. Alright? You stay over there, right?" he said, pointing again to the east, beyond the Chrysler plant. "Well, that's where you should be protesting."

Mike saw the tape recorder that I was holding into the fray and looked at me exasperatedly, hoping I might hear him out. "Louie, Louie," he shouted.

"They don't even understand what's going on over on the other side of the bridge. The plant's not going to go back that way." He gestured toward the east. "The plant's going to come back this way!"

I didn't understand why he was saying this or what he might mean exactly. I did recognize some of the basic social dynamics at play. Hostilities between relatively affluent and poorer blacks have a long history in Detroit. Through much of the last century, middle-class blacks in the Motor City have strived to mark their distance from less well-off blacks—living in exclusive neighborhoods and asserting their class distinction through membership in particular churches and civic organizations.[2] And neighborhood residents might easily take the Mack Alive membership, with its obvious resources and political clout, as a group of T-shirt wearing elitists, bent on a kind of cultural colonialism. But obviously, there was more happening here as well. Mike seemed to know something that others didn't, but I wasn't sure what. And I wondered, What did the Chrysler plant have to do with any of it?

Before I could ask him, Mike turned his attention back to the folks from Mack Alive. Seeking out Pitts, he asked, "Hey, hey, excuse me, my brother, hey, can I ask you a question? You don't stay on this side of the bridge, right?"

"Yes, I do," answered Pitts.

"Where do you stay? You stay on this side of Saint Jean?"

"Yes, I do. Born, raised, graduated from high school, junior high school," Pitts said.

"Well, do you understand something? On that side—"

Pitts interrupted him. "Do *you* understand that you don't have to tolerate liquor stores being put in your community?"

"Why don't you let me, why don't you let me finish something first—"

Pitts interrupted him again. "Look, you screaming and you boot dancing and you buck dancing for Louie, how many scholarships has Louie given out? Hello! How many scholarships has Louie given out? How many school programs has Louie ran?"

"Well," Mike answered, "what has the government done? We got gambling casinos; they ain't doing a doggone thing! Y'all don't even understand! You all don't even know what's going on!" Mike tried to continue, stuttering urgently, as if he were warning a pedestrian of an oncoming car.

"No, *you* don't understand!" Pitts again interrupted. "You standing on the wrong side! Dancing for Louie, Tom!" With this Pitts turned his back and walked toward the other side of the street, where increasing numbers of green T-shirt-wearing Mack Alive members were gathering, along with a couple of minivans out of which people were unloading public-address equipment. Mike stepped off the curb and leaned into the street, yelling after him, "Oh yeah! Oh yeah! You calling me an Uncle Tom then, right?! No brother, I ain't no Uncle Tom, I ain't no Uncle Tom! You all don't even know what the hell is going on! Why don't you protest the casino then? Why don't you protest the crack houses then?!"

As neighborhood residents emerged from their houses and collected on the sidewalk in front of the Admiral Theater building, a kind of improvised counterrally began to assemble. Some from the immediate vicinity had started making signs of their own. On the backs of broken-down cardboard boxes they wrote, "Go home, Mack Alive!" and "Leave Louie Alone!"

There were sets of camera crews from two local news stations to cover the rally. A reporter from the local Fox News affiliate inserted herself into the mix, and people eagerly gathered around her. The tall man named James, who had up to this point been yelling at the growing Mack Alive contingent across the street, quickly stepped in front of the reporter's handheld microphone. "I don't see nothing wrong with the store. Because first of all, the building's going to bring jobs to the community, that's one. Two, we don't have to send our kids way down to the street to go to a decent store, that's another thing. We don't want to have to go across the bridge. And Lou did more than just open up this. He did things for the community. And I don't know why they want him to leave." Mike had now seen the reporter and rejoined the conversation: "Lou is just trying to stay in the community. Trying to do something. Now there's a whole big thing about liquor. They have liquor stores up there, they have liquor stores over here. No one's protesting them."

By now Nafso had also arrived. He was standing in front of his building with his arms folded against his chest and his legs locked in a wide stance. On either side of him stood his two adult sons, and all three of them were warily watching the Mack Alive protesters assemble their public-address system. One of the counterrallying residents pulled Nafso over to the reporter, who asked him how he felt about the protest. "I think that they are taking the wrong attitude. It really is a different picture here," he said. "We're trying to develop the area here. We're not trying to hurt the area. That is not our intention. You know, if we're going to be excluded from the liquor, let's do it in general to everybody, not just to me, exclude me out. I went and got petitions from the neighborhood; nobody showed up against me. OK? Within my area nobody showed up against me. And you know, I'm not just building a liquor store, we're building a store in here with it. We're not just selling liquor here, or just advertising liquor, or selling to minors; we're not doing that. . . . You know, you're excluding me, being racial against me for what I'm doing. I'm not doing nothing wrong. I'm here building. I've been here for twenty-three years. I didn't go nowhere. I'm here every day, with the people here. I know them by names, I know their kids, I grew up with them. So I'm not trying to hurt nobody here. And they don't feel that. If they did, they wouldn't have even signed that petition. If they were against me, they wouldn't have signed up, and they wouldn't all be out here now."

One of the Mack Alive protesters, still in front of the building, shouted through the din that people from the neighborhood were "hoodwinked." Nafso protested. "No, everybody would not have come out here, and you can ask the people here. And that's the proof. I want to ask you a question. If I did that, would all the people be here, knowing that? They're all here, they're all walking up here now, because they know what my plans are."

"Lou's not bringing people out here," James added. "They coming out here. These signs not bringing him here. He would be here, regardless of these signs. This is the community speaking."

"Our neighborhood, and our opinions," Mike chimed in again. "We will express our opinions as far as our neighborhood is concerned. We are the community, the people who live here. That live right here!"

A young, neatly dressed woman who was standing close by spoke up. "And it's been approved by the city of Detroit," she said, noting that she used to work for the city planning department. "This development has been approved. I mean, you're for a beer and wine license, but you're against a liquor license. I mean, how ridiculous is that? So you're going to stop the tax revenue from coming in through this building, removing the eyesore from the community, eliminating the other jobs and other businesses that could move into the building and generate income. They not protesting the crack houses in this neighborhood. I don't understand it. This building has been vacant almost twenty years. I went to the movies here when I was a kid. It's been burned down and vacant for all that time. Now that he's trying to invest the money in it, they want to protest it, and that's not fair. That's income tax and property tax that you're losing out on. I mean, you don't protest none of the drug houses around this area. And they're not bringing any benefit to the community. At least he is bringing some benefit to the community. I don't understand it."

Community and Truth

The counterrallying group from surrounding houses was expanding. There were now close to seventy-five people on the sidewalk in front of the Admiral Theater, nearly matching the number of Mack Alive protesters. Many of them were bringing beer bottles, mostly forty ouncers, out of their homes to parade in front of the building in direct defiance of the "Denounce the 40 Ounce" signs carried by the Mack Alive contingent. With the public-address system set up, Mack Alive gatherers, now a sea of green T-shirts, were in formation on the grassy vacant lot across the street from the theater, and the counterrallying residents, with Nafso standing in the middle, were spread along the front of the building; it was a face-off over Mack Avenue, car-carrying trucks loaded with Chrysler Jeeps roaring in between.

Throughout his fractured commentary and vociferous response to Mack Alive's protest of the liquor store, Mike kept mentioning the Chrysler plant across Saint Jean. But I still wasn't clear what role it played in any of this. What could the Chrysler plant possibly have to do with the protest of a liquor store? When I had an opportunity to ask him about it, Mike demurred: "Oh, man. Well, that's a whole story right there. . . . I don't even think I want to get into that." I suggested that we walk up the block, where others wouldn't hear us. In spite of all the noise from traffic and scores of hollering protesters, and that we were standing now about fifty feet away from anyone else, Mike talked in hushed tones. He told me that he had reason to believe that the Chrysler plant was hoping to expand its facilities to the west, and that this would, of course, destroy the whole neighborhood. Looking first to his left and right, he said that he had seen a set of building plans, and that he was sure these had a lot to do with Mack Alive's decision to protest Nafso's new store. "If they so worried about substance abuse," he asked rhetorically, "then why doesn't Mack Alive protest all the drug spots in the neighborhood?" He suggested that it was because drug spots aren't "in the way;" they aren't an impediment to the plans of the empowered, established, middle-class black community on the East Side.

Mike emphasized that none of the Mack Alive protesters were from the neighborhood, but that a couple of them were in city government, and that one of them was a state representative. He assured me that a number of people in the neighborhood felt that folks from Mack Alive really only wanted to gain or retain control over property in the neighborhood so that they could either sell it to Chrysler at a huge profit or build market-price housing in anticipation of the future gentrification of the area.

A bit later on, when I was talking with Nafso and a few others from the neighborhood, including Cynthia, a former employee of Lou's other store on the block, the same concerns emerged.

NAFSO: See, they want property. You gotta understand, they want property on Mack. The city, see that's all city people there. Alberta Tinsley and them are all part of the city. They need property. See, they want the neighborhood to go down, because they want to come this way.

LUKE: With the [Chrysler] plant you mean?

NAFSO: Either with a plant or they want new housing. They want to tear down every three or four houses here and give it to, like, private sector, like they're saying, and build up-to-date subdivision-type homes.[3]

JAMES: (Turning to the gathered counterrallying residents) And not give them shit.

NAFSO: Not give them much. Because once they run away businesses, residential goes down. That's part of any neighborhood, any community. It's not about liquor. Why do they OK beer and wine, and not liquor? Drink five beers as opposed to liquor? I mean, you're contradicting yourself. I mean, that's really the fact. Cynthia, Cynthia. . . . Explain to him what their plans are. . . . You know probably more. . . . Tell them about what you heard about them wanting to take over the property here.

CYNTHIA: Yeah, they want to build new homes in this area over here. We don't need more money [people with money] over here.

NAFSO: See, they're saying they want to take from Saint Jean out to Cadillac. That's what I was told they were going to take.

CYNTHIA: Yeah, that's what Chrysler wants to take.

NAFSO: They're not going to hype all that for liquor. You know, if you want to change, she's a councilwoman, right? Why don't you change the ordinance on the distance between liquor to liquor? She's so eager, right? Don't even do this. Change the ordinance, you're all done. I can't get a license then. Right! Because if the community don't want you. If you don't want me here, then I shouldn't be here, you're right.

CYNTHIA: Right. We want him. Everybody signed that petition. We want it. Most of the people over there don't even live over here. How can you tell us what we can have over here? You can't. If we want it, we should be able to have what we want.

Nafso's son, who had been standing by like one of the Queen's guard, finally leaned in: "They are from the other side of the bridge. These are not people from this area."[4]

"I'm telling you, in a few years, they are going to be building cars right here on this dirt!" yelled Mike. Nafso added, "That's a true note. Just put that in your file for a while. I mean, that's how news happens. Mark my words . . . if they [Chrysler] become solvent again, they're going to be spreading out over this neighborhood."[5]

The many uncertainties and suspicions that neighborhood residents shared about the Jefferson Avenue Chrysler plant, and its relationship to entrenched city politics, were not without antecedents. After Chrysler had nearly fallen into bankruptcy in the 1970s building big gas-guzzling New Yorkers, it devoted the old Jefferson plant, which opened in 1907 as the Chalmers Motor Corporation, to constructing a new line of subcompact Omni-Horizons. But when sales of these did not meet the expectations of company executives in the mid- and late 1980s, Chrysler decided to phase out the line of cars, and the old plant along with them, opting instead for a new plant, to be built on adjacent property, that would be technologically more advanced and would churn out sport utility vehicles, for which a market was just emerging in the early 1990s.

Like numerous urban renewal and community development plans that came before it, the rebuilding and expansion of the Jefferson Avenue plant, which commenced in late May 1989, would require the displacement of a well-established local population. And previously undertaken projects were already unflatteringly coloring perceptions of the city's relationships to big business. In 1981, for example, the wholesale demolition of 1,500 buildings and the removal of 3,400 people to make room for the General Motors Poletown plant had completely wiped out one of the city's oldest and most politically active neighborhoods, near the Hamtramck border. Some home buyouts in the proposed Poletown area turned into protracted lawsuits, and the city eventually paid more than $100 million for the land.[6] Many of the people who had been longtime residents of the neighborhood and had financial or emotional investments in the community felt that they were duped. Residents and community leaders complained that the rug was pulled out from under them by an unholy congress of the mayor's office, city council, and General Motors Corporation leadership, which had shrouded itself in secrecy while executing its plans.[7]

In the late 1980s, informed by lingering outrage over the Poletown demolition, residents of the neighborhoods surrounding the Jefferson Avenue Chrysler plant worried that Mayor Young and big business interests in Detroit were hatching a similar scheme that would destroy their neighborhoods.[8] Most troubling for the residents who lived around the Chrysler plant, though, was that the city and Chrysler Corporation seemed to be conspiring behind their backs. As a *Free Press* story reported, residents were worried that "the city [was] keeping them in the dark about its plans while it [was] taking steps to evict them."[9] Some in the immediate vicinity expressed their concerns during a mandated hearing on the environmental impact of the proposed project. In an apparent reference to the relocations forced by the General Motors Poletown plant, a woman who had lived in the area for thirty-four years told city officials, "You all are doing to us what you did to Hamtramck. . . . You all are ripping us off."[10]

The neighborhood's resentment of the Chrysler plant's renovation and expansion was exacerbated throughout the construction process, over the course of which rows of homes were razed and replaced with "noise walls" along with earth berms that the remaining neighborhood residents worried would further erode their property values. The actual demolition and construction processes were also disruptive, shaking old houses like earthquakes and filling backyards with dirt, mud, and water from sewer lines.[11]

This history of eminent corporate domain was doubtless informing the assuredness with which James, Mike, Nafso, and others imagined the future further expansion of Chrysler, and the extent to which they imagined that Mack Alive was somehow involved. As neighborhood residents' suspicions about the possibly nefarious agenda of Mack Alive continued to stew, the organization's leaders took the stage, each speaker passing the microphone to the next.

Wyche, Mack Alive's director, was the first to address the crowd. "It is our responsibility as a community to demand what we want," she began. "And if we don't want liquor stores, we don't have to have liquor stores. Do you hear me?" Reaching out to the counterrallying residents and condemning Nafso at the same time, she offered a potentially unifying plea: "This is our community, we live in Detroit," she said. "But Mr. Louie lives in West Bloomfield! Take your liquor store to Bloomfield, Louie! This is our community." She preached to the gathered masses on both sides of the street, hoping to appeal to their identification with the city, to their citizenship in the African American community. When she yelled, "Whose community is this?" those rallying from both sides of the street shouted, "Ours!" in unison. But each side imagined different adversaries. Some of the counterrallying residents looked at each other with sardonic smiles as they participated in her call and response. Wyche continued: "Giving somebody a piece of cheese and a loaf of bread is pacification. Hello, do y'all hear me? Giving somebody a job is great. But you got to empower them! You want to give us something, give us ownership in your building!"

At this point all the Mack Alive protesters cheered wildly. Sensing that she was on to something, Wyche ululated to the crowd, "WoWoWoWoWoWo! . . . Ownership!" Shelving her worries about the proliferation of liquor stores in favor of an emphasis on African American economic entitlement, she repeated this two more times. "Give us ownership, Louie!" she screamed across the street to the cross-armed Nafso, standing again between his two sons. "Give us ownership. Give us stock in your building! Twenty percent! Thirty percent! If you really want to do something for this community, let the people invest in your project and own in it. At the end of the day, we take something away!" The suddenly explicit emergence of Wyche's interest in "ownership" at a rally purportedly about the moral liabilities of liquor only confirmed the suspicions of many of the counterrallying residents that the Mack Alive protest was much less about a liquor store than about the plans of the organization to seize control of the blocks around the Admiral Theater building.

For counterrallying residents, it was perhaps particularly irksome that the eloquent voices speaking on behalf of Mack Alive were using the language of "community" and racial solidarity to plead a case that they felt was essentially divisive and partisan, motivated by the avarice of a dangerous alliance of municipal and corporate interests. When Tinsley-Talabi began to speak, she continued to invoke the essential parameters of *belonging* within the community, drawing more directly on the protest's volatile racial politics, and articulating the specifically African American interests of the city's governing bodies.

She held the microphone to her mouth and, as Wyche had before, ululated to the crowd. "Wowowowowo! We call upon the ancestors today! It's not just us but the ancestors are looking upon us. We will have a victory. Everyone here knows that the fight to get rid of alcohol and tobacco billboards started on Mack Avenue. . . . And I'm not mad at nobody across the street. You know why? Because you're my brother, and you're my sister too. And we love you. And I'm going to tell you something. . . . We're here for you. You need to understand that. I'm on the Detroit City Council, and I want you to know that the Detroit City Council supports what we're doing today. And we're going to go before that board of zoning appeals, we're going to go before the building safety and engineering and whoever else to make sure that this does not happen."

Her exasperated call "upon the ancestors," and invocation of a unified African American "brotherhood," was reminiscent of other calls to collaborative spirit and action that have been delivered from the pulpit and podium. But the councillor's explicit references to the state, and her involvement with government and various offices that might play a role in preventing the opening of the liquor store, are claims to administrative power not just made in the name of but also to some extent *hidden behind* her celebration of fraternal love. At stake here wasn't just what would happen with Lou's Motor City Marketplace. The struggle at Mack and Saint Jean was also a discursive one over who controls the terms of belonging in the black community in Detroit, who gets to say what *community* is, and who gets to say who is in and who is out.[12]

When Tinsley-Talabi had finished speaking, the public-address system began blaring civil rights–era soul music. James Brown screamed across the street, "Brother, we can't quit till we get our share / I worked on jobs, used my hands / But all the work I did was for the other man. / But now we do things for ourselves / We tired of beating our heads against the wall, and working for someone else." In a scene of classic comic resistance, several older men dressed in dark three-piece suits and baseball caps had pulled their cars in front of the theater building, poured themselves plastic cups of beer, and were skillfully twitching, spinning, and swiveling their hips to the music.

When James Brown was taken off the public-address system, a stout woman with a powerful voice, an older member of Mack Alive, picked up the microphone and yelled, "Community!" The Mack Alive crowd cheered, and she yelled again and again, "Community! Community! Community! Community!" After a pregnant pause, she continued in the curved tones reminiscent of a sermon: "Community does not just mean you happen to live in the same neighborhood. It doesn't necessarily mean that I do business in a particular neighborhood. Community has to do with similar *values*, similar ways of thinking about the children. And so in that respect, we don't just become a community because we're bounded by certain streets. We become a community when we are a community unified with one purpose. . . . We want to build this new East Side on a sure foundation. We have no problem with the Admiral Theater going to be the marketplace. Wonderful! But what kind of a marketplace? What kind of a community will we have in the next twenty years? We have an issue with liquor. Not based on your right to drink it. . . . But based on our right to say what we in the community support. So this doesn't have anything to do with a person's rights. What it has to do with is community! A unified purpose! It has to do with us as a people, called by a holy name, standing before the oracles of God. Hallelujah! We need not continue to be ashamed. We have lived here all of our lives. I grew up here. Hallelujah! I went to the Admiral Theater! Saw Batman and Robin! Hallelujah! This may not be the same community. Not in terms of unified purpose. But we are, as the song says, coming back again! Hallelujah!"[13]

As she finished her remarks, Marvin Gaye's ringing falsetto rose over the public-address system: "Brother, brother, there's far too many of you dying."

With her head thrown back, her palms and extended fingers raised to the crowd, the speaker would seem to be suggesting that "communal" ties among those "called by a holy name," explicitly exclusive of Nafso or others standing before different gods (or at least worshipping the same differently), trump the expediency of "rights"—especially one's rights to drink or to sell drink. But more than this, such community ties afford those who can claim membership within this community of "shared values" the means either to exercise or remove rights from others.

Yet what gives her the right to make this assertion? As she would tell it, not simply a presence in the neighborhood but rather, and more important, a past there—a lost but also found and recoverable past. The weight, for example, that attends her habitation of the Admiral Theater in its former incarnation, when movies were still shown there, affords her and her "community" a sense of manifest and nearly sacred belonging. Her contention that she and her people "are coming back again" would seem to suggest that the theater is hallowed ground, a promised land, of sorts. In a city that is so actively trying to re-create itself, where histories are mutable and always subject to revision, as Detroit's tercentennial celebration reminds us, claims on the future run first through the past.

In light of this, perhaps the most striking thing about the final speaker's language is its similarity to discourse that is associated with whites who fled the city during the postwar era and who are now courted by a construction boom along the river and a number of market-price housing developments in the lower East Side. Here, potential buyers, who thus far are mostly young white professionals, are enticed to come back to a differently imagined promised land—the city that their community long ago left behind.

Everyone who was at the rally shared in a general uncertainty about the future of their community and their lives in Detroit. All were, in different ways, struggling to make spaces for themselves, to find places to which they could lay unequivocal claim in the midst of multiple and perhaps inestimable encroachments. In hotly contested language slung from one side of Mack to the other—in both desperate cries for ownership and secret fears about the undisclosed plans of the auto industry—African American residents of the lower East Side (living on both sides of the Chrysler plant) expressed fears that their futures were not safely in their own hands.

Even with all the organization's political and economic influence, Mack Alive's effort to thwart Nafso's plans ultimately fell short. The store was eventually built and is now a fixture of the neighborhood landscape, where folks from around the corner as well as workers from the adjacent factory stop to buy food and drink. But even with things more quiet on Mack and Saint Jean, such small businesses are still at the center of cultural negotiations of community belonging and ownership in Detroit; it is around them, and in their distinction from residential space in the city, that tensions surrounding race, class, capitalism, and community are most focused. And as the preceding section makes clear, this is not only the case for voices that are vested with institutional authority or legitimacy.

As we now head deeper into the lives of Dude, Rodney, and others circulating through Detroit's street drug trade, lessons from the Admiral Theater showdown—about the nature of community, ownership, and capitalism—should help us understand that African American drug dealers in Detroit are not doing what they do and inhabiting the spaces that they inhabit either incidentally or in any sort of simple opposition to the purportedly "mainstream" or "central" interests of their communities. Even as they share senses of vulnerability and histories of exploitation, oppression, and uncertain entitlement, these communities themselves are multivalent; relationships among groups of people within them are characterized by shifting allegiances and centers of political influence.

In the midst of historically informed contests over community belonging and ownership, the concerns of young drug dealers are the same as the concerns of others in the black community in Detroit. They seek control over their economic and cultural destinies, and they seek to find and create spaces around which their identities might coalesce. As later chapters will demonstrate, these efforts may involve assertions of subversive control over entrepreneurial space from which the African American community is otherwise largely excluded. In other cases, the daily practices of young black drug dealers may be assertions of domain in residential districts where their senses of control have been threatened or where their families have struggled to remain. Or such practices may signal the upending of the dichotomy between retail and domestic space altogether, through the illicit commercialization of residential houses. As young drug dealers live and work in Detroit, they don't just seize these spaces, giving them order or throwing them into disorder. Rather, they give new shades of meaning to places at the center of social hostilities in Detroit, and thereby create new kinds of cultural space where old social and political conflicts find new reconciliation.

PART II

Dreamhouse

Memories of the outside world will never have the same tonality as those of home and, by recalling these memories, we add to our store of dreams. . . . Daydreaming . . . derives direct pleasure from its own being. Therefore, the places in which we have experienced daydreaming reconstitute themselves in a new daydream, and it is because our memories of former dwelling-places are relived as daydreams that these dwelling-places of the past remain in us for all time.

—Gaston Bachelard, *The Poetics of Space*

Oh no! None of that! This ain't no motherfucking spot. This is a home! You hear me. This is a home!

—Ruby Freeman, to her daughter May, at discovering that May's boyfriend had brought drugs into her house

5

Families and Fortunes, Spots and Homes

In 2001, when everyone figured that he was on the cusp of reelection to a third term as Detroit mayor, Dennis Archer, a popular city leader and a rising star on the national political scene (he was president of the National League of Cities), declared that he wanted to spend more time with his family and would not run again. There was a sort of giddy response among a familiar and usually percolating list of mayoral contenders in the city: city council members, district attorneys, businesspeople, and church leaders. And within a couple of months two men emerged as genuine, if in many ways antithetical, front-runners: Gil Hill, the seventy-two-year-old president of the Detroit City Council, who had been a Detroit police officer and had sat on the city council for the previous twelve years, and State Congressperson Kwame Kilpatrick, the thirty-two-year-old son of Caroline Kilpatrick, an influential member of the U.S. House of Representatives.

After a close fight that went down to the wire, a visibly exhausted and apparently relieved Hill conceded victory to Kilpatrick. The six-feet, five-inches, three-hundred-pound, diamond-earring-wearing Kilpatrick rode to the mayor's office on a wave of popular interest in a young and revitalized leadership, and his pledge to shift the concerns of the mayor's office from the importation of big business into the central business district (a long-established and seldom successful means to revitalize the city's tax base, and one that had already been pushed to extremes by mayors Young and Archer), toward a more explicit concern with the provision of mundane services and the improvement of quality of life in the city's poor African American neighborhoods. This was especially reassuring to black residents of Detroit, giving them a sense that the mayor was distancing his office from suburban corporate interests, and untangling the complex and mysterious webs between them that had left residents, like those counterrallying against Mack Alive, feeling so insecure.

It is a measure of the desperation of Detroit's residents that the centerpiece of Kilpatrick's campaign to revitalize the city's neighborhoods, for which voters had such high hopes, was simply an acceleration of the previous mayor's imperative to tear down vacant houses. It was something of a grotesque irony that the city's most publicized and sustained program for neighborhood *improvement* had in fact been its housing *demolition* program. While campaigning, Kilpatrick wholeheartedly embraced the cause but nearly scoffed at the languid pace with which Mayor Archer had pursued his home demolition agenda. From the stump, Kilpatrick promised, with a bizarre air of utopian ambition (as if he were climbing to the proverbial mountaintop), that within the first eight months of his tenure he would raze five thousand buildings, which would equal nearly half the estimated number of abandoned buildings in the city, and would surpass Mayor Archer's cumulative totals by close to 500 percent.

The purported benefits of the teardown policy would be in its elimination of "dangerous" or "hazardous" buildings from residential areas. But there was a pervasive understanding that the underlying aim of the program was to destroy housing that could easily be used as space for selling drugs. Justifying his intentions for abandoned houses throughout Detroit, Kilpatrick said, "This is where drug dealers stash their drugs, this is where people stash guns, this is where girls get abused."[1] The city's program was based on simple, mechanical reasoning: if empty houses are a problem, the solution must be to destroy them.

Even so, at what may be the tail end of Kilpatrick's administration, not all residents of areas of significant teardown feel unequivocally happy about the program. Without a redevelopment or renewal plan in place, the systematic razing of abandoned houses has left whole blocks looking like images sent back from the Mars explorer. For those living in the scattered remaining houses, surrounded by landscapes of upturned dirt where old homes used to stand, life "on the block" has become surreal.

Moreover, and maybe more significantly, the mayor may not be doing much about the drugs, guns, and crime that he hopes to curtail. His demolition policy has taken down plenty of houses that surely would become, or that had been used as, sites for drug and money exchange. But in its invocation of the hazards of residential drug dealing, the program also profoundly misapprehends the nature of the relationship between houses, families, and the drug trade in the city, and misdirects its already-sapped energies. For in most cases, houses that are being used as centers of drug transaction have not been sitting abandoned for long stretches. They are much more likely to be inhabited, well-maintained houses, for which the occupants are paying rent or even mortgage. They are often replete with lawn ornaments and the scattered toys of small children.

For families that are involved in or rely on income from the underground drug market, household spaces are shaped by the sharp juxtaposition and commingled proximity of the intimacy of family life—small children playing with one another, birthday parties, holiday meals, and the gathering of friends and relatives—against the cold calculus and public spectacle of profit generation, the face-to-face and hand-to-hand exchange of small crumpled bills carried in sweaty and desperate hands, or smooth currency just drawn from an ATM machine, for pebbles of crack, packs of heroin, or bags of weed. In many cases where drugs are being sold out of a house, the people in and around these enclosures invariably form households that are essentially public, commerce-driven, drug-dealing spaces at the same time that they are intimate and familial.

Belying the complexity of this commingling of intimacy and enterprise, people involved in the drug trade—young and old, men and women—stubbornly articulate a colloquial distinction between "homes" and "spots." In the local parlance, spots are interior spaces primarily devoted to drug dealing. According to the stereotype, they are ramshackle, dilapidated, and dangerous—not suitable for consistent habitation, especially by families with small children. So while common understandings of the private home are that it is above all else *private*, spots are public and profitable retail spaces. Though they are inconspicuous, hidden from the view of legitimate institutions and regulators, they are shaped by their permeability to market traffic.

But households that are the loci of drug trade interaction almost always foil the distinction. They tend to cloud the categories of residential and commercial, private and public spaces; they are synthetic places where new shades of significance are attached to homes: where profitability, intimacy, public intrusion, and domestic exclusion go hand in hand.[2]

As the conflict between Mack Alive protesters and neighborhood residents over Nafso's liquor store makes clear, Detroit is a city shaped by a history of conflicts over domestic and commercial spaces, where there are deep tensions over the seemingly systemic exclusion of blacks from the small business districts in predominantly African American neighborhoods. Here, in the shadow of corporate and political agendas that may wrest domestic spaces from their owners, or recalibrate their monetary values, senses of control over them are frequently tenuous. And distinctions between residential blocks and commercial thoroughfares entail an expanding index of hostilities and suspicions, between blacks and nonblacks, city and suburb, and neighborhood and government. All these overlapping tensions—between domestic and commercial, stable and fluid, and familial and entrepreneurial spaces—take on particular importance in drug houses. In redefining residential space so that it is commercial *and* domestic, public *and* private, drug houses may be taken to represent a sort of unwitting or even deliberate subversion of these oppressive distinctions in Detroit. The paradoxical domestic spaces that young drug dealers inhabit, moreover, create and reflect subject positions that encompass seemingly contradictory ways of being. Young drug dealers are always moving and staying still, making themselves visible and invisible at the same time, and in the process creating a new politics of identity and space that allows them to imagine transcending historical power struggles in the inner city.

The story that follows is about a family that is deeply embroiled in the drug trade in Detroit. This family wakes and sleeps at the moving nexus of home and spot. Their story is also a window on to the "dream-space" of the home, as Gaston Bachelard imagines it, where memories of former dwelling places shape future dreams. For in their narrative, it is around homes and households that the contours of family take shape, memories of loved ones are sustained, and aspirations are expressed. It is around such spaces that dreams emerge and flourish and are suspended or stolen in capricious turns of events.

Detroit Deliverance

While Dude was still locked up at the detention facility, he had given me directions to his mother's place so that I could visit her there. Just as he instructed, I parked right behind one of the black Lincoln limousines belonging to the people next door. A middle-aged woman was outside hand washing a white limo in the driveway, and I could see her speculating about my possible purpose for approaching the front door of her neighbor. Was I a social worker? A salesperson? A police officer? I smiled at her and casually said hello as I walked to the front porch. She gave me a cool nod and went about her business.

A couple of blocks north of Six Mile, off Gratiot, all the houses look the same: one-and-a-half-story brick bungalows with Teutonic trim around the windows and aluminum awnings over rectangular cement porches. There are no abandoned buildings or vacant lots on the block, and everyone's yard is trimmed neatly. The neighborhood has an air of middle-class symmetry and domestic propriety, in great contrast to the blocks just south of Six Mile, where it seems every third house is burned out, and garbage and broken furniture are heaped in dissolving piles on the sides of muddy curbs and overgrown lots.

"Who is it?" yelled Ruby Freeman when I knocked on the door. Dude had phoned his mother to let her know that I would be stopping by to discuss the research project that I was doing and get her signature on some forms. "It's Dude's friend, Luke," I called back. "From the youth home!" She opened the heavy door and stood in front of it.

Ruby is a big, round woman with widely set protuberant eyes and a jutting square jaw. She was leaning on the doorknob, holding it tightly with fingers that were sticking out of a plastic wrist brace, wearing light blue house slippers and a bobbed wig streaked with reddish highlights. She smiled broadly at me. "Hi there. Come on in," she said.

The house was dark and hot, filled with thick, sour air that smelled like old bandages. There were three little kids in the living room, scooting around on plastic toys and grabbing one another in affectionate headlocks. I looked down and smiled. They stared, and the oldest of them took a startled step back across the sticky floor. "Oh, these are my grandbabies," said Ruby, with a grin and a roll of her eyes. "Their mamas are taking advantage of me." Ruby lived in this small three-bedroom house with two of her daughters, twenty-one-year-old May and nineteen-year-old Felicity, and their three kids, a three-year-old boy, a two-year-old girl, and a toddler, whose soft curly locks twisted around his earlobes. Ruby turned the television from a soap opera to a cartoon, and the kids drifted toward it like moths to light and settled on the floor without taking their eyes from the screen. Ruby asked me to fetch the cup of ice that she had left by the couch, and we sat down at the plain white table in the kitchen. Across the room, through the suffocating early summer heat, one of the stove burners was flaming at full blue tilt, the knob on the range broken off. Small impetuous roaches were scurrying across the floor, up and down the walls in the house, and around the table's legs.

I asked how she was doing. "Oh, I'm depressed," she answered, dispensing with any pretense. Dude had already told me plenty about Ruby's circumstances, and I was hardly surprised to hear that she wasn't feeling especially well. Dude's father, Marvin, had died only a few months before, and though Marvin and she were not living together, his death had been hard on the whole family. But more traumatizing for Ruby was the situation with her son Elvin, who had learned earlier in the year that he would spend the rest of his life in a Michigan prison.

For all of this, Ruby said that her health was her greatest difficulty. "'Cuz, you know, I need to be going to dialysis three times a week, and it just be making me so tired after a while." She crunched another mouthful of ice. "Also I got this problem with my wrist. I don't know what it is. Some kind of arthritis or something." I asked if she had been waiting for a kidney transplant, and she said that she needed to lose a lot of weight before that would become a possibility. "The worst thing is, I can't drink no water. 'Cuz my kidney's can't do nothing with it. Then I get lots of fluid in my body and I get poisoned."

Ruby had lived in the little house north of Gratiot only a few months, she told me with a measure of defensive embarrassment, as I clumsily shook a cockroach off my briefcase. "Why did you come up here?" I asked, knowing that she had previously lived in southeast Detroit. "Ohhh, that's a long story," she replied. "But mostly, it's quiet up here. People don't bother you. They stay in their own business and stay out of mines. . . . They ain't that friendly up here, but there just ain't so much drama. You know, the landlord won't do nothing to keep the place up. And I can barely afford rent with my welfare check and the little help that I *do* get from May and Felicity. And anyways, I don't like it, mind you, but it's just more peaceful than down there. Nobody talks to nobody up here. It's easier that way, you know. That way you don't got to get into no mix with nobody. More private."

"Things were pretty crazy down there?" I asked. "Whew! You ain't lying," she said. "There's only one thing I know about that whole area," Ruby told me.

"Wild. All anybody doing down there is slinging drugs and getting wild. . . . I know. I spent near my whole life down there. And I just thank God I come up out of that neighborhood alive."

Ohio Valley Blues

In the summer of 1970, when she was fourteen, Ruby rode with her father and older sister Lois in the family's Ford station wagon from her home in Mobile, Alabama, to visit her sister Jessie Lee in Detroit. The car ride was long and hot, over the western edge of the Smoky Mountains and through the humid Ohio Valley, and Ruby had made the trip to Detroit under trying circumstances. Her mother had passed away only a few weeks earlier. So with the weight of this loss on their shoulders, the three Freemans headed north as mourners, to convene with Jessie Lee, the oldest of Frank and Mary Freeman's seven children.

Ruby, a hazel-eyed, light-skinned, and carefree teenager, imagined this to be a brief and isolated departure from the rhythm of her adolescent life in Mobile. She figured it would be one among several recent incomprehensible events and rituals—along with visiting her mother in the hospital, when she was surrounded by medical machinery, and then standing at her funeral as she was laid in the ground—that would pass, the significance of which would recede in the distance.

Mary's death had come quickly. Preceded by only a few days of visible illness, it had been a shock to her husband, children, and perhaps Ruby, the youngest of Mary's kids by eight years, more than anyone else. Until her hospitalization, just before her passing, Mary had been a strong maternal presence in the Freeman family, the stricter and more demanding of the two parents.

She and her husband had moved from rural Louisiana to Mobile at the end of World War II, following the opening of well-paying and steady jobs at a paper mill in the area. For as long as Ruby could remember, her father worked at the mill, and her mother stayed at home caring for the children and helping out at the Baptist church that the family attended. "Mama was a churchgoing woman," Ruby said, the soft contours of her Alabama accent still faintly evident. "We was always going to church. Now, she worked a little before I was born. But from the time I was able to remember, she was strictly a housewife and a churchgoer. I didn't see where she had *time* to work outside the house. She always stayed busy. If she wasn't cooking, she's cleaning, she's washing, or she's ironing. Then there always was something at the church, or church programs or something. And then, for us kids, it's either a day for worship or I got to go to choir practice. . . . You know, you want to be playing, and you don't want to quit playing to go do this or do that. But shoot, you couldn't miss church. If you miss church, then you couldn't go to the show. And I was wanting to go to the show every Sunday. So I had to go to church."

Ruby was careful to insist that, contrary to the stereotype of the northern-dwelling Southerner, she was not born on the wide floorboards of a share-cropper's shack. "And it's not the country, OK?" She pushed back from the table, held her hands to her belly, and laughed. "Oh, Lord," Ruby said. "Every time I be talking about my home, everybody be calling it the country. And I always be saying, 'No it was not.' I was raised in the city. Mobile, Alabama! Born and raised right in the city. Now we got sidewalks, cars, stores—just like everybody else, OK?" She rolled her eyes. "We got lights, OK?" Indeed, childhood in Alabama was a time of suburban comfort and plenty for Ruby. Not long after her father and mother had moved from Louisiana to Alabama, they had accumulated enough money to buy a house with two large adjoining lots, where Frank eventually built two other houses, in which all of his children lived. Ruby remembers that the property "was sort of toward the back of the city, not too far from the dump, you know. But it was nice! It was just like a nice, regular old suburban neighborhood."

Although through the preceding three decades there had been strong patterns of African American migration between Mobile and Detroit, Jessie Lee was the first of the extended Freeman family to make the trip to the Motor City. One of her closest friends from Mobile had driven up in the mid-1960s and had opened up a beauty shop on what was then the bustling East Side, and business had been good. Not long after her friend settled in Detroit, Jessie Lee joined her. She had been trained as a cosmetologist and eagerly welcomed the opportunity to settle in what was, at the time, considered a city of relatively harmonious race relations and ample opportunity for socially and economically ambitious African Americans.

On arriving in Detroit, Jessie Lee moved into the upstairs apartment of a two-family flat in one of the oldest neighborhoods on the East Side, on Pennsylvania Street near Kercheval. Soon, her brother Al and his wife joined her. Al had worked as a mechanic in Mobile and, during that period of growth for Detroit's auto industry, had an easy time finding employment in one of the Ford Motor Company assembly plants. He and his wife moved in next door to Jessie Lee on Pennsylvania, renting the bottom half of a two-family flat.

Other than it being the home of her older sister and brother and a niece and nephew of around her age, Ruby didn't know a thing about Detroit then; for her it held neither promise nor despair. But Ruby enjoyed the first few days of her initial visit outside of Alabama. Her sister's apartment was only a couple of blocks away from the Detroit River and a small marina where some of the city's wealthier residents moored their boats. She could take long walks along Kercheval Avenue, where there were multiple record shops, soda fountains, and hot dog and ice cream vendors.

Nonetheless, she was dismayed to discover, on the morning of her third day in Detroit, when she awoke after a restful night's sleep, that her father and sister Lois had left for Alabama and, very pointedly, left her behind. "They brought me up here, and I just thought I was coming to visit. They didn't say nothing about it, but they was trying to get me up here to live. And so what they did was they waited 'til I was asleep. They waited until I fell asleep up in the room, and they all crept up out on me. They all got into the car; they was long gone by the time I knew they'd left. Oh boy! When I got up looking for them, I had myself a fit!" Frank, along with his two older daughters, had in fact conspired to deliver Ruby to Detroit and into the care of Jessie Lee. Grieving the recent death of his wife, and overwhelmed with the change this had wrought, Frank felt he couldn't care for his teenage daughter.

For Ruby, this would mark the beginning of a long and conflicted relationship with Detroit. Having never left Alabama and having just lost her mother, Ruby was shell-shocked to find herself stuck in one of the country's largest cities under the supervision of an older sister whom she didn't know well and with whom she had difficulty getting along. She remembers calling home incessantly to talk with her father and pleading with him to allow her to come back down to Mobile. "I called my daddy every day, two or three times a day, like clockwork," she told me. "He say, 'You gonna call me like this, you might as well come on home.' So he finally sent for me. Jessie Lee and them drove me back, just so they could keep an eye on me. But it wasn't long before I was back."[3]

*   *   *

Six years later, at age eighteen, Ruby found herself living back in her sister's neighborhood in southeast Detroit. In the intervening time, she had been traveling between Mobile and Detroit often, usually to circumnavigate the claustrophobic disapproval of her father or one of her older siblings, none of whom could effectively assuage the pain she felt at losing her mother. Twice she had departed one or the other place because she was pregnant. The first time was with a daughter, whom she left with her older sister in Alabama. The second pregnancy was by an old childhood friend with whom Ruby used to share a swing set in Mobile. It resulted in twins, whom Ruby named Elvin and Evie, and with whom she once again left for Detroit. With two small children only beginning to toddle about and their father still down in Alabama, Ruby was lonely and restless.

It was around then, and not by coincidence, that a man who lived around the block struck her fancy. Marvin Robertson was the older brother of one of Ruby's best friends. They were two of six children from one of the largest and most notorious families in the neighborhood. Nearly everyone in the Robertson family was involved in drug dealing, and the family's reputation for rowdiness, fisticuffs, and illicit "street" activity preceded them. While Marvin's mother strenuously disapproved of her children dealing illegal drugs, her struggle to keep them from it was a losing battle. Daisy Tinsley, city councillor Tinsley-Talabi's youngest sister, who had gone to school with the Robertsons and had often seen them in the neighborhood, remembers that they were "always out in the street, yelling and carrying on. We all knew that they were into something."

Marvin's sister, Elaine, had been a pretty fast mover in the dope game and had taken Ruby under her wing. As Ruby put it, "Oooo, she was something else. She likes to go and have fun. And I was the dull type. I was Miss Square. I'd say, 'Girl, you know I don't do none of this.' I didn't smoke weed. I didn't drink. I didn't do none of this. Got with Elaine, I started smoking weed, I went to drinking some bahama mama panama papa!" Ruby laughed and yelped. Her eyes watered, and she stopped talking for a moment to catch her breath. "Yeah . . . Elaine wasn't no joke. She knew some big-time peoples. She was bigger than Marvin. Marvin was just somebody out here selling for somebody else. Whoever was the man at the time. But Elaine and her boyfriend, they were selling weight out of their house. Now that was one house I was scared to go to, and whenever I'd go with her to her boyfriend's house, I'd always stay outside. He stayed over here in the Burns and Mack area. Seemed like he was always in jail, but every time he came out they was making money. And I'm not talking about no three, four thousand dollars either. Making every bit of thirty, forty, fifty thousand. He knew who to get in touch with. And Elaine stayed into it a lot."

Ruby scratched the back of her neck and pulled her wig forward. "Man, but Elaine couldn't make it last. She ended up getting killed coming from the store. See, Elaine could only see out of one eye. The other one was made from glass. There was another man she was with, and they was selling drugs out a house she had over on the West Side. And she went to the store, and whoever planned this had to know Elaine had one eye. Some young boy killed her. Asked her to walk to the store with him. They had got into it about some drugs. But Elaine carry a gun with her, and it's hard to get a drop on Elaine, and he ain't but a young punk too. So he had to have got her from the blind side of her eye. Talked her into walking through the alley. Pulled a gun out and shot her in the head. Coming from the store." Ruby frowned. "That's part of why I don't fuck around on the West Side."

With Elaine's death, Ruby felt especially drawn to Marvin, and before long they had moved in together into an apartment in a four-family flat. But that arrangement didn't last long. A few weeks later, Marvin started selling crack out of the house, and Ruby quickly found another place to live. "Just because I didn't like that. You can't sell in the house with me. Once I got somewhere to go, then I'm out of there. You know, I wasn't about to deal with that. Seems like every time we turned around, he was into it with somebody. You know, and I'm not into that. I'll move. You can stay if you want to, I'm gone, 'cuz I ain't for this. I mean, he started dealing in there . . . and then I went to Piper Street. We found a house there, and I was in love with it. We was buying the house too, Marvin and me both. I loved the house, until Marvin got there and got to knowing everybody—and everybody up and down there was selling drugs—so it wasn't long before he was doing his thing there too."

Like so many people in poor Detroit neighborhoods, where most residents are renting their homes, Ruby moved around frequently from apartment to apartment, from house to house, usually followed by Marvin a short while thereafter. His arrival would, in turn, often provoke another departure. "Marvin had a lot of jobs, he just never kept them. He used to work at Ford's. He was working carpentry. He was always at that every summer. Then in the winter, he had them jobs too. He kept those kinds of jobs. But *real* jobs? . . .

They about like six months and then bang, he get fired or he quit, 'cuz he so used to the street, so used to keeping his own time and doing things his own way. He would always be selling drugs again before long. I can't say where he was doing it. But I know he was doing it. I ain't that stupid. He was selling them little McDonald's spoons. That tooting stuff. He would try to hide it from me, but I knew."

An Old Coat

By the time she and Marvin had moved into the house on Piper, Ruby was pregnant with their first child, a boy they named Forrester. And two years later, while still living on Piper, they had another child together, a daughter named May. Then, when May was only four years old, Ruby and Marvin assumed guardianship of Dude. He had been born in Detroit to Ruby's niece—her sister Jessie Lee's daughter—but Dude's mother had left Michigan under dire circumstances, heading for Alabama after amassing a gambling debt while shooting dice with men from the Kercheval neighborhood and refusing to pay. Knowing that Dude's mother was both in physical danger as a result of this and that she had long been struggling with an addiction to crack, Ruby volunteered to take custody of Dude. At the time, she wasn't sure whether it would be a temporary measure or a permanent arrangement. But after Ruby had been taking care of Dude for a couple of years, she formally adopted him, and has since considered him as much her own as any of her biological children.

With the growth of her family, it became more difficult for Ruby to move away when Marvin would start dealing drugs in the house. And as the kids grew older, and Ruby and Marvin continued struggling to make ends meet, the family became increasingly involved in the drug trade, in ever more compromising ways. Several months after they moved to Piper Street, Ruby discovered that her eldest son, Elvin, who was eleven at the time, had been selling drugs for Marvin around the corner from their house.

"Marvin just had to go and meet everybody on that damned street, and they was selling all over the place. God! Seems like every time we look around, someone knocking on the door, wanting something from Marvin. That was bad enough, but this is what got me: you know I would do anything to get the kids them little allowances. They got to the place where the other kids was wearing these brand-name clothes and gym shoes, and here my kids go noticing Payless now; they was fine with it before. 'I want shoes like that.' Well, I teach them that you save your money and you can get this. So my son started delivering newspapers. And soon he's wearing all the name-brand stuff. I'm wondering, 'Oh dog, come on!' This boy wearing stuff like this just doing the newspaper route and with the little bit of money that I'm saving? It could be done, but it didn't seem right. It took me a while, but I come to find out, my son was dealing drugs."

I asked why she felt it took so long for her to make this discovery. "I don't know," she shrugged. "I guess I was in my own world with Elaine and all that, and Marvin was getting on my nerves with his drunk butt. You know, trying to keep him in line every time he get drunk, he wants to fight. Lord, that's all we did was fight 'til I finally decided to hit back." Ruby knew that she could be acquiescent with Marvin, but drew the line when he would threaten her children. "In case he wanted to hit the kids: that wasn't working. 'You not going to touch my kids.' So we got to scrapping and going on, and I found out, 'Hey Marvin, I can handle your ass a little bit.' Not if he's sober, then I can't do nothing with him. But as long as he was drunk, I was handling him. And the major fight we had, I never had to worry about him putting his hand on me no more. He told me I was crazy. Huh, I don't care how crazy, 'cuz when it comes to me and mines, I will fight for mines. Marvin never touched 'em since. He has to fight with the dog. But he won't mess with the kids no more. Elvin got to crying about that: 'Mama, please make him leave my dog alone or I'm gonna kill him, I'm gonna kill him.' So whenever he gets drunk, Elvin would go take his dog, put him down the street somewhere."

Ruby shook the last ice cube from her cup and chewed it up. She told me that her fluids had been in surprisingly good order that morning at dialysis, and she wanted to reward herself with more to drink and a bunch of fresh green grapes. I ran to the corner store and bought her a bag of ice and the least rotten grapes I could find. When I returned she had moved to the couch in her living room and had put a plastic tub at her feet, where she told me to drop the ice. As we talked, she would occasionally reach down and grab broken cubes to refill her Styrofoam cup. She held the just-washed grapes in a bowl on her lap.[4]

"Now, I knew Marvin was messing around with Big Mike; I mean, that was his hustle right then," Ruby told me. Big Mike, Ruby explained, was in

control of most of the illicit drugs circulating through the neighborhood, and
Marvin had begun selling crack for him out of their home on Piper. "But
what got me, when he started really getting in my children's business. . . .
See, Big Mike had Evie selling too. Yep, sure did. She was only twelve years
old. Now he already had Elvin down there. And Elvin done talked Evie into
holding a sack. Getting it off for him. And she did. Mmm hmmm. A twelve-
year-old girl, didn't even have her period, just standing out there on the corner with a pocketful of rocks. But, you know, she come and told me. And I
got off into Big Mike's ass about it. You don't come to where I'm at and get
my daughter into that! Got her selling out the house, sure did. Lord! Me and
him fell out real good. Because, you know, she didn't have the sense to know.
She was just a child."

After discovering that Evie had been drawn into the dope game, Ruby and
Marvin's relationship grew especially tense, and eventually, Ruby took occasional refuge with a man named Booker, with whom she had been flirting at
a liquor store in the neighborhood.

Recalling this episode, nearly ten years removed, Ruby seemed suddenly
on the verge of tears. "I think the real reason me and Marvin broke up, me
and Marvin separated, was when my daughter died. Elvin's twin, Evie. She
died at fourteen up in Booker's apartment, and I kind of lost it, you know. I
just wasn't myself. And a lot of times I think back. I try to remember, where
was the kids at this time? I glance around like, 'Where was you all at?' You
know, 'cuz I was in the ozone. I still carry her coat everywhere I go. When I
go down to Alabama, I bring her coat with me. I didn't even let go of that for
a second for the first year after she had died. It's summertime, and I'm carrying that coat to the corner store . . . I got it hanging up now right in there."
Ruby, who was now sitting on the worn couch in her living room, let her
head fall to the right, and she looked into her bedroom. She pointed, and I
could see the closet door leaning open, revealing an old brown coat, lined
with clumped, blond synthetic fur, hanging from an inside hook. She smiled
faintly. "Yeah. She died in my arms," Ruby said. "Evie was asthmatic, and we
had just went to the doctor and he had said, you know, she had to stay away
from dairy products, and white bread and stuff like that, and they was taking allergy tests. And she knew she couldn't eat it, but for some reason she
had wanted herself some liver cheese. . . . Dude was in there with her. He
used to follow her around like a puppy dog. Needed to be near his big sister.
So there she was, sitting there eating some liver cheese and talking, when

she went into an asthma attack. She was choking and falling out. I hear her choking and I come running in. She lying on the floor now. Choking. Can't hardly breathe. She said, 'Mama, Mama, I love you.'"

Ruby's voice was steady, but she was wiping streams of tears from her cheeks. "'I love you too, baby,' I say. 'I love you too.' I try to get the asthma machine; I bring the machine in, bring it over to her, but it acted like it didn't want to work. She's in my arms now. Her eyes rolling back. Lord, I'm saying, 'Come back! Come back!' I'm trying to blow in her, you know, give her mouth-to-mouth. But then foam come running out of her mouth. I just . . . tssss . . . lost it right then and there. And I wanted to go with them when they finally come and get her in the ambulance. I went to the hospital with her. But they wouldn't let me ride in the back. They made me ride in the front with the driver. It took forever. I guess 'cuz I'm panicking. It seems like we never going to get there. And when I gets to the hospital, they wouldn't let me in. They saying, 'Well, we're just trying to do everything we can for her.' I don't know, I just, in between there, I couldn't tell you too much. I just lost it. I just wasn't me. I was . . . I don't know. I had to ask Forrester, 'Where was you when Evie died?'"

Evie's death hangs like a dark cloak over this period in Ruby's life. But for everything that it obscures, it marks with sharp clarity the commencement of a constellation of circumstantial changes for her. In Ruby's estimation, the most important of these was her decision to leave Marvin. "When Evie died, I just left. Marvin had starting selling out the house by then. We ended up losing it to taxes, and I didn't even care. Dang, all that money we spent on that house. . . . But I was in my own world, and he was there selling drugs. Him and Elvin. So I end up with Booker. That's where Evie died, that's how I ended up there. At first I was just seeing him, because, you know, he was always flirting with me, but when Evie died, I was there. Evie was there in his apartment when she died, and I never did leave. . . . Dude went with me everywhere I went. So no matter where I go, I always had Dude with me. Elvin and Forrester was always at the house with Marvin. So I just, I just wouldn't go back. Not with Marvin selling up in there."

Ruby looked disgusted, and twisted her large body back and forth on the croaking plastic couch. "'Cuz she died where I was at, and that's where I stayed. She was with me at Booker's house. After that I basically moved in. . . . I would go home and make sure the kids had something to eat, or to see if they needed some money. I tell them to come to me, 'cuz I just didn't want to see Marvin no more for a while. Matter of fact, we was the last people in there, ain't nobody in the building; they was fixing to tear it down, and I just wouldn't leave. I stayed where she died in my arms. Right there in that building. And if they hadn't torn that building down, I wouldn't have moved out of there. I had found a place for us to go, but I just couldn't move. That was the last place Evie was alive, and I just couldn't leave it. Couldn't leave her memories. We was the last ones in there. 'Til that wrecking ball hit them bricks, that's when I left."

Ruby said she felt like she might be sick and looked like she was going to fall on to the floor. Desperate to hang on to the last material vestige of Evie's life, her worn and matted coat, but unable to inhabit for long the memories that it would jog, her shoulders heaved, and she sobbed quietly with her head in her hands. "That's it," she said finally. "I don't want to talk about it no more."[5]

Ironing Shorts

Months before Ruby and I sat talking in her house, before I had even met Dude, I had heard his name bandied about by staff people at the detention facility. I remember the first instance, as I was walking down a central hallway on the day following his latest release—his sixth to date. The clean-shaven, bald-headed staff person who was assigned to escort inmates to and from the bull pen in the basement for court dates, transfers, or other hearings, exited the second-floor elevator and spotted his colleague, Ms. Bailey, down the hall. She was just about to begin a shift on the unit at the facility where Dude had, until that afternoon, spent the previous two months.

"Guess who just left," he called to Bailey.

"Who?"

"Your man, Freeman," he answered excitedly.

"Ooooweee," squealed Bailey. "Thank the Lord! I couldn't stand another day of that evil child!"

Over the next couple of months I would occasionally hear other staff people mention "Freeman" with a trace of both foreboding and relief in their voices. Other residents' indiscretions would frequently elicit dismissive comparisons to Dude, whose reputation as a "wild child" and "hopeless case" simmered at the detention facility long after his departure.

Dude's and my paths didn't cross until a few months later, when he was again locked up. This was, as it happens, his seventh trip there, and he exhibited a calmness and sense of resolution that was likely born of his long familiarity with the place. When he introduced himself to me, I had no idea that he was the notorious Freeman of whom I had overheard so much.

Not long after I had had my first lengthy conversation with Dude in the detention facility, Bailey, a portly woman of a little over five feet, with dark skin and a sizable gap between her two front teeth, called me up to the monitoring desk at the front of the unit and warned me against getting involved with him. "Luke, you need to be careful with that boy; he's got no soul. He's an evil child," she said. I asked her how she knew that. "Look at his eyes. You see how when his mouth smiles, his eyes don't? . . . It's too late for that boy; ain't no hope."

Was it too late for Dude? He was only sixteen; it seemed early to call his cause lost. It was true that I could see something incongruous in his face. Even when he smiled or laughed, Dude's eyelids hung heavily over his pupils. And in the symbolic economy of skin tone, Dude was likely stigmatized by his dark black color. But the prejudice against him must have been strong for Bailey to see an absence of hope. Even in the confines of the detention facility, Dude was so obviously someone capable of unfettered love, misery, and joy. Where so many young people locked up there were deeply preoccupied with the cultivation of a certain kind of social hardness and would break down in tears only behind closed doors, expressions of toughness and tenderness were seamless for Dude. He would declare his love for the shifting membership of his family, people who watched his back, and me eventually, with the blunt force of a punch. While, as a writer, social worker, academic, and friend, I was caught in an almost impossible web of multiple identities and institutional affiliations, and my attention was often as much on cultivating an appropriate social persona as on the people around me, my guard was always relaxed with Dude.

Dude's seventh detention was the first time that he had faced relatively serious charges. In this case, the court accused him of carrying a concealed weapon without a license. In the detention facility he was always reminding me of his innocence: "They never had nothing on me. They never caught me with no handgun. They found that bitch in the bushes. Not in my hands." But as a practical matter, the question of his guilt didn't merit too much consideration. He didn't have the resources to contest the charge in his juvenile court hearing, and his appointed attorney advised him to plead *no lo contendre*. Dude's concern, rather, was with what sort of sentence awaited him. He knew that there was a reasonable possibility that he would be disposed to a residential treatment program for juvenile offenders, but he hoped that he would be sent home on some sort of probation.

As with many children and young adolescents from poor black communities in Detroit, Dude spoke with well-reasoned detachment about his predicament and had a precociously sophisticated understanding of the systematic inequities and bureaucratic capriciousness of the criminal justice system. Indeed, even his early childhood idealization of the police, informed by exposure to the drug trade through his immediate family, betrayed a wary and worldly fascination with the blurry margins between state racism, corruption, and justice.

"My sister had this place on Van Dyke," Dude explained, while we sat in small school desks in one of the cheerfully decorated, fluorescently lit classrooms at the newly opened juvenile detention facility in downtown Detroit. "Really, we was all living there. My mama, May, May's man Droopy, Felicity, and my daddy even was there, and this was after they split up, after my sister Evie had died. . . . We had us this big old motherfucking house. It was tight. I had my own room and shit. Come to be, we was selling dope right next to the police." Dude placed small torn pieces of paper next to one another on the desktop. Pointing first to one and then to the other, he said, "It was like this: the police, like the police live here, and our house is here. But see, this the thing, they didn't tell on us. We was rolling out the house for at least about a good two years and it's like, them motherfuckers didn't . . . well, they used to do insurance frauds. So we had something on them, they had something on us. We ain't fuck with them, they didn't fuck with us." I interrupted with some degree of naive incredulity, "The cops used to do insurance frauds?"

"Yeah, man! Man, one night, they had a motherfucking U-Haul. Well, they had Mustangs, two of them; they had one Mustang kind of parked on the curb, kind of parked off into the street, the other Mustang behind it. They ran that motherfucking U-Haul right into both of them; smashed both of those motherfuckers. They collect the insurance, and shit, they riding brand-new cars now. They used to do *scantless* shit. Sell dope and shit. Once upon a time they were selling weed out the house. Like I say, they didn't give a fuck. But back then we was selling dope right next to the neighborhood watch. Neighborhood watch was the ones really calling the police on us. They was white people. They been living there before we even came over there. Long time. They was old, went to the Catholic church right there on Sylvester. Know what I'm saying? The police wasn't calling the police on us, the police that was living next door to us. It was cool with them, know what I'm saying. Shit, they used to send me to the store, play their lottery, y'know, I bring them back their money. It was just like that. Send me to the store, buy them pops. They'd say, 'Hey Dude, go to the store for me, baby.' I go to the store for them; it wasn't no big deal."

Dude's enthusiasm seemed to be welling. "When I was little, something that always inspired me was to be a police officer. I used to see them raiding the house. And that shit was cool. That shit was cool as fuck. They coming in there, and, really, I'm fascinated with guns. Fascinated with them. I love guns. They come in the house, put your ass down on the ground, kicking motherfuckers and shit. Yeah, I like that type of shit, know what I'm saying? Something about being in the police." I asked him how many house raids he had been in. "Oooh, Luke, plenty of times. Man, so many times, it's pathetic. I wasn't no taller than this desk," he said, slapping his hand on the top of the school desk into which he was tucked. "Little, just little as hell. The first time I was in a raid, I was little, so I can't remember very well." He paused for a moment, looking up at the textured drop ceiling. "I couldn't even count them. . . . I remember this time, I was living in an apartment building, police raided the whole damn place. They was selling shit out of every floor. There was the blow house on one floor, the smoke house on another floor, and we was selling dope out our floor. That thing got raided all the time. So shit, if I tried to give you an estimated count, I say eight times or better I been in the house when it got raided. . . . Police just running in the house; it was exciting to me. I been in a lot of raids, growing up. A lot of them motherfuckers."

I asked him to describe one of them to me in more detail. "More detail? Hmmm, I got to think about which one to tell." He looked around ponderously: "This when my sister, she was the big lady; she had affies.[6] Man, my sister was the shit. After she had my first nephew, she kind of feared, she couldn't do it. She couldn't see herself going to jail, and leaving her kids on

her mama. And if her mama died, and she in jail, then what? Where they going to go? So she was kind of scared, so she got out the game. But my sister
had ten thousand dollars when she finished. She had ten thousand of her
own money. She ain't even rolled that long."

Dude smiled, suggesting a reluctant touch of jealousy. "But anyways, I'm
upstairs, just came in the house. My brother Forrester, he on the front
porch. So it was like, I was upstairs, ironing my shorts, on the bed. I'm ironing the fuck out these shorts. And something was telling me, hurry up and
iron them shorts, and get your ass up out of here. Then I hear, boom, boom,
boom. Real loud noise downstairs. At first I'm laughing and shit, thinking it's
my niggas downstairs playing and shit. But I'm just ironing. Something tells
me to look out the window. And I look out the window, and I can see through
the trees the top of a blue van. I'm like, what the fuck? But I keep ironing.
I look out the motherfucking window again. I look, and I say, 'Damn, that
look like a police van.' Now, police always used to come to my house. We
used to just be there wilding out, shooting off the porch. We was so bad back
then, and like I say, the neighbors used to call the police on us. We had a
stereo and kept a speaker in the window, listened to the radio all night; you
would hear the radio rapping. So it's like, I'm thinking, Oh they done called
them again 'cuz of that. So I open the door to the room, and I kind of walk
down the stairs. I was creeping down real slow, and I look. I say, 'Damn, we
getting raided.' And it's like I froze. As soon as I try to walk back upstairs, she
bust through the door and point a big-ass chrome .357 at me. She yell,
'Freeze, come here.' And I'm like, 'I hope this dumb bitch don't shoot.'"

Dude jumped out of his chair and stood before me in a black jumpsuit
that draped around the tops of his shoes. He thrust his head forward and
opened his eyes exaggeratedly, so that his dark irises were framed all around
in white. He put his hands over and behind his head. "So I'm like this, coming down the stairs," he said. Dude tiptoed toward me, with bent knees, and
then fell out laughing. "Oh, man, scared this bitch gonna shoot." Dude slid
back into his chair and recomposed himself.

"They got my mama and everybody and shit. Mama like, 'I ain't moving
out the chair.' She had just got on dialysis; that's when she really getting sick.
She was sitting in the chair. They like, get up ma'am, and all this. Mama like,
'I'm not fixing to get up, y'all crazier than a motherfucker,' know what I'm
saying? And then at that time, my daddy was living on Van Dyke with us too.
So they had my daddy and shit, and my sister Felicity, she was selling dope

for my sister May. And we had one window in the back room. It had one little hole in the corner, where the glass was missing. Felicity had heard them when they came in, and she threw the dope out of that window. These motherfuckers start kicking out windows and shit. Kick out the back window. I'm out there, they got me handcuffed, they take me back to the house. Then they take the cuffs off me, they had put my mama in some handcuffs, took her out to the van. So to the rest of us, they like, 'Y'all stay in the house, don't nobody move, we're coming back to get y'all.' Look, after they left, I kind of crept to the door and kind of stuck my head out, and now everybody on Van Dyke was out there. Everybody. Motherfuckers pointing. I crept to the back, I jumped out that motherfucking back window, and I was gone. I mean I jumped out that back window, Luke, I was out of there. Know what I'm saying? But when they raided, hey, I didn't give a fuck, I was laughing. They was telling me to stop laughing. 'What you laughing for? Ain't nothing funny.' But they didn't find shit. 'Cuz the dope was in the backyard. It was in bags in the backyard. You know them little purple bags that come with a bottle of liquor, I think it's Crown Royal? May had it in one of them bags, and Felicity threw it out the window. Little CR bag, threw it out there."

Dude leaned back in the little desk and smiled with bemused satisfaction. "That's some crazy shit, ain't it?" he said. "My sisters are nuts," he exclaimed proudly. "May done settled down, but Felicity is still out there, Luke. I'm telling you. Really, they both crazy."

Too Much Furniture

Though she is five inches taller than he and probably outweighs him by around a hundred pounds, Dude and his sister Felicity share the same dark and luminescent skin, and both have eyes that slant slightly upward. Born to Ruby's niece three years before Dude, Felicity spent most of her life away from her biological mother and under the care of other relatives. When I met her, she was living in Ruby's house with her infant son, Nay-Nay. The first summer that I knew the Freemans, Felicity was working part-time at the new baseball stadium, cleaning up during and after the many summer Tigers games. On days when she wasn't working, she would usually sit in the house, sleeping or watching soap operas and cartoons on television. When I would visit the house in the afternoons, often to help Ruby with shopping or other errands, Felicity would be in bed with Nay-Nay, the lights off and the door closed.

Through her early childhood, Felicity swung between Alabama and Detroit like an unbalanced pendulum. "I was born up here in Detroit, when my mama was still living up here," she reported. "And I went for the first time down to Alabama when I was five. Then I came back up here when I was six, then I went back down there when I was like seven, I was back up here at eight, then back down before I was nine. I came back up here at ten years old. I was staying at my cousin's house on the East Side 'til I was thirteen, but she said she couldn't put up with my behavior, 'cuz I was going from school to school, talking back, this and that. And she had just found out that she had cancer, too, so she said she just couldn't do it, couldn't do it either. So the only choice was for me to go back down South. That was the summer of '92, when I went back down there. I went with Auntie Ruby, because she went down to take care of my grandma. We went down there together, and on the way down Ruby asked me if I wanted to come stay with her. And I was like, yeah, anything better than being down here."

Felicity shrugged casually, as if she were mulling options on a fast-food menu. "By this time, Auntie Ruby was staying in this big old house on Van Dyke. Really it was May's house. May and her boyfriend Droopy's house. . . . There was a whole bunch of us up in there: me, Forrester, Dude, Marvin and his sister was even staying there sometimes. Ruby had just split up with this other man, Booker."

Felicity recounted how she had started dealing not long after moving in with Ruby, when she was around thirteen years old. Sitting in their hot living room, wearing the blue shirt and khaki pants required of Comerica Park employees, she told me that drug slinging was the best opportunity for a young person in the neighborhood to make quick money. When she first got into it, she was one of many adolescent women in the area who were dealing crack on the street, selling off single rocks at a time to customers without much money. "There was a lot of girls doing that. There was probably as many girls doing it as boys back then, because girls, you know, was less obvious. So I wasn't thinking about it really. It wasn't nothing special." Soon Felicity was working in houses, taking advantage of secure familial connections. "My sister's boyfriend, his name was Droopy. Well he and I first went out, we had our little thing, but he was May's boyfriend at the time. And he was making good money. I mean, he wasn't small timing it like these niggas out here now. He was making it. And I wanted to make it too, so I started working for him. At the time I was like fifteen, I needed money, wanted to go places, wanted to buy this and that. You know, so that was my hustle. I enjoyed it. I was young, and it kept money in my pocket; working for him I was making a good four or five hundred a week."

Droopy had occupied another house on Van Dyke, just up the street from where Ruby and everyone else was living. It was a big single-family house with running water and electricity, out of which Droopy was operating a pretty fast dope business and into which he installed Felicity to manage the operation in the house. I asked her if she was at all worried for her safety, or if she felt vulnerable as a young girl in the dope game. She threw her palm at me dismissively: "Nah. . . . Not really because, you know, when you young you don't be thinking about the dangerous part of it. Well, I had heat [a gun], 'cuz it was like I was in the spot. I was working in the spot down the street from the house. Well, when I first started working there it wasn't a spot, it was just the house, but when we moved down the street on Van Dyke, I was still selling there. Heat, electricity, all that was straight. Furniture. And I had my friends over and everything. So it was all good."

But it didn't remain "all good" for too long. Droopy's dominance of the market in the area was soon provoking the animosity of other upstart dealers in the neighborhood and, as Felicity told me with characteristic nonchalance, "There was some gunplay and all that." With neighbors now taking notice and fearing for their safety, the police started snooping around more often. Concerned that he would be subjected to more rigorous investigation and not wanting to relinquish the market space to his competitors, Droopy decided to move all of his trade into the big old house down the block on Van Dyke, where everyone was living. He then unceremoniously burned his dope house to the ground.

From when she was young, May had been an assertive and enterprising person. She had inherited Marvin's light, glowing complexion and his blue-green eyes and, as she describes it, had most of the neighborhood's young men at her beck and call. And while she associated her involvement in the drug game with her involvement with one such solicitous man, she was clearly more in charge of the operation than he. "You know, every girl wants a bad boy. You know how that feeling go. Well, this boy was bad. He sold drugs; I sold drugs. I mean it was like I was on top of the world with him, you know. Like nothing I wouldn't do for this man. We just living the life. And, you know, I took care of my mother and them. When we moved, I moved them up out of where we was [on Piper] into a better house."

May nodded enthusiastically and habitually clicked her pierced tongue against her front teeth. Her three-year-old son, Deon, pushed the door open and toddled into May's room, which was upstairs from Ruby's and Felicity's rooms and decorated with colored scarves and posters on the wall. "See, when I moved Mama," May continued, "we had material things, not like that used-up, raggedy-ass furniture and stuff that's sitting downstairs, the broken stove and all that. We had better things than that. I bought my mother a refrigerator with two doors that run all the way to the floor. Bought her that. And her room was *straight*, trust me. We had *too* much furniture in that house, if you ask me. And I furnished the whole thing. There wasn't nothing in that house anyone can tell me I didn't buy. And everything was for my mother."

Having heard from Felicity that they were selling drugs out of the house on Van Dyke, I asked May if this house was "the same drug spot Felicity told me about?" May recoiled at my indiscretion and categorical confusion: "No it wasn't no spot. We basically did weight. We sold a little stuff. We sold out of the house. But it wasn't like a dope, like a dope house. Like I say, everybody stay with us. We had my brothers, Felicity, my mother, my father, my cousins, their friends. So basically it was just the family place, I didn't turn anybody down. But then Droopy had a little other girlfriend—a little older girlfriend. He used to be staying over at her house. He used to spend nights at our house sometimes, every now and then. But like I say, it didn't really matter 'cuz I was making so much money I didn't have time for him anyway. I had about, I would say, five thousand a week. And like I say, we had so much stuff. There wasn't nothing anybody wanted for. You had it. Name-brand everything. The babies stayed fresh. You name it, we had it up in that house."[7]

Mama's Cane

Unlike Dude, Ruby didn't find anything the least bit amusing about police raids, and in spite of all the material comforts that May and Droopy's money might have provided, Ruby could no longer endure the constant harassment of the narcotics division. After being handcuffed by the police and dragged outside in front of her neighbors, Ruby packed her few bags with her few easily moved possessions and left Van Dyke. As always, she stayed on the move. Ruby found a small, sparsely furnished rental unit on the northeast side of town, on Seymore Road. She thought that leaving the lower East Side would put some distance between her and the spider-webbed drug-trading networks in which members of her family were entangled.

Unfortunately, this didn't work out as she had hoped. Only a few months after Ruby left, May and Droopy were evicted from the house on Van Dyke after Droopy started smoking too much of his own supply. Meanwhile, May had given birth to a son, and she had stopped slinging drugs. Soon she and Droopy were sleeping most nights at Ruby's house on Seymore, along with Forrester, Felicity, Dude, Marvin, and his sister Lydia, who was herself addicted to crack.

While none of the family members were selling drugs out of the house on Seymore, it wasn't long before the more pronounced and pervasively "Blood" influenced gang culture of the northeast side of the city became a problem for the household, and especially for Dude and Forrester, both of whom, attesting to their identification with the lower East Side, had long claimed affiliation with the (Crip-associated) Gangster Disciples.

Like most kids growing up in Detroit, Dude's involvement in drug dealing emerged independently of his involvement in any gang activity in the city. Before he was thirteen years old, he and several of his friends had formed an incipient little group, which they called the Playboys. They all had rough, home-hewn tattoos put on to their arms, with little bunny-head silhouettes and the word "playboys" written in clumsy cursive. At the juvenile detention facility, Dude pulled back his jumpsuit sleeve and rubbed the coarse, lined image with his index finger, barely discernible against his dark skin. "With the Playboys, we was neutral, right. And it's like, when we was growing up down there on Van Dyke, it was the S.U.N.s. The S.U.N.s was Crips. So we used to always say, 'Fuck a Blood.' It really wasn't, we wasn't really initiated into it like that. Know what I'm saying? We call ourselves neutral. We was out for the hos. Getting money and hos. So that was our whole motto: being a playboy. Me and my niggas, we rode under the six [pointed star], but you know we never really put ourselves into representing and shit, like to the fullest."

Dude held out his hand to shake mine, and twisted my fingers around into a palsied gnarl. "That's Folk up. See you got the fork right there," he said, pointing to my fingers, which seemed to have arranged themselves into a shape vaguely reminiscent of a three-tined fork. "See, if I wore a hat, I turn that motherfucker to the right. That mean, shit, you letting niggas know what you represent. Bloods to the left. Crips and Folks, they're to the right. I didn't consider myself in no gang. I considered myself representing. There's a difference. Gangbanging is just straight up, 'I'm Folk nigga, and this and that.' Me, I wear my hat to the right, walk down the street. You know what I'm saying. I see a slob [a derogatory term for Bloods], he notice me and I notice him, it's on. But I just consider myself representing. Just getting money, representing. If I'm in a room, and it's a room full of Bloods, and they be like, 'What you representing?' I be like, 'I'm representing Folks.'"

While I stayed in my seat, Dude rose and walked to the chalkboard, and drew a trident, pointed up, in white chalk. "That's for them hard-legged ass niggas. Gangbanging is stupid," he said. "Gangbanging ain't going to get you money. So fuck that gangbanging. Everybody who survived that shit back in the day, they realize, like, that shit ain't get me nowhere. I almost got killed. If I want to do something, just go on ahead and make some money, and represent. That's the new generation, they mainly trying to get money. Get money and represent they shit."

But for a Folk or GD, representing in the lower East Side would entail much different risks than representing in northeast Detroit. Here, where groups of kids walking home from school are often a roiling mass of red and black hats, bandanas, T-shirts, and jackets, any signification of alliance with Crips could be a distinctly provocative and foolhardy gesture. When Ruby and then her children moved to northeast Detroit, entanglements with local Bloods followed soon thereafter. "My sister, she was kicking it with one of them slob niggas. And he bought her a ring, but he thought he was going to get some pussy or something, and he didn't get that. So she told him, 'It's over. I don't want to go with you anymore.' But, like I say, he had even bought her a ring, so my man was pissed off. So comes to be, he throws a brick through my mama's window. And I was there. I hear the brick come through the window, smash the glass, and land right in the living room. Right on the floor, sitting on the rug. I'm the only one home, so I run out there, ba, ba, ba. Luke, I'm telling you, man; I'm throwing them. I'm crazy. I lay the mother-fucker out. Out cold. I whupped his ass good."

Around a week after this incident, at just past noon, Dude came home from a quick trip to the store to find May talking to the same young man on their front porch. He could hear that their voices were raised. "I was like, 'Man, I'll come up on that porch and beat your ass again,'" Dude told him. "He like, 'Whatever, this and that,' and then some guys in a van pulled up. They all jumped out the van and, shit, walked alongside of my house. It's like I turned to look at him and I turned around, got hit. Knocked me on to the ground." Dude punched his right fist into his left palm, and threw his head to the side in pantomime. He lay with his face on the ground, his cheek hot and buzzing from the blow. "When I came back up, I grabbed my mama's cane; it's like the first thing I seen. I just split him, just beating him. But then after that they was all on me. All come out of the van and was just beating on me. I have to say, you know, I was being watched over then, you know, just to be alive." Later, Dude was watched over by more than a celestial guardian. When word of the gang beating reached his brother Forrester, a small troupe of young men from southeast Detroit made their way up to Ruby's house on Seymore. "My brother Forrester, know what I'm saying, he had that AK. And he brought some people around. So when all them came around again, we was waiting, ready to attack them bitches."

Ruby was in the house when the gunfight ensued. She was sitting on the couch, with her customary cup of ice, watching one of the several soap operas to which she has been long devoted. Forrester, Dude, and some others from the old neighborhood were settled around the outside of the house, on the porch and the front steps. When the same van that had brought Dude's assailants pulled up in front of the house, Dude's brothers and friends opened fire. Ruby heard bullets ringing through the room and fell behind her stuffed reclining chair. "Oooweeee. I was screaming like a crazy woman," she told me. "Oh Lord, yes. But I didn't get hurt. And none of my peoples got hurt. . . . I'll tell you one thing. Now as far as anyone else getting hurt, let me just say: Forrester can take care of himself." Ruby chuckled wryly. "I'm not going to say nothing else about that."

Only a couple of months before the shooting on Seymore, Marvin's mother had passed away after a long struggle with heart disease, during which she had been in and out of the hospital for months on end. She had left the house to the care of Marvin and his older brother John, and, in the weeks after her passing, Marvin had moved from Seymore into the old Robertson house. After her living room was riddled with bullet holes, and even though she had some ambivalence about it, Ruby decided to leave Seymore and, reversing their usual order, follow Marvin into the house at the intersection of Parkview and St. Paul, right around the corner from where she had lived with her sister Jessie Lee when she first arrived in Detroit.

"After all that shooting up, man, I left that place. I grabbed Dude, Felicity, and May, and I went to Marvin's house. Marvin had already left Seymore; now that his mama had passed, he was doing her house. They open it up as a little spot. Well, they was selling big-time drugs up out of there after a little bit now. Before I even get there, I knew I didn't want to go; I already knew what they were doing up there, but it felt like I didn't have no choice. . . . I asked him to stop selling as long as I was in that house. And he did that . . . sort of. See, Marvin moved into the building across the street, and he got himself a job as the apartment manager there. But how long do you think that job lasted? Before long, Marvin was selling out of that building too! You know, he had Forrester and all of them selling out of the building. So he could say that he wasn't selling in the house. But still and all, the customers knew him from *this* house. So they still knocking at *this* door, where *I'm* staying. And I'm supposed to send them over there! I don't even want to have a conversation with these people. Come on now. I knew damn near everybody that came to the door. And then all I didn't know, I got to know! So you know, they was still. . . . You still was selling out the house! That's all that mattered. So I had to get out of there. That's when I come up here."

When she decided to leave the Robertson house, Ruby considered heading back down to Mobile. She could move in with her first-born daughter, Sarah, and take some of the younger children with her. It was an enticing possibility. But ultimately not one she could pursue. With Elvin's relatively recent conviction, and with her concern that she would not be able to convince Dude to accompany her, Ruby was resigned not to leave Detroit.

Her prejudices against moving to the West Side would preclude it as a possibility, so from the house on Parkview, Ruby left for as far away as she could reasonably go without leaving the East Side of Detroit. While the rent would likely be a stretch, she moved into the small brick bungalow in the northeast corner of the city, next door to the owners of a limousine service. "But Dude and all of them wanted to stay with Daddy down on Parkview. Then he supposed to go to school down at Southeastern High from there, and I got on Marvin, 'cuz Dude wasn't doing it. So that's when I put him over in Osborne High School. But what good it do? He didn't go there either. At least he did step a foot every now and then in Southeastern. But he didn't want to go nowhere near Osborne. Thinking I'm trying to do right by his little ass! Lord. Mmmm. That boy just didn't want to leave Parkview. Didn't want to leave the game."

Coda: In the Youth Home

Before the napping inmates were startled awake by the unsettling odor of jail-prepared food wafting off the stainless-steel lunch carts—wheeled out of the elevators and down the echoing central hallway to which all the units were connected—the boys and girls were all locked in their rooms and lying, many of them facedown, on their small beds. Their heads were covered under blue-green sheets, and the unit commons were still. Many of the gray-clad guards had fallen against their chair backs, with pens in hand or with their black hats crumpled forward, their mouths agape and their throats rattling with breathing amplified by desperate, insubordinate slumber.

In the midst of this quietude, and under the watchful eyes of cameras hung from the corners of the rooms and surveying the great hall, Dude and I crept from the unit and went to the empty gymnasium. We sat on the rubberized floor, leaning against the shelved hard-plastic bleachers. Earlier in the day Dude had learned that he would be released on probation. Beyond all his wildest hopes, he wouldn't even have to wear an electronic tether. He would need to attend a few classes and some structured probationary activities, but, with this light disposition, Dude felt that he had dodged a bullet.

He still wasn't sure when and if his actual release would be authorized, when he would walk through the front doors and into the hot sun, which he hadn't felt in three months. The uncertainty of the wait seemed to make him somber and reflective in the final days of his most recent stint at the detention facility.

I asked him what he planned to do when he got out. He looked up at me and smiled slyly. "You know, it's time for me to get serious, you know. . . . I ain't going to be playin' no games. Up in the youth home a nigga can start thinking like a kid, because that's how they treat you up in here. I done asked God for a lot, and he gave it to me. Got me out of this mess. So now, you know, I got to hold up my end of that bargain. . . . I'm a grown-ass man, and now it's up to me to do what I need to do."

Dude leaned back and with his voice muddled by its return off the bare

cinder block walls, recalled his past and plotted his future. "Early as I can remember my daddy was selling dope. My brothers, my sisters, mother. They
all taught me this game. And I really learned the game from the hood where
my daddy was living, from down there in that old neighborhood. Everybody
from that area, they grew up together. It wasn't like a nigga just came from
like down the way, and just moved over here and just grew up. Them type of
niggas, we ran them out from over there. You know what I'm saying? You got
to get your ass from over there. This is a family-owned thing, here, you know
what I'm saying?"

Dude and his brothers Forrester and Elvin used to have a "motto" celebrating their mutual dependence. "We used to have us a little saying, 'OFF.'
O . . . F . . . F. . . . Means 'only fuck with family.' That's our clique. Only
fuck with family. You ain't family, we ain't messing with you. You know how
it is with big brothers. You want to be like your big brother and shit. It's like
my brother Forrester, he rolling for these niggas. He used to give me something, just to keep me from stealing cars, shit like that. He ain't fixing to give
me nothing free, 'cuz ain't nothing free in the world. So he was giving me like
$35 off a $100 sack. Bring him back $100, keep $35. But then after a while
I was like, 'Fuck that, I need more.' So then I started with more. I was getting $80 off $200.

"And the whole time, I wanted to be like my big brother Forrester, you
know what I'm saying? I'm like, this nigga ain't stealing, this nigga ain't doing this, this nigga ain't doing that. But then after a while, after no more
dope weren't coming in, or after he weren't really making no more money;
shit, he was doing basically what we was doing. So I'm looking like, shit, this
nigga another one of us. I can be better than this nigga. I can go out there
and get my own; it was like I just felt that it was a need for me to handle my
own business, go out there and get my own money, instead of depending on
another nigga to get me something. Even though my mama used to tell me,
you better start to act your age, you know, act your age. I'm like, fuck
that. . . . I'm fourteen, but I'm acting like I'm about eighteen. And ever since
then, I been acting that way, and people be like, 'How old is you, nineteen?'
'I'm sixteen!' Niggas be like 'What? You sixteen; oh, you can't hit this weed.'
'Man, you crazier than a motherfucker,' I say. 'You got to pass me that blunt.'"

Dude fell silent and looked pleased. On the other side of the cavernous
space, the gymnasium supervisor, who had fallen asleep with his chin dug
into his palm, which was supported on his knee at his bent elbow, grunted

and snorted and shifted in his seat. Dude didn't seem to notice. "Then it go to my oldest brother, Elvin," he said. "He was still selling dope, but he was doing it right. That's why I think, if he was out of prison, walking the streets with me, half the shit that's happening, or half of the people I be around, it wouldn't even be like that. It wouldn't even be that type of party. My big brother never play that shit. With him, it's like if I'm out there slinging, *sling*, know what I'm saying? If I be like, 'I want to go with you on this lick.' He be like, 'No.' No. So it was like, he loved me, know what I'm saying? I ain't saying that he like, 'Well, I'm your big brother and you ain't fixing to do this,' but the shit he was doing he wouldn't let me do it. The only thing he was going to let me do was sell dope."[8]

I asked Dude if he had thought about selling dope on his own or setting up his own operation outside the family. But he seemed headed in the other direction, toward home. "Funny thing, man. I was rolling for these cats. They went down to Columbus, set up shop down there, and I didn't want to go. They left me a house. I had all this money. I was fucking this little redbone who come from the West Side, little light-skinned chick. And I had her rolling in there for about a day, and then I was like, 'Fuck this house.' 'Cuz, man, it's like the house I was selling dope out of, we was still paying rent to the owners. My nigga, he was paying them $400 a week. Every Friday. The owners knew we was selling dope and they was like, fuck it, sell dope, just don't tear up my house. We had the bitch fixed up. You would come in, chill, sit back, watch a little cable. Go in the refrigerator, there's food in that mug. Ain't no spot, this our house. We was paying them $400 a week. And I was like damn, I barely making $1,500, and you want me to pay you $400 a week? Fuck that. I go up to my daddy's house, go home, and sell all the dope I want for free. So it's like I stop selling dope up there, I just shut down operations.

"See, Luke, I just couldn't fuck with it." Dude shifted around on the floor, so that he was facing me. He crossed his legs and played with his oversize, facility-issue gym shoes. "At that point in time, I was on that other-other. 'Cuz, like, I want to sell dope and move. Sell dope and move. Sell a rock here, sell a rock there. . . . I ain't going to lie, the money was getting to me. Nigga, fourteen, fifteen years old, handling $800 just, shit, that's a lot for a fourteen-year-old to have. Eight hundred dollars, I'm fucking females, I can go to the mall anytime I want to. I had to learn that you ain't going to accomplish shit just out there ripping and running, spending all you can spend. 'Cuz like I say, there was times I think I done spent like $50 on food, and I ain't even hungry. I just wanted to be moving, 'cuz I just wanted to be out spending money. And I was too greedy to be spending four hundred a week on rent."

"Man, Luke," said Dude, with a quiet smile and determined shake of his head, as if to ready himself for a more serious disclosure, as young inmates would often do when talking about home and the expansive spaces they might inhabit after their release. "Like, fuck this man," Dude continued, dreaming now of spots and homes. "When I get out, for real, I'm fixing to just get with my family, my niggas, sit there and just roll. Make my money, stack my shit, stack my shit, stack my shit. I mean, shit Luke, you've seen the house we living in. It used to be that I'd say, 'Well, the only reason I'm doing this is that I'm trying to get something a whole lot better. Buy my mama a brand-new stove or something, a brand-new refrigerator.' But then, instead of doing that, I end up doing other things. And then I still tell myself, 'Well, I'm selling dope to take care of my mama.' But that ain't even the truth. I'm selling dope to really just to be selling. . . . I look at it now, doing my days locked up in here, even when I was at home, I look at selling dope, like, 'Damn, I'm selling this shit for nothing.' And now it's gotta be different, Luke. Forrester's on the run, Elvin's locked up forever. And now my daddy gone. That was my mans. I remember him, sitting in the hospital with his stomach cut open after they found that cancer. Man."

Dude laughed and pressed a tear away with the tip of his finger. "He was fighting 'til the end. I remember he called the nurse a stupid bitch, I remember that. And then he died the next day. That was my mans. Well, I got to be the man now, Luke. But it's like, I'm not selling it for nothing, 'cuz I'm getting paid, but then what are you doing with your money? You ain't doing shit with your money. You ain't saving it, you ain't buying what you supposed to buy. You ain't doing nothing. So what are you gonna do, overcome it or become it? What you gonna do, man?"

6

The Thickness of Blood

Dude was sent home from the detention facility on a boiling hot day in early July. After waiting for several months for his case to be resolved, and then waiting weeks for the details surrounding the assignment of an electronic ankle tether to get sorted out and eventually dropped, his release seemed to come suddenly and catch him off guard. He learned only two days before that he would be sent home on the appointed day, and even then he was reluctant to take much stock in the likelihood that he would actually walk through the facility's front doors.

That morning, I found Ruby in the lobby of the facility. She was sitting on one of the foam blue chairs that are fixed to the floor in formation, tossing ice into her mouth from a white foam cup. She had gotten a phone call from the special services provider on Dude's unit the night before, and had been told to come to the facility early in the morning to pick him up. The next day she caught the bus and rode down Gratiot Avenue, a huge thoroughfare that angles across the city's grid on the East Side, from downtown to the northeast corner of Detroit. She had already been waiting for nearly an hour when I showed up and sat down next to her.

She said hello quietly, as if she were out of breath. I tried to reassure her that it always takes a long time for kids to get through all the weigh stations on their way out the facility door, as they are moved from bull pen to bull pen, as mysterious papers are signed and procedures observed. "Yeah, they lock 'em up quick, but they take forever to release them," she agreed, as she compulsively pulled apart and pressed together the Velcro strap on her wrist brace.

"Lord I'm thirsty," Ruby said, after an awkward silence, "and I'm stuck with this ice again. . . . You know, I just love watermelon," she said, staring absently out the window of the detention facility waiting room. "It's my favorite food. And I just hate that I can't eat it." She seemed to be talking only to assuage her nervousness. "I always say that if I want to just kill myself, I'll just get a big watermelon and a jug of water and go out happy. . . . I tried that once. When I was real down, I just got myself a big ol' water-melon and sat down there eating away. My daughter came in and saw me; she said, 'What are you doing?!' I said, 'I'm eating myself a watermelon. Now leave me alone!' Oh Lord. I was sick. They had to rush me to the hos-pital, to the emergency room. I was falling out, sick as a dog. Couldn't breathe, my heart was all messed up. . . . So I'm not going to do that again. I'm done with all that." Ruby laughed and looked away, and we fell silent again.

At around three in the afternoon, after Ruby had been sitting in the lobby for several hours, talking with other mothers there, and after she had worked her way through several cups of ice, pushing the limits of her allowable liq-uid intake, Dude walked slowly and stiff leggedly through the bright red door, under the metal detector, past the sheriff's desk, and toward me. He was wearing a dirty orange Giants baseball jersey along with jeans that he had turned inside out because they were so filthy. The stench from his clothes was nearly unbearable. His pants had been caked with mud when the police dragged him along the ground in the process of arresting him and stuffing him into their cruiser. And his shirt, which had been tossed several months before in a heap of other detained kids' clothes and locked in a closet, had adopted the pungent odor of stale, stress-induced sweat, ex-creted by kids who had just been handcuffed and whose minds and adoles-cent bodies were tense and afraid. He reached his hand out and shook mine, twisting our fingers into gang signs, as he had done countless times on the unit, and then stood silently with his arms to his sides. Ruby said, "Hey, aren't you forgetting something," and reached her arms out to hug him. "But my clothes stink," he said. "Well, I don't care about that," Ruby responded, clutching him against her torso.

We decided that I would drive everyone home, so Dude and I left to retrieve the car. Nearly every day, when I had seen Dude in the youth home, he had asked me what the weather was like outside, and over the spring and summer I had made inept efforts to describe it as unpleasant, to reassure him that he wasn't missing anything. So I was excited to walk out with him on this hot, sunny day. When we swung the doors open, the air fell on us in heavy blankets. "Luke, it's too hot out here," he said. "You wasn't kidding. Shit, it's nicer in there."

On the way to Ruby's house, Dude sat in the backseat, behind his mother, while she yelled back at him, over the sounds of traffic on Gratiot and wind coming through the windows, about her expectations of him during his probation. "You going to be doing all kinds of stuff," she said. "Just 'cause you coming home doesn't mean it's going to be easy. After a little bit, you might be wishing you could go back up into the youth home." Ruby paused strategically. "So tomorrow, you going to the morgue."[1]

"What? Tomorrow?!"

"Yeah, and then on Saturday you going to a gun awareness class at the district court. And then next week you going to basketball camp."

"I ain't going to no basketball camp," protested Dude, who happens to love basketball.

"Yes you is. And whatever else they tell you to do. This is intensive probation, man. We got to keep you busy: basketball camp, football camp, we got to keep you busy." Dude was quiet in the backseat and wore a big dismissive smile.

"The most important thing," she said, "is that you are not allowed to cross Gratiot. I don't care who's down there, or what you think you want to do. You ain't going down to them neighborhoods; not Parkview, not Kercheval, not Mack. None of it." Dude didn't bother launching a protest. But of course, he was formulating a somewhat different prescription, with his own hopes and ambitions.

As I dropped them off at the house, Ruby walked toward the porch while Dude and I arranged to meet a couple of days later. We shook hands and hugged, and he walked slowly onto the porch to greet Felicity, May, and his nephews and niece, who were sitting on their mothers' laps under the aluminum awning, trying to escape the heat. As Dude settled onto the cement steps of the front porch and looked out into the street in front of Ruby's house, it seemed obvious, however, that he wasn't yet home.

A Drive with Ruby

When I returned to meet Dude, Ruby told me that he had left. She sounded frustrated and discouraged, breathing a heavy sigh and looking around distractedly. She told me that she knew that he had gone to the morgue earlier in the week, but that he hadn't come back home in a few days. "Are you worried that he's not OK?" I asked. "You see I'm worried, don't you?" she said impatiently, shaking her head. "But I don't know what to do. I can't chain that boy down. If he needs to be moving around, he's going to be doing it." Ruby shrugged her shoulders and slapped her hands onto her thighs. "That's always the problem with these boys. Moving, moving, moving. Can't stay still. Don't know where they're at. Boys in the city; they're on the move." She told me to keep trying and assured me that she'd call me if he showed up.

I hadn't heard from her, but about a week later I stopped by again. I knocked on the door, and Ruby called wearily, "Who's there?" When I shouted my name, she sang "Hey!" with a ring of familiarity. She came to the porch and told me that she had no idea where Dude was, that he had been by recently, but only for a couple of hours, and that he had been gone again for the past two days. Ruby said that his probation officer, Ms. Clementine, had stopped through and seemed upset that he wasn't around.

She invited me to sit down in the living room and offered me a glass of water. Ruby came back from the kitchen, limping slightly on one of her legs, which had been bothering her since four that morning when she left the house for dialysis. She turned the small oscillating fan that she had propped on an old milk carton toward her and sank into the black couch, which seemed to be molting its upholstery. "Do you wanna go try to find him?" she asked, sort of tentatively.

"That would be great," I said. "Are you sure you're up for it?"

"Oh, please!" she answered. "You know, the only time I look forward to is leaving to go for dialysis. Come pick me up in that shuttle, you know I'm gone. I don't care if it's three-thirty in the morning. Whatever. I know most people don't wanna do that one bit. But it's the only time I can get out of the house. Plus Chuck, he drive the clinic shuttle, and that be my boo right there, boy. We just talk and talk." Ruby smiled, a little embarrassed. She grabbed a bottle of prescription medication, which was filled with Tylenol 4s that she had picked up that morning on her way home from dialysis. She plopped a wig on her uncombed hair, and we left.

Ruby and I drove from northeast Detroit, heading southwest into the Kercheval and Pennsylvania neighborhood, where Ruby figured we'd have a good chance of finding Dude. We stopped first to see Dude's older brother Forrester, a few blocks north of Kercheval. We pulled up alongside the big gray house where he was living—and making a living selling dope—and honked the horn. Forrester peeked out the front door, bald and moonfaced, and came outside when he saw his mother. Ruby got out of the car, and they laughed and hugged in front of the house. When she introduced me, he stepped forward and shook my hand with an air of cautious but smiling formality, like a schoolboy. Forrester said that he had seen Dude early the previous day but hadn't heard from him since then and had no idea where he might be.

"Alright, then," said Ruby. She reached into her purse and pulled out the small prescription drug bottle. "See if you can do something with these for me, baby," she told Forrester. He took them quietly and dropped them into his front pocket. "OK," he said, chuckling a little and glancing over at me.[2] Ruby told him that she would make a dinner plate for him, and he said he'd show up at her house to pick it up. They hugged again, and both blushed and looked away from the other.

From Forrester's house we made our way a little farther south, to the homes of a couple of Ruby's old friends from the neighborhood, both of whom she hadn't seen since moving away several months earlier, but who she figured might have seen Dude around. Again, neither knew where he might be.

We turned on to Parkview and rode slowly down the block where Ruby had recently lived with Marvin. The empty lots in the neighborhood were especially lush, and the old trees made a high, opaque canopy over the tall grass fields.

When we got to the corner at St. Paul Street, Ruby asked me to stop the car. "See, there it was," she said, as she pointed out the car window, to our right. The corner was vacant of any structure, as were most lots on this and the surrounding blocks. But here a sheath of freshly spread dirt, with large tractor tire tracks still visible in it, covered the vegetation. "Ooo, that sure is a shame," she said, her voice suddenly breathless with emotion. Ruby began to cry in the way she often did—with almost no perceptible change in her face, only lots of tears, and a faint wind-rustled quiver in her voice. She explained that the house had been burned down earlier in the year. Marvin, who had been in and out of the hospital receiving treatments for stomach cancer, finally succumbed to the disease, and two months later, his mother's house had been destroyed in a fire; the charcoaled remains had been sitting there ever since.

I asked Ruby what had happened. "Like I say, when Marvin had left me he was doing his mama's house," she said. "They open it up. I already knew what they were doing up there. But after all that shooting up there on Seymore. I needed to move on." "Did Marvin's mama know that they were using it as a spot?" I asked. Ruby dropped her elbow out the window and let her head fall against the rest. "His mama was dead then," she replied. "She's dead. But oh no. Oh none of that. None of that! They was doing good if they snuck a smoke in there when she was alive. None of that. She was already dead and gone when they did that. Marvin's brother John had fixed it up for his sister Denise; she was in jail. When she come out of jail she needed somewhere to stay. So they fixed the house up for her. And she got up there, and you know, it's not too long past before she let niggas come in there and sell drugs. Just niggas from the neighborhood, be up in there slinging.

"And when Forrester found that shit out, he went over there and put them out. But then he started selling drugs there. Marvin was hardly there by this time; he was so sick already. Already mostly in the hospital. So . . . that was really Forrester's spot. And that's when all the trouble started. 'Cuz, see, the other big spot right then was just around the corner. When Forrester opened the house, he made a little bit too much money, if you know what I mean. And then everybody wants to get jealous, and here comes the shit. This is where Jarhead comes in at."

Ruby intoned his nickname, Jarhead, with unfettered revulsion. He was a young man—she guessed in his late twenties or early thirties—who had been running an active dope and weed house a couple of blocks away from the corner of Parkview and St. Paul. According to Ruby, he was the scourge of the neighborhood. Though no one would pin anything on him, everybody around knew that he had murdered at least two other young men in the neighborhood. And his reputation as an arsonist was beginning to precede him. Though Forrester had stopped using the Robertson house as a dope spot when Marvin passed away, it was, both for its history and potential, still the target of Jarhead's destructive interests.

As Ruby explained to me while we sat in the shade of the car, "Jarhead burn the motherfucking house down. And Forrester and them wasn't going to stand for that shit. And his *Grandmama's* house too. I mean, the dope game be the dope game. But now you messing with family. Now you messing with memories. So they did what they had to do. Now I can't say for sure what gone down. But I can tell you this much. Forrester and them wasn't going to let nobody get away with that."

Though her family's drug dealing there had frustrated her, Ruby was in deep mourning as we sat in front of the rectangle of dirt left after the house's charred remains had been cleared away. For her it was a space still imbued with warm memories of family. It was where everyone within the Freeman clan returned to find a sense of direction and refuge. For Dude and Forrester, of course, their grandmother's house was both a familial *and* economic refuge. But while it was clearly in violation of both Marvin's mother's and Ruby's wishes, the establishment of the house as a spot did not dilute its potency as a familial space for them. And the revenge that Forrester sought from Jarhead wasn't just for the loss of a drug spot, it was for the loss of his grandmother's house, for the loss of her history.

"Well, Jarhead," Ruby continued, "he got his. And now, he in a wheelchair. See that's what I'm saying, Jarhead done did all this. Shooting up, threatening people. And I mean, he shot a lot of people up, shot they cars up and shit, thinking that he the shit. If you shoot at somebody, they gonna shoot back. You see what I'm saying? Now, here are the rules in the street," Ruby said, slicing the air with her swollen fingers. "And Jarhead acting like he all for it. You out there like Jarhead, you got to be all for it. It's the law of the street, far as with the dope guys, that they take care of they own. You know, if they got a beef, they deal with it theyself. But with this shit with Forrester, Jarhead decided to go the other route. When somebody shot at him, he took it to the law." Ruby let out a dry, cynical chuckle. "And the whole time, he ain't one time told the cops what *he* did. And I'm telling Forrester this shit, you know, that now that the law involved, you can't be messing around. But Forrester don't play that. Forrester's gonna handle his own. And he did handle his own. But what he don't understand is that anytime you hurt or shoot somebody, you stupid for staying around. Now whether he did it or not, I really don't want to say. But if he did it, he should be gone. You don't stick around here, like he be doing.

"Now we got Forrester on the run from the police, but he just sitting up there in that house, coming over to my place to get a plate. Shit. I don't need all this stress. I be telling them that they're gonna stay around Detroit, they should just call the police themselves. 'Cuz I'll call them in a minute. Like that time they was in the house on Parkview selling out of there. I called the police. Marvin was so pissed, he had Forrester wanting to jump on me. I say, 'Come on with it. . . . Not only would I slice you, I'll call the police back, tell them why you jumping on me.' And they didn't believe me. I called the damn police. I said if you don't get this shit out of my house right quick, I called the police and I told them what they was doing. They got everything out of there.

"I can smoke with you, I'll hang around with you, but you can't sell this shit in my house, not with my kids around. I got that, and that's a strong thing. Now the drug thing, you can do what you want to do, just not with me. I got to leave here. I don't want no one to come in here and say, 'I'm taking your kids.' I love them too much for that.

"But it ended up they was selling everywhere I went anyways. If it wasn't them, then the kids was doing it so. . . . Lord have mercy. I mean really, you got to lay your head down. Like on Parkview I was scared to go to sleep every night up in there! So finally we ended up where we at, thank the Lord. Now you can just lay down and go to sleep. And you don't have to worry about nobody and no drugs, see what I'm saying?"

Before we pulled away, I asked Ruby where her sister Jessie Lee's house was, where she had first lived when she came to Detroit, if it was still standing. Without turning toward me, and waving her finger out the window in an even arc, she said, "Oohh, that's long gone. . . . She took the money they was giving for these houses over here. . . . Just like most of them down here. Marvin's mother was one of the only ones to stay, along with Mattie Mae and old Al across the street." Ruby pointed at the two houses around the corner. "That's when this neighborhood turned. Right then, when they bought all them houses and tore them down. Then this neighborhood bust wide open."

Market Value

In 1976, during a wave of city-sponsored community development, a proposal was drawn up for a modern supermarket and shopping center with an address on Kercheval, near Pennsylvania Street. At the time the proposal was submitted to the city, there were four large occupied commercial structures along Kercheval that would have to be destroyed to make way for the supermarket. More complicated and costly for developers, however, were the thirty-three occupied residential houses within the project boundary. Even though the city plan deemed thirty-one of the thirty-three structures "substandard," all were homes to people in the neighborhood.[3]

For these folks, the project created a sense of both great possibility and significant disquiet. Home owners were careful to demand more money for their properties than the developers were initially offering. Ruby's sister Jessie Lee rejected the city's initial efforts to purchase her home. But when the developers were able to provide more money, she accepted their offer and with the income managed to purchase a small house on the border of Grosse Pointe, an upscale suburb. Many households located just outside the development's official perimeter were also sent letters inquiring about their interest in selling. Marvin's mother was one of these, though she flatly wouldn't divest herself of her old home, no matter the circumstances or the offering price. Several of the residents on the periphery of the development who refused to part with their homes became members of a citizens' district council, the creation of which was mandated at all redevelopment sites by 1968 state legislation. Down on Kercheval, the citizens' district council included Marvin's older brother Peter, who lived in their mother's house, as well as Mattie Mae Lacey, a sixty-year-old single woman who lived across the street on Parkview. Though they were plenty ambivalent about it, some citizens' district council members had hopes that the demolished houses in the neighborhood wouldn't be lost for nothing, that this development might be the beginning of something wonderful for the neighborhood.

Unfortunately, as the bulldozers were rolling over the last of the houses that would need to be taken down, the whole project became mired in local entanglements and conflicts. Samuel Franks lives in a small apartment facing his mother's house, where he grew up, and with a view that goes behind the house to the wild green field extending across the obsolete sidewalks along Parkview. When I went and spoke with him, on a warm late summer day, Franks stepped onto his front porch and surveyed the vacant blocks across the street. He shook his head in apparent disgust. Though he wasn't an official member of the citizens' district council, his recently deceased sister was, and both he and his mother, who still lives on McClellen, were actively involved in the council's politics and policies. I asked him how members of the citizens' district council felt about the project. "We wanted the development; we wanted it bad. We was fighting hard for that grocery store. Because there really wasn't anything there after the riots. There was some stores, but you had to go past the Chrysler plant to get groceries. And we was tired of that. Tired of having nothing over here. Finally we was going to have something going on right in the neighborhood." When I asked him, in light of this, to explain what happened to the project, he looked a little annoyed. "You know what it is same as I do, man. It's all political." He stared hard at me, with a furrowed brow, and I asked him what he meant. "You know, man. It's all the same stuff, the same shit that's going on right now: where we, the people in the community, don't know what the fuck is going on, and there are just a few people making all the decisions. The reason that the development never happened was purely political. . . . You know, certain people wanting to maintain control over everything, so that they can exploit it, make whatever of it the hell *they* want. And you know we so close to the river, and Belle Isle and all that. That's what really makes them want to take control of this area. I call this the 'Holly-hood,' you know. They gonna make a show in this hood." Matie May Lacey, meanwhile, said she has no idea why the development failed. "You know, you try to talk to some of these people, and they just don't answer you straight. . . . All I know is that it was better before they come through with this."

Though a wooden sign was pounded into the ground on the corner of Mc-Clellen and Kercheval, proclaiming the imminent arrival of a neighborhood shopping center with a Farmer Jack grocery store as the centerpiece, this never happened. Instead, in the opinion of many in the immediate vicinity, the abandoned development tore apart the cohesiveness of the neighborhood and, perhaps more dramatically than any other factor, led to the proliferation of the street drug trade in the area. Still looking out the car window, with the sun warming her in the reclined seat, Ruby recalled that before the demolition at McClellen and Kercheval, "everybody was together and everybody was like the type, you know, that didn't want mama to know what was going on.

"Everybody was gonna know what was going on, because everybody was close. You see what I'm saying? People, they knew every nook and cranny around there. Anything happen, trouble 'round there, they know, whether they talk about it or not, they know. If you stand on the porch and yawn, they would know. But like I say, it was nice, it was fun, everybody would get out and cook. You know the neighbors coming over, asking what you're doing with such and such. It was, in my view, it was nice. And when they started buying stuff up and tearing stuff down. . . . That all changed. That's when the drug game bust wide open. When that happened, everything was wide open. They was out in the street with it. After everybody moved out, before they tore those houses down, it was open season for the drug people. What can I say? There was a little apartment building over here before the little homes, the nursing homes got here. Right across from the Catholic church down there toward Jefferson on Parkview. They had that lit up. Lit up! That was silly. They was bumping everything in there!"

With the physical geography of the area reconfigured, with the creation of empty lots between theretofore clustered houses, and with the stalled and mystifying promises of a supermarket and shopping center fading on a plywood sign, a different sort of market, one well suited to the physical and social spaces recently carved into the neighborhood, took firm root around the intersections of Kercheval and Pennsylvania.

As the afternoon turned to evening, Ruby was dubious about finding Dude. We drove back up to Mack Avenue, toward the Burger King, where we thought we'd get something to eat before heading home. Then, though we had more or less given up on finding him, we both simultaneously spotted Dude standing in front of the East Side Medical Clinic. I turned the car around and we pulled to the side of the road and waved for him to come over. He laughed sheepishly when we jumped out to meet him but then gave Ruby a warm hug, turning his cheek into her bosom. Dude shook my hand in his customary manner and explained that he had just dropped a urine sample at the clinic, after an hour-long, "boring as hell" lecture about the dangers of drug abuse, attended by himself and two other probationers, both of whom fell asleep within ten minutes of sitting down in the clinic's classroom. Ruby told Dude, with less a sense of admonishment than fatigue, that we had been driving around looking for him for the better part of the afternoon. But Dude didn't seem especially concerned.

He said that he was waiting for his friend Treb to come pick him up and take him to a house on Pleasant Street. "Pleasant," Ruby said gravely. "What you doing down there?" Dude shook his head with an air of absentminded indifference, as if he hadn't heard her, and turned away. Ruby stared at the back of his head with a fixed but soft gaze, all too happy to play along. Dude didn't say anything, and didn't look back. "We going to drive you down there," said Ruby. "Come on, get in."

When we arrived Dude hopped out of the car in a hurry, scurried through the knee-high wildflowers in the adjacent lot, leaped onto the porch, pounded on the door, and ran up to the second-floor apartment of the old yellow house. Ruby sat still in the car, save for her incessant fidgeting with the Velcro straps on her wrist brace. "I don't know what to do with this boy," she said quietly. "Mmm, mmm, mmm. So I guess this where he be at. Yup. That boy doing his thing." After all of her irritation at not being able to find Dude earlier, Ruby sounded faintly proud of him now. Of course, she hoped that he would complete the requirements of his probation and make something of his life that wouldn't involve dealing drugs in the old neighborhood. Yet she also admired and seemed in some way to love him especially for his industriousness and stubbornness.

A few moments later, Dude came back out of the house with two $20 bills, which he handed to Ruby, telling her that it was all he could give her then. "I would have more," he said, "but I'm dealing with this probation all the time, every day. . . . I ain't got time to be doing much." Ruby thanked him, and then kissed him on the cheek. She told him that his probation officer had come by the house several times, and that he had better start coming home at night or he was going to violate.

"I'm going to be there tonight, Mama, I put that on everything," he assured her.

"Yeah, right. I'll believe it when I see it," Ruby shot back, rolling her eyes and touching her fingertips softly to his wrist. Dude smiled broadly and giggled at the ruse. She knew that he was already outside her grasp, that he was determined to create a new home in the old neighborhood. Here's where Dude was going to settle down and stay moving, where he would try both to make his mark and disappear, embodying the seemingly contradictory dream-space of spots and homes in the Detroit dope game.

Dog Days at Jackrabbit's

The corner of Pleasant and Kercheval is a little less than a mile to the east of Indian Village, roughly in between its edge and the disappearance of

Kercheval into the Chrysler plant. Characteristic of the lower East Side of Detroit, its qualities conform to an advanced phase of urban decay, described elsewhere as the "green ghetto."[4] Most of the many vacant lots in the area have been cleared for over a decade, allowing thick foliage, trees, and shrubbery to grow unimpeded. During the warm and humid Detroit summers, the contiguous parcels overflow with tall prairie grass and wildflowers and would look like woodland meadows if not for the sidewalks circumscribing them and for the evenly spaced fire hydrants that line the parameters of city blocks. The ruins of slat-sided houses, jutting, groaning, and leaning away from their foundations, are strewn with accidental awkwardness amid the fields and weeds. On the hazy, heavy-aired day when I returned to visit Dude at the corner of Pleasant and Kercheval, the urban prairie extended up both sides of Pleasant for around 150 yards and came to a stop on either side of the street at a pair of old, rectangular two-family houses.

On the east side of the street was the yellow house where Dude had been working. A couple of days before, he had called me out of the blue, from his friend Treb's cell phone, and said I could meet him at the house on Pleasant. He had given me precise parking instructions, and when I got there I did just as he said, pulling my car to the side of the road about 25 yards past the house. To my right, across a trash-covered field, I could see the back porch of city councillor Tinsley-Talabi's house. "Right under her nose," I thought to myself.

Typical of two-family flats in the area, the house had two doors on the first floor: one that led upstairs, and another that led into the downstairs apartment. The doors were sheltered by a dark porch roof, which had a balustrade around the top for the rectangular upstairs balcony. The yellow house's porch steps were twisted and cracked from exposure, and rang like taut drums as I climbed them. The door leading to the upstairs was on the right. It was old and heavy, reinforced with gray weathered plywood, over which a rusted steel mesh had been nailed. There was a one-inch-square opening in the middle of the upper panel, against which one could press one's face and look through the mesh into the stairwell, or shout up toward whomever might be in the second-floor apartment. I leaned into it and yelled "Hey!" through the screen. "Who is it?" came Dude's familiar voice. "It's Luke!" I shouted, trying to be both cool and audible.

Dude thundered down the stairs and pulled up the weathered four-by-four beam that had been braced between the stairwell and the door, and stomped back up to the second floor. I pushed open the door, which squeaked off the jamb, falling into the stairwell, and walked into the foyer. After the first four steps there was a landing, and the staircase made a sharp left turn and led up to the front room of the second-story flat. Most of the boards for the landing were gone, leaving a gaping opening. There was also an oversize mirror, approximately four feet squared, propped on its edge against the landing's rough framing, so that people on the second floor could see around the bend in the stairs to the front door. I had to negotiate the stairs carefully, with the missing boards at the landing and the frameless mirror leaning gingerly in the corner. At the top was a gate of black steel bars secured with a keyed padlock leading to the front room of the apartment. And poking through the bars were the black, twitching, wet muzzles of three pit bulls that Dude and Treb had been raising in the house. The dogs spent most of their time in this front room, and consequently the pale hardwood floor was covered with a sprawling archipelago of dog shit, steaming in the stifling Michigan heat. From the dog room, there was a pair of French doors leading to the main living room, where there were two plush white couches at right angles to one another, facing a nineteen-inch television. Dude, who had rushed up the stairs in front of me, opened the French doors and plopped himself on one of the couches. "Sit down, man," he said with an impish grin, suggesting that he sensed I might be uncomfortable. He told me that he had just been to the weed house on Holcomb, around a block away. "They got the 'dros right now," he said as he dumped a dime bag of weed on to the coffee table in front of him. "Man, you got a television, Playstation. You all are set up here," I said. "I told you, dog," said Dude, with a proprietary smile. "This ain't no spot, nigga. This a motherfucking home." Dude pointed me toward the rooms in the back of the apartment, each furnished with a narrow, bare mattress. "We got bedrooms up in this piece, Luke."

At twenty years old, Treb was both Dude's elder and had been something of a mentor for him. Tall, light skinned, and muscular, with broad and handsome features, Treb was quiet when Dude introduced me to him, hardly looking up. Chewie, who was sinking into the corner of the couches, with his arms extended at his sides, was more talkative. He reassured me in a clogged-nose whine that he was one of Dude's oldest friends and that if I was Dude's man, it was cool with him if I hung around at the house. The three of them had known and looked after one another for years; they had gone to the same elementary school and had been playmates, friends, and rivals ever since.

When I showed up, there was the usual midmorning lull in customer traffic at the house. Treb went into one of the back rooms (where the dogs also spent a lot of their time) to chop up an eight ball of crack into the nickel and dime rocks that they would sell over the course of the afternoon. Dude, Chewie, and I sat in the living room, not saying much; the two of them were dazed from the marijuana and stared passively at the television, where Dr. Phil was haranguing guests on *Oprah*.

Later in the day, when customers came to the door and knocked, the dogs barked furiously and rushed across to the gate. For the previous several months, Chewie, who had invested the least in the crack supply in the house and thus had the lowest stake in the operation, had been doing the retail work. He would yell down to the front door from behind the black gate, telling whoever knocked that they should come up. Throughout the cooling afternoon, customers would hop over the landing and climb the steps to the gate, where they would tell Chewie what they wanted and then wait for him to retrieve the specified amount from the bedroom table, where the dime and nickel rocks were laid in a pile.

Most of the customers were from the neighborhood, like old man Walker. He had known the boys working at the house since they were small—Dude, Felicity, and May had played with his daughter when they were all young children—and he had been a steady customer since they opened up shop on Pleasant. Walker pounded on the door and yelled, "What's going on up there?" from the porch, affecting the inquisitorial tone of a police officer. Dude, who had left the four-by-four beam leaning in the corner, laughed and told him to come up. Walker jumped up the stairs, two at a time, and stood lock legged with his hands through the gate. He smiled slightly, and with his eyes shifting to and fro, nodded hello in my direction, touching the brim of a tweed riding cap that sat on his graying Afro. "Oh, that's my man Luke," said Dude. "You ain't got to worry about him." Walker nodded again and laughed. "Anymore," he said, "you just never know what might be going on." He told Dude that he wanted two rocks and handed him a $20 bill. Chewie seemed irrevocably sunk into the couch and was laughing at the television. "Y'all ain't fucking around up here," said Walker. "You know the vans is out."

The police raid vans would make frequent sweeps through the neighbor-hood, storming known dope spots, and if the cops appeared quickly we would likely have to jump from the second-story windows to make a quick getaway—something that the boys were not eager to do, and that I was pretty sure would leave me with a broken leg. "For real?" asked Dude. "I seen them over on Crane," sputtered Walker. "Alright then; good looking," said Dude. Overhearing them, Treb moved quickly to stash the crack supply be-hind the house. Dude turned the television off, and Chewie and I flew down the stairs and out into the street. Dude followed us down, but stayed behind and jammed the wooden beam back into place behind the closed front door. I could hear him pounding it into position as Chewie jogged up the road toward a relative's house a few blocks away. I waited for Dude, who emerged from an upstairs window, swung his body over the short balcony covering the porch roof, and, as if he were a pirate scaling a mast, climbed down one of the wooden pillars in front of the house.

Dude and I got in my car and decided that we would drive around the neighborhood for a bit, checking to see where the vans were, if they had found their targets and might already be preoccupied enough for Dude to go back to the house without too much worry. Dude leaned the seat way back so that he was nearly sunk beneath the passenger-side window.

We drove past the vacant lot where his grandmother's house had stood only a few months ago and where Ruby and I had stopped to talk. There was the squat four-family apartment building where he had stayed with his mother when he was just a baby and the building where his father had lived and sold dope after separating from Ruby. We hadn't seen any raid vans or even unmarked narcotics cars, but the streets were peculiarly quiet, which made it seem likely that word had gotten out and that they were still on the prowl.

We circled back to the intersection of Kercheval and Deleware streets, and came to Jackrabbit's liquor store, surrounded on three sides by over-grown vacant lots. Besides a day care center that is three blocks to the east, Jackrabbit's is the only commercial establishment (and nearly the only still-standing building) on the long stretch of Kercheval between Indian Village and the Jefferson Avenue Chrysler plant. From early in the morning until well past dark, there are gatherings of men and women around the front door of the store, along the front wall, and in the vacant lots on either side of the building, talking with neighbors, meetings friends, getting something cool to drink, and buying and selling crack, weed, and heroin.

Before the Chaldean owners had purchased it, over a decade earlier, the store had been run for about twenty years by an African American man who had grown up in the neighborhood and become a Golden Gloves, Olympic, and eventually professional boxer. His nom de guerre was Jackrabbit. In its heyday under his management, in the mid-1970s, the store had been a center of black entrepreneurial pride in the postriot neighborhood; there had been a two-story mural celebrating African American heritage, featuring Kwanzaa colors and the visages of notable African Americans, painted on one windowless side of the two-story brick building. But by summer 2000, the mural had long since disappeared. The building was textured with peeling paint, the remains of the words "Jackrabbit's Liquor" only faintly visible in once-red block letters that are nearly faded to white.

Dude would often wile away the early morning hours at the store, talking with the owners or store clerks behind the bulletproof glass separating the cash register and hard liquor from the rest of the merchandise and customers. "I'm out here before anyone," Dude told me, as we parked the car alongside the store. "Even if I be at my mama's, sleeping on the couch, I just get up, eat me some cereal, and catch the Gratiot bus to Cadillac and Harper Square and that motherfucker drop me off on Deleware, right there. Right there on the block. I'm there early as fuck, so when I get off the bus, soon as I get off, I go to the store. Even the Arab in the store knows I'm the first one on the block," Dude told me. "I'll be standing outside the door, I'll yell, 'Sam, man, let me in, man.' Joe'll open the door, let me in before they open. We'll be chilling back there. He'll say to his cousin, 'Jimmy, take over,' we go in the basement and blow some blunts. I'm not bullshitting. Me and Joe. Know what I'm saying? We real cool." Dude sat in the car with the door open and his feet already on the pavement.

"Do any Arab or Chaldean store owners sell drugs?" I asked him.

"Basically, I don't know, man. If I can walk in the store and I can see a baller-type nigga behind the counter, like how we be behind the counters, then I would say the owner might be doing something."

In most such stores, the glass wall separating customers from the employees and owners is an unbreachable divide, with store owners almost never venturing into the retail space during open hours, and with the space behind the counter completely off-limits to customers. But Jackrabbit's, for Dude and other dope slingers in the area, was much more fluid. "Like one day, I'm sitting behind the counter, and Joe sitting back there with me, real early in the morning. Just him and me, and he peeped the feds. They came in that bitch low-key as hell. Joe says to me, 'Dude, Dude get out the store, get out the store.' I run from behind the counter and, shit, through the side door and shut that motherfucker, and walk right past those motherfuckers. Feds coming up to the front counter just then, but they don't see me back there. I walk out the store. I come back an hour later, Joe's like, 'Remember when I was telling you to leave out the store? The feds walked in this mother-fucker.' I was like, 'For real?' He was like, 'Yeah, you didn't peep him with the glasses?' That's how he talks; he talks funny as hell and shit. So Joe, like I say, the hood, *this* is the hood, Luke, this is the motherfucking hood. Right here. Joe's store. Call this motherfucker Jackrabbit's. And this the heart of the hood. This be where everybody come together. This where business hap-pens. Where money comes in and out. This where everybody be seeing everybody. How niggas say they from the hood and they don't know this nigga that live on this block, or they don't know old girl over here. Ain't none of that. Everybody know everybody. Ain't nobody don't know nobody around here." Dude pushed the door the rest of the way open, and stood next to the car. "When I'm locked up," he said, "I bet you everybody in this whole fuck-ing neighborhood know I'm in jail."

Dude's attachment to Jackrabbit's liquor store, with its multiple informal and legitimate economies, is hardly unique. Young African American drug hustlers all over the city spend time in and around liquor stores that are owned by ethnic whites and Chaldeans—selling drugs and playing key roles in the ordering and defining of the social spaces surrounding these busi-nesses. Dude's attribution of such importance to Jackrabbit's signals a num-ber of things: the store may be the "heart of the hood" simply because it is the only widely shared public space in the neighborhood, because it is where everyone interacts with and learns about the well-being of everyone else.

But as the heart of the hood, Jackrabbit's is not simply an institution that sustains the social life of neighborhood residents. It is also a locus of danger, tension, and conflict. Indeed, it is precisely in its multiple meanings, in its harboring of both conflict and conformity, that it makes sense as the heart of the hood for Dude. It is emblematic of the neighborhood, in other words, because it symbolizes the contradictions and social tensions that underlie all social interactions there. It is both legitimate and illegitimate, at the center and the periphery of economic and social activity. In this multivalence, in both its symbolic value and in the practical space that it creates, Jackrabbit's upsets conventional schemes for understanding inner-city neighborhoods, where distinctions between those on the margins and those in the mainstream are presumed to be clear.

Inside, there were several isles stocked with corn chips, cookies, and cans of soup, and a glittering wall of liquor bottles and cigarette packages behind the glass-partitioned counter. "You want anything, man?" Dude asked. I told him that I might get myself something, but he insisted that it be his treat. I pointed to a bottle of grapefruit juice, and he grabbed it out of the cooler. He pulled a soda from the neighboring door. As we left, Dude held up in either hand the grapefruit juice and the Pepsi that he had gotten for himself so that Joe, who was standing behind the bulletproof glass, could see. He shouted, "What up though, Joe!" Joe nodded back with a quick tilt of the head and a half smile, and Dude walked out of the store without paying. As we walked through the front door I registered my surprise with Dude. "I told you, Luke; Joe's my man. I pay when I want to pay."

Outside, Dude and I stood along the front wall of the store. A few other young men had started gathering along the street side of the building, hoping to get a sense for where the narcotics officers might be and when it might be safe to go home again.

Dude and I were shuffling toward the car when we saw two black vans swing on to Kercheval, looking like sharks with prey in sight and going so fast that they nearly tipped onto two wheels. "Man," said Dude, without raising his eyebrows, "you about to see this bitch get raided." We scrambled into the car and sped around the corner while others dispersed in every direction at once. As we pulled away, the vans came to sudden odd-angled stops in front of Jackrabbit's. Dude and I circled back through a few minutes later, and saw that the back doors of both vans were open, and three young black men were leaning against the sides of one of them, pressing their palms against it, getting patted down by Kevlar-wearing, dark-blue-uniformed police officers. "Who's gonna get taken down?" asked Dude rhetorically, while he peeked over his shoulder. "Not me! I know that!" Dude's loud exclamation seemed both at odds with and fueled by his addled bearing. We returned to the house on Pleasant, where we'd keep watch through the windows in case the vans continued their hunt.

In the afternoon, with customer traffic not picking up after the raids, we left the house and drove around the corner to pick up Dude's Aunt Lydia, Marvin's younger sister. She lived in the neighborhood and would make daily visits to Jackrabbit's, to pace along the sidewalk there and sell crack, which was often supplied by Dude or Treb. Dude told me that sometimes she would turn a trick or two with passersby. "Whatever she has to, to get them rocks," he said. "She just like the rest of them from my daddy's family, they all smoking rocks." We pulled up in front of the small house that she was renting with her boyfriend, and Dude went out to get her. He pounded on the front door and turned toward me, still sitting in the car. He rolled his eyes at the absurdity of having to wait for his aunt, and of his facilitation of this degrading episode in the first place. Eventually, her boyfriend answered the door and told Dude that she would be out in a minute. Dude stood with his hand in his pocket, clenching the wrinkled plastic bag of nickel rocks that he had taken from the stash at the yellow house. Eventually, Lydia emerged wearing a tight white blouse and red cutoff sweatpants that she had fringed provocatively up the sides of her thighs. She leaned her head into the car, smiled a mostly toothless grin, introduced herself to me shyly, and climbed into the backseat. We drove around the block and headed down Pennsylvania toward Kercheval. On the way toward Jackrabbit's, Dude and Lydia talked about the family. Darla, Lydia's little sister, had just gotten out of jail again and was staying with Ruby until she could find a place. "She big as hell, too. Fat," said Dude. "I know that's right," answered Lydia, laughing. "But she going to thin out, just wait a minute. Just wait 'til she get her hand on some rocks."

Dude instructed me to pull over across from the store. Lydia climbed out of the backseat and walked purposefully across the mostly deserted street. "How long is she going to be down here?" I asked. "Oh, she going to stay here all day," he answered. "That's my auntie, she down here every day, all day long, getting these sacks off. She don't give a fuck." Lydia walked over to a pay phone that was sitting stump-like in the middle of the sidewalk, about twenty feet from the storefront, into which a skinny man was leaning. She twirled around to its far side and rested her back against it.

While there were several cars parked across Kercheval with the drivers sitting in them, waiting to get served by one of the dealers working on the corner, foot traffic was still slow. There had been a hoard of customers early in the morning, before the raid vans came, and they were probably still high. There would be another wave coming around later in the afternoon, Dude said. "She going to get that sack off. I know that."

He looked at her with a mix of sympathy and curiosity as she settled into position against the phone booth. Dude was obviously conflicted about sending her out to the street, and his voice betrayed his sense of responsibility for her and wry confusion at her circumstances. She was family, after all.

The Chosen Family

By late October, Dude had been out of the detention facility for four months. The blue cornflowers and tall umbrellas of Queen Anne's lace in the fields on Pleasant had mostly gone dormant, and the long grass was lying on its side under fallen leaves from the sycamore and oak trees on the edge of the road.

Though usually cold by then, a strange wave of warm and wet air had blown into the city with a stormy, overcast sky as I drove to the block on Pleasant and parked beyond the yellow house, where Chewie and several young kids from the neighborhood were shooting dice. Typically, Chewie was losing his money, and when I walked over to the curb where they were playing, he asked me if I had a quarter he could drop. I obliged, knowing that my empty pockets would keep me from getting in too deep.

Chewie had a basketball with him, and I picked it off the curb and dribbled around my legs. Being a decent basketball player was probably one of my most important assets in Detroit. Though my game was mostly slow-. footed fundamentals and not hard to ridicule, it was effective. Having made quick work of the quarter. Chewie turned from the game and smiled at me suspiciously. "I can tell you can't hoop," he said. "Dude said you had a 'J,' but I'll fuck you up, for sure." Chewie rose up from his knee and asked me if I wanted to play him one-on-one, assuring me that my "youth home game ain't no good on the streets." We walked down Pleasant, a couple of empty lots past the yellow house, to an old wooden light post, against which a slanting and rusted rim and square piece of particle board, flaking apart like a piecrust, had been nailed at about nine feet above the ground.

As I chucked the ball back to Chewie, zero-zero, up to ten, Dude pushed open the screen door of the blue and gray house across the street and walked on to its crooked porch, where he silently sat down on a plastic chair and watched us play.[5] Dude shook his head occasionally as I pulled in front. When I was the first to reach ten points, he threw his arms up in mock disgust.

I hadn't talked to him in a couple of weeks, and while Ruby had seen him briefly when he would grab a change of clothes or do some laundry, she wasn't in consistent touch with him either. As the thickening clouds finally broke, the rain sounding like radio static on the dried leaves below, I went over, drenched in sweat and water, and sat next to him on the porch. Dude said that I had only been lucky to beat Chewie. "I told him you got a 'J,' but you couldn't fuck with me. I mean, really, Luke. You can't play. . . . If it wasn't raining right now, it would be on. I'm telling you." We both laughed, for not entirely incongruous reasons, and Dude slapped my hand, as if to gain my acquiescence. "What are you doing over here?" I asked, wondering why he wasn't across the street, working in the yellow house. "See," Dude explained, "my man Billy had came to a stalling point."

Not long after Treb had set up shop in the yellow house, a man named Billy rented the top floor of the blue two-family flat across the street. Then, a couple of months after Billy arrived, Dude's friend Aisha moved from the first floor of the yellow house into the first floor of the blue house, which was in obviously better shape. Through the late summer and fall, as Dude settled back into the neighborhood, he developed a friendship of sorts with Billy and began spending almost all of his time around the house.

Dude said that Billy, whose lanky frame and smooth features made him look much younger than his thirty years, was still working with a few thousand dollars, and that he, of course, still had the house, but that friends of his from when he was young had taken a lot of money and dope from him. "You know everybody comes to a stalling point in the game. . . . He had his car, his house, he still was paying his bills, but he was like, you know, falling. And he used to see me every morning. You know, it was still summertime, so I used to be out there early. And he used to just see me out there. . . ." Dude pointed across the street. " 'Goddamned,' he used to be thinking to himself, like, 'Damn, that's a little dedicated motherfucker.' I used to be out early in morning, just sitting there by myself. One day I came over here to buy some weed from him. I started back across the street, and he was like, 'Hey, man, you want to smoke a blunt?' "

Dude and he talked and hit it off immediately. "I ain't no people person. And he ain't no people person. That's why he liked me. 'Cuz he wasn't a people person neither." Dude said that Chewie had started rolling for Billy, holding the house down while he was gone, on weekends mostly. "So I was over there at Treb's spot, I still was rolling. But that spot been getting slow as hell. I was bored, getting tired of watching Jerry Springer. I came over here, and Chewie was up, watching porno flicks on the DVD. You know, I go up-stairs, we kicking it. I fall asleep over here . . . and when I woke up there wasn't nobody in the house. You know, the sack was there on the table, so when someone came to the door, I answered the doorbell, grabbed the sack, and I served them. Then later, I came back with all Billy's money or what-ever, gave it to him. And then it's like, it's just like it all came together so quick. Like within a week we was just sitting down having a conversation. Smoking a blunt in the house. He say, 'Dog, you know what? I like you.' Say, 'I like you a lot. I ain't saying you got to roll for me.' He like, 'Look, stick around.' He say, 'Stick around, dog . . . whatever I got, you got.'"

Dude said that after not too long, he was spending more time at Billy's house than in Treb's spot across the street. While Chewie was handling most of the door traffic at the blue house, Dude was helping Billy organize the transportation of larger quantities of dope and weed from their supplier to the various spots where Billy had younger people posted.

"Billy always say, sit down and listen motherfucker, you ain't going to get nowhere if you ain't going to listen. That's why there's that much love for me. Right, I'm sixteen. Shit, a sixteen-year-old person, all they thinking about is how many blunts they can smoke, how many bitches they can fuck. But I'm me. Not trying to stick my chest out like I'm a big bad motherfucker. You got to stand your ground, but you ain't going to let yourself know that you like Mike Tyson or some shit. Niggas don't like fake niggas. Niggas like niggas who bring it real and keep it real. . . . You know, we been fucking with that 'E,'" Dude continued.[6] "We doing that shit all the time now, and that shit will make you say some shit. . . . You know what I'm saying? Billy be like, 'Man, there's so much love,' you know. Saying shit about how we going to be niggas for life and shit. How there is so much love."

He told me about how Aisha had moved into the first-floor apartment of the blue house, and how he started hanging out there also, with Aisha, her daughter, and other women, girls and young children from the neighbor-hood. Indeed, Billy's house had assumed fairly rigid gendered divisions. The upstairs was a strictly male domain. Meanwhile, Aisha would frequently have many women friends over to the first-floor apartment, and it was often full of young children; guests were greeted with the whimsical shouts, screams, and laughs of a nursery school. Dude, Chewie, and others working upstairs would rotate through the first floor, taking breaks from serving customers upstairs. Old man Walker, who lived around the block and was a regular customer of Dude's and Treb's, would often go downstairs after copping dope and hang out with Aisha and the kids, watching television or sleeping off the waning effects of a recent high. "We really a family up in here. That's the family. Everybody in this house," he told me as it continued to rain through the warm October afternoon. "That kind of stuff is meant to be."

As the autumn grew colder and darker, Dude continued to settle into Billy's house, working in the dope game and sleeping most nights in one of the bedrooms there. All the while, Dude's relationship with Billy and other people spending time around the house continued to deepen. Dude was becoming ever more attached to Aisha's two-year-old daughter, whom he called "my baby," and with whom he would spend at least a few hours each day, playing and watching television. The expanding network of friends circulating through the space was no less significant. Dude's old friends from the neighborhood and the new friends whom he met through Billy were fixtures there—all part of the family, the household on Pleasant.

Another Drive with Ruby

Two months later, the anomalously humid weather of October seemed impossibly far away. A colorless, shapeless sky had crept over the flat city, and the cold December wind was gusting from the northwest; the ground was frozen white, and the unplowed streets of Detroit were rutted with troughs of ice.

On Christmas Day, Ruby had managed to gather all her living and unincarcerated children at her home in northeast Detroit, and they were sitting in the dining and living rooms of the neatly swept and mopped house, eating a big Christmas dinner. In the darkness of the winter day, none of them had noticed the unmarked black SUVs parked a couple of houses down. When the police lurched forward, marched out of their vehicles, and kicked open the front door, Forrester threw his plate of food off his lap and leaped toward the back of the house. But Felicity's room offered no way out, and he reemerged with his hands over his head. The police arrested him for attempted murder and led him away in handcuffs.

Only a few days later, I stopped by Ruby's house in the afternoon. She had asked me if I could drive her around to look for some of Forrester's friends. He was now sitting in the county jail, trying to decide whether to plead guilty or face the dim prospects of a jury trial for shooting Jarhead. He had sent letters to Ruby, May, and Felicity, asking each to get in touch with people from the southeast neighborhood who might be willing to offer an alibi for him on the day in question. Ruby wrote all the names down on a small slip of paper, and we drove down to the lower East Side. "Everybody knows that Jarhead is up to no good," Ruby offered, as we were heading down Gratiot. "He's just a two-bit dope dealer. And see, everybody be afraid of him. Ain't nobody never stand up to him. Except Forrester. And that's why Jarhead can't stand him. He just *hates* Forrester. That's why he's trying to put this on him. And he be trying to act all innocent and perfect with the prosecutor."

Referencing her now-crumpled scrap of paper, Ruby directed me down a small side road south of Mack Avenue. There, we found a man named Leroy, who had been repairing a roof and, when we approached in the car, was standing on a front lawn cleaning black tar off his hands. He leaned into the window and listened as Ruby explained the letter she'd gotten from Forrester. He nodded passively and said that he would vouch that Forrester was working with him on the day the shots were fired. We talked to another man named Bruce, who we found walking down the street near where Forrester had been living. He also said that he would be willing to testify. But Ruby said she would bet money that neither would show.

Over the course of the afternoon, as a horizontal blizzard moved in from the west, Ruby went on and on about how much trouble Jarhead had caused and how despicable he had been. "He comes over and shoots the windows out—doesn't even get out of the car. That's what him and his friends do, they get in the car and just shoot out the windows of the house, while they're sitting in there. Oh, he's just done so much stuff." While we were driving around looking for people on Forrester's list, Ruby repeatedly recalled her son Elvin, who had recently been moved from a prison in southern Michigan to a more remote high-security facility. "I've already got one baby locked up for a long time for something he didn't do. . . . I just can't take another one going to prison. . . . I don't even know why people bother talking about going to hell when they die; they already in hell. They ain't no place to go but heaven. 'Cuz hell's right here, hell on earth, purgatory. People talking about the world ending. Shit, if it's going to end, it's going to end right quick. There's just too much bad things happening." Ruby sighed and looked away, toward the wild storm out the window. I could hear that she was crying. "The storm," she said with a drawn voice. "This . . . it's just too much."

While Ruby couldn't help but adopt some of Forrester's optimism—that *someone* on his list would be a reliable alibi—she was now feeling dejected and desperate to keep him out of prison. In the months before Forrester's Christmas arrest, she had lost Marvin. And Elvin's disappearance into the prison system for the rest of his life was, for Ruby, like the death of her second twin baby. It felt to her as if her family, which she had fought so hard and long to maintain and protect in the face of so much difficulty, was slipping through her fingers. In the midst of all this, she couldn't imagine losing Dude too.

As she fell silent, we pulled in front of Billy's spot on Pleasant. I blew the horn, but no one seemed to stir. Then, as if from out of nowhere, Dude came up behind the car, slowly and with a wary and contorted face. Though they hadn't seen each other in a while, he and Ruby didn't bother much with greetings. Dude reached his hand in the car, past Ruby, to shake mine, and then stood next to the window talking with her about Forrester's list of alibis. Ruby told him that we had been trying to round people up for Forrester's court date. "They're not going to come," Dude offered sardonically. "Well, what about you?" Ruby fired back. "I know you ain't handling your business? I can't have you get caught up, Dude. I just can't!"

Dude's intensive probation, which was still active in January and would not expire for another four months, had not worked out as Ruby had hoped. While he had attended school for the first couple of weeks of September, and had dutifully gone to his drug-awareness classes and even dropped (albeit "dirty") urine a few times, he had stopped going to school when things on Pleasant got distracting. His probation officer, moreover, had been making consistent, unannounced visits to Ruby's house, hoping to find Dude there. Ruby had been able to cover for Dude for several weeks, turning Officer Clementine away with stories about Dude being out looking for a job. But exhausted with worry about Dude and everything else, she finally broke

down in front of his probation officer and said that she didn't know what to
do. She said that she needed help. But Clementine took no decisive action.
She told Ruby that there was nothing she could do if Dude wouldn't stay at
home. She certainly wasn't going to go chasing him around the city. It was
her job to help the family, but if Ruby couldn't keep the family in one place,
there was nothing to be done.

Though this was nearly a month before, Ruby hadn't mentioned anything
to Dude. And in the meantime, things had become more complicated. With
Dude standing two feet from the car, leaning back with his hands in his pockets and his head cocked forward so he could see in the window without coming too close, Ruby explained to him that Clementine had called earlier in the
week and that he had to go to court for his six-month probation review.
She said that his hearing would be on the twelfth of the month and that he
should enroll in school. Dude nodded and looked at the ground, and then,
betraying his disingenuousness with a smile, said that he was planning to go
to Ruby's house later that day. "Mmm hmm. Right," said Ruby, sarcastically.

Still, she was able to talk him into getting into the car and going up to Osborne High School, in northeast Detroit. If he hadn't yet violated probation,
enrolling in school would certainly help his case in court. It would at least
give him a fighting chance and give Ruby some hope of keeping him out of
the system.

Housed in a collection of orange rectangles set in what feels like a jum-
bled disorder in the middle of an enormous mowed field, Osborne High is
one of the uglier big schools in the city. Once we made our way through the
metal detectors, past the sleepy guard sitting in an open-door cage at the entrance, and into the building, we signed guest passes and headed toward the
office of the administrator who handles readmissions and suspensions. On
the way, while walking down the long linoleum floor, I asked Dude what he
thought of the school. "Shit. This motherfucker is a skipping school, Luke,"
he said. "Everybody here skips all the time . . . so it ain't that bad." We
walked past a side door that led from a secluded corner to the outside, and
Dude explained, "Like this here. This was my door; I used to leave out of
here every day before lunch."

The administrator, a cheerful elderly woman with a coifed, purplish wig,
fetched a chair for Ruby and sat in her office looking for information about
Dude in her computer. Several students with obvious developmental dis-
abilities filed past into the special education classroom where Dude would

be assigned to spend the rest of the academic year. With a warm, gentle voice, the administrator informed us that Dude had never been removed from the school records and he could start again whenever he wanted. She said that students were in the middle of studying for finals and he probably wouldn't have that much to do. "You shouldn't get frustrated," she reassured him. "You know, because you won't know what's going on. . . . But just hang in there, and in the new semester, things will get better. . . . You know, you are such a nice little guy. Such a nice boy." Turning to Ruby and me, she put her hands on his shoulders and said, "He just smiles when you see him in the hall, never causes any trouble. When he's here he's really fine, just great." Ruby smiled appreciatively. "You just need to start coming here and staying here. That's all that's going to get you on the right track." Dude stretched his mouth into a passive smile and nodded in agreement.

As we walked out of the school, I talked with Dude about how seriously he was taking any of this. I wondered why he didn't want to come to school just for the girls. Making sure that Ruby was out of earshot, Dude told me that he wasn't going to be coming back to the school if he had already violated probation. "That would be just a waste of time. . . . That wouldn't be for nothing. There's only but one reason I'm going to be going to this school, and that's if I don't violate, so that I can tell the judge, 'Yup, that's me. I'm a high school student.'"

Trouble with the State

On the way back down to Pleasant, I offered to call Clementine to check on Dude's probation status. I had been able in the past to use my otherwise frivolous title as an intern at the detention facility to gather information from court and probation officials.

When I finally got in touch with her a couple of days later, the news was not so good. As it happened, Dude had had a court appointment on the same morning that we had visited the school. Either Ruby, Clementine, or the court had confused the date, however, and Ruby was left with the impression that the hearing wasn't for another week. Clementine didn't say whether they would lock him up or not. She didn't think necessarily so, but she couldn't guarantee anything. After recommending that I call back in several days about his potential probation violation, she undertook a thorough defense of her efforts on his behalf to date: "I got him wraparound services, I got him everything that I could. But every time anyone would show up, he wouldn't be there. We need to just get him to stay at his mother's house, so that these people can talk with him, so they can see him. He needs treatment; drug treatment, family counseling."[7]

Clementine's tone was decidedly more hostile when I called back a few days later. She told me that Dude needed to go to the courthouse to see if the referee would give him a new court date. Though it seemed that Ruby and Dude's confusion of the court dates was an honest mistake, Clementine left no question that he had violated his probation and there would be no recourse for him. When I expressed concern with this, Clementine insisted that it would have been "impossible" for Dude and his family not to know their probationary obligations. "I've been calling them, and there has been certified mail sent. There is no way that they don't know about the court dates. I don't know what they're doing—I think they're playing games with me, or something. But they haven't done anything. He needs to address his substance-abuse problem. I mean, anyone that would have the audacity to come into his probation officer's office just reeking of marijuana. . . . I mean, something has to be wrong with him. He has to be completely strung out in order to be acting like that. I told his mother that too. But there's nothing that we can do if he's not going to be at home. I went over there this morning and no one was home—I talked to his sister, and she said that she didn't know where anybody was."

The following day I found Dude in the blue house on Pleasant. It was a day of unchanging predawn light. Everything was deep blue and ashen gray. We took shelter from the cold in my car, and I told him about my conversations with Clementine. "Goddamn," he said. "I swear I didn't know that I had court. . . . That's bullshit, they never sent me no letter. I just called Clementine this morning—because I had the flu. Remember that back pain that I had? That turned out to be the flu, like aching and stuff. So I ain't been going to school or nothing. But I called her to tell her that I had enrolled."

"What did she say?" I asked

He pursed his lips and slapped the dashboard in front of him. "She wasn't even there, man. Motherfuck!"

I tried to persuade him to call her back. It occurred to me that we might convince her that he hadn't deliberately skipped the court date, given that he had called her so recently thereafter. "Luke, think about it, man," said

Dude. "If you the judge, and I'm coming in there for a review, and I ain't done nothing . . . just been doing my thing down here, but I ain't been going to treatment, and I ain't been to see Mr. Frederickson [the drug counselor he had been assigned] in I don't know how long . . . man, you know they was going to lock me up anyways. And I'll tell you right now, I been done all the time I'm fixing to do. Last time they locked me up for some ho shit . . . for some gun that wasn't even mine. And the time before that it was some bull-shit too." I reminded him, sort of clumsily, that he hadn't exactly led an innocent life before being locked up. "Yeah, but that's in the past. Man, I put all that behind me. I ain't doing any of the wild shit that I used to be doing. . . . What's past is gone," he said.

We both sat silently for a while. In a manner uncannily reminiscent of Ruby, he looked away, as his dark eyes filled with tears. "I'm just going to have to go with the flow for a while now. . . . Going to have to lay low. I ain't going back to jail. Man, Luke, you just don't know. I'd rather die than get locked up. I don't care for how long. . . . Just going to have to go with the flow, I guess." Dude looked through the windshield, his eyes surveying Pleas-ant Street. "Man, and then my mama . . ." he said, trailing off. Not sure what I should say, I just sighed heavily. Dude's frustration about his current circumstances was gut-wrenching. He knew he hadn't played the game in the right way, that he had made silly mistakes. And I could see him calcu-lating his errors and their consequences: the lost time, the specter of a life even less visible, and, mostly, Ruby's disappointment. He knew she was in poor health and already stressed by the loss of her other children—to death and prison. The last time he was locked up, he had wanted so badly to do right by her.

Someone from the blue house leaned over the second-floor railing and shouted down to see if we had any cigarettes. Without acknowledging him, Dude punched the car seat and shouted, "Man, I don't want to be on the run! It's already too fucked up out here—it's too much." Dude was quiet for a few minutes, and we sat in the car, listening to the winter wind zip past the window.

Suddenly, Dude spoke again. "Like my man up there who asked for a cig-arette. We call him Eastside. . . . Man, Luke, he's on the run, he's been on the run for over a year. Man, he was on the six o'clock news in Ohio. If he gets caught he's facing the death penalty, you know. That's some shit. And he just got caught up defending himself. He wouldn't have killed no crack-head if the motherfucker hadn't been threatening him and shit. That's just self-defense. And I know that if I get caught, the worst they're going to put me through is some stupid twelve-month shit. . . . But I can't do it, man. I can't get locked up no more. It's just too much if you black, and you ain't born with nothing, you ain't got nothing. There just ain't nothing you can do."[8]

Coda: In the Youth Home

About two weeks later, I got a phone call from Dude. His voice was flat and heavy, each word like a book falling on to the floor. "Luke, it's Dude," he said. "Where are you at?" I told him that I was at the house on Pingree, and since it was unusual for him to call, sort of nervously asked where he was. "At the youth home," he answered. "Oh shit," I said. "What happened? Did they just pick you up?"

"No, man," he said, wanting me to calm down. "Some kind of serious shit. . . . Can you come down here?" I told him that I could be there later that evening.

"I'll explain it all to you then," said Dude. "Just try to come down, man."

At the juvenile detention facility, Dude was ushered almost immediately to the "mental health" unit, where all the residents are in dingy green jump-suits, and where, in contrast to the other two-tiered units, all the rooms are on the ground floor. After the control room guards buzzed me through the slow-swinging double doors, Dude stood up from the corner of the blue rub-ber couch where he had been sitting and walked toward me. He smiled faintly and incongruously, watery-eyed and sad. We sat down at a hexagon-shaped table in the center of the unit, imprinted with a chess and backgam-mon pattern, while other residents were finishing their showers and locking themselves into their rooms for the night.

The story Dude told me over the next couple of hours was full of holes, underdeveloped plotlines, unwieldy motivations, and structural inconsisten-cies. It was, among other things, a work in progress. This was obvious to me, and probably to anyone else who talked with Dude about it at this stage, among whom were the staff psychologist on duty that night and at least one attorney who had spoken with him before I had gotten there; with all of his confusion and uncertainty, Dude didn't know whether the attorney was a prosecutor or public defender.

"Now, let me start at the beginning," he said. He told me that the previous Friday he had been at home, at Billy's house on Pleasant, just hanging out with some of the guys from the neighborhood and others who were living in the big blue house. Eastside was there, along with Billy, Chewie, a man in his mid-twenties called Buddy, and another younger man named Juan, with whom Dude had been spending a lot of time at the Pleasant house. Juan is a few years older than Dude; he had just turned twenty-one that January. The two of them had been riding around frequently in Juan's new Dodge Durango, a gift from his relatively affluent parents, who lived on the North Side, in a middle-class black enclave near Seven Mile Road. That night, he and Dude drove down to the liquor store at the corner of Jefferson and Mc-Clellen, bought a couple of Swishers, and rolled two blunts with the stash from which Chewie was selling. They smoked on the way back to the house and lounged around for a while in the upstairs apartment, listening to music on the little white Bose stereo that Chewie had stolen from someone's truck a few days before. Later, along with a few young women who had shown up at the house, they both popped some Ecstasy. Among these women was Chewie's younger sister Patricia, a sixteen-year-old whom Dude had known since both went to Nickel's elementary school, down near Indian Village. She had brought a couple of her friends, both of whom were older, in their early twenties, over to the house. The music was loud, the Coronas were cold and plentiful; it was a typical house party.

"And I don't know what for, but Juan went crazy," Dude said. "He just popped. I mean he was drunk as hell. Luke, man. He was *dead drunk!* And he just flipped." Dude shook his head in bewilderment and paused for a moment, appraising and assimilating what he had just said. "He came after me," he said, looking straight ahead, bracing his forearms on his knees. "He jumped me. . . . I mean he didn't jump me, 'cuz I could handle myself. But he got me in the head a couple of times pretty good. I was lumped up on the back of my head." Dude was talking more quickly now. "And when he was pounding on me, I grabbed a bottle, an empty Corona bottle, and smashed it over him. I still got these cuts all over my hands." He stretched his hands out in front of him and examined the scabbing wounds that speckled his skin, turning them palms up and down. "So then he took off, 'cuz we had, like, been beating on each other. I don't know where Juan went. Him and Billy and some others went out the front door. But I was pissed!" Dude told me that he walked out the door after them and looked up and down Pleasant, but they were gone. He said that he walked to a neighbor's house up the block on Pleasant. A friend of his named Lazy lived there. And he had a gun, Dude told me. A forty-four. Dude took the gun from Lazy's house and walked slowly down the street with it hanging low at his side. "And I was walking out the door with the gun, the forty-four, and I had just stepped out. I didn't really know what I was doing. I wasn't going to hurt him. I was just . . . I don't know. I just . . . I wasn't sure about nothing. I mean, we were two motherfuckers that was way too fucked up. I mean, we were high as fuck." Dude told me that he walked around the front and sides of the house looking for Juan. He said he yelled for him on the front lawn, and then he walked through the door and up the stairs to the second-floor apartment. "When I turned around the corner at the top of the steps," Dude said, "Eastside came out of nowhere." Dude told me that he kept the gun low, and dangled his arm toward the ground to show me, with his index finger curled at the ready. "I had the gun like this," he said, "and Eastside just grabbed it from me." Dude said that he reached for the gun's barrel and managed to twist it back away from his body. The sharp metal gunsight dug into the heel of his left hand, as he tried to shoo Eastside away with the other. "We tussled over it for a minute, scraping over the gun, he was pulling this way and that, and I was pulling. And then it went off. It shot right into the floor. Damn near blew my foot right off my leg."

"Oh fuck," I blurted. Dude paused again and whistled weakly in disgust. "Downstairs, the girls was hanging out. Janet was down there. Aisha and them, my baby girl. My man Mookie. And Walker. They was all down there." Dude shook his head in acknowledgment and measurement of the gravity of his circumstances and the story he was telling. "The bullet went right through the floor," he said. "It hit Walker right in the top of his head. Come out the bottom of his chin." I winced when he said this, and he stopped talking for a minute. He shook his head, and his eyes began to tear.

"At first I thought that Eastside shot me in the foot," said Dude. "'Cuz the blast was so close to my toe. Mookie and them came running upstairs. We was both still just standing there, frozen. Looking down at the floor. And Mookie said, 'You and Eastside better be going. Walker is dead.' We went downstairs, and that's all I can see. I see his hair, man. His face. I see the way that he walks. I hear his voice, Luke. Man, I see the blood. Thick and rich, spreading along the floor. That's all I see. It was still there on Saturday afternoon. The blood was *thick*, man." Dude put his hands over his eyes, as if literally to push the image from his mind.

Dude said that he left the house immediately and spent the night walking around the neighborhood. He didn't sleep or eat. The next morning, almost unwittingly, he found himself back in the house on Pleasant. He climbed into his bed as it was getting light, and he laid still through the morning hours, not thinking or moving. The police, who had been at the house through most of the night, returned in the late morning and began questioning everyone out on the front lawn and sidewalk. Chewie, Billy, Mookie, Janet, Aisha, and friends of hers who had been at the house the night before were all talking to the cops. While Billy, Chewie, and others who lived in the house didn't identify him, both of Patricia's friends named Dude as the shooter.

Eastside had figured that he would have no problem giving the police a false name and offering a crime report as the others in the house had done. No one giving testimony would implicate him, he knew. And he had no place else to go in any case. But it was Detroit Police Department policy to err on the side of arrest. When Walker was killed, most major cities had homicide arrest rates that only slightly exceeded incidents of murder. But Detroit police officers were arresting, on average, three people for every killing in the city. After offering an unorthodox spelling of the false name that he had given, Eastside became a casualty of the unwritten broad-net arrest policy (which has since been changed after undergoing federal investigation).[9] He was taken to the infamous ninth floor of the Detroit Police Department headquarters at 1300 Beaubien Street, fingerprinted, interrogated, discovered, and summarily extradited to Ohio to await sentencing on capital murder charges.

When the police showed up, Dude might have run. He might have moved quickly to lay low. But the previous night's tragedy had left him numb, confused, and immobilized. He walked outside, down the porch steps, and approached one of the notepad-clutching cops. He said that he was the one—the short, dark-skinned boy that the others had been describing. The four police officers working the scene simultaneously flexed their knees, pulled their guns, and trained them on Dude with locked elbows. He spread his hands, dropped to the ground, and lay with his belly on the sidewalk. "I'm ready to go," he said.

PART III

Time Machinery

Once I counted the walls, the tall windows, estimated the height of the waiting-room ceiling. Eight walls, a ceiling twice as high as an ordinary room, four perverse, fly-speckled, curtainless windows admitting neither light nor air. . . . The room made me feel like a bug in the bottom of a jar. I remembered all the butterflies, grasshoppers, praying mantises, and beetles I had captured on the hillside below the tracks. At least the insects could see through the glass walls, at least they could flutter or hop or fly, and they always had enough air until I unscrewed the perforated top and dumped them out.

       —John Edgar Wideman, *Brothers and Keepers*

Contest means play. As we have seen, there is no sufficient reason to deny any contest whatsoever the character of play. . . . Every place from which justice is pronounced is a veritable *temenos*, a sacred spot cut off and hedged in from the "ordinary" world. . . . Whether square or round, it is still a magic circle, a playground where the customary differences of rank are temporarily abolished.

       —Johan Huizinga, *Homo Ludens*

How can one capitalize the time of individuals, accumulate it in each of them, in their bodies, in their control? How can one organize profitable durations? . . . The disciplines which analyze space, break up and rearrange activities, must also be understood as machinery for adding up and capitalizing time.

       —Michel Foucault, *Discipline and Punish*

7

Playgrounds and Punishment

When Dude finished talking, his wet eyes were perfectly still, fixed on a far wall. He tore at my notebook, pulling the binding and loosening the frayed edges. He looked at me and shook his head. "Luke, man, I am so . . . fucked . . . up," he said, perforating the sentence with dead air. Then he leaned back and bowed his head, digging his chin into his chest. He said he was dizzy and felt like he might vomit.

What might happen to him? Prison? For God knows how long? His mind was ricocheting around the room. Should he even indulge in hopes that he might be sentenced as a juvenile? For all his previous certainty that he couldn't handle even another day in confinement, he was now *hoping* for a bit in the state boys' school. But how could he live with himself in any case?

He couldn't say why he had become so upset with Juan, why he had brought that gun into the house, or what might have happened had Juan been at the house when he came back. He worried about talking with Walker's daughter and son-in-law, who were friends of his from the neighborhood. Should he write a letter, or call them on the phone? What would he say to them? He told me that he hadn't eaten since being locked up, now for over thirty-six hours. And sleep was impossible. He rested his forehead on the backs of his hands, which were crossed, fingers interlaced, on the table in front of him.

"I need you to go to the house," he said, his head still hanging low. "You gotta talk to them. Make sure they got their stories straight, make sure they coming to court for me." Dude's eyes were shut, and he winced when he spoke, repulsed by the sound of his own voice.

Later that night, after Dude was instructed by the attending staff to shower and prepare for lights out, I drove back to Pleasant. It was a clear, cold, moonless night, and the ice crunched like dry gravel as I walked up the steps of the blue house where Walker had been killed. Inside, everything glowed with the diffusion of light through exhaled marijuana and cigarette smoke, which clouded the otherwise immaculate house. Earlier in the day the cops had coated the place in fingerprinting dust, and Billy had just been through with a vacuum cleaner after them. I walked in holding a yellow sheet of paper on which I had written a summary of Dude's version of events and questions that Dude had given me to ask several of the people in the house. Chewie was there along with Billy, Juan, and Buddy, who'd been staying there for the previous several weeks. The four of them were sitting around the white-topped Formica table in the dining room, drinking from bottles of Corona beer left over from the night Walker was killed. Chewie was toying with a CD player that he had lifted out of someone's trunk, rhythmically clicking it open and pushing it shut.

Everyone was quiet when I showed up, staying put in their seats and sipping disinterestedly on their beers. I sat in the one empty chair at the table and explained to them that Dude had asked me to come to make sure everything was all right. Billy looked up brightly. "How is that little nigga doing?" he asked. I told him that Dude hadn't been eating or sleeping, but that I thought he was going to be OK. Juan, who still had a bandage on his face from where Dude cut him with a bottle, pushed away from the table, walked into the living room, and sat on the couch.

"That was some STUPID motherfucking shit!" he said, as he reclined into the sofa. "Stupid as hell," Billy concurred. "Walker, man, everybody loved that cat. . . . And I know Dude taking it hard as hell right now. He loved him as much as anyone."

Billy told me that Walker's daughter wasn't blaming Dude for what happened. "She's real fucked up though, you know. . . . Her old mans is dead, you know, so she hurting real bad."

Chewie asked me if I had seen the hole. "What hole?" "That motherfucking hole right behind you, man." I turned around in my chair and looked toward the floor. The plywood surface was coated with high-gloss, deep red paint and glared under the bare light. "Right there!" Chewie stood and pointed toward his feet. The bullet hole was eerily clean. There were no spare splinters or chips. It looked as if someone had drilled a hole through the floor with a sharp three-quarter-inch bit, at a slight angle, from north to south. The paint around the hole had only peeled up slightly at the edges. "Stupid motherfucking shit," Chewie said.

A week and a half later, when I made my daily visit to the juvenile detention facility, Dude was still on the mental health unit. This twenty-bed ward is tucked behind administrative offices at one end of the building, reserved for inmates needing acute psychiatric evaluation or attention. There are a couple of psychiatric nurses, a psychologist, and a psychiatrist on duty there through most of the inmates' waking hours. These plainclothes staff people wander in and out of the unit periodically and occasionally meet with the kids to assess their condition or administer medication. But those responsible for most inmate contact on the unit are the two or three juvenile detention staff, who are bedecked in correctional officers' garb, and none of whom have any mental health training.

When Dude was there, most of the other kids on the unit were suffering from developmental disorders or other clinical problems, and just about all of them were taking medication to suppress or manage their symptoms. One lanky sixteen-year-old spent hours with headphones covering his ears, thumbing through the thick cardboard leaves of a *Sesame Street* songbook and singing along loudly to the accompanying cassette.

After his arrest, Dude had been assigned to the mental health unit as a precautionary measure. This is often done in cases where juvenile detention inmates are facing especially serious charges and may be traumatized by the circumstances leading to their detention or by their recent incarceration itself. Kids in such situations are usually moved off the unit after several days, as they, at least according to institutional presumption, adjust to the shocking realization that they may be imprisoned for many years. In most cases, they are eager to be with the general population at the juvenile detention facility, to shed the various stigmas associated with assignment to the "nutty" unit, as the kids sometimes call it, and to be out from under the supervision of the relatively more plentiful mental health and juvenile justice staff there. Dude, however, wanted to stay. He was just beginning to adjust to his environment, sleeping for increasing hours each night and slowly regaining his appetite. He was dreading the chaotic general population units at the detention facility, crowded with people always coming and going, adolescent posturing and fighting.

So when the staff psychiatrist began conducting interviews with all the kids on the unit, asking them how they got along with Dude, he became nervous that his move might be imminent. Word spread among the detention staff and inmates that Dr. Lacey—a petite, sharp-featured woman with a fragile voice and a shuffling walk—was concerned that Dude had been pestering other, lower-functioning kids on the unit, and that she wanted him discharged as soon as possible.

When I made my daily visit with Dude on this wintry evening, Lacey was in her office finishing the last of her interviews. Dude and I sat together at one of the three hexagonal tables on the unit, as had become our custom over the past week, and I asked him how his day had been. "Shitty, man, I think they're trying to move me out. . . . Dr. Lacey on some shit about how I be messing with these motherfuckers, but I ain't going nowhere, you hear me?" As Dude was talking, the kid who had been meeting with Lacey emerged from her office and walked into the unit's central space where Dude and I were sitting. He was the only white inmate on the unit, and was uniformly and affectionately referred to as "White Boy" by the others. He came over to our table and sat down. "I think you're leaving, man," he said. "She was asking me all about how you be acting and whether you be bothering anybody."

"She said that shit?" asked Dude. White Boy nodded.

"Fuck that shit," Dude muttered under his breath. I asked Dude if he was all right. "I ain't leaving," he said gravely. "You watch. I'm staying right here."

When Lacey came out of her office and walked across the unit toward the administrative offices, Dude screamed at the top of his lungs but with a kind of robotic evenness: "I'm not leaving! I'm not leaving!" Lacey looked back toward him as she pushed through the bright-red steel door but registered no acknowledgment of what he had said. The next time she came through, about five minutes later, he yelled with the same low, mechanical affect, "I hate white people! I hate white people!" Again, she ignored him; the rest of the kids on the unit looked over toward us, but were quiet. As Lacey disappeared into her office, Dude grabbed a pencil and held it up to his neck, looking at a young African American juvenile detention staff. "I hate black niggers!" he screamed. "I hate black niggers!" The juvenile detention staff, Ms. Winbush, rolled her eyes. She came toward the table with a big smile on her face and sat down next to Dude. "You ain't going to do nothing with that, are you," she said softly. "Why don't you let me have that pencil?" "No," said Dude as he put it in his other hand and held it away from her. "Well, why don't you use it to draw a picture then?" I pushed my notebook over toward him, and he started doodling on the yellow page, rolling his eyes at Winbush in mock acquiescence. He was composing an elaborate image of his name surrounded by a collage of gang signs: five-pointed stars and up-turned forks. As he became more involved in his drawing, Winbush grabbed the pencil out of his fist. "Ha!" she said. "I got it." Dude looked at her with a combination of impishness and annoyance.

Winbush went into one of the supply cabinets and retrieved some of Dude's "hygiene" items, and then set them in front of him on the table. "I am not leaving!" he demanded while pounding his fist on the tabletop. She then went into his room and came out with some papers that belonged to him, and put them on the table too. "I'm not leaving," Dude repeated, and again pounded his fist. "I am not leaving." With a still-broad but increasingly awkward smile, Winbush reminded him that he was not on medication and would be fine in the general population. "I'm not fine!" Dude protested. "I'M MENTAL HEALTH! I'M MENTAL HEALTH!" He yelled again in a deep voice, "I'm not leaving! I'm going to go crazy if you guys try to take me out of here."

"What are you going to do?" Winbush asked.

"I might start with something like THIS," said Dude as he threw all the hygiene and personal items that Winbush had set before him on to the floor. She rejoined impatiently, "You know that you're going to pick this up, don't you?" Dude screamed again, "I ain't leaving." Sensing a standoff, I moved over to one of the rubber blue chairs in front of the unit television. Dude turned toward me and winked, to reassure me that he was in control of the situation. I cautioned him: "Don't get yourself locked in your room, man. You're not going to like it."

"I ain't getting locked up. But I ain't leaving here," he answered. Dude stood and crossed the length of the room, past the observation desk and the shower stalls toward the supply closet, to retrieve a plastic basket in which to put his strewn about things. Returning to the table, he called out, "I'm going to kill myself. I want to die!" Winbush, who had been standing near the observation desk, threw her head back: "Now Demitrius," she said, using the name on his facility file, "why would you want to do something like that? You know that I need to do all this paperwork now. I need to call the nurse in to do an assessment now; you know that, don't you?!" She sounded less angry than resigned, and disappointed with Dude for setting in motion a tedious protocol that the institution demands be observed in response to all suicide threats. Winbush's demeanor changed dramatically, becoming dispassionate and terse. She went to the nurse's office, just beyond the desk. Dude said, "I'm not talking to no nurse! I'm going to kill myself!" The charge nurse, who was a small Asian woman with a thick accent, walked toward Dude.

"Demitrius . . . let me talk to you for a minute. Come with me."

"I ain't going nowhere. Hell no."

"Demitrius . . . come with me. Let's go into the office. I need to speak with you for a minute."

"I see little white people with black uniforms on!" Dude yelled.

"Now, Demitrius . . ."

"They're walking all over the place. But they don't have any feet." He looked at her with half-shut eyes and his head rocked forward. He slammed the table again, "I'm mental health! I'm not going anywhere!" Winbush turned toward everyone else on the unit, all of whom had been sitting at other tables or on the blue chairs.

"OK, OK, everybody get into your rooms."

She instructed Dude to go to his room as well, assuring him that the nurse would talk with him then.

A few minutes later the nurse stood at Dude's locked steel door. She told him that he would need to remove his jumpsuit and put a paper gown over his underwear. "I'm going to give you some medication," she reported, turning toward her office.

"I ain't taking no medication," Dude insisted as she walked away. He started to take off his clothes; first his big green jumpsuit and then his T-shirt. Standing in his room in nothing but facility-issue underwear, he called the nurse back and told her that he was not suicidal, but pleaded with her to allow him to stay on the unit.

"But Demitrius, you are not going through a crisis, you are doing OK, and you can handle yourself in GP."

"What do you mean I'm not going through a crisis?! I'm here for murder. I'm facing adult time. You realize that? That's not some fucking shit I deal with every day of my life. That's a fucking crisis. And I feel comfortable here. I finally got to feeling like I can handle myself and now y'all want to move me. It don't make no sense! There's only seven people on this unit. I just can't see myself with nineteen other niggas right now, in some small-ass unit. I'm telling you, I'll get to scrapping and I'm gonna be right back here!" The nurse nodded patiently and eventually decided to let him stay on the unit for the night; the paperwork had already been submitted in any case. Early the next morning the mental health staff had him transferred to a general population unit, where he would try to stay out of trouble, and where he would wait to hear from a court-appointed attorney.

Playtime

At the Wayne County Juvenile Detention Facility, the passage of time is twisted, Möbius-like, into a paradox.[1] Days at the facility are organized according to rigid temporal schedules. Every ticking moment is accounted for, categorized, rationalized, and summarized. Five minutes for a shower, ten minutes to get dressed, thirty minutes to eat the facility's food, and fifteen to rest. Divisions of time are inscribed on and invested in the bodies and biologies of inmates, in calculations of the need for sleep, food, education, hygiene, medication, and punishment. Unlike in adult jails or prisons, where inmates may languish in their cells for hours or even days on end, time is utterly determined and embodied in the disciplined practices of young people confined at the juvenile detention facility.

But even as incarcerated youth are put through the paces like gears in a clock, as they click through their days, moving on the hours in even increments, young people at the detention facility are always waiting for timely decisions to be made about them. Owing to the fact that the bureaucracy is so entrenched and every decision must move through many clogged channels, kids may wait months for a decision about placement, sentencing, or adjudication that they expect "any day." Young people locked up at the juvenile detention facility are simultaneously bored to stupefaction and racked with anxiety. Even as their days blur together, heavy with a sense of unknown imminence, things might shift unpredictably at any moment, as everyone goes to court, comes back, goes again to court, and comes back again to wait. And of course, not only do detained young people not know the length of time that they will be locked up, and often the length of time that they can expect to be under some sort of state supervision after sentencing, they frequently do not know *what sort of time* they will do. For many young people caught up with the law, this is the defining tension, the question that trumps all others: Will they do adult or juvenile time, or what permutation of either?

And the consequences are dire. As judges and court personnel huddle in front of courtroom benches, haggling in hushed tones over the short arcs of young lives and how they might bend upon judicial discretion, years—sometimes decades—hang in the balance. In many cases, a judge's decision to sentence a young person as a juvenile rather than as an adult can mean the difference between nine months of treatment and schooling in a low-security residential placement—with canoe trips on the weekends and off-campus visits with parents—or ten to fifteen years in a prison populated primarily by older men, surrounded by gleaming concertina wire, surveyed by gun-toting guards wearing reflective sunglasses.

Of course, to the kids locked up at the juvenile detention facility these distinctions seem absurd. Most of them are adolescents: somewhere between children and adults. They are in the nascent stages of understanding their sexual, economic, and political subjectivities. Many are in and out of school. Some are parents themselves, though with varying degrees of responsibility for their children. And just as the categories *juvenile* and *adult* don't adequately describe the complexity of their identities outside the detention facility, these institutional designations present an impossible dichotomy. One consequence of this is that such disciplinary categories are rarely assumed without some kind of resistance or negotiation. While their bodies are docile and vulnerable to the managerial techniques of their keepers, young people who are locked up at the juvenile detention facility are usually strategists in their own institutionalization. Dude's insistence that he *is* "mental health" is plain evidence of that.

But young people do not just play with these judicial categories, whether they are adults or juveniles, in order to manipulate the system to their advantage. Rather, much of their fretting about them is born of their own struggles to make sense of their emergent identities. Thrust into an institutional setting where this artificial distinction has such dramatic ramifications, young people become urgently reflective not just about their judicial standings but also about their broader cultural and developmental places in the world. As kids turn over in their minds their court-assigned statuses—Do they feel like kids? Are they boys or men? Should they be treated like children? When did they become adults?—their recourse is naturally to events, circumstances, histories, and memories that are beyond the walls of the juvenile detention facility.[2] At the same time, while young people in the detention facility grapple with who they are and who they are becoming, they also struggle with what kind of treatment they might truly deserve and what injustices might be wrought on them. If they are "juveniles," does their innocence precede them? If they are "adults," are they already condemned?

One way that young people come to grips with these unwieldy and rigid distinctions, and try to refuse them, is through identification with the so-called dope game—a contest which may or may not be child's play, and through which young people see themselves as both children and adults.

Most young people locked up at the detention facility do not plan to make lives out of the drug trade. In the expansive and optimistic minds of the kids kept there, even those who have long before quit school, drug dealing is nearly always imagined to be a temporary measure, which will be followed by a professional career, like law or architecture, with access to legal money and more broad social esteem. Indeed, for many of the kids at the facility, drug slinging comes even to define the parameters of childhood. Kids often talk about getting too old for the dope game, as if it is an institution from which they hope soon to matriculate. At the same time, they see the advantages of slinging drugs accruing mostly to the young, who have a harder time getting other sorts of work and are not as concerned about the risks of handling dope and illegal money. Yet nearly all the kids in the drug trade tell stories about close friends and relatives in the game, often of their own generation, who have been killed or sent away to prison, not to return until they are middle-aged. The cold, grave epidemiological fact is that between the proliferations of gun violence and the hysteric herding of young black men into the prison system, there are few living models of the drug-hustling adult to which young drug dealers turn in Detroit.[3]

On the other hand, the dope game can also mark one as possessed of an adult seriousness, as "on his business." Many young people who deal drugs on the street are motivated to stay in it by the urgent need to assume primary (adult) responsibility for family matters when older relatives are unable to handle them. Also, as drug markets in Detroit become increasingly fluid and spontaneously generated, young people are much more likely to have more control over the terms under which they are participating. Where they used to find jobs as closely surveilled street runners, working under older lieutenants, participation in the current and more loosely configured drug trade now affords even the most modest young people opportunities to be entrepreneurial, setting the terms of their potential as both capitalists and consumers. Finally, claims to being in the dope game are a means to elaborate "outside" identities that are institutionally stifled in the detention facility. Narratives about being in the dope game thus situate young people in particular places and times, possessed of a measure of social stability and a more developed social identity.

As young people in detention narrate their lives, constructing and deconstructing their places as players in the dope game, they play with and move between childhood and adulthood, or occupy both simultaneously. While Dude waited again for the terms of his punishment to be determined, he was thrust into this institutional confusion, and, to some extent at least, it was through the dope game that he imagined his way out. And, of course, he was not alone.

Learning the Hustle

When I started fieldwork, in the fall of 1999, four months before I met Dude and over a year before Walker was killed, the building with the mental health unit that Dude so loathed to leave was only half built. At that point, the Wayne County Juvenile Detention Facility—or youth home, as it was called—was housed in a pale-beige cement structure, adjacent to the Lincoln Hall of Juvenile Justice in a midtown warehouse district, about a mile and a half from downtown. The now-abandoned juvenile jail has the feel of an improvised encampment, where one might easily lose his sense of direction in a maze of hallways, added to rooms, added only later to other hallways. Near the rear entrance is a solid wall, about twelve feet high, circumscribing a big blacktop recreational square. The main body of the building rises six stories, with evenly spaced square windows. There are walkways that run from this rising monolith, across a broken-apart sidewalk, to other multilevel buildings that are part of the same complex and are plastered with the same glaring beige cement. The main entrance to the facility is through a low-slung annex that spreads out underneath the six-story wing.

When the building's lobby was still in use, brown-clad sheriffs would sit for eight-hour shifts in the dimly lit space, behind an old faux-oak desk, talking incessantly about the previous night's basketball or hockey game or exchanging jailhouse gossip to keep themselves awake. Occasionally they would listlessly flirt with the mothers of detained children, who would sit in one of several orange plastic chairs, watching the *Jerry Springer Show* flicker on a 1970s-era turn-dial television that was hanging in the corner. The air in the building was heavy and hot and smelled faintly of warm meat.

On my second day of research at the old youth home, as I was wandering around the building without direction, through unfamiliar hallways and past mysterious doors, I found myself amid the charter school classrooms, housed on the first floor, where detained inmates would attend classes on weekdays. The rooms looked identical in many ways to those in any other underfunded public school. The walls were decorated with brightly colored construction paper along with pictures of zoo animals and nature scenes that looked torn from a calendar or a *National Geographic* magazine. Inside, the students sat at individual desks arranged in single-file rows.

I walked past one room where the inmates, all young boys, were leaning silently over literature books that I recognized from my own classes in junior high school, around fifteen years earlier. In another one of the rooms, an African American man with a gray beard was scrawling rudimentary algebra problems onto the chalkboard on the back wall.

From down the hallway, I could hear laughing and yelling through the blaring bass beats of hip-hop music. I walked toward the noise and found it coming from a much larger room; I stopped at the doorway and stood against the jamb. The room was lined with old computers—Zenith system 3s—and there were general equivalency diploma (GED) instruction books stacked in twisting piles on the tables. The kids in the computer room were in black, gray, and beige jumpsuits, the colors worn by kids on the fifth and sixth floors of the building—marking the oldest kids and those facing the most serious charges. The phrase "Property of Wayne County Juvenile Detention Facility" was stenciled on all their backs in white paint.

Several of the inmates were gathered around one of the computer screens, playing an electronic solitaire game, and others were scattered around in small groups. On the periphery of the room were three African American men, all in their twenties and dressed as sharp as knives. One sat on top of a desk, with his shiny black leather shoe propped against the back of a chair. The other two were sitting in backward-facing undersized school desks with their arms draped in front of them. The man across the room rocked onto his feet and stepped toward the door, walking with his right hand extended from his pressed black suit. "Hey!" he said brightly as we shook hands, "my name is Mr. Johnson." I introduced myself and told him that I was there trying to get a research project started. "Interesting, interesting," he said, speaking with the speed of an impatient adolescent. "Excuse me, excuse me!" he yelled into the noisy room, as his colleague, Mr. Paley, turned the music off. When the students had given him their attention, Johnson said, "Everyone . . . this is Mr. . . . ." "Mr. Bergmann," I offered. "Yes, Mr. Bergmann. He's from the University of Michigan and he's a . . . you're a sociologist, is that right?" I told the class that I was a cultural anthropologist. "Oh, great!" he said. "Why don't you talk to us, if you wouldn't mind, about whether hip-hop really is a culture. That's something that we've been discussing here. Can you do that?"

Standing next to the bejeweled and immaculately dressed Johnson, I felt more than a little awkward about this, but I plowed ahead into some kind of argument about subcultures and stereotypes. I was acquitting myself pretty well, I thought, when one of the kids in the room, a long, thin boy with half of his hair braided and a slight speech impediment, interrupted:

"What kind of culture are we in here, locked up?"

"Good question!" I said, excitedly, and launched into an overblown, nerve-shaken critique of the notion of "convict culture," and the copious sociology that it had produced. This seemed to leave most of the kids in the room a little disappointed, and I was thinking of rephrasing my response when another kid spoke up. "It's black culture in prison," he said. This encouraged me, and I spouted off a few statistics about the overrepresentation of African Americans in the prison system (at the time, blacks constituted close to 50 percent of prison inmates and were just 13 percent of the population), and how the overall prison population had gone from half a million in the early 1980s to over two million at the turn of the century.

Johnson wrote the numbers down on the chalkboard and recapitulated what I had said. It was at this point that I noticed Rodney for the first time, leaning his chair back in a pose that would become familiar. He was looking agitated. "Think about it, man," he nearly erupted. "What hit the scene in the '80s?" Wearing a black jumpsuit, with long dangling braids sweeping across his shoulders and freckles covering his olive face, Rodney smiled, and rocked his head back and forth while turning to the side, as if he were dancing to a thumping bass line. He looked around the room, waiting for a response. "Yay, man," he finally said (using a street term for crack), laughing, and now rocking his head back and forth a little faster. "Y'all is slow!"

The mention of Yay seemed to light a fuse in the room. A heavyset, round kid in a gray jumpsuit nodded his head and raised his hand. Johnson called on him. "Yeah, the reason there's so many black folks in prison is because no one is giving us any jobs." Another kid, who looked about ten years old and had a squeaky voice, said, "Black kids can get jobs . . . at McDonald's for six bucks an hour." He fell out laughing, along with most of the others in the room. Rodney raised his hand. Mr. Thomas, another of the teachers, pointed at him and called his name. Rodney sat up in his chair and spoke loudly. "For real! I mean, you young, you still a kid, basically, how you going to be making six an hour, when you can be stacking real money, slinging?" Others nodded and giggled. Johnson asked how much they could "really" make hustling. There were groans of longing, missed and missing opportunities, among nearly all the inmates in the classroom.

A tall kid with a big, jagged Afro raised his hand eagerly.

"Bernardo," said Johnson.

"Well, first of all, it depends on what you mean by 'hustling.' I mean, I could be mowing lawns, and that could be my hustle. There's all kinds of hustles out there. It just depends on how you want to make money." There were more laughs and nods in the room. Johnson clarified that he meant drug dealing.

"Realistically," Bernardo said, "I could make one G a week selling rocks. You know, I ain't going to be working at McDonald's making that. You can't do shit else when you young to make that kind of money!"

Rodney said, "Yeah, but you're going to get taxed. You got to pay for the stuff you going to sell. That's going to cost you half, dog. So you ain't making no G."

It seemed now that everyone in the room jumped in. "And you going to get taxed for what you need to live; you need to stay geared, you need a ride." A short kid with a toothy smile agreed. "If you got someone in the spot, you got to be paying that cat, bringing them stuff to eat and drink, you know? At least, that's how I be treating people. You know? And then you might be getting taxed for the rent for the spot or whatever. You be struggling, running around."

"Well, I'm not talking about setting up no spot," answered Bernardo. "I'm talking about sitting up in the piece, collecting each week, or just slinging from the hip, you know?"

Johnson and the other teachers had been following the discussion closely, but not saying anything, when Paley interrupted. "You all think this is the only way for black folks to make money. But look at who you're selling to. Your dads, your moms, and your aunties. Y'all are destroying the black community." Without raising his hand, Rodney disagreed. "Yeah, we doing some of that, but we selling to a lot of people who ain't black, and anyways, someone going to be selling this shit regardless. Regardless! And whoever's doing it, going to be doing it. And whoever be smoking it, going to be smoking it. Regardless. Why are we going to let someone else get that money?" The other students grunted and nodded in agreement. Johnson said, "Well, even if you think it ain't morally wrong, you know it ain't going to work anyways. You keep working in the neighborhood like that, and the police are just going to know you. You know how you all are, with your bling-bling and all that. That's going to make your life impossible, I'll tell you right now." To the loud laughs, nods, and hand-slapping approval among the other kids in the room, Rodney retorted, "Yeah, but we know the police too!"

As the hour drew to a close, Johnson, who had again seated himself on one of the tabletops, approached me with his hand outstretched. "You all need to pay attention," he said to the boys in the room. "This man is going to get his PhD. And you all should be thinking about yourselves as having the potential to get a PhD. And you should talk to this man—you should work with him." When the students stood up to leave, Rodney hurried over toward me. "I want to work with you on this thing," he said. I suggested that we talk about my project the following day, since there would be a couple of forms to fill out; he said I should come up to their unit and hang with them there. Rodney skipped out of the room with the others, and Johnson walked up to me afterward. "That's a bright young man right there," he said, pointing to the door through which Rodney had just disappeared. "You can see that. He's heading in the wrong direction, but he could be a community leader."

The next morning I settled into a seat in a large central room in the school. One of the teacher's aides was there grading papers and told me that the room was the designated "reflection room" at the school, where kids are sent when they are misbehaving in the regular classrooms.

After I had been there for about a half an hour, Rodney came into the room, walking with an exaggerated hop and skip, his braids swinging behind. "Get off my back!" he yelled behind him as he skated to the far side of the room. Thomas, who had been in the GED classroom the day before, came in after him, laughing, and pursued him across the length of the floor. "You guys always want me to make comments," Rodney said, turning away from him, "and then when I make comments you get on me. But now I say I don't want to make a comment, and you say that I can't be in student council; you guys are crazy!" Rodney sat down in one of the plastic chairs, and Thomas leaned over him and told him that he needed to "watch his business."

"I'm on *my* business; you watch *your* own business," Rodney shot back.

"Just be on your business," Thomas answered over him again.

"Y'all want me to talk, right? Y'all always be saying I should be talking in class. Then when I talk you be pulling this. . . . That's some ho-ass shit, Mr. Thomas."

"Just be on your business," answered Thomas lamely over his shoulder, as he walked away.

Rodney saw me sitting across the room, and hopped up and sat next to me, carrying a folded white paper he had brought with him. "They're bull-shitting," he said. "They telling me that I'm a leader and shit, and that I'm supposed to be talking all the time in class. Then when I say something, they don't like it. They perpin'." I asked what had happened. "Man, ever since you came, all they be talking about is the 13 percent of African Americans, and the 40 percent incarcerated, and the overrepresentation and shit. You could tell they don't really know what they talking about. They just got something to go on about now. None of them ever took the time to look it up themselves, to do their own research." I laughed and offered some sort of facetious apology for arming the teachers with those numbers. "The thing is, they ain't just black folks in here. And I think that shit is racist, man. All they do is talk about what's happening with black folks. And I'm tired of that shit."

He handed me the paper he was carrying. "Then they got this thing," he said. It was an inmate newsletter—six two-sided pages called the *Advocate*—that one of the social studies teachers had helped the students put together.

On the cover was an image of a black man in front of a prison cell, with his back turned, and a bar code tattooed across his shoulders. "This is all about only black folks, too. Racist shit, dog. And Mr. Thomas was saying, 'What do you think about this, Rod?' And I don't want to talk about no more of that 'Black Power' shit, dog. That's all they want to talk about. I don't want to hear about stuff that I know more about than they do, man. I think they're retarded; Mr. Thomas must be an idiot. I'm serious. He always wanting to talk about dealing dope. He ain't never dealed no dope! None of them ever been in the game. You see us all in there; most of us in jumpsuits know more about the dope game than these cats. You know that's gonna be true. Mr. Thomas's soft. They all soft as wet bread. . . . They all from good hoods; they don't have no idea what they're talking about. . . . So when they said, 'What do you think about this picture?' I said that the shit was racist. I said what about for the white folks, and Mexicans and Arabs and shit? You know, they's a lot of these other people in here." I asked Rodney whether he thought it might be good or constructive for anyone at the facility to hear about it. "If I sent a petition out to everybody in here, I bet, I guarantee you I could get half the people to sign a form saying they don't like it. . . . But I'm making the most noise, you know. Then these soft-ass hos bring me down here."

Through the door, we could hear the shouts of Mr. Rey, the school's vice principal, "6N, 6N!" Rodney stood casually and shook my hand. He told me to come to his unit the following day, where he would introduce me to the other kids there. In the hallway, everyone else from his unit was forming a line from tallest in the front to shortest in the back, so that attending staff could walk behind them and see everyone's head. The kids from 6N moved forward in unison, like a black, canvas caterpillar.

Signs of Home

In the old facility, the units were wedge shaped, wide at the front and narrow in the distance, so that all the individual cell doors would be visible to staff people sitting at the broad end of the room, usually in front of a glass-walled office. The space felt like a foreshortened fun house. There were big square windows covered with thick wire screens lining the walls, flooding the wide end of the room with daylight. When I first entered the unit to which Rodney was assigned, no one stood to greet me or even did much to

acknowledge my presence. All the kids on the unit were sitting in short plastic school chairs that were arranged haphazardly around and beside a few
metal tables. School had been canceled for the day, so the kids on the unit
were spending their time playing games and shooting the breeze.

Rodney and three others were engaged in a fast-paced game of spades, slapping the cards down with a wound-up snap of their wrists, so that they
would spin and float toward the edge of the table, or sometimes on to the
floor. I walked tentatively toward them, not sure how I should manage the
spatial politics of the room, and leaned against the narrow windowsill behind the tables. Rodney looked at me and seemed vaguely amused, as if he
were watching a sitcom. The others glanced up from under their furrowed
brows, but then looked away again. There was a heavyset kid named
Bosworth, with a round head and a pouting face, leaning forward with his elbows on his knees and his chin hovering just above the table. Around the
table corner from him was Brendan, a small kid with perpetually chapped,
white lips that were stretched and cracking around his crooked eyeteeth. He
laughed with a convulsive tick every couple of minutes at nothing in particular. Across the table from him was a narrow-shouldered Latino boy with
a wispy, adolescent mustache. Sitting behind Rodney, peering interest-
edly over his shoulder, was Nards, short for Bernardo. Tall, long, and dark
skinned, he seemed to have an adenoid problem, and snorted air through his
half-open mouth. He offered a running commentary on the card game, ridi-
culing both teams for whatever misfortune befell them.

As the cards were flying back and forth, Rodney told me to sit down and
kicked a small chair toward me. I thanked him and half-whispered that "I
just didn't want to make anyone feel uncomfortable."

"You're a silly cat," he said, with a chuckle, and told me that everyone else
was already comfortable with me. "Remember, dog, we used to being
watched. We always got somebody looking at us, so it really ain't no difference with one more."

When the last trumps had been collected, and the playing cards were put
away, Rodney and I stayed at the table, along with Brendan. Rodney surveyed the people around the unit—playing chess and cards, writing letters,
drawing cars or practicing their signatures in dull pencil, and flipping
through magazines. "See, most of these cats, they're just small-time niggas,"
he said. "They might have done some little petty stuff. They might be petty
thugs, petty thieves, petty drug dealers, but they're here mostly for some mi-

nor shit. They didn't do nothing serious, really. . . . Not like me. And I ain't no petty-ass nothing. I'm the only one, I'll put that on everything I love. I'm the only one in here who is locked up for anything serious." He paused for a moment, nodding cheerfully. "But," he said loudly and with an edge of compressed giddiness, "I didn't do it!"

"No-oo-oo-oo," he stuttered, and laughed with a squeal. I shrugged my shoulders and said, "All right, man." Thinking that he was virtually admitting guilt, I thought it best for me not to push the issue. But after a moment, Rodney continued: "Probably the only other cat who ain't no petty-ass nigga is my man Nards. I knew him on the outs before I was up in here. You can see he ain't got any money. Raggedy-ass cat. Look at all that hair, man. When we on the outs, I'll be giving Nardo money, man. He's in here for some serious shit. For some felony-type shit. But that nigga is the only one up in here who makes jokes. He's the only cat you can really be playing with. When you say something, he's gonna know what you talking about. He's full of jokes, man. Other than that, dog . . . this place, basically, is a day care center. It's summer camp in here. There ain't nothing hard about this shit. . . . I could do this shit all day, if it wasn't for the not knowing what's gonna happen, you know? . . . As it is, I'm the only one here making real money. . . . We making some serious scril. We got the Jag, the Cadi-truck, the motherfucking brand-new Vette. We got my man making trips down to Alabama. We doing it for real! But I got to get over, man. I got ideas, dog, for making this shit work. . . . I got this girl on the outs. She works at a McDonald's right now, but she's managing. She runs that place, and we going to open an arcade." I asked if this was his girlfriend. "No, not really," he demurred, and then moved on. "See, we need someplace where people are going to spend money, you know, there ain't no receipts and shit when you put a quarter in a video game. Ain't no way they can keep track of how much money you making there. So, you know what I'm saying, we can do our little thing there, be rolling up in there, slinging." He pounded his left fist into his other hand, and said, "I need to get me at least $100,000 before the next year is over. I need at least a $100,000. . . . It's on, dog, we going to get that arcade."

Several days later, back on the sixth-floor unit, after the kids had returned from school and scattered around to talk about life on the outs, Rodney made it his business to offer me an introductory lesson in the Detroit dope game. "OK," he said, "I'm going to explain this to you." He was clear and didactic. "Now there are four different kinds of drugs that are sold in this city: pills, dope, raw, and weed. . . . Now rawheads are the craziest folks, man. They're nuts." Brendan was sitting with us, nodding along. "You know that's right!" he twisted and laughed in agreement. Bosworth, the heavyset kid, pulled a chair up to the table. "I would say that probably 60 percent of raw-heads are white, and 40 percent are black," Rodney continued. "And most of them is factory workers, you know. Rawheads don't be like crack fiends, all broke and shit. They got jobs, respectable jobs, and good money. . . . See, a rawhead be needing that shit. He can't go without it. When he do raw, he's gonna always need to be copping more, and he'll be doing anything to get it." Brendan broke in, contorting his face as if he had swallowed a mouthful of sand. "I'm sick. I'm sick," he said, in a gravely voice, like a jonesing heroin addict. Bosworth tore off the corner of a piece of school paper and began folding it into a small square pouch. "This is how we did them," he said to Rodney. "Oh, yeah, we cross them over like this," Rodney noted, with an excited smile, tearing another corner off the page and folding it in a subtly different pattern. Rodney explained that twelve packs, like the ones he and Bosworth had just folded, make a "B" or bundle. "Small-time hustlers," he told me, "they buy a B for like $50 or $60, and then sell each pack for $10. . . . Some people be selling packs for $12 or $14. But that's bullshit, man. I sell them for $7 or $8, but then I'm not going to get taxed like these small-time niggas out there." I asked Rodney how much he paid for a B of dope. "No, man!" he groaned. "Raw is raw, and dope is dope. You see what I'm saying? There ain't no Bs of dope." Dope, he told me, is crack cocaine. "You can have different cuts of dope, you can cut it once, twice, or three or four times. With baking soda. See, most times you got what's called an eighth, or an eight ball, or an eight." Rodney explained how eight balls are usually divided into either dime or nickel rocks, and how much profit one can expect to generate from selling a cut up eight ball. "It's not hard, see. Drugs are easy, man. Child's play, dog. A little kid could do this. This shit is easy as hell. But you making serious money."

The next day I entered the unit early in the morning. The stale smell from breakfast was still hanging in the air, and sleepiness was returning to some of the kids, all of whom had been awake since six in the morning. Rodney dragged his chair over to the middle of the room, where Nards and Willis were sitting with an active chessboard between them. "Come over here, man," he said. I walked over and sat across from him, slouching over my knees. He had with him a flimsy, yellow file folder, stuffed with tattered papers and Polaroid photographs. On the cover he had written "Dexter Boys" with a pencil, in stylized script, and had surrounded this with the initials "DC" inscribed in Celtic-looking interlocking patterns. "That's you?" I asked, pointing to the phrase on his folder. "For real," he answered. "And this my corner," he said, pointing now to the initials DC, which stood for the intersection of Dexter and Carrington. From the file folder he pulled out a letter that the girl working at McDonald's had written to him. He cocked his head to the side as he handed me the letter, and said that he needed to write her back. Her letter was full of superlative declarations of love and eternal devotion. She assured him that she loved him more than any other woman could, that she would do anything for him, and hoped he wouldn't be too upset that she had written. "I hate it when girls write me when I'm locked up, man. That's why I tell my mama not to give the address out, and I tell them hos not to write. Man, that just makes my heart drop when I get a letter from a girl in here." Brendan agreed, "A nigga just don't need all that distraction. And then all you be thinking about is what you missing."

"Look at this," Rodney broke in, opening the folder again and pulling out a thick deck of fading Polaroid photographs. A couple of the other boys dragged their chairs over and sat in a circle around and behind me and Rodney, their eyes riveted on his pile of pictures. The first showed Rodney standing roughly in the middle of a gaggle of other young men. In the photograph, he is wearing an emerald green fur coat that comes down to his waist. Rodney pointed out his brother, Antonio, standing right next to him, also wearing a fur coat, this one iridescent silver. "Look at this; we got the minks, dog," said Rodney. Willis chimed in with fawning admiration: "Y'all was geared, huh, Rod?" he said. In the photo, both Rodney and Antonio are holding fat wads of cash up to the camera. Behind them is a fabric banner, on which is spray painted a couple of sparkling champagne glasses and a gleaming white Mercedes-Benz. After everyone in the circle had seen the photograph, Rodney peeled it off the top, and held the next photo out toward me. In this one, he was standing alone, in the same mink coat, behind a messy pile of bills, over which he was hovering with bent knees and a pulled-lip grimace. His hands are out to his sides, with his palms forward and his index fingers curled into the shape of a little "d," for Dexter.

The images Rodney was passing around captivated the other kids on the unit. They held them in their hands and smiled, and at the same time, wanting so badly to step into the photographs, they frowned and shook their heads in delicious frustration. They all told stories of being at the clubs where some of the photos were taken, and Bosworth and Brendan rushed to their file folders to retrieve their own sets of pictures showing their own wads of cash and piles of money.

As the boys on the unit handed each other's Polaroids around their loosely gathered circle, they each hoped to show the others their points of contact with the outside world. Here they were without stenciled jumpsuits on their backs, without case numbers hanging over them. Here they were before their futures had been put in the hands of overworked judges, tired advocates, and court-appointed attorneys with questionable degrees of commitment. Here they were with their boys, their girls, and their family members. Here they were in their neighborhoods. Indeed, for most of the locked-up young African American kids, streets and corners were the most important points of explicit identification. Bosworth was often called "Fenkell" by inmates at the facility, after a street in north Detroit. Brendan was "Six Mile." Nards was "Livernois." If ordered according to nickname, the kids on the unit would map every quadrant of the city.

Rodney's preoccupation with writing DC on everything he could get his hands on reflects a similar impulse. Every day at lunch and dinner, he would sit down in front of one of the small empty Styrofoam trays that had been set out on the unit tables and with his plastic "spork" dig the initials DC into the bottom of the widest food well. On his paper cup, he would scrawl the same with one of the black pens he seemed always to have pilfered from the staff desk at the front of the room. And he wasn't alone. Before the ritual recitation of grace at mealtimes, plastic utensils chirping through Styrofoam sounded like singing sparrows all around the unit.[4]

Games and Contests

Only a few days after Rodney had disparagingly described the youth home as being like a day care center, he was playing his daily chess match with Big Willis Harrison. Willis had been at the facility for only a couple of weeks, and Rodney had taken him under his wing as soon as he had arrived, offering him jail-wise advice and teaching him to play chess. Willis was a quick study; on this day he was beating Rodney, who was growing restless and frustrated.

"This is some ho-ass shit," Rodney said. Willis laughed like a foghorn.
"What's the matter, man?" he asked.

"You're on some dick-handlin' bullshit, man," Rodney shot back.

"What, you losing?" Willis asked, facetiously.

"You moved out of turn!" Rodney yelled, and reached over to reposition Willis's queen. Willis slapped his hand away. "Quit, cheater!" he screamed back.

Rodney looked down at the board and then swiped his arm across it, knocking all the pieces on their sides and on to the floor. He strode defiantly off to the other side of the room.

As Willis's booming laugh followed him, Bernardo walked through the main unit door, from the hallway into which the elevator opens. He was wearing street clothes and brown corduroy trousers that gathered over his floppy white basketball shoes, and was followed closely by a juvenile detention facility staff member, a light-skinned black man with a bald head. I hadn't even noticed Bernardo's absence, but the kids met his return with an ominous silence that fell suddenly and evenly over the unit.

Early that morning, before the others had risen from sleep, Bernardo had been led from his room and taken by van to the Frank Murphy Hall of Justice downtown. He'd already been convicted of armed robbery, and this morning he had been sentenced—maybe months in the reform school, maybe years in prison. When he returned, Bernardo moved toward the center of the narrowing unit and paced around without pattern. His usually audible breathing was heavier and wetter now; in the stillness of the room it was more a sniffle than a snort. While everyone's eyes were on him, no one said a word.

Bernardo walked over to the far corner of the unit's wide end and sat in a creaky fold-up chair. He dropped his face into his hands and started to whimper. From our seats we could see his shoulders heaving and hear his squeaking efforts to keep himself from sobbing. He was crying puddles of tears. The other kids sighed, shook their heads, and raised their shoulders as if against a cold wind. Eventually, Rodney broke the silence among the small group of us who were sitting there. "Man, this don't look too good," he said. Brendan licked his lips and agreed. "It's fucked up," he whispered. Bernardo had been hoping for some sort of residential juvenile placement or possibly even a probationary term, but his current mood made this seem unlikely.

Everyone shuddered to think of themselves in his place. Of course, many would make the same early morning trip in the coming weeks.

Several days later I visited the unit in the afternoon. The boys had finished their day in the school and had gone to their rooms for the mandatory "reflection" period, when most kids lie on their cots and sleep soundly. The main unit room was empty then, except for Bosworth and a short but muscular fifteen-year-old named Raul, both of whom were "doing detail" on the unit—folding newly arrived clean underwear, socks, and towels into tight little bundles to be distributed when the others awoke from their slumber. They both greeted me enthusiastically when I arrived, each shaking my hand and snapping their fingers afterward. When they had finished arranging the laundry, the three of us sat and talked as the guard unlocked the unit rooms and the other kids slowly emerged. Bosworth and Raul were old-timers on the unit. Each was there for unrelated carjacking charges, and both had already been found guilty in adult courtrooms and would be sent soon (neither was sure when, and neither was sure for how long) to the Michigan Department of Corrections. Raul had played linebacker for the junior varsity football team at his high school, and he explained to me that he hoped somehow to play football again after his likely release (barring any disciplinary issues) in around six years. Bosworth, an inveterate drug dealer in Detroit, told me that he wanted to study architecture after getting out of prison. He was a star geometry student in Mr. Bradford's math class at the youth home, and during free times he would often draw floor plans of potential "dreamhouses," in consultation with the other kids on the unit, who would hurl suggestions for the dimensions of game rooms and wet bars. Raul told me that it was Bosworth's seventeenth birthday, and Bosworth smiled shyly.

The others were now mostly out of their rooms and sleepily gathered on the far side of the unit, lying in chairs with their backs in the seats and their heads propped against the back supports. The din of laughter and talk was growing louder when Bradford, the math teacher, was let on to the unit carrying a stack of hot pizzas. He had ordered them for Bosworth's birthday, and brought them up as a surprise. Everyone sang "Happy Birthday" with different degrees of silliness, seriousness, and tonal integrity, as Bosworth put his forehead down on the table in front of him and covered his head and ears with his hands and arms. When we were done singing, he picked his head up, still blushing, and nodded coolly without looking at anyone in the room.

After we had eaten, as the other kids on the unit sat down in front of the television, which was set on a rolling cart in one of the front corners of the main room, Rodney grabbed a chair and dragged it away from the group. "So, man, come over here," he said. I drew another chair next to his and sat down with my notebook on my lap. "I got to talk to you," he said. "So when you come to my court date, are you just going to sit in the back and observe, or are you going to be talking or what?" I told him I just planned to observe and asked if that would be OK. "Yeah, yeah!" he said excitedly, rocking back and forth, and smiling as if we had just hatched a plan. "That's cool," he said. "Now let me ask you something. Do you think I should write a letter to the judge? 'Cause I been thinking about that, but I'm not sure what kind of let-ter to write." I suggested he talk to his lawyer. He had told me that he had a hotshot lawyer whom his mother's boyfriend, Johnny, had gathered the money to hire. The fact that Rodney had a retained attorney put him in the minority on the unit, where most kids were often complaining about the in-eptitude, unavailability, and apparent indifference of their court-appointed lawyers. Rodney reflected for a moment: "Yeah, I don't even want to mess with him about that; he's already got that stuff. I gave him letters from every teacher I've had in here: Mr. Bradford, Mr. Schrock, even them ho-ass Black Power cats." Rodney giggled and punched his fist into his open palm: "But see, we got this thing locked down man. We already got this shit beat! There ain't no *way* they can say that I did this, no way!" As Rodney started to talk about his case, he talked more hurriedly and became harder to follow. He told me that someone had been shot on the corner of Dexter and Carring-ton, one of the busier drug corners in his neighborhood, where an Arab-owned gas station is the locus of all sorts of neighborhood activity. "But I didn't do it, man. I couldn't have done it. I wasn't even in town. I was up in Grand Rapids, 'cuz see . . ." He gathered himself to start again. "See, a bunch of us from the neighborhood had been gambling on the street with these other guys, from somewhere else. And we found out they was gay, and they was, you know, coming on to us. So we wrecked those faggots. We stomped 'em!" he said excitedly. "And that was on that corner, right near Dexter and Carrington, right there. And then they filed charges against us. Now they just know me on that corner. I mean they knew me from before, but they knew me for sure after that. So when my man got shot, first one they going to blame is me. But here's the thing. When they put that gay thing on me, I took off, man. I went to Grand Rapids, where we got people, 'cuz I had missed one of the court dates, and I was just like, fuck it, I'm gone. . . . And that's when this other shit happened." He paused in momentary reflection. "I think that's why it would be better if I was being tried in adult court. 'Cuz, see, we got this beat on the evidence. They don't got shit on me. I was out of town. They got one witness who said that whoever did it was like 6 feet tall, and I'm only 5'10". And one time this cat said that whoever did it was wearing a hat, and another time, that he had his hair all braided up. Now how's he going to see someone with a hat covering his head and see that his hair all braided up at the same time? I'm telling you . . . if this was adult court, there wouldn't be nothing they could do. They would have to let me go. But with juvy, they care more about who you are, you know. You know, making you a good person. That's why I'm getting all these letters and shit. You know, you need to show them that you going to do good, even if they ain't got no evidence."

Shifting to the side, Rodney said, "Let me ask you something: Do you believe in God?" I told him that I wasn't sure. "You don't?" he asked, laughing sort of incredulously. "Well I do. Straight up. I'm a firm believer in God, and I pray a lot. And one thing is, I'm afraid to go to hell," he said. "Do you believe in Hell?" he asked. "I don't know," I persisted. "You don't know? . . . Well I don't want to go! You know, we don't live on this earth for too long. What's the average life expectancy? Like sixty-five years, right? That's really short compared to, you know, after that. And I just don't know about . . . I guess I don't know about selling dope."

"What do you mean?" I asked.

"I don't know . . ."

"You feel sort of conflicted?"

"Yes, exactly," he said. "I feel conflicted! Because I know it's a sin. And the Bible says, obey the law of the land. So I know it ain't right. But then I also know that the Bible says that no man should judge another man. And I know that as long as you right with the Lord, you know, when it's your time to go, you gonna be OK. You gonna be OK. That's why I'm saying, I'm not doing this shit forever. This is just to get me started. I'm thinking that I'm gonna be a lawyer or some shit when I get older. So you know what I'm saying? I got time to get right with God still. . . . But, like you say, I feel conflicted now."[5]

A few weeks later, I was sitting on a courtroom bench next to Rodney's mother, who was wearing a bright red, full-length dress. Rodney had told her that I would be there, and though I had never met her before, she gave me a warm hug when I introduced myself. "You know, I get nervous before I come in here," she told me. "So I'm feeling sick, I'm sick in the body," she said. "I mean, I raised four kids by myself. And none of them be getting into trouble. It's the damn hook been dragging us in here for years. All these cases." Leaning toward me, she added, "We beat 'em all, though. Just like we'll beat this one!" The prosecuting attorney, a bearded white man, was wandering in and out of the courtroom, and she leered at him. "Ohhhh, look at him," she said loudly enough for him to hear. "He will have to answer. Some day, he will have to answer for his actions. Jesus will see us through this. Yes, we are bathed in the blood of Jesus!"

Finally, Rodney entered through a door in the back of the small court-room. He was dressed in a big boxy suit that his mother had brought for him, and he had his hair pulled back tightly, in a single long braid down his back. He saw his family when he walked into the room and broke into a wide smile, and then sat down at the table next to his lawyer, an African American man whom his stepfather had retained for the case.

Rodney had been counting down the days to this court appearance, making ever more elaborate plans for what he would do when he got out. The night before, he had gathered all of his pictures and papers from the charter school and handed them to me to give to his family. He told me that there would be a huge party at his sister's house when he got home, and he said I was sure to have a lot to write about if I could make it.

After Rodney was settled in his chair, the judge entered the room and sat with his arms crossed in front of him. Sounding annoyed, he announced that the state had not been able to produce its witnesses. Rodney's lawyer stood and asked that the charges be dismissed. The judge responded, without looking up and almost under his breath, by asking for his calendar. He flipped through the pages and then said, "February eleventh. We'll postpone until then." Rodney shook his head, looking down at his crossed fingers, weighing the prospect of yet another three months behind bars. He stood and looked toward his family, winking awkwardly before disappearing again through the back of the courtroom. Whatever his fate, he would need to wait to learn it. His mother bolted out and ducked into a bathroom a few doors away. The sounds of her retching echoed through the halls.

8

Across the Street

In the blue light of a cloudy dawn, early in November, all the kids at the youth home were herded into idling vans parked outside the rear entrance to the facility. They were driven, most still half asleep, the mile and a half distance to the brand-new Wayne County Juvenile Detention Facility on Saint Antoine, right across the narrow street from the towering Wayne County Jail. There had been talk for the previous fifteen years about building a new facility, and as conditions in the old youth home continued to deteriorate, with overcrowded rooms and crumbling infrastructure, the city and county finally managed to appropriate funds to complete the project.

From outside, the new juvenile detention facility strikes an almost deliberately comic contrast with the adult county jail across the street. Where the jail is a twelve-story monolithic concrete rectangle with narrow slit windows, the juvenile detention facility is low-slung and sprawling, faced in mottled brown ceramic-looking tiles. Standing out on the sidewalk, the windows look large and square, with pleasant turquoise-hued hanging blinds. The waiting area is lined with enormous street-level picture windows. It has elegant carpet and is furnished with comfortable blue chairs, and there are houseplants in the corners.

But from the inside, behind the steel doors that lead out of the waiting area, the contrast between the two spaces dissolves. The two-tiered units at the juvenile detention facility are designed according to adult correctional facility specifications. Each is equipped with multiple cameras, and officers in a central room fortified with television monitors control all the doors.

From the individual cell rooms, the windows are all too high to look out of, and the only access to fresh air for young people locked up at the new facility is on the roof, in a brick-enclosed cell that is covered on top with a perforated sheet of metal. It all amounts to a far cry from the expansive yard and big clear windows at the old youth home.

With the move to the new facility, the tension between adult and juvenile institutions—and the fluidity of the boundaries between them—only became more pressing. For many of the kids incarcerated there, the move to downtown Detroit was eerily reminiscent of other early morning visits that they had made to the city's "criminal justice complex" for hearings in one of the adult courts there. It is hardly surprising, then, that in retracing their tracks to adult court, young detainees' sense of proximity to the complex of adult facilities in their new digs was especially acute. And suspicion was running high among the kids that the decision to position them close to the adult courthouses and jails was a reflection of the increasing likelihood that they themselves would soon end up within one or more of them. While movement between the juvenile detention facility and the county jail would still require a short ride in a locked van, their new proximity seemed to make the dire prospect of "adult time" all the more real. But just in case any had not taken note of this possibility, the juvenile detention facility staff people were quick to point it out.

On only the third day that the new facility had been open, Ms. Bailey was assigned to the lead position on the unit where Rodney was kept. In the new building, all the sixth-floor charges, who were still wearing their stenciled black jumpsuits, were assigned to the unit called "Bill Pickett," after the famous black rodeo cowboy.[1] Bailey congratulated them on the cool name of their unit but assured them that she had no intention of being their rodeo clown. After the kids on the unit had eaten lunch, she took some time to make clear to them her use of the institution's "level system." The system penalizes detained kids for all sorts of indiscretions, from fighting, to swearing, to talking out of turn, to absconding with another kid's juice carton. Depending on the severity of a situation, the loss of a level can mean the revocation of special gym privileges or restriction to one's room for days at a time. In all cases, level docking is seen by inmates as a subjective measure, the fairness of which depends on the integrity of the staff person on duty.

Bailey, who had worked at the facility for close to ten years, turned the television off and strode to the front of the room. She introduced herself to the

gathered inmates, most of whom were already familiar with her from previous episodes in the facility. "I respect you," she said. "I really do. I feel for
you all. I have kids of my own, so I know how hard it can be. And I know my
kids would have a hard time up in here. But let me say: just like I respect
you, you need to respect me too. You need to do what I ask, when I ask, and
we won't have any problems. One thing I won't stand for is all your filthy
talk. . . . I mean, I can say 'motherfucker' in one hundred different ways, but
they say that I need to curtail that. And if I have to curtail that, then I feel
that you should have to curtail it also." Rodney, Willis, Raul, and the others
on the unit all laughed and nodded in agreement. "You all need to understand where you are," Bailey continued with a preacher's enthusiasm. "You
aren't in any day care center anymore. Look at this place," she said, waving
her short arms around the room and glancing up at the barred second-tier
walkway over her head. "You know what's right across the street from you
now? That's the real thing right there, and the only difference between this
and that place is the school. Right next door, and you need to understand
that, 'cuz they are setting you up in here. I'll tell you, you don't even know it,
but they are *setting you up* in here. They're just getting you ready to go across
the street." The kids on the unit again all nodded appreciatively. "I'm just being real," said Bailey. "I'm just being for real."

At the old youth home building in midtown Detroit, when detained kids
would mention the adult justice system, they would usually name a particular courthouse or jail—"Frank Murphy" (the Frank Murphy Hall of Justice)
or "the 36th" (the Thirty-sixth District Court). At the new detention facility,
all this institutional complexity was reduced to one phrase: "across the
street." Conversations among both kids and staff people there were often
abuzz with invocations of across the street, what might be happening there,
who might be heading there. And where the move downtown had been a
foreboding possibility for many young people facing transfer to adult court,
there was some reassurance, however deluded or misguided, in its physical
distance. In contrast, the move across the street seemed both ominous and
easy—only a few steps away.[2]

As detained kids adjusted to the new facility, new faces appeared and familiar faces left—some without anyone noticing, others with more fanfare.
Bosworth was sentenced to five years in prison and shipped up to Baldwin,
the minuscule rural town in northwest Michigan that had been awarded one
of two contracts to build what Michigan's Republican governor John Engler

was calling "a punk prison."[3] After his sentencing, Bosworth rushed back to the unit to collect the personal effects that he had left there. He smiled nervously, and looked flushed as he pulled some school papers, his drawings (all the dreamhouse floorplans he had drawn for other inmates on the unit), and a Bible out of his room, and tripped down from the second tier and toward the red door at the front of the unit where Mr. Lyle was waiting to accompany him to the Department of Corrections van downstairs. Several of the other kids on the unit, who had known Bosworth for several months, gathered around the door and, one by one, threw their arms around his shoulders. His eyes were red and tearing as the door shut behind him, and the room was stricken with a solemn weight for the rest of the afternoon, as the boys sat lifelessly in front of the television.

In contrast, Brendan had left early in the morning, when everyone was still asleep. And in the ever-shifting personal landscape of the unit, where relationships are both intensely intimate and always provisional, his absence was hardly noticed. Bernardo was also gone. He had left just before the move from the old building, like Bosworth, bound for Baldwin, likely doing a three-year bit. And over the course of the first month in the new facility, a new group of kids were sent to Bill Pickett.

Clowns and Gods on Pickett

In a space already unsettled by the convergence and blurring of different kinds of time, most of the kids on Bill Pickett found themselves facing cases that explicitly inhabited the strange terrain between the adult and juvenile systems, tilted one way or the other by whim, fancy, and fortune.

From my first introduction to him, Branford Wilson was perhaps the most well-mannered inmate I had encountered at the facility. After I had been conducting fieldwork there for a couple of months, most new arrivals initially assumed that I was a counselor or caseworker. Branford figured that I must be a lawyer and walked up to the front of the unit while I was talking with the facility's quality assurance specialist. He stood quietly with his hands folded until there was a lull in the conversation, and then asked if I could help him with some "law book questions." I explained that I wasn't a lawyer and probably couldn't do much, but that I'd be happy to listen to him.

In spite of my discouragement, he smiled and nearly sighed with relief at the prospects of having someone hear his story.

Sitting in the crowded unit, in the din of BET on television, excited card games, and arguments over the inequitable distribution of juice, Branford launched into a seemingly well-rehearsed recapitulation of his situation.

After a group of his friends robbed and assaulted a pizza driver (he was unclear about who among the group was most to blame), Branford was convicted in juvenile court in Detroit and spent three years at the Maxey Boys' Training School in the Michigan countryside. Then, after completing the reform school program, with numerous delays resulting from his strained relationship with one of the psychologists there, he was released to a supervised, independent-living group home on the West Side. He was, without question, a model resident in this placement. He found employment, completed the GED, and was even particularly helpful for younger people in the program. Yet he was intensely eager to leave. He had a daughter living in the city and needed to make more money to care for her, and he wanted to be with his daughter's mother. Branford believed that the only way he could take care of his responsibilities was to get out of the group home. With the tacit agreement of group home workers, who told him that they would complete paperwork indicating that he had finished, Branford left the supervised independent living situation only a couple of months before he would have been released. Unfortunately, the paperwork was never filed, and as far as the courts were concerned, he had gone AWOL.

He had been living under the law since then—trying to keep a job and lead a quiet life. Without a state identification card or a driver's license, he had managed to stay out of the view of the police and courts for nearly four years following his stint at the group home. Then, within a month of his nineteenth birthday (and the closing of his juvenile file), Branford was flagged by a city police officer for speeding. He tried to outrun the cops as he exited a freeway in Detroit, but was arrested and thrown back into juvenile detention. Now, though, he had adult fleeing and driving without a license charges and his juvenile AWOL case.[4]

Branford told me that although he was nineteen and had been consistently employed at a stamping plant since leaving the group home, he was worried that his juvenile judge, an inveterate and notoriously draconian adjudicator, would send him to boot camp to serve a six-month sentence. His

Michigan Family Independence Agency caseworker had met with him a couple of times and, short of having the case dismissed, was transparently hoping for him to go into some kind of juvenile placement, which would involve much less paperwork and actual face time for the worker than would probation, a preferable disposition in Branford's eyes. Ironically, one of Branford's most pressing interests was for his *adult* charge (which was likely to result in a probation sentence) *not* to be dismissed, since he figured it might supersede his juvenile charge.

I told Branford that I'd be happy to write a letter on his behalf, but that given the judicial-bureaucratic complexity of his case, I doubted that it would do much good. A few weeks later I attended his juvenile hearing to see how it might be resolved. Branford's mother, who looks just like him, and his girlfriend and daughter were there. They entered the third-floor courtroom along with a teacher from the detention facility charter school and Branford's Family Independence Agency caseworker. An appointed attorney, whom Branford had met on his previous trip to court, was also there. The prosecutor, a tall man with round shoulders, stood tiredly across from them; his presence, in a case where so little real harm had been done, seemed particularly awkward.

The hearing commenced with everyone introducing themselves as the judge leafed through Branford's thick file. "Let's see, hmmm," she contemplated. "Where have you been? You were at the state boys' school for some time," she mused. Branford answered, "Yes, ma'am." She stopped flipping the pages and looked down through her round bottle-bottom glasses: "It seems that you've been missing for thirty months!" she yelled, staring in absolute stillness at Branford. "I have a little theory that for every day you're missing, you should spend an equal amount of time in detention." Everyone in the room was silent, and Branford looked nervously toward his lawyer.

"And I'm inclined toward boot camp!" snapped the judge. "For you, Mr. Wilson, that would be quite a stretch of time, wouldn't it? I think boot camp might do you a lot of good."

The court-appointed attorney tried to suggest that Branford had been out of trouble, reminding the judge that he had been working. The judge asked where, and Branford answered that he hadn't been working since he was locked up, but that he was working before.

"You were working when you were picked up?" she asked, rhetorically. "It doesn't look that way to me. It looks like you were trying to run away from the police." She asked the prosecuting attorney whether he had any thoughts about what should be done with Branford. "It doesn't matter to me what happens," he said. "Whatever your honor deems appropriate. . . . But I would add that I feel that I'm sitting across from a man." The prosecutor turned back toward the people assembled in the courtroom and laid his eyes on Branford's girlfriend and daughter. He continued: "And a man wouldn't run like that, or would know not to run. A man would know what his responsibilities are. And here they were not fulfilled. . . . That's all that I would add." The judge nodded her head in agreement.

Indeed, no one would disagree that Branford had become a "man" in the years since going AWOL. He was two years older, had been working hard, and had been caring for his child. But how could his recent emergence as an adult have anything to do with a two-year-old juvenile charge? If he was a man now, shouldn't these juvenile charges have been dropped? Shouldn't he simply be charged in the adult system with fleeing the cops and driving without a license? Instead, the prosecutor in juvenile court seemed to be invoking Branford's "manhood" as an exacerbating factor in the juvenile case against him. All of which was more than a little confusing for Branford. For weeks on end, while the judge took his case under advisement, Branford was in a sort of no-man's-land where his institutional designation as either a boy or man might turn like a vane in the wind.

Before Branford's case was resolved, in the middle of winter, a sixteen-year-old named Cedric Mann showed up on the unit. He seemed cool and calm, and given his circumstances, he maintained a remarkable self-possession. Everyone on the unit had seen him on television a couple of nights before he appeared up on Pickett. As reported in the news: Cedric and his best friend, Justin, both African American, had caught a cab in front of a liquor store in the city and were on their way to a house party in Southfield with their high school friends. At some point during the drive, as the cab slowed to a stop, one of the boys in the backseat pulled a gun from his jacket, pointed it at the back of the driver's head, and shot him. The cabdriver, who was an Arab resident of Dearborn and the father of young children, died instantly. Then one of the boys reached into the pockets of the dead man and took $60 in cash. It was a brutal murder committed by affluent kids, seemingly for the sake of a few bucks.

Rodney had sort of attached himself to Cedric, mostly because Cedric was an accomplished chess player and provided a relatively rare challenge to Rodney's chess-playing supremacy on the unit. Over the first few days of his incarceration there, Cedric beat everyone he played, including the most skilled staff people, each several times.

But many of the other kids on the unit weren't sure what to make of Cedric. He had been an honors student at Northern High, in the suburbs. Yet he was charged with this grisly murder. When he first arrived, most other inmates kept their distance but were also captivated by him. They seemed both envious and disgusted.

But for all the mystery, intrigue, and outrage surrounding his case, the fact that most titillated others on the unit was that his lawyer was Otis Culpepper, the famed Detroit defense attorney. Culpepper, who is known for his signature alligator-skin cowboy boots and tailored suits, had earned a reputation as one of the most skilled defense litigators in the city through the multiple exonerations that he achieved for various high-level members of the Young Boys Incorporated, the notorious Detroit drug gang. For kids on Pickett, landing Culpepper as an attorney was a sort of miracle, a kind of holy and wholly transformative deliverance; Culpepper was a savior. And Cedric knew it. Though his current circumstances had plunged him into episodes of deep uncertainty about his station in life, his past, his faith in a Christian God, and his future, Cedric was also profoundly confident that he would either be exonerated altogether or be sentenced as a juvenile, simply for Culpepper's representation.

Meanwhile, Justin was represented by Neil Rockind, another famous attorney in the metro area (nicknamed "The Rockweiler") who had made his name as one of the most effective criminal defense lawyers in the state. For Cedric, Justin, and their two lawyers, their joint trial became an irresistible game. The two camps decided that through their trials (which were separate cases but tried simultaneously in the same court room), each would accuse the other of pulling the trigger and taking the money, and both hoped that as the case moved forward each side would cast doubt on the guilt of the other. In the end, if all went according to plan, each would cancel the other out. Cedric and Justin, best friends for years, were tight-lipped about all of this with everyone else in the detention facility. As the trial progressed, both would spend the day in court, through their high-priced representation, accusing the other of the crimes in question and imploring their juries that the other deserved to pay a price. But at the end of the day, the two would come back to the detention facility, change out of their courtroom jackets and slacks, and sit in their jumpsuits playing chess together.

When Justin was convicted of manslaughter and given a ten-year prison sentence, both his and Cedric's camps were elated. Given all the testimony and evidence against him, the jury finding was a major victory for Justin. Cedric might have been especially happy, though. For in the playing of each defendant against the other, the seriousness of this conviction meant that if he was not acquitted altogether, Cedric would likely be convicted of a much less serious crime and might hope for a nearly dismissive sentence. And so it happened that not long after Justin was sent off to begin his term, which may not end until he turns twenty-seven years old, Cedric was transferred to an open-campus, low-security juvenile placement in nearby Ann Arbor, where he was to serve a nine-month sentence. He was allowed to leave every weekend to visit his family, and on weekdays he would enjoy frequent field trips with other kids at the placement.

At the detention facility, kids seemed always to be talking about their efforts to secure retained lawyers and the liabilities of various and sundry appointed attorneys contracting with Wayne County. Most of the young people there were left with no choice but to accept appointed council and assumed that this representation would be only minimally adequate. None were optimistic that these attorneys would vigilantly represent them. But detained kids facing serious charges were loathe to dismiss the possibility that they might land the services of a good lawyer. For some, this was the only hope of avoiding a long-term sentence in the adult criminal justice system.

Fredrick Nelson came from the housing projects of Inkster, Michigan, about thirty miles west of Detroit, and from a hardworking but impoverished family. His father was a maintenance man for an apartment complex, and his mother worked as a maid in a hotel. Meanwhile, Fredrick had been working in the drug trade on the grounds of the housing project where he lived, starting when he was only twelve years old, with cousins and other young people in the neighborhood. In Lamont Gardens, as the projects are called, so many kids were slinging drugs off the curbs that competition was fierce among them for customers; the arrival of a slow-driving addict looking for a fix would mark the beginning of a footrace toward the side of the road.

Fredrick had been locked up since just before I first visited the facility, on a first-degree murder charge, after someone looking to score some crack had been beaten to death by a swarming group of young drug dealers in the Inkster projects. Fredrick was fifteen, barely literate, and possessed of such a simple, sweet naïveté about the world that it was nearly impossible to imagine him playing a significant role in the killing, but then it was just as easy to imagine him being led to do almost anything. He was moody like a little boy, and I would often see him go from hysterical laughter to brooding quiet, and then to soft tears that he'd shed in the corners of the unit.

When Rodney, Cedric, and I were occupying our customary places on Pickett, sitting on the blue couches under the rising stairs leading to the balcony and the second-tier rooms along it, Fredrick came up to us and said, "Look, look what I got." Rodney mocked him. "Get the fuck out of here, Ink," he said. Fredrick laughed with goofy exuberance. He held out a clenched fist, turned it over, and opened his fingers, keeping his hand low so that others on the unit wouldn't see. He had crushed a yellow crayon, taken from the art supply bin, into small nickel- and dime-size chunks, which could nearly have passed for the real thing in a quick, dimly lit transaction on the street. "I got the rocks," he said. Rodney and Cedric leaned forward excitedly and grabbed his hand from below, fingering through the waxy bits of crayon. "This is how you chop up?" Rodney asked caustically. "Shit, I'd sell each one of these for two apiece." Ink looked disappointed, but then realized that Rodney was only joking. He laughed again and sat down on one of the blue couches adjacent to the stairs, looking off into a corner of the room.

His head swiveled again toward Cedric. "You saw Culpepper today?" he asked. Cedric nodded. "How much you paying him?" No response. "A lot, huh?" Cedric nodded again. "Like 5,000? . . . 10,000? . . ." Cedric didn't say anything. "Damn! More than 10,000!" Ink erupted in a nervous, toothy smile. "What, like 20,000?!" "More than you could ever afford," said Cedric. "How much would it cost to get, like, a pretty good lawyer?" asked Fredrick. Rodney answered, "What you mean, 'good lawyer,' dog? There's a lot of different lawyers out there. . . . I mean, you could get you a decent attorney for 5,000. But you got a murder rap, dog. So the way I see it, that ain't really gonna do shit for you. And that's if you could get that." "Damn!" said Fredrick, helplessly. He looked off into the bright unit room, not focusing on anything. He held his index finger to his mouth and chewed on the frayed edge of his fingernail.

Among nearly everyone who had been on the unit for long, Fredrick was beloved. None had much hope that this overgrown child would end up anywhere but in an adult prison, where, most staff people and other inmates speculated, he would quickly be subjected to physical, emotional, and sexual abuse. Still, he would rehearse this conversation with Rodney and Cedric many times over the course of his incarceration, with unflagging, if sometimes vulnerable, optimism. The patent unfairness of his situation made the looming impact of his family's destitution seem impossible— somehow still something *someone* could remedy. But while he was optimistic, he was reflective about the relative likelihood that he might wind up in prison and the consequences that this would have for his life. While hanging out on the unit one day, he told me: "If they let me go, give me some little juvenile thing, I'm going to be doing good. Hang out with different people. Do good in school, you know. . . . But if you get sent to prison, fuck it, you going to be booming. I'm gonna be right back out there on the street. Doing what I was doing before. Prison just give me time to think about how I should do it. How should I dodge the hook, stay hot. Prison really . . . it ain't really about nothing. Only thing they doing is giving you some time to think about what you did. They ain't really doing nothing. They just getting you built. Getting your anger up. Getting you ready to get booming again."

His conundrum was a common one. And the larger significance of his circumstances were clear to others on the unit: Institutional designations of childhood, and all the legal benefits associated with such designations, were much more likely available to those with money. While the innocence of childhood might easily be lost in the legal system, it could also be bought.

Intentions of a Little Man

Dude's first hearing was nearly a month after his incarceration at the detention facility. Through the first month that he was locked up, Dude had been optimistic that he might be tried as a juvenile. He hoped at the least that people likely to be testifying in his case would describe his participation in Walker's death in the most diminished way possible, or that they might simply lie on his behalf, put him somewhere else, or not talk at all. After his transfer from the mental health unit to Bill Pickett, he settled into a relatively calm routine for a couple of weeks. The unit's special services representative, whose major responsibilities included granting phone calls to inmates and processing their complaints, appreciated Dude's long familiarity with the facility and standard protocol there. He took a particular interest in Dude's case, and allowed him frequent phone calls to Ruby as well as Billy and others in the house on Pleasant where Walker was killed. During this period on Pickett, Dude even spoke several times with Juan (who had been the object of his frustration the night that Walker was shot), and Dude felt that Juan and he had come to a kind of understanding about the unfolding of events on that night in January.

As the weeks passed, Dude became increasingly convinced that he would probably serve some time in some sort of institution—but he was also confident that he would not be doing adult time. Even after he had been loaded into a van and taken two blocks from the detention facility to the Thirtysixth District (adult) Court for a pretrial hearing, where he waited for an entire day in the bull pen without ever being arraigned (as happens frequently in the court system), Dude returned to the detention facility with a bolstered spirit.

"When I was in the Thirty-sixth today, I talked to everybody in the family," he told me that evening. "Billy, Chewie, Treb, all of them over there on Pleasant. There's a phone in the room where they quarantine you at or whatever, and I was calling from that, just over and over. When the time would run out, I'd get right back on the phone. . . . They was all crying and saying that they can't believe that I'm locked up. Like, it's just something that they can't even put they minds around, and then that gets me to crying." Dude shook his head, "I'm telling you, black people. . . . When we need each other like that, we like that!" He clapped his hands together in a clasp and curled his fingers around one another. "Billy, especially," he continued. "He showing me so much love. It's like, 'How much you need? You need to get this lawyer. You need to get some clothes.' I was talking to Buddy, and he said, 'Don't worry, man. I'm going to go to the mall and get you something, so that you be looking geared at court.' I said, 'Don't worry about getting me no fancy stuff. I just need me a little shirt, some cheap pants. I'll be straight.'"

But Dude's good mood didn't last for long. As the days and then weeks went by, the promises that Billy and others had made, to help him pay for an attorney and get him clothes for his court appearances, went unfulfilled. He wrote them letters, but didn't hear back, and even with opportunities for phone calls, wasn't able to reach any of them.

The day before his rescheduled pretrial hearing, several weeks later, Dude was poring over copies of the witness statements and police reports that his appointed lawyer, a Jamaican woman named Ms. Housewell, had given him. He had me read them to him over and over again, even though he had already read them and understood them all better than I. He went through them repeatedly, trying to determine which statements to take seriously and which to disregard. And he kept asking me how he should think about dealing with them, what angle he should take. "Luke, man," he said, "this got my mind all fucked up. I can't even think straight right now. This just got me so twisted around." Dude found Buddy's statement particularly troubling, as it didn't say anything about any struggle between Dude and Eastside, and it bluntly reported that Dude had shot the gun through the floor of his own volition.

The following day, on the third floor of the Thirty-sixth District Court, which was filled with construction dust from the rising football stadium next door, Dude was once again scheduled to have a pretrial hearing, to determine the merits of a second-degree murder charge for his accidental shooting of Walker. Not long after I got there, Ruby showed up from dialysis with a little bag of food to stabilize her blood sugar. The prosecuting attorney had arrived nearly ten minutes before. This would be her first case in the Wayne County courts, after her recent transfer from Oakland County, a conservative suburban district, and she clearly was eager to make a good showing. Billy, Aisha, and Dude's erstwhile girlfriend, Janet, all arrived before we went into the courtroom. Janet was crying quietly from the moment she took a seat in one of the back benches and broke into heaving, screeching sobs when Dude entered through the bull pen door just to the side of the judge's bench.

The first witness to take the stand matter-of-factly recalled the widening pool of blood haloed around Walker's head after he was shot. Leaning away from the witness, Walker's daughter began to whimper and then started moaning uncontrollably in her boyfriend's arms. The court bailiff stood close and then insisted that they leave, escorting them out of the room. Dude fidgeted with a pencil that his lawyer had put in front of him, digging his thumbnail into the eraser.

The judge was a lovely young woman whose soft demeanor belied her tendency to hand down tough sentences, especially when minors were subject to adult convictions. In Dude's pretrial hearing, she listened to the mumbled testimony of only two witnesses before declaring second-degree charges appropriate. With this, Dude might face a prison term that would be decades longer than for manslaughter.

Two days later, when I saw Dude at the detention facility, he was serving the second day of a two-day "isolation," where he would be locked in his room for twenty-three hours of each day, for starting a fight with another kid on the unit after returning from court. Dude was lying naked on the floor of his cell, wrapped in one of the sheets from his cot. The staff person on the unit, Mr. Mallard, opened the door for me and told Dude that he had to get up.

"Freeman," he shouted with a hint of frustration, "someone's here to see you."

"Fuck you," Dude answered back from under his sheet. "I don't give a shit."

I went in anyway and tried to talk with him about what had happened. He sat up, with the green sheet falling off his shoulder, but he didn't say anything.

We had been sitting in silence for around a half an hour when Dude slowly stood up and began piling all his personal belongings—homework papers from the facility school, drawings, and letters—into a plastic laundry basket for his evening inspection. He stepped into his black jumpsuit and shuffled to the end of the second-tier walkway. He stood there at the top of the stairs, then dropped the basket in front of his feet and kicked it away, so that it somersaulted down, scattering a waterfall of papers over the stairs and on to the floor. Mallard grabbed an "Unusual Incident" form from behind the front desk and yelled for Dude to pick everything up. Dude grunted and began kicking his things into a pile, pushing them with his foot into the tipped sideways basket. He lifted it and started walking toward Mallard, but before he got to him, he passed the kid with whom he had scuffled the day before. Dude dropped the basket again and threw himself on to the other inmate, pounding him in the face before he was knocked to his side and fell against one of the tables. Mallard and the other staff on the unit rushed over and each grabbed both of them from behind. In response, Dude's stay in isolation, without a visit from the social work or mental health staff, was extended for two more days.[5]

On April 10, about four months after Walker was killed, Dude was back in court, this time for a plea hearing. When I arrived, early in the morning, Dude was sitting in a courtroom behind the partition reserved for people already in custody. He stared at me intently but didn't say a word, and I could see his hands were shaking. As I was walking toward him, Ruby lunged at me. "God, am I glad to see you . . . come here." She grabbed me by the arm and led me out of the courtroom. In the hallway, all the potential jurors from two other cases were sitting around, leaning their backs against the walls, looking bored and angry. Ruby broke into tears as she tried to explain that Dude had told her that he had been offered a plea arrangement. The others in the hall turned toward us as she struggled to explain that he could take second-degree murder for ten years or go to trial, and he didn't know what to do. The night before, when the plea was offered, he called Ruby from the detention facility and was asking her to make the decision. But she didn't know what to say. She couldn't advise him to agree to spend ten years in prison. Yet she was terrified that he might be gone twice that long if he agreed to a jury trial. She was crying now, almost hysterically, and wanted me to talk with him and help him decide. We walked back in, and she introduced me to the lawyer, Housewell, who explained the deal that was on the table. With a shrug of her shoulder and a pleased smile, she said that she didn't think it was a bad offer. He could get eighteen to thirty-four under normal sentencing guidelines, and this would ensure that he would do less than that.

Ruby looked down on Dude, who stared up at her, clearly scared, but brave—not knowing what to do, needing to make a decision about possibly spending the next ten years of his life in prison, right there and at that moment, with everyone standing around him and no one knowing what to say or being willing to make the decision on his behalf. It was anguishing. With pinched emotion, Ruby whispered, "What do you want me to do? I can't tell you what to do. You gonna have to decide this for yourself." Tears were rolling down her face. "I don't know. You gonna have to do this." She took a step away from him. Sitting with his hands in his lap and looking especially small in the stuffed courtroom chair, Dude looked up, wide-eyed and closed-mouthed at all the adults standing around him. "I'm not taking any plea," he said.

After rejecting the plea, Dude had several weeks to contemplate his situation before his trial began. On a stormy afternoon in late spring, he and I talked in one of the classrooms at the detention facility.

LUKE: What's been going on?

DUDE: Shit. I been thinking hard. Reality kickin' in every day more and more. I can't get mad, like I say, when I catch attitudes. Got to stay calm. Like Elvin [his older brother] say, "Home is why you scared." 'Cuz he knows I'm scared of missing them streets. Know what I'm saying? But it's about the time too, 'cuz it's about prison. I know I done changed. You leave for two years and go to a placement, you gonna come back thinking more positive and more better, know what I'm saying? You won't just hop back out into the streets. Like if I got out right now, I know I'd go right back into the streets. Wouldn't be no different. So I'm looking forward for some time, I'm just not looking forward to no time in a motherfucking prison. Fuck that. Prison. That's the big P word. That's a hell of a motherfucking boot. Got the raw quarantines [isolation units] and all that type of shit. They got Elvin. They got Forrester on second-degree. His ass might as well be in there for good. I can just imagine . . .

LUKE: What do you mean? What can you imagine?

DUDE: 'Cuz. To be truthful, all odds are against me right now. I don't got a paid attorney. That's for one. Then I'm black. That just gives them more of a reason. Then they like . . . who knows? They done took all them statements. . . . I don't know if my lawyer knows what she's doing. I'm trying to, you know, be a lawyer my damn self. That'll help a little bit. I mean, God forgive me for lying, God forbid me from lying. But, you know, God know the truth. [Dude extended his arm toward me, and we slapped hands.] I done confessed the truth to him. So you know, let the shells speak, you know. That's how I just feel, you know. I confessed the truth with God. God don't look at you from the outside. He look at you from the spirit in. He know I got a good heart, got good intentions. My intentions was not to shoot Walker, even though I shot through the floor.

The point of it is, like, if you kill and it was an accident, but God allowed it to happen. . . . They say the sin of killing is death. Killing has a punishment of death. But if He let it happen, if He allowed it, I could be forgiven. I could hopefully still come home. To the temple. That's how I took it, with this case, you know. You got to have faith to beat this case. And it ain't even about so much the beating it. . . . You know, you gotta do some punishment for doing what you did. I'm just hoping that punishment don't be prison. I mean, I can deal with the punishment of going away for five years in a juvenile system. Know what I'm saying? I'm just looking at the world. Now if I was older. Send me to prison. Send me where I got to go. Know what I'm saying? But I'm young. I just made bad mistakes, bad choices.

LUKE: Well, where do you think it's fair for you to go?

DUDE: I don't think I should go to prison! I'm a fucking juvenile. I may be slinging like a man, but that don't mean that I'm an adult, in terms of going to prison. That don't mean that I need to be going to prison. 'Cuz like I say, you know, it wasn't intentional, it wasn't on purpose. What happened was an accident. But I just think of the word accident. I say damn, what the fuck is an accident?

LUKE: What *is* an accident, do you think?

DUDE: What happened that night. That's how I look at it. That was an accident. Car crashes, them not accidents. That was meant to happen. What happened that night, it was an accident. So I was thinking to myself all day. I can't go out the world ass-backward. Can't do it. Least for myself. I was saying to myself, I want all these wonderful things *without* selling drugs. And this was shit I thought about when I was in the streets. So I made a mistake, now deal with it. Just don't go out the world ass-backward. Don't just stick your chest out there like you the man, "Yeah, I done killed somebody, yeah." Like maybe a month ago, maybe two months ago, I say, "Yeah, I killed a motherfucker." I thought I'd feel like I was the man if I did go kill me a nigga. It's different when that shit happens to you in reality. That shit different as hell. That's always going to be with you. Always. Always. . . . The more I think, I just got too much to live for, too much to do, besides being out there slinging, getting high, and trying to get the Benz. You know, if you gonna get the Benz, do it the right way. Get myself out of this and make it right. Fuck that, I can't let myself go ass-backward. I be thinking, what kind of legacy you'll leave on if you die? What would be said at your funeral? "He was a good person." No. "Dude Freeman opened up many community centers to help young teens in trouble." No. Know what I'm saying? I want to be somebody like that. I would come in this motherfucker [the juvenile detention facility], say to kids here, "Look, y'all ain't bad. Bad is for the motherfuckers who is dead and in prison. That's where the bad motherfuckers at." These boys do not know, Luke. They don't open they eyes, them boys is fucked. With a hard dick. I'm telling you, they fucked.

For all the months of anticipation and anxiety, all the fretting about how his sentence might turn and handwringing about his own sense of what punishment he might deserve, and whether he was more appropriately considered a child or an adult and in what contexts, Dude's trial proceeded with alarming speed. Only three witnesses were called to testify by the prosecution, and they simply repeated what they had told police in their statements at the crime scene. Dude's attorney cross-examined them only minimally, as there were few contradictions in their remarks to exploit. There seemed to be no doubt that Dude had fired the gun; there was also no question that he hadn't meant to kill Walker. The issue pressed to jurors in Dude's trial concerned whether or not he had the intent to harm *anyone* with the gun. Did he return to the house on Pleasant with a chrome forty-four to kill his friend Juan or only to scare him? If he had intended to kill Juan, then Walker's death would be reasonably interpreted (according to legal statute) as the effect of an *intent* to murder, and thus appropriately penalized with a charge of murder in the second degree. But this, of course, was impossible to say. The testimony was suggestive of various things, but hardly conclusive.

So the major fulcrum on which the case turned was discursive; it hinged on interpretations of "intention" and our imperfect capacity to understand the relationship between what people do and their will to act or make willful choices. For the prosecutor, this was doubly important, because she not only was trying to attribute willful intent to an obvious accident but also an adult's accountability to a sixteen-year-old kid, whose capacity for fully endowed intention wouldn't be clear.

With so little testimony, it seemed that the most influential phase of the trial would likely be in the closing arguments, when the prosecutor would make every effort to shape the categorical parameters of adulthood to match Dude and his circumstances.

Dressed in a sensible business suit and wearing her blond hair down, the prosecutor delivered her closing arguments with a determined and ungroomed Michigan accent, pacing in front of the jury and pointing down toward Dude with her bejeweled index finger. "No one knows when the end of their life will come," she began. "Walker sure didn't know. Walker had no idea that the evening of January tenth would be his last." She circled back behind the prosecutor's table and leaned on her hands. "Walker had no idea that on January tenth he would live his last moments: moments spent grasping for breath, grasping for life—a nightmare created by the actions of a little man with a big gun."

The prosecutor picked up a white piece of paper and held it out in front of her face with a bent elbow. "This is the result: an autopsy report. A human life turned into a piece of paper, a number. This is all that's left of Walker. And it happened because this man was mad." She leered at Dude. "And we all know he got mad. He murdered someone. He went and got a gun, went and got a gun. Thank God Juan wasn't there," she paused and thrust her finger toward Dude. "Because HE was mad. A little man was mad. You need to remember that this is not television violence. There's nothing fictional about the ground that Walker lies in. There's nothing fictional about this piece of paper."

"The judge will instruct you in two crimes," she said, addressing the jury, "and you need to return the right conviction. He will instruct you in involuntary manslaughter. But this was not a negligent situation. This was a deliberately created situation. This little man made a horrendous choice. A series of horrendous choices. And through no fault of his own, Walker has been reduced to a piece of paper. A human life has been extinguished, and there will never be enough justice for that. Never."

She stared back at Dude, who was looking down at his clasped hands on the table in front of him, diminished in the oversize green suit that Ruby had brought for him to wear and the black dress shoes that we had gotten at Payless the night before. "Sympathy is not permissible," she shouted. "It's inappropriate for you to look and say, 'Oh, he's a young man.' Don't let him deceive you! . . . He's no child. He's Mr. Bad with the gun. The defense will say, 'Oh, this poor boy. . . . He's a juvenile. He has no direction.' Well, he was an adult that night, and he did adult actions."

"An adult *that night*"? Was the prosecutor leaving open the possibility that Dude might be a child in other moments? She seemed to be implying that his status as an adult should be measured not by qualities inherent to him but by behaviors expressed by him in a particular moment. But does the possibility that one might slip into and then out of adulthood (based on particular and in this case quite obviously aberrational behavior) actually support the prosecutor's argument that Dude is unequivocally and categorically *not* a juvenile, but rather a "little man"? Does it strengthen the case for sentencing someone who had just turned seventeen to spend the next twenty years of his life in an adult prison? It would seem more effectively to make the opposite case: that Dude was someone still in the midst of becoming an adult, still not fully transitioned from the blur of adolescence.

Then there are also questions about why Dude's accidental shooting of Walker should be considered an "adult action" in the first place. What his actions demonstrate is a formidable lack of good judgment. But then, *most* serious crimes committed by young people reflect an absence of good judgment. This is part of what makes them demonstrative of a *juvenile's* sensibility. Meanwhile, what makes for a fully functioning and accountable adult is their good judgment. Most courts give special dispensation for older people who are proven not to have such judgment—through claims of "insanity" or "incompetence." Yet with respect to distinctions between juveniles and adults, and certainly in Dude's case, this is not really an axiomatic presumption. In contemporary legal discourse as it is actually practiced in courtrooms, or at least as Dude's prosecutor was practicing it, adulthood stands as a proxy not for a fully developed accountable person possessed of all their faculties but for the *capacity for intent*. In this context, the central question is not whether a supposed offender knows what they are doing—the ethical dimensions of their actions—but whether they *mean* to do what they are doing. If we try to make sense of the prosecutor's assertions, the best we can do is accept that adulthood is equated with intent, with the making of choices, regardless of how irrational, nonsensical, or "childish." Of course, even very young children make sophisticated and willful choices—not to take their medicine, for example. Such a capacity for intent, however, would never compel a reasonable person to attribute adulthood to small children.

The only thing that emerges clearly from this is that the justice system's understanding of childhood and adulthood is deeply muddled. It is both institutionally rigid, demanding that a categorical distinction be made (with extraordinary consequences), and plainly contradictory. For young people negotiating this hazardous terrain, this is profoundly confusing. In reflecting on his case and hoping for a juvenile sentence, Dude said, "Now if I was older, send me to prison. Send me where I got to go. . . . But I'm young. I just made bad mistakes, bad choices." Reasonable enough. But it is precisely the invocation of choice that the prosecutor uses to support an adult conviction and sentence.

For Dude, choice, intent, and accident are not mutually exclusive. Dude's assignment of Walker's death to an accident (and his acknowledgment of bad choices), and his circular definition of accident as "what happened that night," would suggest as much. For Dude, moreover, it is clear that questions concerning the constitution of moral personhood are fluid. There is no contradiction for him in acting willfully and being not yet grown-up. As other remarks of his would suggest, he sees the terrain of adulthood and childhood as slippery and ever-mutating, even as he tries to imagine himself fitting into and around these stiff judicial categories: "I don't think I should go to prison. I'm a fucking juvenile. I may be slinging like a man, but that don't mean that I'm an adult, in terms of going to prison."[6] For Dude, the patently obvious fluidity of his status as neither simply a juvenile nor an adult does not diminish the consequential weight of institutional categories. Prison, for him, is both where "bad" people go and an institutional strategy for defining who is "bad." In the shadow of possibly going to prison, Dude was clear: he is "a fucking juvenile."

In the end, the jury returned a verdict of involuntary manslaughter. And despite the efforts of his lawyer as well as multiple therapists and social workers writing on his behalf, Dude was sentenced as an adult, to a minimum of ten years in the state penitentiary. Though he will be eligible for parole in 2009, the stronger likelihood, given the rarity with which inmates are released early, is that he'll be locked up until 2018, when he will be thirty-four years old.

The prosecuting attorney was clearly upset. Though she had fought for a second-degree murder charge, Dude wouldn't be the boon to her fledgling career that she might have hoped. After the verdict was read, she collected her papers and threw her briefcase over her shoulder with the impatience of a child needing to use a bathroom. After court officers led Dude away, for a speedy transfer to Jackson State Prison, Ruby and I stayed behind, sitting in silence on a courtroom bench. The jurors emerged from their quarters and filed past us, looking at Ruby and then quickly away.

Coda: A Sunday Night

Luke, what's up? How's everything going out there in that cold world? Still the same, huh? Shit ain't change in here much. Coming up on a year that I been locked up. I'm still in the hole. I'm hoping they going to let me out on the 20th, so I can go to the yard. But if not, you know me. My mama wrote me, and told me to tell you hi and to give her a call. When you do, send her my love. Did you get the last letter I sent you? 'Cause in the hole, these people be on some other stuff. Oh, my mother also told me that Lydia is off crack. That's a real good thing. I hope she can get her life right. But other than all this prison crap(!), I'm tight. You know, the same shit. Well, player, I'm about all out of words. Plus it's late as hell, and now I'm getting sleepy. So when you get this, hit me back as soon as you can. Peace and love. Your lil' bad-ass homeboy, Dude.

PART IV

Owners, Occupants,
and Outcasts

The ordinary practitioners of the city live "down below," below the thresholds at which visibility begins. They walk—an elementary form of this experience of the city; they are walkers.

—Michel de Certeau, *The Practice of Everyday Life*

The city can be known only by an activity of an ethnographic kind; you must orient yourself in it not by book, by address, but by walking, by sight, by habit, by experience; here every discovery is intense and fragile, it can be repeated or recovered only by memory of the trace it has left you.

—Roland Barthes, *Empire of Signs*

9

Neighborhood Watching

After the second suspension of his trial, when he wasn't sure at what point he might be released, and when he was especially eager for a sense of connection to his family and life outside the detention facility, Rodney arranged for me to visit his younger brother, Antonio, at their house off Dexter.

The block where Rodney's family was living, on Wadsworth, is typical of the Dexter neighborhood: a few vacant lots and a mix of two- and single-family homes in various states of upkeep or disrepair. When I arrived to meet Antonio, the violet winter light made the brick covering his house look like yellowed newspaper. The stairs leading up to the porch were falling off their risers and tilting toward the street. On the covered porch, against the wall, sat an old plaid upholstered couch that was wet from melting snow, and there were a few brightly colored toys scattered across the floorboards. The large front windows were covered from the inside with opaque black plastic, fixed there with masking tape. There was a black Ford Expedition in the driveway.

I waited in front of the door for nearly a minute before Rodney's mother, Maria, opened it. She looked at me and smiled enthusiastically, remembering me from Rodney's courtroom hearings, and invited me in. Rodney's stepfather, Johnny, was reclining on the living room couch, looking at a football game on television in the almost completely dark room, underneath the fluttering garbage bags blocking the window light. "You're probably here to pick up the pictures, aren't you?" asked Rodney's mother. I followed her into the dining room, where there were photographs and letters, shoe boxes filled with various correspondence, and dirty dishes stacked on the table. On the wooden trim between the living and dining rooms, Maria had affixed, in chronological order, descending from the top of the jambs down toward the floor, all the name-tag stickers that she had worn while visiting Rodney at the detention facility. Each had both their names written in broad magic marker. And in the dining room she had taped to the walls letters that he had written to her onto which she had written loving responses. She noticed me looking over all the exhibited material. "Oh, yeah, I hang on to everything," she said. She began to flit around the room, fingering through collections of letters and collected bills, into which she had deposited old photographs of Rodney that I was figuring he had told her he wanted. "He needs to understand that those are demons in that youth home," she said as she was gathering the photographs. "They are not people, they are just demons inside the bodies of people. Rodney needs to have faith. He needs to understand that there is no judge higher than the Master."

I nodded and smiled, and asked if she knew if Antonio was around. She said, "Oh, yeah, you were supposed to meet him . . . he's at Malachi's house." Rodney had told me that Malachi was their godbrother, one of their closest friends in the Dexter area, and that he had been giving a lot of dealing work to younger kids on Dexter. Maria began sorting through more papers looking for the number. "He lives on McQuade. . . ." Unable to find it, she wrote down several other phone numbers: her daughter's, Antonio's, and her own, on the back of an envelope.

"Rodney doesn't want to hear from me," she mused as she referenced her address book. "He and I aren't getting along right now . . . he's mad at me for turning him in. . . . But I told him, there ain't no reason for you to be running. You didn't do nothing. And if he hadn't run away when the police came, he would be *out* right now. . . . And I told him, don't run when they come to get you. . . . I just keep telling him he needs to keep Jesus with him, he needs to read in the Bible. . . . But he just says, 'Aw Mom, I don't want you talking to me like that.'"

Johnny, still reclining on the couch, said something about getting a new lawyer for Rodney. But Maria threw her hand toward him in disgust. "Oh, that's Johnny; he don't be doing nothing. Just be messing around on me behind my back."

"I don't mess around," he protested weakly. Maria ignored him.

"I ain't getting no new lawyer . . . he just going to take forever getting to know the case. . . . This one's going to finish this goddamned motherfucking thing!" She softened her voice and asked if I would bring some medication to the facility for Rodney. She handed me a bottle of cold medicine, a jar of facial cleanser, and the stack of photographs, and then showed me to the door. As I walked on to the porch, she said, "So Luke . . . is Luke your only name? . . . It's not Lucifer, is it?" I turned around, probably red-faced, and laughed. "No, John is my middle name."

"Wow, two Bible names! Your mama musta known what she was doing," she said.

Later that afternoon, after delivering the photos and facial cleanser to Rodney and again arranging over the phone to meet up with Antonio, I returned to the house. Rodney's mother answered the door with an unlit cigarette dangling from her lips. She invited me to sit down next to her on the couch, where she had been watching *Scarface* on the new television that her daughter Julie had given her.

Picking up where she left off, Maria began once again decrying the detention facility's roster of demons. But in this case, as it would be through innumerable subsequent interactions that we would have, the subject of her derision became the city generally. "We got to get out of this city," she demanded. "I'm not from this place, I don't even know my way around. . . . Antonio and them, they know this place, but not me. I'm from Niles, Michigan. You know where that is? It's way over on the west side of the state. And it's nice and quiet there. This is just a wicked city . . . the whole place, and all the people who live here. And the police and the judges, they all demons, you hear me?" She got up from the couch and began pacing back and forth across the living room floor. She raised her voice. "Matthew say, 'Judge not, that ye be not judged. For with what judgment ye judge, ye shall be judged!' . . . I'm *quotin'* now," she screamed as she swiveled back in the other direction and, catching me totally unprepared, slapped the back of my head so hard that my neck whipped forward and I nearly fell onto the ground. "It say in Romans, 'Who art thou that judgest another man's servant?' . . . These are demons, and they are judging us! Well, our Father will handle them! You know where they going!" Though I ducked a bit this time, she slapped my head again, for emphasis, as if it were a pulpit.

"And all these niggers. . . . See, I grew up with white people," she said.

"We're not black; we're Indian and German and black. You didn't know that, did you?" she asked rhetorically. Patting my hair back down, I assured her that Rodney had told me that they were part American Indian. "But all these stupid goddamned niggers," she began gesturing toward the dark windows at the front of the house and swinging her long straight black hair to her other shoulder, "you know, they got to get perms to make their hair straight. But not us. We got this natural! Mmm hmm!" I nodded. "All these niggers around here, I answer them with Jesus . . . we all bathing in the blood of Jesus! I'm quoting there. That's what's written in RED! . . . All the niggers around here, they all think I'm a witch . . . 'cause I be talking Jesus to them, you hear me?! I be quoting, and they afraid of that. They afraid of the ones who really know."

Given racial politics in the metro area, it shouldn't be surprising that in proclaiming her distaste for and distinction from the city, along with its people and politics, Maria spoke perhaps most passionately about her family's complex racial history and identity. For Maria, though, the family's persecution wasn't just at the hands of a few people in the immediate vicinity, or even the institutional prejudice of the police department and court system. While all of these weigh in her measurement of her family's difficulties, it was the city itself, in a kind of imagined cosmological coherence and subjectivity, that emerged as their most oppressive foe in her estimation. "It ain't just the neighbors," she told me. "The police be bothering us all the time. They know, if you a Phelps, they going to be fucking with you. Those goddamned motherfuckers! That's the reason Rodney is locked up right now. They know that he knows the Lord, and it scares the motherfucking shit out of them. So they do whatever they can to bring him down." Maria sat back down and reached around to the edge of the couch to retrieve a small bag of weed and rolling papers. She rolled a joint as she talked. "Same with the judge." Maria grimaced when she said his name. "Cagney. That judge is a demon. There ain't no way you can judge, there's only one judge . . . and he loves us all, but he especially loves *his* people. The people in this city, the people in Wayne County, they don't understand anything, they don't understand the truth . . . they afraid of the truth . . . the niggers." She pronounced the word with a hard "R," to make clear its racial referent. "All they care about is money and material things." She told me repeatedly that she needed to leave the city and the county, and that the "niggers" there would never leave her or her children alone. "I tell you, I'm going to get the fuck out of here. I'm not saying exactly where I'm going; everybody around here be too nosy. I might go out with my daughter, Southfield, or Royal Oak. You know, she and her man just bought a house out there. Yeah. See, it might look like we don't have nothing, but they don't see, you understand. That's how we're blessed. You seen that Julie's driving a Jaguar. You see her driving the Vette. That's not nothing, you feel me? Mmm hmm. . . . But I'm not saying where I'm going. You'll know, 'cuz I'll be gone, but I ain't saying shit about where I'm going."

She turned around and pointed toward the wall. "See this wallpaper in here," she said. "Rodney put this up. He helps me so much; you know, did you know that he's a mother's boy? . . . Not like Antonio. He's all over the place. I don't know what to do with him. He gets a goddamned 4.0 and is hanging out on the streets all the time. He's up on Dexter. Goddamned Dexter. That's where he is. Mmm hmm. That goddamned street corner up there. Every damn day, he's up there, messing with all them niggers on the corner."

Maria pulled air through the dwindling roach between her fingers. "But Rodney, he helps me clean up and take care of things," she croaked, trying not to exhale the smoke. "We had a darker wallpaper up, but we had to take it down because it was too fancy, and the neighbors would start to think we had something. I mean, look around. You can see that it's a poor neighborhood. I don't know if you realize, but this is the ghetto right here. That's where we at. So we keep all the windows closed because everybody be staring in here, and looking at my daughters." Maria pushed down an unruly corner of one of the garbage bags. "Thank God for Rodney," she said. "They know how good he is, and they just don't want to leave him alone. Sometimes it feels like they won't stop 'til they get him. But we have to trust Our Father."

Maria twisted the smoldering dregs of her joint into an ashtray and laid her head back, looking dreamily at the ceiling. A few moments later, she closed her eyes and fell asleep. I tiptoed out the door so as not to disturb her, and drove up Dexter, looking around for someone who might be Antonio.

Hitting Corners

Maps aren't to be trusted. At least according to the activists, poets, and philosophers who argue against the oppressive, planning pens of cartographers, the only way to know a city is by walking through it, breathing its used, already-exhaled air, smelling, hearing, and moving among its people. But the drawing of maps is not always an oppressive gesture. It is not always an abstraction of lived experience that disguises the play of power.[1]

When he was locked up at the juvenile detention facility, Rodney would scribble on prison-issued, wide-ruled lined paper, drawing the streets crossing Dexter, and marking with small *X*'s and dark circles the significant points of interest there, most of them places where drugs were sold.[2] At the epicenter of the neighborhood, where I was told everyone would gather, and where Rodney would figure prominently when he was released, was the corner of Dexter and Carrington. "That's where I'll be, right there," he told me, tapping the tip of his pencil against the map he had made.

For Rodney, everything fell into order around "DC." Just north of Dexter and Carrington's intersection, he had told me, was a residential crack spot that had been open for years, surviving untold raids, temporary closings, and changing of hands. To the southwest were a few other corners devoted to the dealing of various drugs—a weed corner here, and a raw heroin corner there. On DC itself, of course, a customer could probably get just about anything they wanted. People were bumping weed, yay, raw, and sometimes even powder cocaine. He told me that there was a gas station there, and a brick wall behind it, where he used to sit, and where he'd be sitting again, he assured me, when he got out. Around him would be other "Dexter Boys," people from the neighborhood, or people who used to live there, and even a few of their friends. All "down for Dexter," and all, in various manners, situated within the ebbing and flowing tides of drug exchange within one of the most notoriously dangerous and drug-infested neighborhoods in the city. Indeed, their devotion to this space, Dexter, and one another would seem suggestive of a familiar kind of sociospatial delimitation, of the circumscription, boundedness, and intimate finitude of their "set." This, of course, jives both with popular cultural and sociological imaginations of young men in the inner city, according to which they are often the inhabitants of an impenetrable as well as inescapable cultural and geographic underworld, where prevailing "codes of the street" are like coils of concertina wire.

We might suppose that this would hold especially true for young men in Detroit, where the cultural and geographic distance between the "inner city" and areas beyond seems so pronounced. But the experiences, sentiments, and daily practices of the Dexter Boys actually suggest something different.

To identify with Dexter is to identify with a space that is imbued with potential profitability from a (black) market that is defined by trajectories connecting the neighborhood to the wide world beyond. For young people working on the streets there, Dexter is not only the setting of nostalgic memories and myths of origin, it is situated in a cycle of earning and spending. Dexter is a place for business. Or as Rodney once told me, "Dexter is home, but Dexter is all about getting money." For Dexter Boys, identification with Dexter is hinged precisely on its permeability, on the possibility of their movement through and out of the neighborhood, and across traditional categories of spatial dimension and division in the Motor City metropolis.[3]

Rodney moved the curtain covering the small trapezoidal window in the door and peeked through. I hadn't seen him since the day he was released from the youth home. This was nearly six months after his case was supposed to be settled, but various procedural delays, none of which were his fault, had kept him locked up. When the county prosecutor finally got his witnesses to court, their testimony was so inconsistent that Rodney's case was dismissed within half an hour. And now, three weeks later, Rodney was back in the house on Wadsworth. He had white medication on his face for his acne—a remnant, he insisted, of the stress of being locked up and having to eat grease-fortified detention facility food. He pushed the door open and turned immediately toward the couch, where he had been sitting when I knocked.

His mother was in her bedroom, a small space just off the living room, listening to the radio. I got up and looked in, and asked how she was doing. "I'm feeling sick today, Luke. My body hurts . . . 'cause I'm anemic, you know." She hardly took a breath. "We haven't had the damn water turned on in over a month." Rodney's family had been using bottled water, from five-gallon jugs, to cook, clean, and flush the toilets for that long. She told me that they needed thousands of dollars to get the water turned on. "And Johnny's not going to pay that shit. He's just out spending his money messing around with other women! And if I had that much money, Lord knows, I wouldn't be spending it on a damn water bill here! I would get the hell out of this place. Move out of this city!"

When Maria's boyfriend, Johnny, discovered the house while driving through the neighborhood it had been sitting empty for years, and the title was held by the city. Maria explained: "Because this place wasn't even a home when we came here. It was just a broken-down, abandoned old shit-hole. You hear me? That's right, motherfucker. There wasn't nothing here, and we came in here and made a home out of this place! We made it nice in here. Rodney put in this floor. See the linoleum? Fixed the damn windows." And while Rodney and his family had attempted to pay off some of the back payments from previous inhabitants of the house, they had long ago fallen way behind. "See, they told us over and over that they was going to kick us out of this place, and then I wrote a letter to the city, and then they said, 'No, we ain't never going to kick you out.' So then I'm thinking, they ain't never going to auction this place off. We done finally got this wicked city to listen to us. And the Lord's people was going to finally win. Now, living with no running water, I just don't know; we can't live like this for too much longer."

Rodney sat uncomfortably while his mother talked. He played with the worn upholstery hanging off the couch. "You want to go hit a couple of cor-ners?" he asked, with an almost embarrassed smile. He stood and bounded up to the room he shared with Antonio on the second floor to put on some brand-new sneakers and a clean white T-shirt. "Let's roll."

"We out!" he shouted, for his mother's benefit.

When Rodney and I settled into the car, we looked at each other like kids who've just figured out how to cross their eyes and are struck by the novelty of seeing double. We hung out together almost every day while he was in the detention facility, but we were seeing each other in a completely new light now. For all the many hours that we had spent in one another's company, we were both a little uncertain about how to be "on the outs." When Rodney had been locked up, our interactions were mediated by powerful institu-tional and logistical constraints. We were useful to one another in that set-ting in particular ways. Rodney had become my first key informant, and as an intern at the facility, I could be a source of some help to him as well.

But now our dependence on one another would be much different, and we would need to learn to trust one another in the face of new vulnerabili-ties. He was taking an obvious social and legal risk in allowing me to hang around with him, in bringing me into the neighborhood and becoming to some extent responsible for me there. And where I was deeply dependent on him, Rodney also saw all sorts of potential advantages in associating with me, beyond his excitement at having his hood represented in a book. He fig-ured that I could help him get through school, deal with the authorities, and, in his wildest fantasies, maybe even figure out how he could make more money in the drug trade.

For all of our interdependence, though, when Rodney was out on the street he held his cards extremely close to his chest. Occasionally, for weeks at a time, he would recede into the distance, not wanting to talk at all. He was always careful not to let anyone on Dexter, including me, understand all of his maneuvers in the drug trade, or what his gestating plans might be. He treated all of us like potential saboteurs. But there were also episodes when he would approach me with alarming sincerity: when he was worried about his family, couldn't sleep, or was in some kind of trouble. In these moments, he would be totally transparent, and would expect the same of me.

As Rodney pointed the way, I drove to the north end of Quincy, a narrow residential street in the neighborhood. I pulled to the side across from a parked Chevy Suburban, rumbling with its heavy engine and the bass booming in the back. Two other young men sat inside. Ebo, as Rodney called him, had lived in and out of the area for several years, inhabiting a number of abandoned houses at various points on Quincy and proximate blocks, and turning them into sometimes-lucrative dope spots. Recently, he had been living in and working out of a small gray wooden house that looked like it belonged on a turn-of-the-century Nebraska prairie, and that had been standing empty longer than anyone could remember. Inside, Ebo had stashed pounds of weed, and was mostly selling to other neighborhood residents and young people working in the drug trade in the area. Next to him sat Dante, a nineteen-year-old who was living with his mother and older brother on the bottom floor of a two-family flat on Quincy Street and was working sporadically on the corner of Dexter and Carrington.

Rodney flashed his hand above the window, signaling the "D" with his fingers. Ebo flashed a D back toward us, no doubt assuming that I was a customer, and we pulled away. Rodney had me turn left, and we drove down Carrington and out toward Dexter, three blocks away.

Social activity around the intersection of Dexter and Carrington takes shape around two small businesses that sit across the four lanes of Dexter Avenue from one another. On the east side of the avenue is a six-pump gas station owned by a Muslim Arab family. There is a six-feet-high cinder block wall separating the gas station parking lot from an abandoned house on

Carrington. The wall is covered with crude graffiti, and there are several names scrawled in black spray paint that I recognized, including Antonio's and Rodney's. There were a few people leaning against the window of the gas station next to the metal-and-glass front door. A sixteen-year-old called Loc, with training dreadlocks and a newly attempted mustache, sat on the narrow perch of the gas station's windowsill, emptying a Swisher Sweet of its tobacco filling onto the asphalt below. He remained on the relative periphery of the drug trade on Dexter. Loc wasn't especially ambitious and didn't seem to care what he sold or who he was working for; he worked when work was easily available to him.

Oscar, a twenty-four-year-old with well-groomed short hair, was sitting across Carrington, leaning against the low chain-link fence surrounding the St. Clare Episcopal Church, a dark stone building dating from the 1920s and rising no higher than the illuminated gas station sign. He shifted a brown paper bag into his left hand and swung his right arm high in the air, flashing the D for Rodney's benefit. Oscar and Rodney went way back. He had been a neighbor of Rodney's when both boys lived with their families in Ecorse, and he had briefly dated Rodney's sister Princess. Oscar, whose brother lived with him in the neighborhood and worked at a Chrysler plant in the suburbs, was one of the few Dexter Boys to maintain steady legitimate employment; when I first met him, he had been driving a garbage truck for the city. Rodney and I pulled into the parking lot, and got out of the car. Rodney slapped hands with Loc and Oscar, who were staring at me suspiciously.

"Check this out, man," Rodney said, as we walked into the station's ministore, where there was a diminutive Arab man working behind the thick glass-cage counter and another moving boxes through the back room stock door into the glassed-in room. Rodney yelled at the man in the doorway, leaning over boxes of bottles. "Hey, man! Yooo hoooo? Hey!" The other, certainly hearing Rodney, didn't pay any attention to him. Rodney walked toward the back of the store, where all the beer and soda pop is stored in glass-door coolers, and grabbed a Coke. He walked back to the counter, then picked up a bunch of candy bars and threw them down in a heap in the cardboard bin where they had been arranged. He shouted toward the guy behind the counter, thrusting his index finger toward him: "This guy's a ho-ass nigger. . . . HO-ass nigger!" and then strutted toward the door. The man behind the register shouted back, "Hey, are you tough? Huh? Or are you just acting tough?" He smiled faintly when he said this, and puffed out his chest and raised his bearded chin provocatively. Rodney nearly erupted with glee, laughing in an affected falsetto, and pushed open the door, leaving with his Coke in hand.

On the other side of Dexter is the Party Time liquor store. Like most liquor stores in Detroit, Party Time is owned and run by Chaldean Americans. It is one of only a few sources of groceries within a couple of miles, though the selection is obviously thin, and has a steady flow of customers moving in, out, and around its front door, especially early in the morning and late in the afternoon, when people are getting off work, and through the evening, when many local residents come to the store to buy beer and liquor.

As with the gas station on Dexter, most of the illicit drug sales that were happening around Party Time involved small amounts of either crack or weed. Timmy Mason, a baby-faced and stick-thin fifteen-year-old with a round globe of an Afro, was there. We had met in the detention facility several months earlier, after he had been picked up on some petty drug charges. He emerged and ducked again into the store while we were standing in the gas station parking lot. Timmy was working hard, moving dime bags of weed and small chunks of crack, which he'd cop from any number of people in the neighborhood, including Rodney. Marley stood close by, wearing a woolen hat and laughing so loudly that we could hear it over the Dexter traffic rushing in between. Marley, whose long dreadlocks slithered out from under his hat, would often work alongside of Timmy—taking alternating customers through the afternoon—until Timmy would have to go home to allay his mother's worries about him hanging out with older people on the streets. Marley had something of a paternalistic relationship with Timmy, who was nearly ten years his junior. Though Timmy probably didn't need it, Marley liked to imagine that he was looking after him during their hours in front of the liquor store.

Rodney seemed a little disappointed that there weren't more people on the corners at Dexter and Carrington. He said that it was pretty slow right then, too early in the day, and suggested that we head down to the Coney Island restaurant on the corner of Providence and Dexter, where many of the young people from the neighborhood had recently begun spending time.

On Dexter, there's not much between Carrington and Providence. On the west side of the street, after the Episcopal church, there are vacant lots for several blocks. It is the same story on the east side of the street until just before Providence, where there's a dormant storefront church in a single-story, rectangular cinder block building, and then the crimson-roofed Neighborhood Coney Island Restaurant. Indeed, the stretch of Dexter between Carrington and Providence is such a no-man's-land that it would be relatively rare for the young men out on Dexter to walk the 150-yard distance between the two corners. They generally prefer to head over to residential side streets and move from north to south, where they can more easily duck out of sight, or stash drugs or cash that they may be carrying with them.

But Rodney and I raced down in the car, and turned left into the Coney Island parking lot, where there was an older Albanian woman, the wife of the store's owner, engaged in the seemingly futile task of sweeping tobacco debris, dirt, and other detritus out of the corners of the large parking lot and toward the street. In the restaurant's small vestibule, between two sets of glass and aluminum double doors, stood Z and Kilo, passing a blunt back and forth through the almost completely opaque haze. Z is twenty years old, and dropped out of Central High School in the eleventh grade. He moved to the Dexter area a few years earlier to live with his girlfriend, the mother of his daughter, who was attending Wayne County Community College on the East Side. He was supporting them both with occasional dealing work that he'd arrange with Malachi or others in the neighborhood. Kilo, a long-faced and ebony-black nineteen-year-old, had been kicked out of Northwestern High on Grand Boulevard and was living with his mother and older brother on Quincy Street in a two-bedroom bungalow. A small bearded man called "Corn Meal" stood just outside the exterior door sucking on a straw from a big cup. He was looking out to the street and straight ahead simultaneously, with his protuberant and severely walled eyes. Corn Meal had been diagnosed as slightly developmentally disabled, and was treated as a well-liked pet by other young people on Dexter. He slept most nights on the couch at his aunt's house, only a few blocks from the Coney Island, where he whiled away most hours of the day. Across Providence a young man of Arab descent, whom the Dexter Boys called Fred, was sweeping in front of his family's liquor and convenience store, on the ground floor of a four-story apartment building that many years ago had been used as a Masonic meeting place.

We drove up Dexter and then turned right on Glynn, a couple of blocks north of the Coney Island. We weaved around some of the run-down residential side streets, and then came out on Dexter again. Rodney had put a tape in the deck—Jay-Z, who could be heard coming out of nearly every other car that spring—and he told me to make the same circle around the block. As we rolled to a stop at the intersection of a couple of small streets just off Dexter, Rodney looked over at me with an impish grin and told me to wait a minute. He craned his neck to see if anyone was coming, hopped out of his seat and walked to a stop sign at the corner, reached up behind the metal octagon sign, and pulled something small down with him. He smiled at me and walked back to the car. Plopping himself back in his seat, he held out a square folded paper—stuffed with powdered heroin. "We going to go talk to a rawhead," he said, matter-of-factly. "It's going to cost you $10."

We turned a corner and drove down McQuade, which runs parallel to Dexter, and is lined with an awkward combination of one-story bungalows and square two-family flats from obviously different and architecturally disparate eras. Many of the houses are visibly suffering from long years of neglect, and the neighborhood looks patched together with a sort of harried randomness. As we approached the intersection of Providence Avenue and McQuade, we passed a diffuse group of young black men and boys moving along the sidewalk in front of three or four houses on the block; Rodney told me to pull over.

Malachi was sitting on the stoop of the small duplex that he was renting with his girlfriend, the mother of two of his children. Chubby and bald, he had what looked like a day's worth of stubble growing out of the back of his head. As we got closer he smiled and said, "Roudeeeeeee," in a sustained, high-pitched, gravelly note. Rodney had talked a lot about Malachi when we would see each other in the detention facility. In November, Malachi had been shot in the head outside a suburban strip-club that the young men and boys from Dexter would often visit. At the time, and through the uncertainty and unreliability of information filtered through multiple family members and neighborhood contacts, Rodney had been grief stricken, thinking Malachi would likely die.

But miraculously, the bullet had hit his skull at a tangential angle and lodged against it; I could see the round scar and small bump formed by the remaining shrapnel that rose up and interrupted the smooth curve of his shining bald head. Malachi was older than most of the other young people working the drug trade in the area. He had recently turned twenty-five, and had been like an older brother to Rodney and Antonio when they were young, and were new arrivals in the neighborhood.

In the fluid structure of the drug trade on Dexter, Malachi represented a measure of relative stability. There was general consensus that he was managing the heroin market on this block, and that the others there, for the moment and to a degree, at least, were working for him. When Rodney and I arrived, this included a cast of four: Rasheed, Antonio, Z, and Kilo. Rasheed (whom everyone called Sheed), tall and lean with a heavy, wooden brow, chiseled square face, and thick wide mouth, was walking behind an abandoned brick house on Providence out of which all the windows had been torn, counting unfolded bills. He had first met Rodney almost ten years before, when they were both prepubescent kids playing in the neighborhood. They would ride bikes together, jumping dirt piles and skidding to stops with their feet dragging.

Antonio was sitting on the side of the curb in the late winter sun with his elbows on his knees, pulling apart a swollen red maple tree bud. Z, with an open expression and a small mustache trimmed down just above his upper lip, sat a few feet from Antonio, resting back with his palm on the ground. Kilo, around the same age as Z, had a small black mountain bike and pedaled around in circles in front of Malachi's house.

Malachi stood from the stoop and delicately slapped Rodney five. Rodney introduced me to him and he measured me cautiously as we shook hands. It was midday, and Malachi and the crew working with him were waiting for his heroin connection to bring another bag of raw-pack bundles into the neighborhood. "Are there any clio around?" asked Rodney. Malachi said that there was a guy parked down the street named John.

At the end of the block, just about a hundred feet away, Rodney and I could see a municipal van with a yellow light and an aluminum extension ladder on the roof. Rodney walked over to the driver's side of the van and knocked on the window. A middle-aged African American man with graying temples and gold-rimmed bifocals unrolled his window with tight turns, and raised his eyebrows. Rodney asked, "Are you John?" "Yeah," he said cheerfully. Rodney handed him the paper raw pack and said, "I want you to check something out for me. I want you to tell me if this is any good." John said, "Alright," and took the pack into the cab of the van. Rodney led me to the other side and pointed to the door. "That's you," he said. I opened the door and sat in the seat next to John. Rodney walked off to talk with the other boys on the block.

With just the two of us sitting there, John reached around behind his seat and pulled a metal contractor's clipboard case onto his lap. He opened it, lifted out a yellow legal pad, pushed aside a bunch of small hand tools, and took out a round mirror. He opened the pack and poured the white heroin on to the mirror, and chopped it up with the edge of the unfolded paper. "Man, when I first saw y'all, I didn't know what was going on," he said. "No offense or nothing, but when I seen you, I thought, 'Man, are they taping me or what?!'" He told me that he had been coming there for several months. "You know, it helps if there are people you can trust," he said. "I got a family and I got a job to maintain, you know." He lifted the mirror to his nose, looked quickly to either side, as if for traffic, and inhaled the small amount of heroin in two strong snorts.

Rodney came up to my window, after having walked around and talked with the other guys on the street for a while, and I unrolled it. He asked John if the stuff was any good. "'Cuz that should be the best right there."

"Yeah, that's real good," said John. "'Cuz I, you know, I already had some dope this morning. And usually, if I done it in the morning, I don't get that same hit the second time. You know? Well, you don't know . . . do you?" He chuckled again. "Usually I don't feel that hit in the back of the head like that. Definitely not that fast."

Rodney looked pleased. "Yeah, it's good, ain't it?" He looked at me. "Are you ready to roll?" I nodded and got out of the van.

As Rodney and I walked back toward my car, he shook his head in disappointment. "Man, you perpin', dog!" he said, leading the way. "I mean, you ain't say nothing, did you?"

"I don't know," I stuttered defensively.

"That's the whole point, dog. If I give a rawhead a pack, then he gonna talk to me. He has to. You basically just bought that conversation, dog. 'Cause the whole point is that he's gotta talk to you about the raw! Damn, I go to all this trouble to set you up with somebody, give him the pack, and then you ain't even say nothing to him!"

"Well, I talked to him a little," I said, sounding pretty pathetic.

"Man, this ain't even going in the book, is it?"

"No, it will!" I tried to assure him. Of course, it was only at this point, as he spelled it out to me, that I understood the sophistication of Rodney's specific ethnographic plan, of his keen interest in who might represent Dexter, and how—as he pulled the pack down from the back of the stop sign and arranged this meeting with a heroin customer near Dexter, where I unwittingly bartered heroin for an interview.[4]

Suburban Nights and Ghetto Dreams

The second week in March, not long after Rodney had taken me from corner to corner in the neighborhood, defining the congruent parameters of the drug trade there along with points of contact and significance for the Dexter Boys, he and I were once again driving through the neighborhood, running errands. This had become something of a routine for us in the early days after his release from the detention facility. Rodney had left the institution with a focused determination to get somewhere, and to get there quickly. He had lots to do. At his insistence, we had started meeting at the house on Wadsworth with stacks of GED books, which we would spread on the coffee table in front of the television in the living room, peeling back a corner of one of the plastic bags over the windows to let in more light. We would labor through this material, section by section, until Rodney would lose patience, usually not too long after beginning. Rodney found the GED lessons either insultingly rudimentary or totally mysterious; he remarked on numerous occasions that the grammar tests were racist, probably designed to trip up people just like him, who were used to speaking black English. As Rodney would try to fight through these frustrations, he asked me to repeat for him how long it would take to get into college and the various possibilities that this would afford him.

And of course there was other business to handle. After one of our study sessions, Rodney and I drove to a Michigan Secretary of State office to procure a driver's permit. On our way, we circled through the neighborhood and came across Sheed, who was standing on Providence, a block off Dexter, with his back turned toward the street, looking with serious downcast eyes at a stack of dollar bills that he held close to his chest. Rodney asked me to stop the car and then leaned out to ask Sheed if he wanted to smoke a blunt. Sheed looked at me with concern before recognizing me from our couple of previous meetings in the neighborhood; he smiled back at Rodney. "Maybe later, man," he answered. "I gotta take care of this right now; I'll be done after one o'clock."

As Rodney and I pulled away, I asked him if it would be OK for me to spend some time out on the street corners with the boys on Dexter while they were slinging. Sitting back in the passenger seat of my car, he curled his mouth to the side and clicked his tongue. "You know, man, I don't know if I would be comfortable with that right now." Rodney shook his head, and just as I was feeling like the wind was knocked out of me, he continued, "What you need to do is come out with us, dog. You know, when we go out. . . ."

"Yeah," I said, much less deflated.

"I'll tell you what we're going to do," he said, turning toward me. "We going out on Monday. See, every Monday we all be going to the clubs," he explained. "Every week, man, we be going to this club in Southfield, and usually we hit the titty bar before that. And, you know, you probably want to see the places where we be hanging, right? We gonna bat it up; you're going to come with us this week. That's when, you know, everyone can really see you; that would be a good way to break the ice. . . . If you want to see us on the set when we working, you got to chill with us when we not working." I agreed enthusiastically. Rodney looked me up and down, taking in the tattered New York Mets cap I was wearing and the dusty Doc Martens with yellow stitching on my feet, and said: "But first we're going to get you something to wear."

On the appointed Monday, I met Rodney at his house, where I changed into a Rocawear outfit that he had picked out for me during a trip to the mall the previous weekend.[5] With me dressed from head to foot in iridescent-gray denim, with new white tennis shoes, a polyester shirt printed over and over with the message that "It's not where you're from, it's what you Roc," and with a matching hat that Rodney expertly tilted to the side, we drove off, hitting corners and killing time until more of the Dexter Boys would be ready to leave for the clubs in the suburbs. When we turned from Providence on to Dexter, Rodney noticed that there was a big gathering of folks at the Coney, and we pulled into the lot and went in to see when everyone would be heading out.

As one walks into the Coney Island on Dexter, a glass partition is immediately to the right of the entrance, beginning from just beyond a seldom-used narrow brown door on which is pasted a small paper sign preempting possible inquiries about the use of bathrooms; "Toilet has been stolen," it reads. There are two cash registers behind the glass, and there are small stainless-steel troughs through which money can be exchanged. A couple of feet above the counter, holes have been drilled in a scattershot pattern

through the two-inch-thick transparent curtain, only enough so that customers and employees of the restaurant are barely audible to one another as
they yell back and forth. And in between the two cash registers is a bulletproof lazy Susan, a clear plastic box that pivots around, and through which
food and utensils are pushed to customers in the dining area. This is the
only consistent sort of interaction across the two sides of the glass. The
employees of the store never cross the glass divide and only clean the place
after they've closed for the night. The dining area is by and large conceded
to the people who spend time there, most of whom are Dexter Boys. The
staff who work at the restaurant, almost all of whom are members of the
family that owns the place, make no effort to intervene in the use and, more
frequently, abuse of this space at the hands of the young men on Dexter.
Young people from Dexter, in turn, feel a sense of propriety about the dining
space in the restaurant. They roll marijuana blunts on the condiment counters and make mixed drinks for themselves on the booth tables while the
owners and staff people watch from behind the nearly soundproof glass
membrane.

Most of the six or seven people in the restaurant had seen me with Rodney already, but the few who hadn't shot me long looks, which Rodney de-
flected with the customary reassurance that I was his "man from the youth
home." Behind the bulletproof glass, a white man with a shaved head looked
at me, and then turned his co-worker with a bemused expression. Malachi
was sitting in one of the shallow white corner booths with a long bottle of
Belvedere Vodka in front of him and a small glass container of Everfresh
fruit punch to chase it down. He was on a riff, simultaneously yelling and
laughing at Antonio, who was sitting across a small isle from him looking at
the ground with a reluctant smile. "Ton couldn't even get his dick up," he
was saying. "Hey Rod, remember when we went to Atlanta? And Tonio was
with that ho and he couldn't even get his shit up?" I had sat down in a booth
on the other side of the small dining area, and Rodney was standing at the
front of the brightly lit room before one of two small condiment counters.
He laughed appreciatively as he split open one of the Swisher Sweets and
sprinkled the contents of a dime bag into it. Rabbit, a small and slope-
shouldered sixteen-year-old with little square teeth and bright red lips who
had lived around Dexter when he was young but now lived with his well-off
mother in a nice neighborhood in north Detroit, walked around the room
with a tall can of beer in his hand. A light-skinned and handsome man called

Hector, who was wearing a jeans outfit almost identical to mine, sat back and read a tattered copy of a hip-hop magazine that had been circulating among the others there.

"Antonio's a fucking fag!" Malachi yelled and chortled. Sheed was there also and laughed along. "Something was wrong with that ho," Antonio said, while shaking his bowed head. "That ho was off." Hector's brother, a dark-skinned young man named Shell, with an exaggerated laugh that invariably showcased the two long spikes that were all that remained of his front teeth, broke open another cheap cigar at the booth table where he was sitting. He recalled the evening in question, remembering that he and Sheed had had several other "$500 hos" in their rooms at the Atlanta hotel where a large group of Dexter Boys had gone to watch the NBA All-Star basketball game a couple of months earlier. "We didn't have no trouble with our hos, did we Sheed?"

"We fucked the shit out of them bitches," Sheed answered, blinking his glazed eyes.

Goal Post is one among several strip clubs that line the southern side of Eight Mile Road, the dividing line between Detroit and the northern sub-urbs. On the northern side of the boulevard are mostly car dealerships and family-friendly franchised eateries, like Bennigan's and Applebee's. The jux-taposition of the two sorts of retail spaces, with their overdetermined con-trivances of familial morality (on the north side) and extrafamilial vice (on the south side) neatly reinforces common stereotypes differentiating the city from the suburbs.

Rodney directed me toward a back alley behind the club, where we parked, and where he pissed against the back wall before we went in. Though the management is white, Goal Post is a black titty bar, where pre-dominantly African American patrons come to see predominantly African American exotic dancers. The enormous bouncers at the door knew Rodney by name as we walked in and didn't pat him down, as they had with some of the older customers entering before us. We sat down in front of one wing of the stage, just underneath one of the greased poles that rose into the ceiling. Sheed and Antonio were already there, sitting with beers in front of them. Rodney and I sat down next to them, and Rodney pulled another Swisher out of his pocket and began rolling a blunt on a magazine in his lap.

But just as the end began to glow red, one of the largest of the stable of

African American bouncers walked over and pulled the blunt from his lips.
Rodney was outraged, yet quickly realized that he was fighting a losing battle, and suggested that we cross Eight Mile and head for Nickels in Southfield, where others from Dexter would soon be gathering in any case.

Like several of the other clubs that young people from Dexter frequent,
Nickels is on the first floor of a not especially well-appointed hotel. When
we arrived, at around 11:00 P.M., there was already a huge crowd assembled
in the low-ceilinged rooms, which would have looked like large classrooms
had the fluorescent overhead lights been turned on. Malachi and many others from Dexter, several of whom I had not yet met, were hovering around
the bar, and Malachi bought me a Long Island Iced Tea and handed it to me,
winking and raising his glass.

By one-thirty that morning Rodney was drunk. He had disappeared from
the room where I was standing with most of the other boys from Dexter.
When I went into the other larger room where a disc jockey was playing music, I found Rodney floating toward me from a writhing mass of bodies and
an impenetrable wall of noise. As he drew closer, I could see that he was being carried above the ground by two huge bouncers, each holding him under
the arm as he kicked, struggled, and pleaded to be left alone. I let them pass
me, and then followed them out about twenty feet behind. As he was being
led through the hotel's hallways and into its lobby, Rodney pulled out of the
loosening grip of the bouncers and threw himself onto a guy in a gray sweatshirt, with whom, it turns out, he had gotten into some sort of scuffle in the
club. As Rodney and the other guy continued grabbing and throwing
punches, one of the big bouncers managed to toss them, along with Antonio,
who was standing by at this point, into the closed front doors of the hotel,
which swung open as their bodies thudded against them, allowing the three
fighting boys to roll out onto the sidewalk.

Soon, Antonio and Rodney had dropped their expensive leather jackets
and were together pummeling the young man in the gray sweatshirt, who
had fallen on to the ground in a crumpled heap. A woman friend of his stood
nearby and screamed at Rodney and Antonio to stop, as other Dexter Boys,
having heard what was happening, pressed their faces against the inside of
the hotel doors, which had been closed and locked to prevent more participants from falling into the fray. A friend of the guy in the gray sweatshirt
came at Antonio from behind, but was dispatched with a single blow to the
face.

Antonio stood over him and looked over at Rodney, and then back toward the hotel windows. Dexter Boys were leaning against the glass doors of the suburban nightclub, and there was a gathering mass of onlookers who were shifting uncomfortably, like birds in the surf, not sure whether to intervene. He yelled to the surrounding crowd, with his arms extended like wings and his fingers articulating D for Dexter on either side: "I live for this shit," he shouted, nodding his head exaggeratedly. "I really do. . . . We living for this shit. DC, baby! We Dexter out here, baby."

What Antonio "lives for," of course, is not just fisticuffs in a parking lot, but rather the entire social context in which this drama unfolded: among the Dexter Boys and signifying Dexter at this club in the suburbs. It is precisely this convergence of social elements—Antonio's identification and invocation of Dexter, with all its associations with the drug trade, and evocations of the inner city—in this *extralocal* context that is so important for him, and in which the other Dexter Boys, peering out from the lobby and pounding on the windows, take delight.

Antonio's proclamation signals a key preoccupation of the Dexter Boys: movement between city and suburb. Antonio's announcement of the arrival of Dexter in the suburbs, "We Dexter out here, baby," is a celebration of exactly this; that those from Dexter have come out to the burbs, and that whatever it is that divides the city and suburb is easily and routinely traversable for them.

While the distinction between city and suburb has powerful resonance for the Dexter Boys, they are not imagined to be in a simple opposed relationship to one another. Where the Dexter neighborhood is a locus of both domestic and business activity for the Dexter Boys, the suburbs are a locus of recreational activity for them. This much was, in any case, clear in Rodney's insistence that I visit the suburbs with the Dexter boys before I spend time on Dexter, in their "working" environment. For the Dexter boys, the suburbs are part of the geographic parameters of their spatial practice, a divided but navigable space that they move in and out of consistently. Thus, in their experience of them and their relationship with one another, city and suburb are not part of a dreamed, diasporic trajectory (according to the still-mythologized destiny of the successful black family): from the South, to the city, to the suburbs. For the Dexter Boys, rather, the suburbs are at play in their everyday lives in a manner that does not necessarily upturn but instead confounds their conventional associations with domestic space, work, and recreation.

Where prevailing sociological preoccupations with young urban drug dealers in the inner city emphasize spatial circumscription, the Dexter Boys' sense for the parameters of their community is fundamentally tied to a spatial transgression not simply of the policed order of their neighborhood but of the broader cultural and political divisions between city and suburb in the Detroit metro area. For the Dexter Boys, community identity is connected to a geography that is at once bound by four discrete corners and that crosses and flaunts well-worn social spatial boundaries and borders across metro Detroit.

Near a Church

A few months later, in early July, the Coney Island on Dexter looked deserted. There was a lone car turning behind the building, circling around the drive-through lane; but there was no one else. No one stood in the parking lot or vestibule, and there was no crowd in the booths as there had so often been in previous months.

Up the street, Antonio was standing in front of the abandoned two-family flat on Carrington, just on the other side of the cinder block wall at the edge of the gas station parking lot. The old beige brick house had been bought recently by St. Paul's church, an African Methodist congregation housed in a beautiful, cubic synagogue just a block up Dexter, as a long-term financial investment. The house was missing its front doors and was still full of the dissolving belongings of the previous inhabitants, who had clearly left with no time to spare. Antonio, who was holding a yellow Styrofoam "to go" container from the Coney Island filled with wet sausage and pancakes, pushed through the low chain-link fence around the front yard and climbed up the cement porch steps; he sat on a milk container and picked at his food with his fingers. Ebo had been sitting on one of the wide slab ledges of the porch, taking cover from the sun with Oscar and Loc. When I traipsed up to the porch and sat next to Antonio, Ebo was reprimanding him for buying food at the Coney Island.

"Y'all too crazy, man. You and Rodney. Y'all looking for trouble. I'd stay the fuck out that place right now." An informal neighborhood prohibition against going into the Coney Island had been in effect for about two weeks. It was around then that a young man called JW, tall and thin with sharp features, a pointy chin, and a big Afro, was in the Coney Island with Frank, another Dexter Boy, lounging in the booths, sipping beer as the sun set over the houses on the west side of Dexter. As it grew darker, several people whom they didn't recognize came into the restaurant making a lot of noise. When one of the video games in the corner ate one of the strangers' quarters, they began punching and kicking the machine. JW, feeling protective of his neighborhood hangout, told them to calm down, and soon they were enveloped in an argument, and then a fistfight broke out. The biggest of the men from outside the neighborhood knocked Frank on his back, leaped on him so his knees were pinning down Frank's arms, and began beating him in the face. JW bolted out the door and grabbed a gun from the glove compartment of his car. He stormed back in and pointed it at the big guy, who was still pummeling Frank. When the heavy turned and saw the gun pointed at him, he jumped off Frank and lunged toward JW, who shot him in the leg, accidentally hitting Frank in the arm with the same bullet. The big man groaned and grabbed at JW, who pulled the trigger again and hit him in the middle of his face. He folded onto the ground and lay dead on the red-tile floor of the Coney Island.

Everybody scattered. JW disappeared. Frank went to Henry Ford Hospital to get his wound treated. Reclining on the porch of the abandoned house, Ebo and Oscar were recounting this particular detail with a sense of incredulity. "Shit, man, I ain't never would have gone to no Henry Ford Hospital to get my shit dealt with. . . . I would have just let that shit drip-dry and then wrapped it up," said Ebo, miming the procedure by twirling his arms around his leg. Oscar added, "Just let that shit drip-dry, you know. Now, you know, he going to get called into the First Precinct, man. And you know, he going to say who done it."

"No, he ain't," Antonio objected. "He know the rules."

"Fuck the rules," insisted Ebo. "When they got you down at 1300 Beaubien, and they telling you that you are an accessory to murder, you gonna say something. You gonna say whatever the fuck's gonna get you out that motherfucker."[6]

"Yeah, man," Oscar agreed. "JW is hit man. The game is over for that motherfucker. He off of the D. He through on Dexter, man."

"But he still hanging around, man," Antonio said.

"Yeah, I just talked to him yesterday," said Ebo, with a falsettoed tweak of disbelief in his voice. "He not going anywhere, man. If I was him, I would be going to New York. I would go there and just blend, you know. I would at least be going to Canada or something; get the fuck out of the United States."

"Hell, yeah," agreed Oscar. "The hook going to be watching too. They know that the suspect always. . . ." Ebo finished his sentence: "Return to the scene of the crime. . . . Exactly. And they got him on murder one, premeditated and shit. 'Cuz he was there and then he left to get the heater. Oh, man. I heard they was talking twenty-five to life. Twenty-five to life, man. And how old he now? Twenty-six? Yeah. When he get out, *if* he only get the twenty-five, I say *if* . . . he going to be fifty-one by the time he gets out. What you gonna do when you be fifty-one, got no education, got no idea what the fuck is going on, man?"

Timmy was rushing around beneath us, grabbing from a stash of rocks that he had piled behind the gas station dumpster and then meeting customers around the corner on Carrington, in front of the house where we were sitting or in the vacant lot behind the church, spreading for nearly an entire city block and bisected on an angle by a worn dirt path between tall blades of city grass. At one point, Timmy moved half of his stash into the recesses of a clump of weeds and flowers growing through the fence behind the Episcopal church on Dexter and Carrington. "Look at that little nigga," said Ebo. "I wouldn't never stash my shit next to no church. That is some stupid shit. Look at him over there. You know that God's up there looking down on that little nigga, saying, 'Boy, what the fuck are you doing? What the fuck is the mattah with you, boy?!' I wouldn't never stash my shit next to a church. You have to be some kind of crazy motherfucker to do that!"

"I mean, my man's got a good mama; she makes that bread. She takes care of him. Whatever he wants, she gonna get it for him. Watches out for him, keeps him in school. Keeps him geared up. That house she got up there, shit. He living large up in that piece. That shit might as well be in Grosse Point!"

When he was locked up at the detention facility, Timmy and I had hung out often, and I had spoken with and visited his mother on his behalf. She was living in a big brick house in an anomalously immaculate neighborhood in northwest Detroit that had long been a refuge for city-dwelling members of the African American middle class. After leaving Timmy's father, a crack addict and drug dealer, Timmy's mother earned an associate's degree from a community college and got a job at an insurance company, where she had been working for several years. When I met her, she was earning a good salary and was living comfortably with her three children.

"And he still down here," said Ebo, "he still down here. Taking the bus down here every day. Working hard, stashing his shit in front of the church!" The others laughed aloud. "Man, they's some niggas into some dumb shit out here, man," Ebo continued. "Some dumb-ass, old-school shit. I'm getting tired of this shit. I got to move on. They's a bunch of young cats, like youuuu," he said, pointing admonishingly at Antonio. "It's like it's a virus. Like it be some kind of disease. I fixing to go to school, man. Get on my shit, get me a tight-ass little job, you know."[7]

Antonio snorted in protest, but Ebo continued his lament. "I been doing this shit since I was thirteen, man. For eight years. Nobody doing shit out here, though. I mean, I'm bored of this shit man. I been bored of this shit for a while." Loc said that he's been going to school. "What?!" Ebo roared incredulously. "You going to school? Where you going to school?"

"I'm going to Wayne County Community, man. I been going for a couple of semesters. I just be taking major classes, like general stuff. The problem be with financial aid. They wouldn't give me any of that shit. They say that my old girl makes too much money." I asked what his mother does. "She's a nurse. She works up at Henry Ford, but she have like two other jobs."

Ebo was continuing with his unhappy disquisition about the dope game on Dexter. "Man, nobody likes to talk about going to school out here, man. They be talking 'bout girls and Ecstasy and cars—you tell them that you want to go to school, and they're like, 'I'm not talking to you.'"

"You know that's right!" concurred Oscar. He had been working for the sanitation department as a garbage collector and seemed to find it agreeable. "I just cruise around all day with a bottle in the cab. Me and the cat I be making my rounds with, nobody bugs us, we go as fast or as slow as we want. And I make damn good money. Keep my little hustle on the side." But with city budget cuts, even at that time of relative prosperity, Oscar had been suspended for the past couple of months and was waiting for a call back to work. "I got applications in at Chryslers, too, 'cuz I know a couple of people down there from my brother. So right now I'm waiting on that and waiting on getting reinstated at sanitation. . . . But I know I got to be working. I ain't so stupid that I think I can just make it out here on the streets. You know, your shit might blow up, and then you gonna think for a while that you can really make it. But your shit's gonna shrink just as fast as it grows, dog. You'll go from making Gs a week, to making nothing. Just like that. Man, this shit is just boring. . . . People think that they gonna be coming up in the game, ain't doing shit. Just the same niggas out here, year after year. Not doing shit."

Antonio had his fingers in the tray in front of him and pushed a piece of sausage around in pools of syrup. He guffawed at Oscar's pessimism. "You're crazy, dog! Shut the fuck up, man."

"You and your bro, dog. Just keep going to the Coney, then, man. Keep acting like fools. Y'all too nutty."

"Shit, the Coney's ours, dog. This our spot. You can't be scared of your own spot, man." Antonio set his tray of half-eaten sausages and pancakes on the porch floor and rested his head on the windowsill behind him; he shut his eyes for an afternoon nap.

10

Of Hot Dogs and Heroin

Let's pretend there's a way of getting through into it, somehow. . . . Let's pretend the glass has got all soft like gauze, so that we can get through. Why, it's
turning into a sort of mist now, I declare!
                                        —Lewis Carroll, *Through the Looking Glass*

In late summer, I went to the Coney Island on the corner of Providence and
Dexter to get a cheeseburger and some lemonade for lunch. By then the hullabaloo over JW's shooting had settled down, and the little eatery had again
become the epicenter of public activity in the neighborhood. The booths
were crowded with people from the area, most of them older and haggard
looking. A gray-headed man and a woman wearing a wide-brimmed pink hat
sat in the back corner, leaning up against one another, and both picking at
an order of dark beef strips and eggs with hot sauce. Another woman, an ac-
quaintance of theirs with light skin and a soft face, who might have been in
her seventies, sat in a booth across the aisle from them and sipped clumsily
on a fifth of V.O. Scotch. She looked at me when I walked in and watched
as I stood in the short line in front of the bulletproof glass counter. Her head
wobbled on top of her thin neck. Her eyes were red and unfocused. "Vote!"
She yelled at no one in particular. "Vote! We got to vote," she continued. "Go
to school!" Some of the others in the restaurant twitched in apparent agreement. Others looked away in embarrassment. "Mandela! Mandela! Mandela!"
she chanted. "Free Mandela!" She was now looking right at me, the only
white person in the restaurant, besides the pale-faced Albanians behind the

glass. "I'm a respected woman," she insisted, thrusting her extended index finger toward me. "I been coming here for a long time. Ever since they opened. . . . I know these people!" she yelled, pointing now at the owners of the restaurant behind the glass at the counter. "And they know me! I'm a respected woman!"

I nodded and stared ineffectually, registering the racial tension in the room, the disquieted sense of vulnerability that the woman must have felt sitting in a white-owned business, inspiring her to blurt out an assortment of imperatives to social responsibility, black liberation, and defensive claims to her own respectability. Indeed, what was I doing there, and what were the real terms of belonging?

Through the following months, as winter descended on Detroit and warm interior space became especially sought after, the Coney Island fell into a protracted period of shifting claims to ownership and belonging. During these dark days, the Dexter Boys took more frequent physical refuge in the restaurant. But their occupancy of it was not just for shelter from westward winter storms. As the Dexter Boys moved into the Coney Island, they brought their work with them, and the restaurant became a blazing heroin spot, an efficiently run indoor market where customers would come less for food than for a cure for their daily dope sickness. And in instigating this transformation, the Dexter Boys challenged notions of ownership and belonging on the corner of Dexter and Providence, if not inverting, than certainly reconfiguring a space that shaped and symbolized racial politics in their neighborhood.

While it is evident from their exteriors (the traffic flowing around them, the talk about them, and the ink spilled over them) that small retail businesses are the loci of struggles over space and community in the city, their more formidable social power is inside, over the threshold. In most cases, the physical configurations of such small businesses, the arrangement of walls, aisles, kitchens, and dining rooms, and the social spaces and practices that take shape around them, can be taken to reflect in microcosm divisions and tensions that define the Motor City.

As I've begun to suggest, the emblems of this kind of spatial arrangement in Detroit are the ubiquitous glass curtains that hang across the front ends of almost all small retail businesses in the city, creating carceral divisions of interior space. Indeed, small retail spaces in Detroit can be taken to signify all sorts of things for the black community, and for the Arab, Chaldean, and Albanian American communities as well. What a telling metaphor, for example, these glass curtains are for the lack of access that African Americans have to commercial activity within their own neighborhoods, in perhaps the most black-identified city in the nation. We can imagine such spaces reflecting, reproducing, and shaping all sorts of social and cultural divisions that characterize widespread inequities between suburban business owners and city residents, between African Americans, Arabs, Chaldeans, and ethnic whites. Suburban residents with access to the small business community in the city, and many forms of symbolic capital and substantial real capital, are situated on one side of an impenetrable but transparent curtain, making relations of power inexorable but transparent. Meanwhile, neighborhood resident customers are confined to the other side, always already suspected of being dangerous, potentially criminal, but of course always entitled to exhaust their meager incomes on products that are cataloged and arranged by the store's owners. As the objects of fear and unspoken reproach, neighborhood customers suffer a grim everyday indignity, and in many Detroit neighborhoods, the bulletproof windows in retail stores have attained an almost folkloric symbolic potency.

But to the extent that these divided spaces reflect and reproduce social inequalities, symbolizing differential access to certain kinds of capital and power and shaping the identities of those who move through them—to the extent that they are involved in what Michel Foucault has called a "microphysics" of power—they are not just metaphors for exclusion.[1] On the contrary, the everyday occupancy and use of such bifurcated spaces by people from the neighborhoods around them is always, of necessity, a complex embodied engagement with tensions between the distinctions that these spaces represent: city versus suburb, black versus other, ownership versus occupancy.

The Coney Island on Dexter might be taken as an especially illuminating example of social dynamics unfolding out of such divided interior spaces. For on Dexter Avenue, the interior of the Coney Island restaurant is a particularly rich and richly inhabited public space. It is not simply a place designed for the efficient distribution of low-cost consumer goods, within which people swarm past one another, stopping to talk for a few moments, holding lottery tickets and cold six-packs of canned Budweiser. It is a space that was designed for and encourages lingering interactions, as people sit and eat, take shelter from the heat or cold, or find someone with whom to share a blunt, a story of daring, or more pedestrian exploits.

In the case of the businesses on Dexter with which the Dexter Boys are interacting, and around which they are consistently working and playing, the politics of social space are contested not only through explicit disputes over ethnic white ownership, zoning conflicts between retail businesses and residents, or breathless claims to community loyalty and suspicion that are amplified and shouted from on high. Among the small retail spaces on Dexter that are populated by the Dexter Boys, meaningful negotiations of social spatial politics happen perhaps most vividly through mundane, unremarkable interactions among people inhabiting, making use of, and moving through these spaces every day. The manner in which the Dexter boys are able to incorporate the Coney Island into their everyday lives, where they are able to push against its divisions and the distinctions between ownership and occupancy embedded in it, opens for them the possibility of moving past such divisions, of finding an in-between space that is neither on one side nor the other of the restaurant glass.

As I was waiting for my food, several Dexter Boys, including Rodney, who had been circulating around the corner of Dexter and Providence, came into the store. Antonio and Malachi led the way for the others, all of whom were to some degree involved in an extended slapstick row between Dante and Marley, a regular source of entertainment for these two, and everyone else within earshot. "You got me all fucked up, motherfucker," Dante was in the middle of saying as he entered the room. Malachi assumed his usual position as the wise arbitrator in other people's disputes and doin' of the dozens, sitting in a booth between the two contestants and offering a running commentary of approving laughter and tired groans.

"That's all I got is hos—different ho every day. Every day! I'm not saying you don't have some hos," Dante said, looking with mock sympathy at Marley. "I'm just saying I got a lot more hos than that."

"Everybody's got hos," Marley retorted. "I mean a ho will do anything you tell her to do. You want her to suck your dick, the bitch will suck your dick. Shiiit—anybody could get a ho." Malachi recalled an episode where Marley had sex with a young woman from the neighborhood and attempted to keep it a secret from the others. In a gravelly belly laugh, Malachi remembered how Marley "fucked this one ho, but was embarrassed to have everybody know!" "Shit," he continued, "if you don't tell your mans that you fucked this ho, that means that you respect the ho more than your mans. You s'posed to come back to the hangout and tell everybody when you fucked the ho. That's what you supposed to do." Marley rejoined, "Well, ain't this the hangout? Everybody here know I fucked the ho now." The others hooted with delight.

Dante looked down at his watch. "Come on, right now! It's two-forty, let's see how long it takes for me to get a ho. Let's keep track, right now. I guarantee you I'll have more hos than you. . . . Man, you got me all fucked up, man," he said grabbing napkins from above the trash receptacle, and wiping under his arms and above his protuberant belly. Rodney looked at Dante as if he was a circus curiosity and tapped me on the shoulder. "We out," he said.

Rodney was working in Malachi's crew, filling in for Kilo, who needed to go downtown to handle some business with the probation department. Over the course of the summer, Malachi's previously modest heroin market on McQuade had swollen. Drug customers were coming from all across the West Side, and increasingly from the western suburbs to cop dope from Malachi and the crew, and as word spread, the management of traffic had become a more complicated logistical affair. Cars were flying down Dexter and hitting the corner of Providence with a glaring disregard for how conspicuous they might be on the big thoroughfare. In an effort to keep things more discreet, members of Malachi's crew had begun hanging out toward the corner of Providence and Dexter. And in the cooling glow of the springtime murder at the Coney Island, the Dexter Boys working on the corner were soon spending most of their time moving between the Coney Island parking lot, where there was the cover of presumably law-abiding pedestrian traffic, and the far corner of Dexter and Providence.

Rodney was making the most of his afternoon shift, keeping a cold Corona beer in the bushes next to the restaurant. He was staying busy, moving between the Coney Island's parking lot and its interior, watching through the big square windows for heroin customer traffic heading down Dexter. Most cars would come to a crawl around the intersection, with the drivers looking over both their shoulders for someone who might be selling. Usually they would end up parking on Providence, on the east side of Dexter, and would walk toward the vacant lot across the street, through which Sheed was circling at regular intervals. One of them drove right into the Coney lot—an older white woman in a beat-up Pontiac with disheveled hair that trailed out the window after her. Rodney furrowed his brow and waved her off impatiently, shouting, "No! Over there!" in muffled, monosyl-labic bursts. He and others working for Malachi then were attempting to conceal themselves within the Coney Island foot traffic, but were worried about too many conspicuous cars pulling into the lot. The driver looked ad-monished, and slowly turned out of the lot and across the street, where Sheed was waiting in front of one of the abandoned houses on the other side of Dexter.

Rodney came into the restaurant, where I was sitting and watching the street. He plopped himself into a booth behind me and took a roll out of his pocket to count. "You see that stupid-ass bitch?" he said, as he fingered through small wrinkled bills. "Dumb, man. We tell them not to come into the lot. They acting so stubborn, though. I'm telling you, man, this ain't how it's going to happen. I ain't going to be fuckin' around down here too much longer. I got some other plans, dog."

"Where you gonna go?" I asked.

Patting the cash that he had pushed back into his pocket, Rodney broke into a furtive smile. "Man, what you asking so many questions for?"

Shelter and Comfort

A couple of months later, in mid-autumn, Sheed was at the Coney before seven o'clock in the morning, just as the sun was rising behind thick blue clouds to the southeast. The sour smell of cleaning fluid hung in the air, mingling with the aromas of greasy food and corn syrup. Sheed sat with a breakfast special in front of him and his two-year-old little brother, whom everyone called "Little," alternately tucked under his arm and standing on the seat next to him. Little already had features that made him easily recog-nizable as Sheed's kin, and Sheed had taken special care to dress them both in matching outfits, with blinding white tennis shoes. Each had their hair in neat braids angling across their scalps and dangling like ornaments on to their shoulders. Sheed had cut up the small pancakes on his plate and was feeding them to Little, who pulled the pieces of food off the plastic fork, and chewed and pulverized them with a big sugar-expectant smile.

Shell was standing at the front of the room, feeding quarters into the "Cruisin' the World" driving video game that the owners of the restaurant had installed just to the left of the glass partition and narrating his success for the benefit of anyone else in the room. He stomped on the floor pedal and pulled the shifter down with a violent thud. "Look at this, Little!" he yelled behind him. "Ain't nobody can whip this shit like me." Little swiveled around on the booth's bench to watch Shell playing the game. "Lookit! It's blue," he said, pointing at the car Shell was maneuvering through the virtual landscape. "Yellow," he said, pointing at a competing car. With Little distracted, Sheed hunched over his legs and pulled a wad of cash out of his front pocket. He held the money in his left hand and pulled bills rapidly into his right hand with his thumb as he counted. When he came to the end of the stack, he evened the edges of the bills on the table.

For the previous several days, Sheed had been working the morning shift in Malachi's crew, and he had moved the trade further into the Coney than it had been theretofore. Customers would regularly amble into the store's parking lot and often come into the dining area looking for one of the young men who might be dealing there. Shell was working as the lookout and the babysitter for Little when Sheed needed to make a run across the street. Sheed was paying him $50 for the shift, which would last until precisely one in the afternoon, when others would arrive to take over.

As Shell was adding another set of his initials to the high-score list on the driving game, a man from the neighborhood called Red, for his gray-flecked but otherwise bright orange hair, walked into the restaurant. He lived in a small apartment down Providence in the only still inhabited building on the block, paying $150 in rent each month for the squalid room where he was staying. He came in with his hands in his pockets and his head hung low, his bright green eyes and youthful, freckled face obscured by a ragged red and white beard and sagging white hat, cast toward the ground. His big beige boots curled at the toes like a court jester's, and he picked them up flatly, so that the ends of his feet never touched the ground. Sheed acknowledged him with a grunt, and Red pointed two fingers of his right hand, mumbled "two," and hobbled to a booth across the room. "It's going to be just a minute, dog," said Sheed. "Alright, then," Red answered softly and appreciatively. Sheed put his wad of cash back into his pocket and looked across the street through the big windows. He pivoted out of the booth, and Shell swung away from the video game after him. "Luke, can you watch Little?" he asked, as he was bouncing out the door after Sheed. Little and I chatted about the colors of the cars on the video screen while the others were gone.

Ebo, whose souped-up Suburban was gleaming in the Coney parking lot, sat sleepily in the back of the room and had been uncharacteristically silent. He looked up and noticed Red sitting quietly in the booth. "Hey, my man with no toes," he said, stretching his arms over his head and arching his back, trying to wake himself up. Red chuckled bashfully. "That's right. I got no toes."

Sheed and Shell walked back into the restaurant after fetching two packs of raw from the stash sitting inside the window of one of the abandoned houses on Providence. Hector, who was arriving early to work the afternoon shift for Malachi, from one in the afternoon to as late as he might feel like working, followed them into the store. "What up, Red?" he asked cheerfully as Red got up to leave the restaurant. "Hey Ice," answered Red. "Where's your auntie at?" Hector's Aunt Patty lived in a small apartment building a couple of blocks away from Red, and they had both been copping heroin from Malachi since he had been managing the raw trade in the neighborhood. "Oh, I ain't seen her since yesterday."

After Red left, everyone in the restaurant marveled at his circumstances and resilience. "That man been stabbed twice, been shot, had his arms broken six times," said Ebo. He raised his left arm, "Had this one broken three times," and then his right arm, "and had this one broken three times. And he got no toes. They froze the fuck off his feet. You see how his boots are. And he fucking with the heroin. Damn!" Ebo held his index finger to his head as if shooting himself. "After living through that, the man needs to be numb, dog," Hector said.

The young Albanian American woman behind the counter leaned forward and yelled through the holes in the glass. "Hey, Shell!" Shell came over to the window, where the young woman had placed pieces of plastic-wrapped chocolate in the bulletproof lazy Susan and given it a twirl. "It's for the baby, not for you," she said with a bright smile and in a nasally New York accent. Shell grabbed the chocolate and handed it to Little, who was hanging both arms over the back of the booth.

At exactly one o'clock, Sheed took the growing wad of cash out of his pocket, handed Shell $50, put Little on his hip and headed for Malachi's house on McQuade to pay him his portion of the daily take. Shell left to get a beer and then take an afternoon nap after his early morning workday. Through the window, Hector watched his little brother walk around the outside of the Coney Island and toward the liquor store across Providence. He shook his head in disapproval. "You know, Shell ain't doing shit out here. Just risking everything. I mean, if you going to be in the game, you can't be acting a fool like he always be. I mean, he started drinking before he started working this morning. And now, where he going? Look, he going straight to the liquor store, and he going to get drunk, and then he going to be going out on the street and be acting a fool. Shit, he got this girl pregnant, and he ain't going to be doing shit for this girl. He was just in the joint for a few years, for some stupid dope shit. And he still on parole. If he gets caught again, he talking about some real time. They don't play."

Ebo saw the young Albanian woman through the glass and called to her in a flirtatious, singsong voice: "Hey Polly! You looking good today, girl!" Polly leaned forward, her long simple pigtails framing her round, vaguely handsome face. From the corner booth where he was sitting, Hector yelled, "Hey baby!" The usually tight-lipped Polly broke into a wide wooden smile and said something playfully dismissive as she turned back around toward the kitchen. I told Hector that it looked to me as if Polly might like him. "Oh, I'm just playing with her," he said. "We all be messing around with her all the time. 'Cuz she can take it, you know? You seen her say some shit right back to me. The whole family here, they real cool with all of us. They Albanian, but they from New York, so they see the world just like we do. They talk like us and shit. . . . They smoke weed and everything. They be saying, 'Hey, you know where we can get some weed at?' And shit . . . well, Polly don't smoke, but her brothers do."

Shell came back into the restaurant along with Kilo, Z, Rabbit, and several others from the neighborhood. He was carrying four forty-ounce bottles of malt liquor in his arms, and had balanced a sleeve of plastic cups among them. He sat down and started pouring everyone drinks. The small cups reminded him of those that were used at the Jackson State Penitentiary, where he had been locked up for two years. "This shit's just like in the back forty," he said, referring to the state prison. "I don't want to be back in the back forty! All you be seeing is niggas. Take a shower and look to your side, and you see another nigga. Take a shit and look to your side, and you see another nigga. When you eat, you sitting next to a nigga. When you look out the window, you see the yard, you see the wall. I want to look out and see Dexter, and Providence, and Chicago, and Carrington!"

Kilo and Z came to work in the afternoon. They were becoming the regular afternoon crew, with Hector filling in some days, supplementing their work, or working as a $50 per shift lookout for trips to the other side of Dexter to retrieve packs of heroin. The Coney Island on Dexter had now become the spot where drug customers would congregate to place and receive their small narcotics orders from the dealing kids. Any effort to steer customers away, to send them down Providence toward McQuade, as Rodney had done a few months before, was completely abandoned.

With the cold winter weather settling over Detroit, the Dexter Boys were themselves also gathering with increasing frequency in the warm Coney Island dining room. Malachi came through in the afternoon, wearing a fat maniacal smile with which everyone was familiar. His eyes were half shut and exhausted again. He saw Polly behind the counter and cocked his hat as he crooned her name like an inflated balloon let loose. "Polly! . . . How you doing, though?" He noticed a band-aid on her finger. "Did you cut your hand?" She nodded from behind the glass. "You did? Let me know who did it and I'll slap them around." She smiled. "Are you cooking?" She shook her head and pointed back toward her brother, who was scooping chicken meat into a piece of pita bread. "You're not? Oh, your older brother is cooking. . . . That's cool, I know he could cook. Where's your brother Larry, I haven't seen him in ages, man?"

"He's outside, cleaning up," she yelled back.

Larry, the eldest son of the Albanian owners, had been sweeping the parking lot with a straw-bristled house broom. With the job half done, he rested his elbow on the top of his broom and smoked a cigarette near the back corner of the building. His blue eyes were half shut against the cold wind and stray smoke, and his thick features were screwed into a fighting scowl. He wore a gray sweatshirt over his drab buttery apron with the hood covering his shaved head. Antonio had just arrived on Dexter and was sidling toward him as Malachi and I stepped outside. "Hey, skinhead," Antonio said. "Fuck you, with your fucking ridiculous hair," Larry answered playfully. Antonio shook his half-braided Afro from side to side and smiled, with the big spaces between his white teeth showing. "This is going to be a beast. But you are one ugly motherfucker," said Antonio, sounding genuinely sympathetic. He clicked his tongue and stared up at Larry, who cocked his head like a bird and looked back impatiently at Antonio. "You're not so hot yourself, you know," he said, with a rapid-fire unfolding of breathy vowels and closed consonants that sounded like a mix between a Bronx and Albanian accent.

From behind we heard muffled shouting coming from Dexter Avenue, and the four of us turned around. A black-and-gold police car had stopped in the middle of the street, with other traffic crawling cautiously around it, and the dark-blue-uniformed driver, a white man with coifed blond hair and stereotypically menacing reflective sunglasses, was leaning toward the open passenger window. "You all need to buy something if you're going to be standing around there," he shouted from his car. Malachi pivoted around, looking as if he was relishing the provocation. "He's my GED coach," Malachi yelled back, pointing down toward me with both his arms raised. "We was just talking. We going to go in and buy something!" The police officer pulled his head back into the car and yelled for us all to get out of there, "all four of you!" Malachi looked both overjoyed and outraged. "He's the motherfucking owner of the store!" he shouted this time, shifting his pointing fingers toward Larry. "How you going to tell him to go buy something?!" But the police officer had driven off.

With raised eyebrows and a round open mouth, Malachi looked back at us, as if he had just seen someone with his pants down. "I'm gone," he said, as he waved his arm toward the street where the cop had been and pushed through the double doors.

Antonio was laughing now, and told Larry that he looked like a crackhead. "Yeah," said Larry. "Standing here with two black drug dealers and another ugly white guy, what the fuck do we look like, bro? Fucking good pals? Please." Antonio giggled.

"Call me a crackhead if you want. But I'll tell you what I can't stand, is being called Arab. Oh my God. People say I look Arab, I will fucking beat the shit out of them, bro. You think I'm kidding; I'm serious. I would rather be mistaken for a crackhead than for an Arab. But, shit. We probably all look the same to you guys, huh?" Larry took another drag off his cigarette. One of Rabbit's friends from the Seven Mile area had shown up and was standing behind Antonio, near the doors, listening to our conversation. "I thought all three of you was Arabs," he said, laughing at his own joke with disproportionate hilarity. Larry looked at him scornfully and shook his head. "Fucking idiot," observed Larry. "Yeah," said Antonio, "I think he's retarded."

"We're Albanians. All of us."

"I know you all are Albanian," Antonio assured him, proudly.

Larry remembered first visiting Detroit when he was four years old. He had come with his two parents and his younger brother Mikey to visit relatives of theirs who were running one of the "A-Eagles" Coney Island restaurants on Joy Road. They had traveled from the Bronx, New York, where they lived among many other close and more distant relatives who had emigrated from Albania (a little county in southeastern Europe, along the Adriatic Sea) over the course of the previous half century. For Albanians living in New York, Detroit has offered considerable opportunity over the last century. The metro area has become home to tens of thousands of Albanians, most with more or less immediate connections to New York City, and a great many involved in Detroit's Coney Island industry.[2] A-Eagles, a chain of restaurants with franchises across the East and West Sides of town, is probably the strongest testament to this. The storefront of each is emblazoned with an enormous Albanian Eagle, which glows bright orange after dark—a luminescent beacon of nationalist pride and greasy food. But Larry's extended family did not limit its business to Coney Islands. Cousins of his owned an entire city block on the East Side, near Chene and Mount Elliott, and rented the scattered but still numerous habitable houses on their property.

Larry lived with his father, mother, little brother Mikey, and younger sister Polly in a five-bedroom house in Sterling Heights, a suburb to the north of the city, and he drove the family's green Mercedes to work every day, often with either his sister, brother, or both sitting as passengers. His parents had recently arranged for him to be married to a twenty-one-year-old woman whom his family knew from attending Our Lady of Albanians Catholic Church. Larry had only met her after his parents had already undertaken to make the arrangement. But he seemed to think that his bride-to-be would work out adequately. They had spoken a couple of times in the house, when she had come over for tea, and each had found the other a reasonably attractive possibility.

Antonio listened with rapt attention as Larry offered his brief familial history to the two of us, and when Larry paused and turned his back against the wind to light another cigarette, Antonio asked questions like a young child at the zoo. "So how much do your pops pay you to work here?"

"He doesn't pay me a thing," Larry answered with a shrug of his shoulders. "It all goes back to the family, and any money I want I just ask for." Antonio smiled with a mix of doubt and excitement. "So anything you need, you could just ask for it?"

"That's right," said Larry, grinning so that his cigarette dangled precariously from the corner of his mouth.

"So you can't do shit without asking your pops for money first?" Larry reassured him that his pockets were always full. "Anytime I need anything, I can just take it. I mean, I run this store. You see me here all the time. I'm here all night, bro. This wouldn't be shit without me, so we understand each other."

Antonio asked how much money the store pulled in each day, and was impressed with Larry's roughly hewn answer: "more than you make all year." Antonio defended himself by imagining that Larry wasn't accounting for overhead. "Yeah, but you going to get taxed, you got to cop all the food and shit, and you got to account for that." Larry laughed at Antonio's imagination of the congruence between the dope game and Coney Island management. "No, bro," he said. "I'm talking about profit."

Larry said that he eventually wanted to buy the plot of land across the street and maybe open a Chinese restaurant there, noting that there weren't any Chinese restaurants in the area. "Shit," responded Antonio. "I'm going to open me a Coney over there."

"You can't do that," said Larry, laughing. "If you did that, I would have to blow your place up or close this place down. . . . Could you imagine," he said, looking over at me, "if Antonio opened a Coney over there? Nobody would be eating over here, that's for sure."

"You know it," said Antonio. "'Cuz you know my Coney would be straight, man. It would be real nice in there. Real comfortable."

"Shit," objected Larry, looking back at me. "If you think that this place is wild. Can you imagine? We only had one murder in this place. People would be getting killed up in Antonio's place all the time." The three of us chuckled.

"What about that?" I asked. "Were you all freaked out?"

"Lemme tell you something, bro," said Larry. "When that shit happened, we were closed for a total of three hours. Me and Polly were working at the time. I was in the back, cooking, and Polly was up front working the cash register. Polly saw the guys come in; she didn't see the shooting, because when she heard bullets, she just ducked, bro. She ain't stupid. But they still came back and threatened to kill her if she talked to anyone."

"She must have been terrified," I remarked. Larry pouted his lips and shook his head defiantly.

"There is nothing that could happen to my sister," he said. "Nothing. She has no reason to be scared. That's it. The coroner came, took the body away. The police were here, talking to everybody, and doing their investigation. Then we mopped up all the blood, me and Polly. . . . God, bro, that shit was disgusting! . . . And then we opened up again. That night. And we had customers coming through the drive-through. . . . I'll tell you one thing, my pops used to keep four black guys strapped in the restaurant waiting for something bad to happen." Turning to Antonio, he asked, "I bet you guys never knew that, did you?"

Antonio shook his head silently. "Fucking Detroit," said Larry. "This place is horrible: racist, segregated, you gotta have bulletproof glass everywhere, fucking crazy drug dealers and fiends. I'm telling you man, they will take anything from you. We are trying to put in more security cameras to deal with those motherfuckers. They've tried to steal the lights, they've tried to steal the signs. Right now, the toilet's not working because one of those motherfuckers, in the middle of the night when Mikey was here, went into the bathroom and disconnected the entire motherfucking toilet—walked right out of the store with it."

"Man, if they could," said Antonio, "they would steal your sign and sell it to the Coney Island down on Linwood." We all fell out laughing.

Larry threw down his cigarette and ground it into the pavement with his tennis shoe. "What do you know about Ecstasy?" he asked either of us. I told him that I knew about it from when I was in high school, in the late 1980s, and that I knew it was making a comeback. Antonio said he didn't know shit about it, except for the fact that everybody on Dexter was doing it. "I know, bro, I got to get in on that," said Larry excitedly. "That's what I want to do. You all have it fucking easy out here. You're not sweeping the fucking sidewalks and shit. I want to get in on some of what you're doing. I mean, not out of the store. That's strictly business. . . . But if you hear anything, man, lemme know." I shrugged my shoulders, and Antonio nodded indecisively.

Custos and Customers

As they stood in the cold, Larry and Antonio's mutual envy might have seemed quaint. Both were peering over a cultural and economic fence between them, each seeing tamer weeds on the other side. Larry's interest in entering the fray of the dope game, his enthusiasm about the possibility of dealing to the dealers who were slinging heroin in his shop, was met with Antonio's fanciful dreams of opening a Coney on Dexter. Yet for all the silliness with which Antonio offered this possibility, the desires at its root reflected real developments in the Coney Island dining area. There, as the days of winter dragged on, what had been the inchoate, improvised dealing activity around the Coney Island restaurant was becoming more and more formal and consistent. The Dexter Boys were organizing themselves into discrete shifts, clocking in and out at 1:00 P.M., negotiating fair access to profits and equitable treatment among one another. In fact, the retail drug-dealing practices there were becoming increasingly analogous to the legitimate food business around which the place was originally organized. This was not only true of how the goods were bought and sold there but also how racial and class politics infused these interactions. Drug dealing would come to govern the racial character of the space.

Hector slid forward in one of the booths so that his head fell against the backrest. His arms were on the table, and he held a newspaper out in front of him, which he read with half-open eyes. Loc walked in and sat in the booth behind him.

"So what about some work?" he asked the still-languorous Hector. "Who's got the work?" Hector stretched his arms out and finally looked back. "Man," he said with a born-down flex of his upper body, "my shit's slow as hell." Hector had relinquished his shifts for Malachi to try to clear more money working on his own. "I'm trying to get this dope off . . . the shit won't move. Slow as fuck. I just couldn't fuck with Malachi's shit no more. I mean, that's the way that it's organized now, it ain't even fair. You got people working in the afternoon, and they getting all that afternoon traffic, you know people coming in after lunch and shit . . . all them fucking rawheads that be sleeping late and shit. And then those cats that are working on that shift, they just keep working 'til as late as they want. They'll be out here serving 'til eight or nine at night, you know. But if you working the morning like me, you got to turn in your money and all the Bs at one. You going to catch all that early morning traffic, but then you only working so many hours. And I know I'm not making what them cats in the afternoon is making."

Meanwhile, Sheed was selling for Malachi, and business was brisk. He was moving back and forth between the Coney and the area behind the liquor store across the street, where he had put the morning stash that Malachi had given him to work with, tucked into tufts of weeds. Sheed was running around sort of frantically, looking especially conspicuous with his hair in two mushrooming buns on the back of his head and standing a foot taller than most other people on the street. He came into the restaurant, leaned with his elbows against the condiment counter, and counted his money. There were three customers in the room. A light-skinned man approached him and mumbled something about wanting a pack. Sheed yelled at him: "Get away from me, man! I never served you before; I don't know who you is. You can wait 'til somebody else comes at one or something." The man looked around, threw his hands out with frustration, and walked out of the store. "Now you two," Sheed said to two other customers, both dark-skinned men in their late thirties. "You just stay here. Don't be getting up like those other hardheaded motherfuckers. Just wait here. Y'all be doing that dumb shit! Just make like this cat and keep your ass right here." The second of the two, at whom Sheed had not yet yelled, looked nervous and distracted. He stood up and tried to follow Sheed over to the liquor store.

While Sheed was across the street, Hector and Loc talked about how stupid he was for not paying someone to watch his back. He had been paying Shell $50 a day to follow him around, but according to Hector, he "got greedy," and now was working on his own. "He gonna make it hot for everybody, ain't nobody going to be able to work this spot after he blows it up. Fucking bitch. That's why I don't fuck with him," said Hector. "He too greedy. We all out here trying to get on together. That's how we do it. But he trying to work by himself. I'm telling you. If I saw the hook coming down his way, I wouldn't tell them where he is; I wouldn't want to be labeled a snitch, but I wouldn't call out to him or anything. I would just let them move along. He's gonna get caught! It's just a question of when it happens. They don't even want to catch him out here with two packs in his pocket or a small roll, they want to get him when he's reaching into that sack, get him at the house with the big stash. But look at him all out with it like that."

A little later that morning one of the beat cops from the Tenth Precinct, a man named Woodrow, pulled into the parking lot and strolled expectantly into the restaurant. Sheed was already in the Coney Island, and having just counted his stash and restowed it in his pocket, he was again leaning over the condiment counter. Woodrow sat in the back and looked up at Sheed.

Everyone else was silent. Sheed looked back and grinned out of the side of his mouth. Woodrow continued to stare at him, without twitching a muscle, and hardly seeming to blink. Sheed had his eyes lowered and maintained his obstinate grin. Finally, to break the silence, he told Woodrow that he had put in an order and was waiting for his food. Polly was now standing behind the counter, and hearing Sheed, she opened the cash register drawer and handed him $3 and some loose change along with a little receipt card. Woodrow shook his head and ground his teeth so that his forehead bulged. "I know what you're up to in here," he shouted, and stormed out of the restaurant. When he had left, Sheed thanked Polly and pushed the money she had given him back through the glass curtain. His shift for the day was nearly over.

After relenting to requests that Shell had been making of me throughout the morning to take him out to "Funco-land," a video game store in Dearborn, the two of us returned to the Coney Island in the early afternoon. "Damn, motherfuckers making it hot," said Shell, as I maneuvered toward one of a few open parking spaces. There were people sitting behind the steering wheels in about half the cars in the lot. In a new clean Cadillac, an elderly looking black man sat low in his seat. He was wearing a dark leather jacket, and his multiple finger rings glimmered off the top of the steering wheel in the winter sun. There was a clean white Saturn sedan, with a young white man with shoulder-length hair sporting a fashionable and cleanly trimmed goatee in the driver's seat. He had wire-rimmed glasses and was wearing a plaid shirt. He had backed his car into one of the spaces on the far side of the lot, so that he could sit and watch the dealers work. He looked hopefully at Shell and me, and then averted his eyes when I looked back as we rolled slowly past him into an available parking space. Next to the white Saturn was a red Dodge Neon with two tiny temporary tires on the back wheels. Its driver, a middle-aged white man in a denim coat, sat in the car smoking a cigarette. There was a city van from the Detroit Public Lighting Department next to the Neon with two men inside—a black man at the wheel and his white colleague in the passenger seat. On the other side of the parking lot, pulled right up to the front door of the Coney Island, was a late-model maroon mini-van driven by a young white woman with straight hair dyed jet black and falling down her back. She was wearing all black and had on heavy eye makeup and dark red lipstick. She looked like a postpunk rock band groupie, but was more likely an art student from some place like Eastpointe or Livonia. She was craning her neck to the right and left, looking back across Dexter, down Providence, and intently through the window of the Coney Island.

"Look at these stupid motherfuckers, Luke," Shell chimed in cheerfully as we were walking across the lot and toward the Coney Island door. He waved both hands in the air as if to exclaim his exasperation with everyone in the lot. "Just sitting there, like they don't have no idea what the fuck's going on. I gotta get ghost, man." Shell skipped toward the Coney to keep up with me.

With cars parked conspicuously in the lot, Z and Kilo were rounding from one to the next, leaning into the windows of each to gather the drivers' orders and darting across Dexter to retrieve packs from the stash across the street.

Inside, the restaurant looked like a bus station, or an airport waiting area during the onset of bad weather. Almost all the booths were occupied, filled with people whose overwhelming inclination toward sleep was staved off only by an equally overwhelming discomfort, agitation, and hope for imminent development. Most were from the neighborhood, unlike those in the parking lot, and all were black. Over the previous several weeks, it had become a widely understood rule and practiced pattern that white customers were not allowed to come into the dining area. They would wait in their cars in the lot or face the angry reprimand of whichever Dexter Boy was at work in the Coney. Kilo and Z, working the afternoon shift, seemed to take particular delight in screaming at any white dope customer who stepped out of their car and toward the Coney door. They would lean in and yell at them like disobedient dogs, and the recipients of these scoldings would invariably skulk back to their cars with their heads hung low.

The people in the restaurant booths were mostly destitute and desperate. Though they sat pressed against one another, no one spoke. One woman sat with her face in her hands, but most looked out of the windows toward the street, waiting for Z or Kilo to cross back over from the other side of Dexter. Shell and I stood in the front of the room, where there was space, and could see Kilo walking several feet in front of Z. Shell said, "Here they come," and a couple of people in booths close to the front stood and craned over to see them. Then others stood. And soon most of the roughly twenty people in the store were standing from their seats and stepping toward the door.

When Kilo flung the door open, the customers suddenly pushed toward him, backing him against the inside of the glass door. He tore his arms away from the clawing horde, stumbling forward over their shuffling feet. "Damn," he yelled, "you all be dumb as hell. Don't be rushing up on us!"

The dope customers slowly backed off. "Sit down!" shouted Kilo, who furrowed his brow and frowned at the fawning mob. "We've told you all before. Why you got to be so stupid!" The others retreated in a cold, held-breath silence and slumped to their seats. As Polly managed the cash register, serving food to cars moving steadily through the drive-through, Z and Kilo each took a side of the room and counted orders.

A half hour later, when the customers saw Kilo returning from the stash around the corner, they all rushed again for the door to get served first. Kilo shook his head disdainfully, but managed to serve them all in what felt like thirty seconds.

With the restaurant suddenly empty, Z and Kilo sat down in distant booths and leaned over their laps counting the money that they had just collected from the customers in the store. Through one of the booth windows looking out on to Providence, I could see Patty, Hector's fifty-year-old aunt and one of the most consistent neighborhood heroin customers, walking deliberately across the Coney Island parking lot, the last leg of her journey from her apartment on Joy Road. She came in through the front doors and said, "Hey baby," to me, with a resigned exhaustion. Kilo said, "Hey Patty," without looking up from the stack that he was fingering through for the second time. "Hey baby," answered Patty. She slouched her long thin body into the booth across the table from me and pressed her sliding dentures back into place with her lips. "How are you doing?" I asked. "Oh, I'm sick today, baby," she said. "But I'm broke. I ain't got shit." I nodded sympathetically, as Kilo pushed his wad of cash behind the cushion of the booth on the other side of the room and rushed out the door toward the liquor store. "Used to be different," she said.

"When I first started using, messing with drugs . . . if you spent your money every day with a person, you could go to that person, ask for some credit, 'cuz you sick, and it's going to be OK. You don't get all this bullshit! Oh, 'I can't do it.' Or just, 'No!' The average dope fiend going to pay you anyway. They ain't going to fuck up. You know, so, you didn't have to go through the kind of shit you go through with these young boys out here now. See they don't give a fuck. They don't use. They don't know what it is. They don't give a fuck. You know, you spend your money, and they say, 'fuck you,' they don't care. So you sick. They laugh and talk and talk to you and shit. Just like you see, I know all them motherfuckers, but I don't ask them for shit. Now Kilo is nice. See with those young boys, Luke, they talk shit to people that use and they try to impress each other. 'Oh, I can talk to that motherfucker like that anytime,' the way they talk, you know, 'that dope fiend bitch,' you know, 'that dope fiend nigger' or 'that dope fiend motherfucker,' and you know. Hey, that ain't cool. Because us dope fiends, as they call it, is the ones that's paying their way. Understand what I'm saying? If it wasn't for us, they wouldn't make shit. So you got to think about things like that. You know you don't be nasty to people. 'Cuz what go around, come around. And that's on the real. A lot of them are in the joint and a lot of them got killed. And these young folks here not even as treacherous as the ones that was down here with the YBI [Young Boys Incorporated]. It's more about business with these boys. It's about getting money. They don't want to go to jail for nothing. They don't want to kill nobody, they don't want to pistol whip nobody. You hear them talking all that shit, you hear them talking about fucking different women and shit. That's bullshit. You know that's . . . sheesh."

While we were both still watching Kilo and the others through the Coney Island window, I asked Patty if she felt that the dealers working there afforded her respect. "Oh yeah, 'cuz I give them respect, they got to give me respect. Yeah, 'cuz I don't play with them. They're kids, but I ain't going to play with them."

"Does it bother you the way they treat other custos?" I asked.

"You know, I don't like how they talk to people, but it's not my business, and I don't want to get out there into it. But I pray the ones that I really like, that I think are nice young fellas and that I really like them, maybe God, maybe He'll save some of them, and maybe He'll get some of them out of this shit. Maybe they, uh, I don't want them to get hurt. You know, get shot, or get their brains blew out, you know, on some bullshit. You know, I hope maybe they'll wake up and smell the coffee. I hope they learn, you don't need to talk to people like they a dog and shit. . . . But a motherfucker got to do something to have some money. They ain't got no place for kids to go and hang out, do things, play ball, no centers or nothing around here. I mean, what the fuck? All these vacant-ass lots and shit. But, hey, a motherfucker got to survive and make some money. So I don't know. It's a tight fight, Luke.

I'll tell you that. It's a tight fight. And I think it's going to get worse before it gets better."

Trespass and Transgression

A week later, just after dawn, Malachi called the Coney and spoke with Polly on the phone. He had been out early and had seen an unusual number of narcotics officers driving freshly painted black cars around the neighborhood and circling in and out of the Coney Island parking lot. He told Polly to tell anyone selling dope in the Coney to take their work and get out. "Tell them I said so," he told her.

Polly called Loc to the glass and told him what Malachi had said. He turned nervously around and spoke with a young man called Jeremiah, a friend of Loc's who hadn't worked for Malachi before, but who had been called as a substitute for Hector, who needed to meet with his probation officer that morning. The two had been selling to early risers out of the store. Loc, in turn, asked Corn Meal, who was sitting there enjoying his daily morning cheeseburger, to tell any dope customers showing up during their shift that they should head a few blocks down Dexter. They would pay him $50 for his trouble.

But in the afternoon, nobody was working down on Dexter. Kilo and Z were moving with agitated strides between the parking lot and the interior of the Coney, looking a little bewildered. There weren't many custos in the store; they were all moving in and sitting down for a minute or two, and then leaving when they realized they were not about to get served.

As it happened, there was no dope to sell. Earlier in the day, Loc had left Jeremiah (only fifteen at the time) with the whole day's stash of heroin, with a street value of around $5,000, and had gone to visit his girlfriend in a different neighborhood. No one, though, had shown up to transfer the remaining bundles of heroin to Kilo and Z for the afternoon shift. By 1:30 P.M., Malachi had come to the Coney. He had just ordered a grilled ham and cheese sandwich when Kilo came in and quietly told him that Jeremiah had gotten locked up and that they hadn't found the bundles of heroin yet. Malachi looked disappointed but was hardly in despair. With the bundles lost, he had much less to worry about than the kids working under him, who would have to make paying him back their first priority when fronted a day's stash.

Malachi sat and ate his sandwich without saying much, then stood and leaned against the condiment counter. He was serious and measured in a way that was disquietingly novel for everyone. "Look, dog," he said to both Z and Kilo, not really distinguishing between the two, "go down there and find out what's going on. Just go look around, man." They walked off on their reconnaissance mission.

An hour later, Kilo and Z came back and said that they had looked everywhere. They had searched in the basement and around the alley behind the four-family flat where Jeremiah lived, where Loc and he had been selling. Z had talked to Jeremiah's mother, and she had said that the cops had taken everything. She also said that they had charged Jeremiah with a violation of the controlled substances act and that they had gotten all the dope. All eighteen bundles were gone. Meanwhile, Loc said that he didn't know what had happened. Z and Kilo said that Loc had seemed nervous when they talked, uncertain about what to say; they supposed he might feel responsible for what had happened, and told him that he should meet them and Malachi at the Coney within a half an hour.

Normally, the boys working a shift will stash six bundles (of twelve packs each) and work from that amount, grabbing frequently from some inconspicuous location, such as an overgrown gathering of weeds or an obliquely arranged dumpster, as customers come and go. They will then conceal the big bag containing the rest of the dope available for that day somewhere else—somewhere less accessible, usually in a vacant house. Consequently, no one could understand why the police caught Jeremiah with the big bag instead of the six bundles. Antonio was sitting in the back of the room. "It's not like he going to be stashing his six and then reaching into the big bag over and over again," he said. "Hell, no!"

Antonio was the first to say, as we were sitting around, that Jeremiah's mother may have been scheming to abscond with the heroin in the big stash. He figured that she might have known where Jeremiah had stowed it and had seized the opportunity, presented to her when Jeremiah was taken away by the cops, to keep it for herself. Everyone knew that she had been fighting an addiction to raw and was hard up for money as well. And as Malachi, Antonio, and others stood around figuring their potential losses, it became more and more clear that this was a strong likelihood.

In the midst of this speculation, Loc walked through the doors. Malachi smiled crookedly at him, with a touch of paternalistic disappointment. Loc stood in front of him and said, "I don't know, dog," and shook his head. Malachi was silent and looked out the window. Loc said, "Man, the hook . . . man, they must have. . . ." He fell silent, shook his head, and shrugged, and Malachi looked back up at him, letting the quiet envelop and constrict around him. "It got to be in the basement somewhere," Loc finally speculated. "Somewhere way in the back. . . . That's the only place it could be."

When Loc left to go back to the house to continue looking for the dope, Malachi said that it seemed to him that Loc might have been lying. "You could see that he wanted to lie about it, so he could hang on to it, and then he thought better of it at the last second. . . . Little bitch!" Malachi seemed to take pleasure in his analysis of Loc's possible motivations.

As Malachi and Antonio talked, dope customers came in and stood in the corners, or sat in booths. Malachi would eventually tell them, in muted tones, that there wouldn't be anything that afternoon, and they would rush out of the Coney, their minds turning about where else to go. "How you gonna let someone who not even on the shift do you like that," resumed Malachi. "I swear to God on everything I love, if his mama don't give up that shit, I am gonna take a baseball bat over there. And I will beat the shit out of her. I swear dog. I'm taking a baseball bat over there." Antonio put his fists on top of one another and swung them down, mimicking the clubbing that he imagined Malachi would give her. Malachi shook his head with resignation, and then he and Antonio left the restaurant to go find Z and Kilo, to see if they could talk to Jeremiah's mother face-to-face. Malachi wanted to get to the bottom of things as soon as possible so that he could go home and take a nap.

Later that night the restaurant was bustling with activity. Malachi and Antonio were back, along with Z, Kilo, and a collection of other young men and boys from the area—Timmy, Marley, Oscar, Hector, Shell, and Rabbit. Kilo and Antonio were flipping cards onto the table between them, betting single dollars on hands of spades. No one had found the missing bag of bundles, even after Malachi and Antonio had been through Jeremiah's mother's apartment, tearing through her things and threatening her with retribution if she wouldn't relinquish the bundles that they were still sure she had taken.

At some point, Antonio and Kilo started arguing over how much money had been on the table in front of them and to whom it belonged. Antonio insisted that he had been shorted $13 somehow, but Kilo wouldn't give him the money. "Come on, I'm serious," Antonio finally said. "That's mine. I need that thirteen, dog." "I'm serious too, nigga," said Kilo. "You lost that shit!" Kilo stood and shoved the cash deep into his pocket, and Antonio grabbed Kilo by his pocketed wrist and tried to pull his hand out. Suddenly, in choreographed unison, they each lunged and grabbed the other by the biceps. They leaned into one another like exhausted boxers, and each tried to shove the other back. They grunted and groaned in each other's grasps, were sweating and straining, slipping off and losing ground, and winning it back with bullheaded determination. The others got out of their seats to avoid being hit as Antonio and Kilo dragged each other across the floor. Malachi tried to get them to stop. "You all acting stupid," he yelled into the fray from the sidelines, laughing but also a little concerned for their safety. "Alright!" Antonio finally yelled. Kilo got off Antonio, pulled $6 out of his pocket, threw the money at Antonio, and then reached down and helped him up. They shook hands and again sat down where they had been before, both completely spent, breathing heavily with their arms over their heads.

Without being asked, Polly put two cups of water through the lazy Susan and yelled, "Are you going to keep playing or are you tired?" As Antonio fetched the two cups of water from Polly and brought them back to his and Kilo's table, two police officers sauntered through the door. Both were dressed in the deep blue uniforms of the Detroit Police Department, and one wore a wool knit cap that drooped over to the side. He came in with his flashlight drawn. "You all in here to buy something to eat? . . . What you all doing in here?" No one said anything. "Oh, it gets real quiet around here when the police show up."

"Isn't that how it's supposed to be?" Hector said.

"I don't know," the cop answered, and frowned, cocking his head to the side. "If you not eating, then you loitering, and I can't have that." He noticed Antonio standing right in front of him.

"Hey Antonio! How's it going?" he said. "You gonna act like you don't know me now? Is that what's up? Where's your brother? I know you ain't up to no good in here."

"I'm up in here waiting on my steak hoagie!" Antonio yelled back, still out of breath. "For real!" he said, gesturing back toward the kitchen and Polly, who was watching through the glass with an amused smile.

"Oh, well, in that case you must be eating a lot of steak hoagies, 'cuz I see you up in here just about every day. You not going to live past twenty-five eating like that. I don't wanna see that no more. You all be up in here too much, and I know it ain't right. And I'm gonna clean this place up. I'm making it my little project. Just so you all know." The other cop, with flattened hair that was stuck to his head in baroque waves, yelled up to Hector, who was standing at the lazy Susan messing with Polly, "Where do you live?"

"I stay on Glynn, right across the street."

"Oh, alright," the cop said appeasingly.

"What about you in the green, the white guy?" the cop asked, looking at me.

I told them that I was a student at a local university, and that I worked with the boys there.

"Well, you got your work cut out for you here," he said.

Antonio, excited from the interrogation, started yelling defensively, "Yeah, that's my GED coach! I'm going to do some tutoring. We out to go tutor."

"It's almost midnight!" the cop bellowed with a laugh.

By this time three other police cars had arrived. Two more sets of white uniformed officers had come into the restaurant. One of them smiled as he walked through the door and said, sort of sarcastically, "Hey, what's going on in here?" Antonio quickly grabbed the food that Polly had prepared for him, and we pushed past the two white cops and got into the car. The black officer with the wavy hair came out after us and knocked on my window. "I just wanted to let you know," he said, "this place is full of narcotics activity. There are drugs moving around here all the time; in fact, they are selling narcotics right out of this store." I nodded, trying to look impressed with this news. "I just wanted to let you know that you should be very careful out here," he said. "These kids will single you out, and they will rob you blind."

End Times

By the beginning of the following week, the crew working for Malachi had returned to the Coney Island. But with the lost supply, the increased vigilance of the cops, and customers seeking dope where there would be less heat, things were pretty moribund. Some drug customers weren't sure what was going on, and would wander in and linger for a while before leaving again, swiveling around, uncertain in what direction to go.

Loc would have to work for some time to pay off the debt that the lost raw represented to Malachi and the other Dexter Boys working there. It would be weeks before he would make any money. Hector, Kilo, and Z would also take a financial hit from the missing bundles, as each was expected to pay Malachi before they could take any profit for themselves. Given his struggles to support his children and the outstanding warrants that he had long delayed dealing with because of the likely consequent jail time, Hector was particularly upset about having to pay Malachi for Loc's mistake. And he was nervous about all the attention that the police had been paying to the Coney and the entire trade on Dexter.

I was sitting with him and his brother Shell when an older woman with white hair framing her smooth dark skin came limping into the restaurant with her cane draped over her forearm. She was wearing a long black dress with a matching wide-brimmed hat. "Hi y'all," she said to Hector and Shell, both of whom said, "Hi, Mrs. Morris," in polite, subdued voices. "Do you know if it's too late to order breakfast?" she asked Shell. He assured her that she could order until three in the afternoon. "I heard something about my nephew," she said. Shell and Hector nodded. "Do you know if they picked up Jeremiah?" "Yeah, they got him last week—on Friday," Hector said. She slammed her cane on the floor and yelled, "Damn! . . . I'm sorry y'all, I know you got to do what you got to do, but I just can't take this anymore! Damnit." Her cane struck the floor again, and she stood looking out the window. Hector and Shell were silent while she waited for her food, and quietly wished her a happy day as she left.

"Damn, you just subbing for someone," said Shell after she was gone. "It ain't even your shift, and you get caught up. . . . That motherfucker is *hit!*"

Polly leaned over the counter and yelled to the guys in the restaurant, "Hey, I need a phone card! Shell! I need you to get me a phone card!" As Shell skipped out of the store to get a phone card from across the street, an older black man with oversize sunglasses came in, with a bucket, scrub brush, and squeegee under his arm. As he made his way around the perimeter of the interior and moved his equipment over the windows, an old-school Buick driven by a middle-aged white woman pulled into the lot. We could see her bright red fingernails through the Coney window and that a young man was sitting next to her, probably her son. Before Hector had even noticed them, the white kid had hopped out of the car and had charged into the restaurant looking to get served. Hector was impatient with his lack of discretion.

"Get the fuck out; go cop from somebody else," he shouted. The white man backed through the doors without daring to look up.

Since then, Hector had been carrying on with a sense of outrage about white drug customers and had managed to pull the man washing windows into the fray. "Here you is, born with all this money, all these options, you going to college and shit, and you decide you wanna go and do raw," he complained. "That's some stupid shit. I mean, we got our own problems, with crack and shit. . . . I know that. Shit, look at some of these motherfuckers from around here."

"Yeah, but crack is done played out," the window washer said. "They ain't so many people messing with that shit. Now you see all these people from Ann Arbor and stuff. I been washing windows out there, seeing all kinds of stuff." The window washer held his tools to his sides and laughed, "Heroin is a terrible thing, man."

"But these white folks got all these options," said Hector. "They stupid, man."

"They not appreciative, you know," said the window washer, as Loc and Kilo came in and sat down. "Like these guys that own this here; you see how I'm doing such a good job. They not going to get service like this from everyone. You see me wiping the corners, going the extra mile to do the job right. But these people don't appreciate what I do, you know. And they making all this money up in here; you know, they not going to be paying me right. That's what I'm saying, white folks just be taking that shit for granted. Shit. They just be shooting up, popping pills, and shit anyways."

Later in the day, after Hector and the window washer had left the store, Loc spotted a black-and-gold cruiser going down Providence toward Dexter; it looked to be headed for the Coney lot. Thinking that it was Woodrow, who Loc and Kilo knew would give them a hard time for loitering, both stood and dashed to the counter to place orders and get tickets from Polly. I was already eating a heaping ham sandwich and sat looking at my food. We were all braced for the imminent entry of the police, so none of us noticed Hector standing on the corner outside, right in front of them. When the police pulled into the lot, Hector tried to play it cool, but they threw him against the car and started digging around in his pockets. Loc and Kilo didn't wait around for their food; they left with their hands in their pockets, walking with stiff legs toward the liquor store across the street. I sat up in my booth seat and watched the police pull a small baggie out of Hector's jacket pocket. His head dropped heavily, at a right angle from his broad shoulders, and the police wrenched his wrists up behind him and cuffed them together. He turned back to look through the square windows of the Coney Island as a hand on top of his head pushed him into the police car. "Call my brother," he mouthed.

As I collected my trash, Polly looked at me through the reflecting glass and shook her head. I moved toward the window and shouted through, "It's sad, isn't it?"

"*No!*" she shouted back through the glass. "I think it's fucking hilarious. . . . I mean how stupid do you have to be? They walk across the street, like, a thousand times a day. You think the cops don't know everything that they do in here? I know everything they do, so you better be sure that the cops know. . . . I mean, there are more crackheads in here than there are customers." I asked why, if she thinks that this is so hilarious, she treats them so well. "I mean, they're all cool. Hector is cool. But they know what they're going to get if they're doing this. You can't feel sorry for them." Still, Polly's callousness sounded forced. Her smile was mechanical and unhappy.

That evening, Hector's Aunt Patty came to the Coney to cop a pack of heroin and see if anyone there had a pair of pliers. She walked in holding her left hand in the air and slumped into a chair, looking exhausted and dope sick. She had slammed her finger in a car door, and her wedding ring was deeply embedded in the broken and swelling tissue around it. She wanted the pliers so that she could cut the ring before it disappeared completely into her discolored finger. Kilo, Z, and Malachi were all there, but none of us had pliers. In any case, we could tell that they would only have made things worse.

"Never mind," she said. "What about a pack? I'm sick."

Malachi said he didn't have anything and told her that he was shutting the spot down. It was too hot; time to move on. A few of us asked if we could take her to the hospital, but she refused flatly, putting her head in her right hand, keeping her left elevated. "Just all this shit," she said. "And now Hector gone. I'm mad as hell. 'Cuz he constantly stays in jail. I wish he would go to work, you know, or try to do something different. Get a job. Take care of his kids. He's got two cute little boys, you know, and yet. Ain't nothing in these streets, you done see that, you been in the penitentiary all these times already. You been locked up five birthdays, your mama sick with lupus. When you going to wake up? You realize every time you get in, you ain't got nobody to do nothing for you. 'Cuz ain't nobody got nothing. So what's up? Why you so ignorant? Can't nobody tell him nothing. He think he know everything. And I can relate to that, 'cuz I was like that at one time, but I keep telling him, 'You don't know everything, baby.' Somebody can always change something. Maybe he'll straighten up this time. I'm going to try to go see him tomorrow. . . . So . . . I'm going to try."

Patty pulled her head out of her hands and pushed herself up from the table. "I'm going to try, I'm going to try," she said, as she walked out the door into the early dark night.

We followed her out into the parking lot, where Shell and Rabbit were outside the double doors. Rabbit had just swallowed his first Ecstasy pill with a whiplash swig from a bottle of Hennessy cognac. Recently after the settlement of a lawsuit that had netted them nearly $100,000, Rabbit and his mother had moved from the Dexter neighborhood to Eastpointe, a modest suburb to the northeast of Detroit. On most evenings and weekends he would make his way down and west toward Dexter, to hang with the Dexter Boys, with whom he would often spend the night, either on the couch at Rodney's house or with one of the other Dexter Boys who still lived in the neighborhood.

Shell had also just popped an E, for which the Dexter Boys had been developing a big appetite over the winter. The theretofore strictly suburban drug, associated among the Dexter Boys with "freaky white girls" at crazy rave dance parties, had been growing in popularity among poor young African Americans all over the city.

While we were standing around in the parking lot, two white narcotics officers spotted us in the white light shining through the Coney's windows. They bounced their car into the lot at a sharp angle and came to a lurching stop a couple of feet in front of Rabbit. Dressed in plain, hip-hop-inflected clothing, two of the white cops who had been in the Coney Island a few nights before stretched Rabbit out against their car, emptied his pockets of $50, but found no drugs. Though they looked at me with particular disappointment, the cops didn't ask any of the rest of us to make the spread-eagled lean against their car—a seemingly arbitrary grace. But when they were through with Rabbit, the police threatened to "beat the shit out of" the other boys if they caught them loitering there again.

After the officers had climbed, red faced, back into their cruiser and sped off, Rabbit and the few others stood around the restaurant vestibule lamenting their luck at having been harassed by the police. Malachi reprimanded them for being too conspicuous. "Y'all acting stupid out here. You know they gonna come fuck with you if you just be out here like that. . . . Damn!" Malachi and Kilo walked across the street and left in Malachi's green Chevy Tahoe, the gold rims shining in the darkness. Shell, Rabbit, Z, and I drifted into the Coney Island.

As Shell, Z, and I sat down, Rabbit remained standing, shaking his tightly braided head, pushing his bony arms into his pockets and complaining bitterly about losing the $50 that his mother had given him, which the cops had pocketed when they left the scene. He walked over to the video game in the front corner, which was always blaring the same amalgamation of German house music and Detroit electronica, and spun the steering wheel with a deep lunge and loud bang.

Rabbit began pacing up and down the spaces in between the orange plastic booths and white Formica tables—dusted with bread crumbs and awash with ketchup smears, puddles of ranch dressing, and gyro sauce—which reflected the pink neon tubes that line the corners of the ceilings and bathed the room in hot light. His eyes looked glazed, and he was mumbling incessantly and low, rolling his tongue over his chapped lips between every few words.

I was sitting in one of the booths, across from Shell, as Rabbit began to preach ecstatically in the aisles, to no one in particular. "I'm from Dexter, and I ain't never had *nothing*!" he said, as he waved both of his hands, flashing the Dexter D. "People just don't know what I'm saying. Dexter forever, baby! I'm from Dexter, and I ain't never had *nothing*! You know?"

Shell, who had much more experience with Ecstasy and was sitting calmly, said, "Sit down, man. Don't let yourself get all crazy. Just sit down, and think about a bitch or something."

"Hell, *no*, man!" answered Rabbit. "Fuck that. I'm from Dexter, the real deal, and I need to say my piece. . . . We going to go get this money! Shell. We Dexter *forever*! We going to get this money! We be out in Bloomfield, baby! We be getting that money, be out in Farmington Hills."[3]

Shell spoke to me in a loud whisper: "This is Rabbit's first time with the E. You can see it making him talk, goddamn. You can see I'm a lot calmer."

Rabbit kept at it. "We all from Dexter here, and we ain't never had nothing!" Several younger boys came into the Coney. They looked like elementary school students, and Rabbit assailed them as well. "Don't fuck around with this dope game, y'all," he said, as the boys looked askance in embarrassment and went to the counter to order. "Y'all need to stay in school, for real!" he continued. "You need to be down at the boys club, practicing your Js and shit, know what I'm saying? 'Cuz you all need to get the fuck out of here, you know," he said, flashing the Dexter D. "Little punk-ass motherfuckers never had shit." He repeated with rhythmic regularity, "We from Dexter, and we ain't never had nothing."

As I was sitting on the booth bench in the dining room, while the sky grew black outside and the fluorescent lights overhead shone with more intensity on straggling Dexter Boys coming through the Coney Island restaurant, a once but no longer heroin spot, the site of frequent police intervention and subtle mediation between black drug dealers and white Albanian owners, Rabbit's riff on the relationship between the city and suburbs rang like the lyric of a Greek chorus.

With his chanting invocation of Dexter, "Dexter forever," all dilated pupils and horizon gaze, Rabbit expressed a sense of intense loyalty to and a pleading statement of cultural and political identity around the Dexter neighborhood. He claimed a sense of pride and authenticity in conspicuous deprivation—"We all from Dexter here, and we ain't never had nothing"—and he imagined a future of collective good fortune.

In doing this, though, Rabbit was not simply imagining a departure from Dexter. He was not dreaming of a transcendent leap to the suburbs. Instead, he was articulating the nature of his and other Dexter Boys' understanding of the neighborhood as one characterized both by its opposition against the suburbs and its imminent potential permeability. He didn't imagine himself escaping Dexter (he and his family, after all, had already moved out of the city) so much as in a continual and fluid movement between Dexter and the counterpoised suburbs. Dexter, though defined by its deprivation, is where Rabbit made at least some of his money and is the home to which he was ever returning, to be with other Dexter Boys, to sleep in his hood. As Rabbit rambled in the dining area of the Coney Island, with Larry and Mikey leaning over the money troughs, their ears titled toward the holes in the glass wall, he expressed a desire to be ever engaged in a de Certeauan walk between city and suburb.[4]

In a context where to be from Dexter is to be in a kind of constitutional categorical opposition to the suburbs and people from the suburbs—"to have nothing" and be surrounded by plenitude, as it were—the Dexter Boys' occupancy of the Coney Island over the fall, winter, and spring months of 2001 might be taken as a reclamation of neighborhood and community space and small business participation. Or it might be understood as a hostile takeover. There are certainly shades of this evident in the Dexter Boys' proprietary habitation of the restaurant, their abuse of its amenities, and their insistence on mixing drinks and smoking weed within it. And, of course, by making a space that to some extent signifies their exclusion from entrepreneurialism and from the benefits of small business ownership, the site of their own enterprise, the Dexter Boys' occupancy of the Coney Island might be taken as a classic act of everyday resistance.

But at the same time, what happened over the course of these several months entailed more than resistance, as an analytic category, customarily conveys. The Dexter Boys were not simply seizing the Coney through force and intimidation, or through subversive strategy. For the Dexter Boys working there, the illicit and parallel occupancy of the Coney Island was both a resistive *and* reconciliatory gesture. The Coney Island was not a front for drug dealing or money laundering. Neither Larry nor his father ever invited or paid the drug dealers who worked in their store, and they would never admit to permissiveness about what happened there. But relationships between the family that owned the restaurant and the dealers who worked there were hardly acrimonious. Rather, as with the relationship between the Coney, the community, and the dealers generally, they were marked by degrees of acquiescence and assistance, and were rife with mutual jealousy, respect, affection, guarded suspicion, and sympathy.

Through practices that were sometimes willful, sometimes incidental, and frequently consequential, the bulletproof transparent partition in the Coney Island—the defining characteristic of the space, separating owners from occupants—became for the Dexter Boys, for a while at least, like Lewis Carroll's looking glass: "all soft, like gauze." With all the messy cooperation and rich analogy between store owners and drug dealers, those purchasing hot dogs and those purchasing heroin packs, white customers in cars and black customers in booths, frustrated and gratified police officers waiting in the back, city residents and suburban commuters coming to cop, the Dexter Boys' occupancy of the Coney Island represented the carving out of a novel kind of space: a space whose soft divisions and gauzy borders troubled the distinction between suburban owner and neighborhood occupant. Here, as keen cultural and political subjects capable of delicate acts of representation and reflection, the Dexter Boys had made a space somewhere in between.

Coda: In a Parking Lot

Rabbit was still sermonizing as he, Shell, and I piled into my car and drove north, toward the house up on Seven Mile Road where Rodney had been staying for the past several weeks, trying to make a go of it away from Dexter. When he answered the door, Rodney held an SK close to his side, with the long black barrel pointing toward the floor. Though his finger curled around the trigger loop, and he carried the gun to suggest its possibly imminent use, he held it like one does an object that they are simply moving from place to place. He leaned slightly to the side, away from the gun, to relieve his arm of the burden of its weight, and it seemed almost to trail after him, like a baby blanket dragged along for comfort. While still menacing, the weapon reflected a worried light in Rodney's eyes.

He ushered Rabbit, Shell, and me through the door and into the house. Rodney, Sheed, Antonio, and a few others from Dexter had rented the four-bedroom house in a quiet working-class neighborhood in northwest Detroit, and had been using it as a base of operations to sell weed back in the neighborhood. Rodney shut the door behind us and lifted the blinds with his index finger to make sure that no one had followed us into the neighborhood. The kitchen was big and clean, and the counters were covered in new white Formica. On a butcher block in the middle were a couple of pounds of marijuana that contacts of the Dexter Boys had bought from traffickers in Arizona. The boys at the house were sitting around the table and laboriously filling little dime sacks with the Mexican weed and then pressing them closed between their thumbs and fingers.

Annie, Rodney's girlfriend, sat in the corner of a couch in the living room with her arms out to her sides. She and Rodney had been seeing each other for the last month, which amounted to quite a commitment from the usually romantically transient Rodney. They had met at a club in the city, and she was immediately smitten, finding him distractingly beautiful and alluringly mysterious. Annie had grown up in a stable working-class home and had never dated anyone like Rodney before. For his part, Rodney had never been this way with other women, as long as I had known him, and even according to his own reluctant admission. Not long after they had gotten together, he told me that he thought he might be in love with her. "She's real beautiful," he boasted unsentimentally. "A model."

It was the combination of his gentleness and roughness that in part attracted him to her. But in the early days of their relationship, especially, it was not unusual for Rodney to get carried away with overcompensating public demonstrations of his independence from Annie. When the three of us walked in, he pushed the automatic rifle under the couch beside her feet and told us not to pay attention to Annie. "She don't know what the fuck is going on," he exclaimed. She rolled her eyes, smirked, and said something under her breath.

Rodney and I sat down at the dining room table, where there were playing cards and beer bottles strewn about. I was wondering why Rodney had carried a gun to the door, or why such a huge gun in any case, and asked him if he was OK. "I'm glad you're here, dog," he said quietly, so that the others in the room couldn't hear. "I been real 'nointed, man," Rodney said, by which he meant some combination of paranoid and agitated. This had become a frequent, almost patterned complaint for Rodney in our private conversations, especially since he had been spending less time on Dexter, trying to find a better way to make more money more quickly, and when he figured talking about his stress might help alleviate it. "They're not fucking around anymore," he said, invoking an Orwellian other. For the previous several months, federal agents from the Drug Enforcement Agency had been after Rodney's erstwhile brother-in-law, his sister Julie's boyfriend, and Rodney was convinced that it was only a matter of time before the feds would be led to him. Rodney was always reticent about his brother-in-law, and that he was telling me all this meant that things must be serious. He rubbed his hand across his belly. "And my stomach hurts, man."

"You're sick?"

"Stressed out, dog." Rodney was prone to stress, but since his release from the juvenile detention facility he had been episodically riddled with anxiety.

Ostensibly, his stress was about making money. After pulling himself out of the heroin rotation on Dexter, he had paid a bunch into the weed that was on the butcher table. But he was still waiting for more of the shipment to come in and was in a financial hole. Meanwhile, he was paying Timmy to get the weed off for him down on Dexter but wasn't happy about their financial agreement. He had been alternately binge drinking himself into oblivion and, in more sober moments, worrying about how to find a more stable source of income.

Antonio, who had been smoking a blunt in the living room with Shell and Rabbit, started fussing about going out to a club. Rodney said that he was on the grind and didn't want to go. But eventually, all four went off to Goal Post. Annie decided to drive back to her mother's house in Wyandotte, south of Detroit.

When Rodney and Antonio were tired of the thumping music and each had sufficiently enjoyed having a desultory body writhe over their laps, they stood and shuffled toward the door. Rodney walked in front, and Antonio followed behind him. There was the usual logjammed crowd around the entrance, with people moving into the club and out into the cold spring night. As Rodney and Antonio drew closer to the club's vestibule, the foot traffic became more congested, with the big bodies of comers and goers pressing against one another, pushing forward and backward like ocean waves against a wading bather. In the dappled darkness, the dimensions of people's bodies and faces collapsed into overlapping, interwoven silhouettes. Rodney and Antonio stepped from the warm, claustrophobic fray through the door and into the night air, and as the silhouettes parted and began again to expand and differentiate with mass and color, one of them, somewhere in front of Rodney and Antonio, collapsed suddenly to the ground. Across the parking lot, in the far corner, the night attendant looked from her square booth, but held still. The fallen man lay with his face down against the asphalt, as blood trickled through a round bullet wound in the back of his head and spread from his face onto the black ground beneath him.

11

Being Seen

That invisibility to which I refer occurs because of a peculiar disposition of the eyes of those with whom I come in contact. A matter of the construction of their inner eyes, those eyes with which they look through their physical eyes upon reality. I am not complaining, nor am I protesting either. It is sometimes advantageous to be unseen, although it is most often rather wearing on the nerves.

—Ralph Ellison, *Invisible Man*

"You see that building with the red roof?" Rodney asked. He had called me from a motel somewhere in Dearborn, but he wouldn't say its name over the phone and he wouldn't tell me the address.

"Yeah, I see it."

"OK, I want you to turn left on the second street after the building with the red roof," he said. "Now you see that building right there with the green walls? Pull in right there." I turned into the parking lot of a dingy-looking motel off Michigan Avenue, just beyond the border of Dearborn and Detroit.

"Yeah, I see you," he said. "Pull in the driveway right there and drive over to the far side of the building . . . way over to the right." I did as he told me. "Yeah, that's right, now park right there. Just pull up and park."

He told me to look up, and I could see a hand curled around the edge of a thick green and white curtain. He pressed his palm against the window to show me that it was him, and I went up to the room and knocked on the door. Rodney pulled the door open and hid behind it as I came inside. All the lights were off, and QVC was on television, where a woman with hair like a frosted Christmas ornament was selling something shiny and available for a limited time only. In the television's glow, the room was an unsettling con-coction of dark greens and shadowy corners. This was his third day here; since checking in, he'd left the room only for brief trips to get more food. There were a few snacks on the table in the corner—some corn chips and a dirty tray from a local Middle Eastern restaurant. He had a black garbage bag with a few pieces of clothing in it, and an extra pair of tennis shoes.

"Some shit happened," he said, with a half smile, as he sat down on the edge of one of two small, crippled beds in the room.

"You want to tell me about it?" I asked. "I don't know," he said. "It's deep, man." Rodney got off the bed and walked around the room; he pushed the corn chips bag across the table and tossed it into the wastebasket. He un-folded the clothes in the garbage bag and then folded them again. "The other night, at the club," he finally continued, "somebody got shot."

"Somebody died?" I asked.

"Yeah, somebody got killed, dog. But that's all I'm saying, man." I looked at him and raised my eyebrows, inviting him to tell me more about precisely what had happened. Rodney shook his head and let out a nervous little laugh. "This is one of them things you don't need to know everything about."

"I don't even want to know what happened, man," I said, turning toward the television.

Rodney sat down again, and put his now-bearded chin into his cupped hand and gazed at the jewelry on television.

"Look," he finally continued, "we was up at the club, man. Coming out of there, and this nigga got shot."

"Somebody got shot in Goal Post?"

"No, dog, right there in the parking lot. We was all on the way out, and this nigga got shot." Rodney was now staring at me with his eyes round like dark moons, looking wary about what my next question might be.

"Man," I started, and then demurred, not wanting to ask him to confirm or deny anything.

"So they're after Ton and me for that shit, dog."

"The hook is after you?"

"Hell yeah. We heard they got warrants for me and Ton. And then we don't know what the fuck is up with that nigga's people." Rodney hesitated and shrugged his shoulders. "That shit's just going to take care of itself," he

added, more quietly. "That's why I'm staying low," he said. Rodney told me
that he was planning to keep moving from motel to motel in the suburbs until he figured out what was really going on and what to do about the whole
mess. In the meantime, he wanted my help.

"I need you to do something for me," he said. "We trying to find somebody." Rodney handed me a small yellow receipt on the back of which he
had printed out a single first name. "You think you can help me find that?" I
turned the paper in my hand and thought of this person, who must in some
corner of her mind have suspected that somewhere, someone would have
her name, and might have already attached to it the gravest intentions.

Finally, and kind of desperately, I answered, "I can't even tell if that's a
woman's or a man's name."

"That's a woman's name, dog. Shit. How fucked up is you, man? We think
she seen what happened, and we need to find her; find where's she's at."

"To find her? What do you want to do with her, man?"

Rodney stood and messed with the folded clothing in the flickering green
light of the television. He shrugged and laughed in a way that sounded like
a puppy's whine. "I don't know, dog. I don't know what needs to happen. All
this shit's just up in the air right now."

"Don't do anything stupid, man," I offered, sort of stupidly.

"Who you telling? We know that this cat's people are going to be trying to
find her, make sure she says what they want her to say, regardless of what
she actually seen. We can't have that shit, man. Nnnnoo!"

I looked again at the name on the wrinkled slip of paper, and told Rodney
that I didn't see how, with only a first name, he would be able to locate this
person.

"It's hard to just disappear," he said.

The Disappeared

In 1963, in a published letter, the writer James Baldwin warned his dark-
skinned nephew that the oppressive element of U.S. society, the white
ruling class, doesn't even see him. He encouraged the young man to understand that his "innocent countrymen . . . do not yet really know" that he exists.[1] In the intervening decades, the battle for social justice in the black

community has often been pitched around matters of social visibility. For many years, Ralph Ellison would say, African Americans have struggled to be seen with the "inner eyes" of the white world.

For young black men, the problem of visibility seems especially resonant. The much discussed and fretted over urban or homeboy style of young African American men is largely in the service of becoming conspicuous and behaving conspicuously. While many, and perhaps especially African American cultural critics, lament the apparently unwitting minstrelsy of the hypervisible young African American man, and see his aesthetics as only more proof that too many of his kind are the ultimate butt of capitalism's inside joke, the compulsion against stylistic understatement is powerful. Motivation toward the most gaudy, conspicuous aesthetics—entailing the immediate display of their spoils, outrageous, blinding bling around fingers hanging on to steering wheels in tricked-out rides that can be heard coming from five blocks away—is many things, but most obviously and simply, a re-fusal to disappear.[2]

For African Americans in the drug trade, though, a kind of shadowy disappearance—controlled but never complete self-erasure—is also an im-portant capacity. As the places in the city that they inhabit embody a para-doxical institutional visibility and invisibility—where houses are spots but also homes, and retail restaurants and liquor stores are just these but also something else—the bodies of young African Americans involved in the drug trade in Detroit are, like pulsars, constantly shifting between visibility and invisibility. And like ghosts, young African Americans in the Detroit dope game inhabit a subjective twilight, living always with an awareness of their own potential slippage into a crepuscular haze, where they might go to prison, die, or just disappear. They are always, because of this, in some kind of confrontation with their own ends, seeing the world without themselves in it.

And as Ellison might suppose, invisibility isn't all bad. Young black drug dealers in the starkly divided and segregated postindustrial spaces of De-troit, for their customary movement between seen and unseen worlds, between their own visibility and invisibility, are not determined by the struc-tural violence that seems in some lights so inexorably to have entrapped them. Their power over their own conspicuousness means, among other things, that they do not understand themselves to be locked into a simple, binary social order where they would be bound to the margins of society. As so-phisticated social actors, they are too agile for that.

Rodney and Antonio were huddled inside a brick house in west Detroit. An-tonio's friend, whom everyone called Pork, was a union construction worker and had been renting the place for the previous several months. The sun was shining brightly through the leafless trees and into the living room of the house. But the two brothers stayed away from the windows. Rodney had given up his short-lived itinerant life in suburban motels a few days earlier, and despite the weight of constant anxiety wrapped around him now, he seemed almost giddy to be out of his self-imposed seclusion. Since leaving the last motel, he and some of his closest friends from Dexter, Sheed among them, had been trying to locate the woman whose name was on the back of the receipt. Not surprisingly, with few leads and nobody whom they would want to approach with inquiries, they hadn't had any luck.

So now they were assuming a different approach. I was sitting in the liv-ing room of the house talking with Sheed, who had been hanging around, and Annie, who had stopped by on her way to class at a local community col-lege. Sheed's younger brother Little was on the floor in front of us playing with small plastic soldiers. Rodney and Antonio had been sitting off to the side on the floor, with their backs against a wall, talking to one another in low, soft voices, and occasionally cupping their hands over the other's ears and whispering. Neither Annie nor Sheed paid any attention.

At one point, the two brothers suddenly jumped to their feet and left the room, disappearing into an adjacent bedroom and shutting the door behind them. They emerged about ten minutes later, each counting out money in their hands. Antonio sat down on the floor in front of a coffee table, and fin-ished flipping through the cash and stacking it on the table. He slid the money into his hand and curled it into a ball before sticking it in his pocket, telling us all he'd be back in a bit and hurrying out the door.

About half an hour later he returned. He sat down on the couch and laid a police report onto the coffee table, smoothing the fold creases with his palm. "Let me see that, dog," said Rodney, grabbing it and bolting to his feet to study it more closely. Antonio got up and walked around the room behind Rodney, reading in a whisper over his shoulder and pointing at the report. The two were quiet for a spell, as they struggled to decipher the significance of this document, purchased for $2,400 from a friend of a friend who happened to work as a clerk in the police department. Antonio snatched the paper back from Rodney and read it again. They disappeared once more into the side room and came out a couple of minutes later, bobbing up and down like kids at a party waiting for cake and ice cream. Rodney thrust his lower jaw out and pursed his lips. "Oh, we got this shit!" he nearly yelped with excitement. "Look at this," said Rodney, holding the document in front of me. "Look at where they supposed to list the witnesses. Look, the report says that there was just one. Only one witness! And then it says that she wasn't even close to what happened! She can't hold no water!"

Antonio tittered nervously. "For real, what she say can't hold no water." Rodney was positively beaming at this point. With only one witness, he figured, it wouldn't matter what had happened that night in the strip club parking lot. It also wouldn't matter who had seen (or thought they had seen) what. Ultimately, it would be this witness's word against his. Rodney said he thought that they could beat the case, if only they could hire a half-decent lawyer.

The road out to Jackson, Michigan, is part of the major land freight link between Detroit and Chicago. As the freeway leaves Detroit, it runs through a deep trough that was unceremoniously cut through established residential neighborhoods to make way for the interstate. Heading west into Dearborn, the highway passes the old Rouge River Plant to the south, with its now-emblematic smokestacks and rows of shed roof hangers. Then it crosses Route 39, which heads north toward the suburban high-rise headquarters of both Chrysler and Ford Motor Corporation, which one can see in the distance, sparkling in the afternoon sunlight. Heading further west, toward Metro Airport in Romulus (a working-class community that sits adjacent to the sprawling network of airport tarmacs), drivers pass parts suppliers and subsidiary companies to the auto industry, many at this point on the brink of closing. Past Ann Arbor, a college town that has recently attracted huge high-tech corporate investment (and lost a fair share as well), the freeway finally opens onto a typical Midwestern big-agro landscape. Cornfields outlined by old oak trees are on either side of the interstate, with the terrain becoming more undulating and forested the farther west one goes.

Rodney was slumped low in the passenger seat as we drove out of the city. And for him, the terrain was defined less immediately by shifts in prevalent industry than by his own relative visibility, which receded and reemerged as we passed through areas of dense and dark population, and then into the small pale townships of rural Michigan. Nothing was more nerve-racking for Rodney than the open road leading into Jackson, where it seemed that white police officers and state troopers always do their most effective profiling. But the discomfort of these rides had become part of Rodney's routine in the last several weeks, a small sacrifice to achieve his larger aims.

"I need ten thousand for the lawyer," he said, as we dipped into the westward lanes of the freeway, leaving Detroit. "That covers preparation and the actual trial, you know. Pretrial hearings, everything. But I already talked to my man, and I think we can beat this before it even gets to trail. So maybe less. Could be even less than that. All I got to do is keep grinding, stay low, stay on the run."

"Ten thousand?" I asked, wondering why he was sounding so optimistic.

"That ain't shit, dog. I can get that. And my man's worth it, dog. For real. He was the lawyer for Julie's man when he got into a mess a couple of years ago. He's a nutty cat. Smart as fuck. Need him. That's why I got this shit in Jackson banging."

In Jackson, Rodney explained, he had family. His aunts, uncles, and mother would be there sometimes. But his cousins were the key. He had two young cousins in particular, still in high school, who thought the world of him. "You know, 'cuz I'm from the city, and they're from out in Jackson, so they think I move real fast. For them, it's like I'm a straight-up gangster, ruling the world. They'll do anything for me. And these white bitches are their girls." Rodney gestured toward the sedan in front of us, driven by a couple of white high school–aged girls from Jackson. Rodney didn't introduce me to them when I picked him up in Detroit, and at this point I knew better than to ask too many questions. As we got into my car, Rodney just told me that we should follow the sedan—but not too closely.

"These are their girlfriends?" I asked.

"Fuck no, dog!" objected Rodney.

"You know like how my cousins worship me? Well, these bitches'll do anything for my cousins. You know, once you go black . . ." Rodney giggled. "So all the risky shit, we got them doing it. Plus, they white, so, you know. . . ."

Rodney's plan, already well into execution, was to ship pounds of weed that he was buying through contacts in the city into Jackson, where he could get his cousins to peddle the goods for a nominal fee. The market in Jackson was wide open, so it wouldn't take too long, Rodney figured, to make enough to pay for his representation in court. Initially, he and Antonio had been planning to make enough to pay for both of their defenses. But only a couple of weeks earlier, they learned that the charges against Antonio had been dropped, presumably because the witness had more definitely targeted Rodney. It was a huge relief to him that Antonio wouldn't be charged as well, but he hated the fact that he couldn't control what this supposed witness might say about him or what might happen as his calculated risk to turn himself in revealed either its wisdom or foolishness.

Not surprisingly, the weight of all this was crushing and was taking a toll. "I'm stressed, dog," he would say, with an air of incongruous invulnerability. Rodney complained during the ride that his stomach was constantly upset and asked if I had ideas about medications that he could take. He said that he couldn't sleep.

"What do you know about dreams?" he asked me, twenty miles outside of Jackson.

"What do you mean?"

"What does it mean when you dream about something? Like with a night-mare. You believe that means something?"

"I don't know, man."

"I been having fucked up dreams, dog. Real fucked up. Dreaming that people keep getting hurt, dog. Pshhhh. Too much stress."

Rodney groaned into the phone. "It's Rod, man."

"What time is it?"

"I don't know, three or some shit." I rubbed my eyes and looked at the clock next to my bed. Three-thirty in the morning.

"Where are you?"

"I'm out here, man," Rodney said, meaning Jackson, but not wanting to say anything more specific over the phone. His breathing was strange, un-even, like a gusty wind.

"Are you OK?"

"Not really, dog. I got shot in the hand. I mean, it ain't a problem, really. It's fine. But the shit hurts like fuck, dog." Rodney laughed spasmodically. "I just drank a fifth of vodka!"

Going to the hospital wasn't an option. He understood that the doctors there would have to report to the cops any gunshot wound that they treated. Rodney's willful invisibility, his effective disappearance, was suddenly in jeopardy. He knew that I was with a med student at the time and hoped that either she or I might have some idea about what he could do.

"How did it happen?" I stuttered, still waking up.

"Man, I was cleaning the motherfucker. Had it in my hand, had that bitch in a towel in my hand, and I was rubbing the shaft, man. That shit just fucking went off. Stupid as fuck, man. Damn! Hurts like a fucking bitch, dog!"

"Did the bullet go through any of your bones?"

"It went through the front, like down by my pinky, came out the back right in the middle, man. Ain't much left of the back of my hand, dog. Blew that shit out."

"You need antibiotics, man. Seriously, you could really get fucked up if you get some kind of infection from this."

"Fuck it, dog. My auntie works at the hospital, she can get some of that shit for me. I'm just going to take whatever she brings home." Rodney groaned again, and I could hear a crashing noise on the other end of the line.

"Did you fall?"

"No, man, I'm right here. I just tripped over this motherfucking towel. We got all these towels out, dog, to catch the blood."

"You should sit down, man, put your head between your legs. You're going to pass out."

"What the fuck?" Rodney laughed, sounding for a moment as if he had no injury, and announced that despite his ruptured, bleeding hand, he could still both stay invisible and was ready to strut his stuff on the street. "I ain't no sucker, dog. Pass out? Shit. I got an all-white jumpsuit on and I don't have a drop of blood on this bitch! You feel me?"

Rodney came back to Detroit a few weeks later—another trip to the city with the white girls from Jackson in tow. In the living room of the same brick house, he and Annie stood with their arms wrapped tightly around one another. His bandaged hand, looking like a poorly treated Civil War injury, hung off her waist. I asked him how the wound felt, and he enthusiastically offered to remove the gauze that he had been keeping over it. As he unwound layers of white material, the bloodstain grew wider and changed color from brown to black. The exit wound had scabbed, and the dried coagulated tissue looked like a pile of untamped asphalt. He held his hand out toward me; it shook like the palsied limb of an old man. He couldn't really move his pinky or ring fingers, but he wasn't too worried. Rodney had heard about a doctor in the city who wouldn't ask him too many questions and charged $350 in cash for X-rays and a quick consultation.

In the waiting room, Rodney recorded a silly, misspelled fake name and a series of random digits where his social security number was requested. The X-ray wasn't encouraging; Rodney's hand bones had been shattered into splinters, and would heal in a fractured gnarl unless he had surgery. But there was no infection. "Fuck it. This shit's going to be fine," he said, skipping out toward the car.

I dropped Rodney off at the brick house, where Annie had been watching television while we were gone. Rodney climbed into her small blue car and threw the passenger seat back as they drove away. After spending several hours at Annie's mother's house in Wyandotte, just south of the city along the Detroit River, he sped off in Annie's car to buy some food at a nearby McDonald's. He had made it only a couple of hundred yards when he noticed that a local police cruiser was following him. As the cops turned on their flashing lights, he raced the car forward, pulled into a driveway, and bumped and rattled onto the front lawn of an apartment complex in the otherwise quiet neighborhood, where most residents were already asleep. Rodney jumped out of the car, leaving the door swinging open, and ran into the closest building, hoping to lose the police. He was sailing through hallways, disappearing around dark corners. There must be a way out the back that would give him more room to run. He thought he might make it. But then, seemingly from nowhere, a burly white man with bare feet grabbed him around the neck and held him still. The Wyandotte cops caught up with him, cuffed him, and put him in the back of their car.

The Restoration

Months later, just before Rodney was led into the courtroom, I sat in the courthouse cafeteria with his lawyer. Annie and Rodney's sister Julie were also there, the four of us arranged around a metal dining table. Though he stood only about five and a half feet tall, not counting the shock of white hair that seemed suspended above his head, Rodney's defense counsel loomed over us. His meaty fingers, banded with multiple gold rings, gripped a cheap plastic pen, and he scribbled on to a yellow legal pad.

"OK," he began, after buying us all a round of orange juice, "I want to try and let you know what's going on here today." He told us that this would be Rodney's pretrial hearing, and carefully rehearsed the procedural details and ultimate ramifications of the day: if the presiding judge felt that there wasn't sufficient evidence to bring Rodney to a full-blown trial in the case, she could dismiss the charges right on the spot. This could be the end of the ordeal for Rodney. The months of living on the run, uncertainty, fear, and incarceration would finally come to an end. The thought of it was almost too much to bear for Annie. Indulging, for the first time in many months, in thoughts of a life lived in the open, with no more visits to the county jail, with Rodney able to touch and hold her, she broke into tears and held her face in her hands. Julie smiled gently and put her arm around Annie's shoulder.

The lawyer cleared his throat uncomfortably and continued: "Now, we got a strong case here, I think," he said. "It seems that they only have one witness. And in her deposition to the police she didn't always sound so secure about what she was saying. We think that she might not be so sure about things. So in this hearing today, it's my job to really exploit that. So you're going to see me asking her some pretty harsh questions. I'm not trying to trick her or anything, but it's important that we know exactly what she saw and that her story is straight. That's my job here today."

In the courtroom, the prosecuting attorney called her witness to the stand. I recognized the name from the slip of paper that Rodney had handed me in his motel room months before. A short, stocky African American woman, she walked stiffly up to the bench and took a seat. She was wearing a gray hooded sweatshirt and loose plaid pants popular among black men those days, with her hair braided in a diagonal pattern across her scalp. Before the hearing, she had been hovering nervously around the courtroom door, talking on her cell phone and avoiding eye contact with anyone there. Now she was forced to look out over a room of potential antagonists. Friends and relatives of the young man who had been murdered gathered in the back of the courtroom, leaning in and holding on to one another, desperate to get purchase on a sense of resolution. Rodney sat passively in a swiveling chair just beyond the bench partition and stared steadily in her direction. She held her head down and answered questions quietly and with few words.

"Were you employed as a parking lot attendant at the time?"

"Yes, ma'am."

"Were you working the night of the shooting?"

"Yes, ma'am."

Though Rodney's attorney was ready to employ every litigious trap in the book to undermine her testimony, she obviated his effort. With her eyes shifting around the room but alighting on nothing, she reported that she had no idea if Rodney might have been the shooter in the parking lot. Without resistance she agreed that this wasn't consistent with her deposition, but that it was the truth as best as she could remember. The friends and relatives of the deceased man grimaced and moaned in shock and disappointment. With all their suffering, even the hollow, grim solace of watching the courts imprison his potential killer was eluding them.

The next time I saw Rodney, he had been out of jail already for several weeks, and was pulled between a compulsion to prolong the celebration of his freedom with episodes of drinking and partying and the shuddering sense that he had just narrowly escaped spending the rest of his life in prison and should somehow turn things around for himself.

Antonio wasn't around. He had been in a terrible car accident with Rabbit and was now sitting in a prison cell in Saginaw, a few hours' drive north of the city. He and Rabbit had been driving around after a long night out and had been chased through the streets by another car, and then, with the police following closely behind, had flipped over as they tried to come off the freeway. Rabbit was killed instantly. Antonio walked away without a scratch, but was immediately put into jail and then sentenced to at least two years in prison for possession of a gun.

But Rodney was keeping his head up. He explained to me that he had a plan. "Real estate," he said. He wanted to start accumulating real estate in the city, and he wanted to start in the Dexter neighborhood. His hope was to begin by opening up a spot or two, having some of the guys from Dexter work in them, and then use the money to accumulate more property, thereby gradually moving from illegal to legal money. "First," he said, "I'm going to get that house on Wadsworth."

Later that day, Rodney and I paced up and down the empty porch of the Wadsworth house, trying to see behind the newspaper and plastic that his mother had taped on the windows years before. He rose onto his tiptoes and looked through the trapezoidal window in the door. The house was dark and empty but filled with jagged and furrowed silhouettes from torn wallpaper and debris. Rodney put his hand on the doorknob, but it didn't twist, so he hunched down and dropped his shoulder against the door, and it fell into the living room.

We could feel a rush of cool and wet air, like it had come from the previous winter. Rodney stepped delicately through the door, and I followed after him. He scuffed his feet against the tiled floor and smiled. "You know, I put this shit down here," he said. "I put all this shit up. The wallpaper, the tiles, and shit." Rodney walked into the kitchen and put his hand against the wall where the name tags that his mother had worn when visiting him at the juvenile detention facility were still affixed in long descending rows.

"She's crazy," he said of his mother, admiringly. He poked his head in the kitchen, tried the back door, which didn't budge, and then loped up the stairs in the living room. On the second floor, the ceilings in his and Antonio's old bedrooms were caving in, and there were paint chips and plaster scattered all over the floors. "This ain't shit," he said. "I'm just going to hire me three or four crackheads, pay them motherfuckers $15 a day. You don't need to pay more. . . . I know how to do this shit. It really ain't no problem. I'm telling you, for $5,000, I'll have this bitch banging."

Rodney looked out the windows in Antonio's room over the backyard and down to the back porch behind the kitchen. "This where they caught me running," he said. "My moms had called the hook, and I'm trying to get the fuck out of here. Julie said she seen the hook come to the front of the house. I'm out this fucking window, onto the porch roof, jump off the porch, and I'm over the fence. I got a lot of memories from this place," he said. "I love this house." As we drove off, he seemed cheerful and assured. We made plans to visit the Wayne County Register of Deeds Office, to have a title search done, to see what was still owed on the house and what he'd have to go through in order to purchase or lay legitimate claim to it. "Yeah, I'm gonna have this bitch banging," he said.

After what he described as the worst year of his life, Rodney's hopes for the house on Wadsworth represented a fresh start. At the same time, his interest in the house reflected a reconciliation of sorts for himself with the Dexter neighborhood and the city more generally. He would take this place back, the place where his family had taken desperate refuge, in which he had invested energy and sentiment, from which his family then had fled, and from which he had run from the police. In his reclamation of the Wadsworth house as a drug spot, the days of his occupancy also would recede into the distance, and those of his ownership would commence.

At least, this is how he had imagined it. As he described his plans to me, I was hopeful but also wary. Since we had first known each other, we had had many of these sorts of conversations, where Rodney would develop an ambitious and far-ranging plan that would finally get him over, that would carry him out of the rapidly turning cycles of solvency and destitution in which he found himself while working in the drug game.

If anything gave me particular hope at this juncture it was Annie. She and Rodney had grown closer over the course of their physical separation while he was locked up, and several months after Rodney had been released they were still together. He continued to ridicule her in front of his boys, maybe even more sharply than before going on the run and spending all those months in jail. Yet she was ever-more expert in dismissing this behavior. And in quiet, private moments, Rodney's tender affection reassured her that all this teasing was in inverse proportion to the depth of his feelings for her.

Early in the fall following Rodney's release from jail, he called me on the phone, and said that he and Annie wanted to talk with me. They were hanging around Sheed's mother's house near the intersection of Dexter and Carrington, and I drove over and picked them up there. Uncharacteristically, Rodney got into the backseat of the car and through the open window encouraged Annie to sit in front next to me. She opened the door and gingerly eased into the seat. "Are you OK?" I asked. Annie rolled her eyes and made a quiet grunting noise, a kind of exasperated sigh. Rodney told me that they had just come from the doctor's office. "What happened?"

"Man . . ." Rodney shook his head and looked toward Annie from the backseat. "Man, we got all fucked up."

"Tell him what happened," Annie said impatiently, barely maintaining her composure.

"We just come from the doctor's office, dog," said Rodney. "Do you think you can sue for a messed-up abortion?" Annie's eyes welled with tears. "We went in to the clinic to get this done two weeks ago," Rodney continued, "but they fucked it up, so we had to go back."

"They fucked it up?" I asked.

"They didn't get it out, dog. . . . That's possible, isn't it? I mean, that can happen, right?" I told them that it was my understanding that it was rare for the procedure not to work. "How do you know they messed it up?"

"Show him the picture," Rodney told Annie.

She reached into her purse and pulled out a Polaroid photograph. The image was hard to make out. But after a moment, from the blur of red, gray, and white, I could discern a glistening, wet fetus, with just the beginnings of arms and legs, cradled in a bloody towel.

Annie told me that she had been having terrible cramps after the abortion, and that she had continued bleeding for longer than she thought was normal. She said that the fetus had finally passed when she sat down on the toilet to pee. Annie collapsed with fear and light-headedness from the shock and blood loss. And Rodney had swept her up and carried her to bed, and then had run a bath, undressed her, and lowered her gently into the water. When she had recovered, Rodney helped her fish the fetal tissue out of the toilet so that they could take a picture of it.

"Basically, we had a miscarriage," Annie said. "And you know, we really didn't even want to have this abortion," said Rodney. "That's why we waited this long. We was twelve weeks. We just couldn't decide what to do. And money be so tight right now, dog. I wanted to think about a way that we could make it work, you know. We just went back and forth."

"'Round and 'round," Annie said. "We really didn't want to do it. We wanted to keep it so bad. Damn." Rodney reached forward and put his hand on Annie's shoulder. "Now it's like we didn't even get an abortion, right. But I lost the baby anyways."

Rodney said he wanted Annie to get pregnant again, and that they both knew that they wouldn't have another abortion. "I'm gonna get my shit straight," he said. "And then we can do this without worrying about, you know, getting our money right, you know? Then we can just start us a little family."

The Rising

Over the next couple of months I was on the West Coast, where I had recently started working. But when I got back to town, I headed straight for the corner of Dexter and Carrington. Rodney's cell phone hadn't been working for a while, which wasn't unusual, but I was eager to hear how he and Annie were doing. Normally, if I would leave town for a spell, I could reconnect with Rodney within an hour of showing up on the corner of DC. Somebody there would have his most recent phone number, would know where I could find him, or would know for how long I should expect to wait for him to come through the neighborhood.

It was a dark, chilly afternoon in early winter, so I wasn't surprised to find the corner pretty desolate. I went into the liquor store on the east side of DC. Ebo was there, looking over the newspapers and bags of chips, staying on the move in the store and keeping warm.

"Hey," he said, almost cheerfully.

I was glad to see him, and we shook hands and hugged each other.

"How you doing?"

"Alright," he answered quietly, looking back over the rows of bright plastic snack bags. I reached down and grabbed some juice out of the cooler to assuage Sam, the store owner, who was looking annoyed that I had engaged Ebo in conversation.

"You seen Rod?" I asked.

Ebo shook his head back and forth uncomfortably.

"Nope," he said. I didn't understand his sudden mistrust of me. It was as if he thought I might be the hook or, in any case, would have no business asking after Rodney's whereabouts.

"Not in a while, eh?" I said, with a slight smile, trying to diffuse the tension.

He continued to shake his head.

"Nope," he said again, with his gaze still cast down toward the Fritos. I walked past him out to the sidewalk.

The wind seemed to have picked up even in the few minutes that I was inside, so I decided not to hang around waiting for anyone else to show up. I'd return soon and find someone who had seen Rodney or could at least help me find him, I figured.

I started walking toward my car, which was parked just a few yards down the block, when I noticed someone waving to me from inside the car parked right in front of mine. It was little Timmy, leaning back in the passenger seat and wearing huge round sunglasses under the brim of a new baseball cap. He was sitting next to a girl who had just bought a bag of weed from him, and they were smoking a blunt, passing it back and forth. Timmy opened the door and said, "Luke, what's up?"

When I had first met him, he was one of the youngest kids spending time on Dexter. Skinny and short and possessed of fine, almost pretty features, his face was round and clean, without any hair or blemish. Now, five years after we met, although still thin and short, scars traced a capillary network across his skin, from fights with knives and an occasional hard-knuckle fist. I leaned against the hood, with my feet on the curb, and asked him how

things had been going. "Everything's straight," he said. "This my girl, Tan-
isha." I asked how his mother was doing. "Oh, she's doing alright. . . . She's
getting used to me bein' down here. Leaving me alone more. She just got
married last week."

"Wow! You like your new stepdad?" I asked.

"Oh, he's alright, I guess. You know she's been looking for someone for a
while. Been too lonely, I guess."

"Your little sister's alright?"

"Oh, she straight. Getting ready to go to college. Thinking about Michigan
State. Or maybe Michigan."

"What you doing?" he asked.

"I'm looking for Rodney, man. You seen him?"

Timmy looked back at me like he couldn't quite hear me. "Who?" he said.

"Rodney. I'm looking for Rodney."

He didn't answer.

"Rod," I said. "Phelps."

Timmy wheeled farther around, and I could see his eyes widen behind his
sunglasses. "He got killed, man."

I stood up slowly, still leaning against the car, and started to cry softly.
Timmy was quiet and still for a minute. Then he said, "Man, I thought you
knew. . . . I thought you woulda had to know. . . . That shit was in November. A month ago. I knew that you would have heard about that." I just stood
there. Each of my senses about him was compressed into an impossibly thin
plane. All at once, I heard his voice, saw his gait, and could peer for a moment into what would be an eternal return, to the instant, after he was long
dead, that I last thought he was alive. Now I was both wanting to cry harder
and not wanting to cry at all, thinking, and no doubt wary, of Rodney's disapproval, that I needed to hold it together on the corner. "He got shot, man,
driving right down Dexter; crashed into the store back there. Right around
the corner. They's still the bears people puttin' up. Right around there, they
still got the bears." Timmy got out of the car and led me around the corner,
to where Rodney's car had crashed into the liquor store after hopping the
curb and sailing through the vacant lot next door. A small mountain of teddy
bears, now gray and matted, were arranged around and tied to the light pole
near the corner.

Staring at the tired, weathered memorial, I thought of others who had
died on Dexter and of how I had reacted when I learned of their deaths,

which seemed always to come on the heels of one another, sickening and startling but then also just a matter of life in the neighborhood: death in the neighborhood. For me, they were always, as a matter of course, a part of the story of the neighborhood and the story I was telling. But Rodney's death was different. Despite my determination to keep myself somehow both on the inside and the periphery of what happened on Dexter, Rodney's death was more deeply a part of my own story.

So strange, then, that almost unwittingly, from the moment that I heard about it, I was writing Rodney's death. Standing in the cold wind and gray light, I was imagining the scene I was witnessing as it might unfold in an abstracted narrative, as I had so much of Rodney's experience, and our friendship before, and I was now so self-conscious about my role in his life, my place in the neighborhood, my place in the lives of all the other Dexter Boys in his absence, the appropriateness of my heartbreak, the grotesque fact that all of this was running through my mind in the first place, that I was nearly paralyzed. How could I mourn someone whom I had been eulogizing from the day I met him? I stood on the corner and put my hands in my pockets, trying to avoid the others.

Marley showed up, and was walking back and forth on the sidewalk. He would skip occasionally from his house down on Carrington to grab bags of weed for customers who were starting to line up around the corner. He came over to me with his arm extended, and we shook hands.

"What's up, man. . . . I didn't even know about it," I said.

"He just finding out about Rod, man," Timmy said.

"Yeah, man," Marley said sympathetically. "Damn, you didn't even know. . . . You come up here expecting to see somebody, expecting to see him riding by, bouncing, and then you find out he gone. . . . I know you sick right now. I still can't even believe this shit."

"I'm feeling pretty fucked up," I said.

"I believe it," he said, shaking his head.

Marley said that he had a program from the funeral at his house, and he jogged down to get it. When he returned, he stood with Timmy in the cold wind and looked over my shoulder as I leafed through the colorful pages, covered with photographs of Rodney and his family. Each of his immediate family members as well as his closest nieces and nephews had written something that was printed in the program.

"Damn, his father wrote something," I said, looking at the image of Rodney's dad, about whom I knew almost nothing.

"Yeah," said Timmy. "He was locked up and just got out on some technical stuff like a week before Rod got killed. He was gonna come up and see him and shit. But he didn't. So the first time this cat's own father seen him, like, since he was born, he sees him in a casket, you know what I'm saying? That's some crazy shit."

"Who did it?" I asked Marley.

"They know who did it. We think it was somebody up the street, staying up toward Davison. They caught 'em right away. . . . But who knows? Could have been anything with Rod."

"He so wild," Timmy said.

"Right," Marley agreed, almost before Timmy had said anything. "Wilding out. So you just don't know. Could have been any ol' kind of shit. . . . He was acting different for the last month. Like he knew it was going to happen."

"Like how? More wild?" I asked.

"No, man," said Marley. Timmy nodded in agreement. "More humble," he said. "Just real calm. . . . More humble." He told me how Rodney had been trying to get a car wash started, right behind the gas station on Dexter and Carrington. He had already bought an old building. "DC car wash," they would call it. Rodney was working on gutting the place and had just finished cleaning it out when he was murdered.

"You knew somebody must have been watching him," added Marley. "'Cuz he was in there working on that car wash every day with a vest on. He was in there cleaning up, taking shit off the ceilings and shit, wearing a vest the whole time. Then he just happens to take that vest off when he finishes his shit there, goes up the street, comes back down, and that's when they get him. You know, they was waiting, watching."

As Marley was talking, several others who had seen me on the corner from across the street, where they'd been slinging at the gas station, walked over—Oscar, Sheed, and Shell. They shouted my name excitedly as they came closer, and when they were standing with me in front of the store, everybody contributed to a flowing, overlapping recapitulation of what had happened. "It was right there," they yelled, pointing toward the Payless shoe store up from the corner.

"Right in front of the fucking Payless."

"He comes out, two guns, from behind the building. AKs. Shooting. And he missed all but that one. Car full of bullets, they only hit him with that one. Come in his back and go up through his heart. That's what it did. It exploded his heart."

"No, man, he made it down the street, and then he crashed his car into the building. That's when he broke his neck. That's what killed him."

"They said he was still alive when he come down here. Woodrow and them come down from the Tenth Precinct. They said he was still alive."

Shell said that he saw me crying, and that he had assumed that being on the corner again was making me miss Rodney. He apologized for not knowing that I had just found out and was telling everybody that he didn't realize that I had just learned about Rodney's death. I could hear him telling the others, "Oh, I know he must be sick."

Where almost all had been suspicious initially, not sure what to make of my and Rodney's friendship, most of the other young men on Dexter seemed to have found ways to make sense of it. Many would call me his "big brother," which seemed genuinely to acknowledge a kind of familial tie and also to infantilize Rodney, farcically suggesting that we were enrolled in the Big Brothers/Big Sisters program. The truth, of course, is that our mentorship was mutual, born for both of us out of a dire self-interest, curious novelty, and finally, after we had known one another for five years, a kind of love. Indeed, as others on the corner that day guessed, I was sick.

Sheed walked around in circles, a head taller than everyone else on the block, with tears in his eyes, talking about how fucked up he was feeling. He told me that he had thought of me the day he saw Rodney lying dead on Dexter. "I thought of all the people who loved him; I knew you'd be hurtin', man," he said. "Seeing you now just takes me right back to that day," he told me.

On the day that Rodney was murdered, Sheed had been working in the shipping department of an auto parts firm, packing and breaking down boxes. One of his co-workers handed him a phone and told him that he had a call. "'Come on Dexter,' that's what I hear. It's my man Tyrone. 'You gotta come up here with Rod, 'cuz they ain't nobody else here. Come on Dexter, hurry up, somebody just shot Rod.'

"It was a sunny day, but cool. A day for jackets. I drove on to Dexter; it was like the Providence parade, times three. That was the most crowded that I've seen our neighborhood. There was people everywhere. Going crazy. Princess was on the ground, on her knees, crying. But there was just so many people up there, there wasn't no way you could get close. Word spread quick, man. Malachi was there. He was shaking his head, hung down, just saying 'damn.' And Kilo. Damn, he was stuck. Sobbing, man. Just sobbing. My mind wouldn't let me believe that this was actually true, until I seen it. It still didn't really dawn on me 'til after I went home, got by myself. I went home and went through pictures, clothes that he left at my house, lottery tickets. I was thinking, He's never going to come get this stuff again. He's never going to be around again, or none of that. Most of the time I still can't believe it. I know it's reality. I know that he's not here. But I still be feeling like someday, he's going to come around or something. . . . But I really know that's not possible."

Sheed's bitterness about Rodney's death was palpable. Nothing in his life, he knows, will ever be the same—certainly not his relationship to the blocks around Dexter and Carrington. "I know ten people that died on Dexter in the past five years," he told me. "I knew these people since I was a toddler, since I was real, real young. All these cats got the same problem. Being seen."

The night before he was killed, Rodney turned to Annie as they were falling asleep. "What would you do if I was gone?" he asked.

"I don't know," she remembers answering.

"Well, make sure you say your prayers every night," he said.

The next morning, Rodney got dressed in jeans, a T-shirt, and a dark hoodie. He left the house to go work on fixing up the car wash on Dexter. Annie had recently gotten a temp job at an office in the suburbs and was planning to drive to the mall to buy some new work clothes. Just before she left, at around 11:30, Rodney reached her on her cell phone, right after calling his sisters Princess and Julie. "I had just been listening to the radio and the person on the radio had said, if you talking to someone on the phone and you love that person, before you get off the phone you should say that you love that person," Annie told me. "When he called me before, I had just said, 'Alright, bye.' I called right back and said 'I love you' to him. He said 'I love you too.'"

Annie was just getting on the freeway, heading toward a suburban mall, when she got a call from Antonio's girlfriend, Annya. "Go check on Rod up on Dexter," she said. "What's wrong with him?" Annie demanded. "I don't know, just go check on him," she answered. Annie called back, but Annya wouldn't say anything more. "It sounded like something was wrong; I could hear that her voice wasn't right, like she crying, or like she had been crying, but she wouldn't say. She kept hanging up on me, and I kept calling back, to see what's wrong with him or what's supposed to be wrong with him. But she kept saying, 'Just go check on him, go check on him.' I was about to crash the car because I didn't know what was wrong with him. I'm flying toward Dexter." Annie got off the freeway and headed into the neighborhood. By the time she got near the corner of Dexter and Carrington, the crowd in the street stretched from the back of the gas station all the way across Dexter and was so big that she had to stop the car two blocks short. She saw an ambulance parked to the side of the liquor store and could see Princess's car straddling the sidewalk. She opened her door, and everyone seemed at once to turn and look at her. But no one said anything.

The police had already pulled yellow tape around the whole corner. She was trying to get a better look, thinking that Rodney might likely be sitting in one of the police cars or might have been injured, when she was taken by the hand and pulled around the back of the store and behind an adjacent house by an older couple from the neighborhood. "I was thinking either he shot somebody or maybe somebody shot him, you know, like he was injured," Annie later recalled. "But it didn't even occur to me that he got killed." Annie moved past the backyard of the house next to the liquor store, through the bushes, and out to the vacant lot where Rodney's car had crashed. "The windshield was cracked, side door was open, and Rod was laying there. I knew he was dead from the moment I saw him," she said. "He was so still. Pale. His mouth was open; there was blood running down his face." Annie's knees gave and she fell to the ground, screaming in the unmowed weeds not far from Princess, who was still wailing furiously. "They got Rod! They got Rod!" Annie cried.

"I had just talked to him, just an hour before," she told me. "I seen them put him in the ambulance, but I didn't get to touch him."

Antonio woke up the morning of November 5, anticipating a visit from Julie and Annya, who would be driving up to the prison in Saginaw that afternoon. "And they usually come, I'm talking literally, when they say they coming, they coming. And it was like three-thirty, they usually gonna break my door and be like 'Come on, you got a visit.' This time, I'm getting hungry, but I didn't want to go to chow because I was going to eat in the visiting room. I'm getting hungry, and they didn't open my door. And I get butterflies in my mind, like damn, something had to happen. You know what I'm saying, 'cuz they would be here. So I went to chow. I went and ate for thirty minutes real quick, came back. Still, they ain't called me. I was watching, it was going on six o'clock. Six-thirty."

Antonio had thought about calling Rodney earlier that afternoon, after someone from the neighborhood was escorted to Antonio's unit in the prison. He thought that Rodney would get a rise out of hearing that he had run into a familiar face. But Antonio changed his mind before going back to his cell, thinking that he could just relay the message through Annya and Julie. "Now it's six-thirty, and if I had been on level two or something, I could have called at three-thirty. But I was on level four. Couldn't make no calls. Now butterflies start really going through my head. Man, why the fuck they ain't coming? Finally, I call to the crib man. The first thing my sister says: 'Rodney's dead.' I was like, 'What? Don't tell me that!' Man, it was like there was a piece of that nigga left in my body, dog. I'm talking about literally, dog. I really didn't know what the fuck to do, man. I'm like, don't tell me that. Man, don't tell me that, dog. First thing she said was it's gonna be alright. Don't go crazy. She thought I was going to go crazy, 'cuz I always said that if something happens to Rod while I'm locked up, it's like, when I get out, it's over with, wherever, whoever. Regardless of where I'm at. So she was like, man, don't go crazy, don't go crazy."

Antonio went back to his cell and told his bunky what had happened. His cell mate helped him prepare a bowl of noodle soup and then encouraged him to eat. But Antonio didn't have an appetite. "I couldn't cry. I basically knew that it was dangerous out there. I kept praying every night because, to be honest with you, man, I knew eventually that it was going to happen. I was praying every night, man: 'Just let him be there when I get out.' Man, I used to be just laying there, like damn, I hope this nigga alright, I ain't talk to him, he ain't come seen me. It just seems, and it's fucked up, but I look at it like a lot of motherfuckers who go to jail, dog, when they come home, there's always a person in their family that's gonna be dead."

Still without shedding a tear, Antonio sat down in his prison cell and wrote a eulogy, knowing that he likely wouldn't get a furlough to attend the funeral: "Tell everybody I say hi and I apologize for not being able to attend the funeral. You know, these Europeans wouldn't let me come because of my custody level. . . . My heart goes out to everyone. I appreciate the love support and respect deeply. . . . I understand that what is done is done, but death is not what a man should fear, because every shut eye ain't sleep, and every good-bye ain't gone."

Antonio was released from prison a year after Rodney was killed. He moved to Grand Rapids with Annya and Julie, about a three-hour drive northwest of Detroit, knowing that the circumstances surrounding Rodney's death would make it dangerous for him in the city still, and knowing that the temptation to get involved might be too much to resist. Only a month before moving to Grand Rapids, he had been shot from close range, the bullet taking out a chunk of his upper lip, slicing through his inner cheek, and knocking several of his teeth out before exiting his face and lodging in his shoulder. He talked now with his jaw clenched and his mouth pouting off to the side.

But nothing was further from his lips than fear. Rather, Antonio's seething quiet anger drenched every room he was in, and everyone swam wide berths around him. He was not simply angry with the people who had killed his brother. Nor did he seem to spare much antipathy for whomever had more recently put a bullet through his own mouth. Mostly, he was angry with Rodney himself—not for being yet another victim of Detroit's pervasive gun violence, but for being murdered on Dexter. "I get pissed at my brother, dog. I say it time and time again: How the fuck you let these pussy-ass niggas get down on you, man? That's just like you letting a fucking baby shoot you, man. It's kind of embarrassing, man, to see a motherfucker that you know, and they say, 'Did your brother get killed up here?' and you be like 'Yeah.' And they be like, 'Man, how the fuck they let this happen to your brother?' It's embarrassing for my brother to die where he died at and how he died, and everybody see this nigga. But at the same time, it's history. This our history."

The poignancy of Rodney's demise on the corner where he had spent so many long days slinging, where he struggled to become part of the legal business community, the corner by which he measured many of his triumphs, and against which he plotted his trajectory, wasn't lost on Antonio. Rodney's death on Dexter had become part of both of their histories in the neighborhood. "It means a lot that he died right there," he told me. "It's history, man, and a motherfucker can never take it from me. This is the same block where we stood. The same block where we lived." In the manner of other generative moments and assemblages on Dexter, around the Coney Island and the corner stores, Rodney's murder made and marked his and Antonio's places on the block. But Rodney's death also meant other things for Antonio's relationship to Dexter.

While DC had always presented certain risks, after Rodney's murder it became an even more dangerous space for Antonio. In turn, Dexter was no longer a part of him in the way that it had been, and Antonio's relationship to the *representation* of the block was changing. Dexter had long been both a sentimental source of personal identity and an exploitable drug market for the Dexter Boys, with monetary utility for young men in the area. Antonio's alienation from the block with which he had so long identified was marked by a deepening transparency of his and other Dexter Boys' instrumental relationships to the streets and corners by which they had mapped their places in the world and judged the commitments of their hearts. Maybe most tellingly, Antonio no longer imagined in Dexter a place with the power of its own personality, its own subjectivity. In the wake of Rodney's death, it had lost its soul; it had ceased, for the time being, to be any place at all.

The day I arrived in Grand Rapids, Antonio got a letter in the mail from Malachi, who had been locked up after a parole violation and would be sitting in prison for the next year. Malachi worried that Antonio would be drawn into the drama of Dexter again and might be hurt along the way. "We love Dexter," he wrote to Antonio, "but fuck Dexter now." Reminiscent of Rabbit's tragic and ecstatic calls to simultaneously love, commit to, and leave Dexter, Malachi's argument wasn't entirely convincing to Antonio, who was less condemning, but who had in some ways a more damning estimation of the sentimental value of the neighborhood.

"It's just a street," he said. "My thing is, I'm not going to say fuck Dexter. Dexter's never done nothing to nobody." Antonio spoke out of the undamaged side of his mouth. "It's just a street. It's just a sign at the end of a pole. It's been there for over a hundred years and never did nothing to nobody. What I can say is fuck a lot of niggas on Dexter. And they know who they is. I don't even have to say the name. They know who they is."

For Antonio, the question remains: in turning away from Dexter, what is there to turn toward? Even two years removed from Rodney's murder on DC, Antonio's future seems inevitably and almost literally a prisoner to his past.

"When Rodney died," he said, "it was like a spirit left out of me. I could actually feel his spirit leave out of me, dog. I don't care about life right now, man. Like literally, I don't, man. If I die right now, I don't give a fuck. When you been through everything that I been through. Motherfuckers scared to go to jail. Motherfuckers scared to get shot. Motherfuckers scared for they motherfucking loved ones to die. That shit, I'm prepared for that shit right now, man. Don't shit faze me, don't shit amaze me. And I ain't just saying this shit just to say it. I don't care. If I was to die right now, I don't really give a fuck."

This was Antonio's tenor most of the time. As others in the family skirted tentatively past him, wary of his explosive moods and fearful for the trouble he might find or engender, Antonio was quiet. He had been voluble when I first met him, almost like an ethnographer in his enthusiasm for parts of the world that were not familiar to him. But he had become more than just taciturn. I had tried talking with him plenty after Rodney had been killed, but it seemed impossible. He was impenetrable. Annya, Annie, and his sisters said the same. Indeed, in the midst of our still-deepening friendship, it may only have been the formality of an interview, for the book that you hold, that gave him momentary pause to speak, and to begin to search for his feelings about his lost brother and abiding "brotherlove." As we talked, he spoke almost faster than his thoughts were able to keep up. Once he had undertaken the search, his will to find a means to express even his confusion was almost desperate.

"The shit, it's crazy, man. . . . It's like it never happened, but it happened. Because, like to this day, by me being locked up, and I ain't saw the nigga in years, it's like he still around, and I just ain't been fucking with him today or yesterday. That's another reason I can't get straight about how I feel, because I miss the nigga right. But it's like I don't look at the nigga like he's dead, because I ain't been around him for two years."

"It makes it harder?" I asked.

"In some ways it's easier, 'cuz I ain't seen him in two years, know what I'm saying? So I don't miss physically being around him. It's going to be damn near three years, and now he's dead. It ain't like I been around you every day, so we got our steady pace of what we doin' and shit like that. And that's why I think, what if this nigga was here? That's all I can think. What if? 'Cuz I done looked at it like I miss the nigga, but it ain't the missin' like I'm never going to see him again. Because . . . just like I was missin' him when I was locked up, I'm still missin' him. I mean, I seen everybody else then, I seen Annya, I seen Julie. Shit. But being locked up, the one nigga I could never see was Rod."

At this point Antonio's voice hit a different rhythm. "It's like I'm still locked up," he said, almost sighing, as he realized that he had found the idea for which he'd been searching. "It's like I'm still locked up. And I know that I can't see him. But the nigga still alive. That's how I look at it. He's still alive but I can't see him. And I'll never see him again. That's why it'll always feel like I'm locked up. Forever. . . . I mean, I'm free, but I'm going to be locked up for the rest of my life."

Coda: Late July

"That would just be too much of a coincidence," Annie remembers Princess saying. "There's no way." Annie halfheartedly agreed. She had been under so much stress around the time that Rodney was killed—not sleeping much or eating regularly. And only a couple of weeks later her grandmother in Alabama had passed away, and she had traveled there to attend yet another funeral. Her body must have been playing tricks on her.

Yet she knew that it was what she wanted. She and Rodney had been told that the baby they lost would have been due on November 9, just four days after Rodney died. Even amid the craziness of his murder, the passing of that day weighed heavily on her heart. After returning from Alabama, Annie visited her doctor. "I just couldn't believe it," she told me. "When the doctor come out and said that I was pregnant, I just . . . I was just speechless." Eight months later Annie gave birth to a baby girl, whose light skin, soft hair, and impish disposition she inherited from her father. And everyone who knew Rodney can see him delighting in our wonder at their resemblance. While we have mourned their separation from one another, her pleasures, discoveries, and still-emerging history are incontrovertibly his.

Notes

Chapter 1: Introduction

1. All names, except of some public persons and those who expressed an explicit wish for me to use their real names, have been changed to protect the identity of the subjects of this work. While I reveal the general geographic locations of many of the scenes that play out in this book, many street names and place-names have also been changed.

2. Baltimore's Harbor Front may be the most famous example, thanks in some measure to David Harvey, *The Condition of Postmodernity* (Oxford: Oxford University Press, 1992).

3. As I describe below, Detroit might be taken as an emblem for this era, as racial spaces were reengineered to accommodate the expansion of the freeway system and all sorts of other corporate interests.

4. See Neil Smith, *The New Urban Frontier: Gentrification and the Revanchist City* (New York: Routledge, 1996).

5. *City Crime Rankings, 14th Edition* (Washington, DC: CQ Press, 2007).

6. The Center for Educational Performance and Information, "Report on Graduation/Dropout Rates for the 1999–2000 School Year," Michigan Department of Education report, 2001.

7. There are several exemplary schools in the Detroit Public Schools system, including Cass Tech, Renaissance, and Martin Luther King, but all of these are magnet schools; only students who do well on entrance exams may attend.

8. Chastity Pratt, "Detroit Schools in the Red; Jobs on the Line," *Detroit Free Press*, March 17, 2004, 8B; and Diane Bukouski, "In Hock: DPS Borrows $160–$200 Million; More Detroiters Still Owe State Takeover Bill," *Michigan Citizen*, May 21, 2006, http://www.michigancitizen.com/default.asp?sourceid=&smenu=1&twindow

=&mad=&sdetail=3041&wpage=1&skeyword=&sidate=&ccat=&ccatm=&restate=
&restatus=&reoption=&retype=&repmin=&repmax=&rebed=&rebath=&subname=
&pform=&sc=1070&hn=michigancitizen&he=.com.

9. I address this in more detail in part III.

10. A report of the Detroit Public Schools system, *Detroit Public Schools Student Information*, collects data from the year 2000 and reports that 91 percent of students in the school system are African American. Four percent are Hispanic and 3.7 percent are white. Just under 1 percent are Asian or Pacific Islander. There has, of course, been a long history of handwringing and ambivalence among the city's black residents about the extent to which public schools in Detroit have been segregated. Some suggest that the school integration busing policies of the late 1960s and early 1970s were the "final push that sent the city's remaining whites to the suburbs." Gordon Trowbridge, "Bussing Battles Spurred Flight: Court Ordered Remedy Tried in Detroit, Pontiac," *Detroit News*, January 21, 2002, http://www.detnews.com/specialreports/2002/segregation2/b02-395697.htm.

11. It is perhaps especially troubling that the two conversations (one about urban revitalization and the other about school reform) are so infrequently linked.

12. Chris Christoff and Chastity Pratt, "Officials Prepare a New Plan for Schools," *Detroit Free Press*, December 4, 2003, 1A.

13. Chris Christoff, "Who's Got Political Muscle? Maybe (Gulp) the Voters," *Detroit Free Press*, December 8, 2003, 1B.

14. Most recent scholarship about Detroit reflects this. See, for example, Reynolds Farley, Sheldon Danziger, and Harry J. Holzer, *Detroit Divided* (New York: Russell Sage Foundation, 2000); John Hartigan, *Racial Situations: Class Predicaments of Whiteness in Detroit* (Princeton, NJ: Princeton University Press, 1999); Thomas J. Sugrue, *Origins of the Urban Crisis: Race and Inequality in Postwar Detroit* (Princeton, NJ: Princeton University Press, 1996); Heather Ann Thompson, *Whose Detroit? Politics, Labor, and Race in a Modern American City* (Ithaca, NY: Cornell University Press, 2001).

15. See Tom Mieczkowski, "Street Selling Heroin: The Young Boys Technique in a Detroit Neighborhood" (PhD diss., Wayne State University, 1985); Tom Mieczkowski, "Geeking Up and Throwing Down: Heroin Street Life in Detroit," *Criminology* 24, no. 4 (1986): 645–66.

16. Gang and drug activity may differ markedly elsewhere. Sudhir Venkatesh, in particular, cites an opposite trend in Chicago, from family and brotherhoods in gangs to more corporate structures (*American Project: The Rise and Fall of a Modern Ghetto* [Cambridge, MA: Harvard University Press, 2000]).

17. Through the first several years of the new century, there have been around ten thousand arrests per year for drug crimes in Detroit, including possession and trafficking charges. The Office of National Drug Control Policy designates the Detroit metro area a "High Intensity Drug Trafficking Area."

18. Orlando Patterson, among others, makes this point. See Orlando Patterson,

The Ordeal of Integration: Progress and Resentment in America's "Racial" Crisis (New York: Basic Civitas, 1998); Orlando Patterson, "A Poverty of the Mind," editorial, *New York Times*, March 26, 2006, http://www.nytimes.com/2006/03/26/opinion/26patterson.html. "Innocent countrymen" is a phrase made famous in James Baldwin, *The Fire Next Time* (1963; repr., New York: Vintage, 1991).

19. Steven Gregory, *Black Corona: Race and the Politics of Place in an Urban Community* (Princeton, NJ: Princeton University Press, 1998), attributes a growing emphasis on the marginalization of poor African Americans to the hugely influential work of William Julius Wilson (*The Truly Disadvantaged: The Inner City, the Underclass, and Public Policy* [Chicago: University of Chicago Press, 1987]), for whom the upward-and-outward mobility of middle- and working-class African Americans created "ghetto communities, socially isolated from the values and resources of not only 'mainstream society' but of the black working and middle classes as well" (Gregory, *Black Corona*, 9). Following Wilson came a great deal of scholarship interested in an "underclass" residing in economically and culturally impoverished communities, much of which was reminiscent of politically regressive "culture of poverty" studies from the mid-twentieth century.

20. Sudhir Venkatesh's valuable work (*American Project* [Cambridge, MA: Harvard University Press, 2000] and *Off the Books: The Underground Economy of the Urban Poor* [Cambridge, MA: Harvard University Press, 2006]) on underground economies illuminates some of the local political dimensions of gang-organized drug dealing in urban communities. But with its underlying orientation to questions of "social control" and "disorganization," it largely ignores questions about cultural meaning and identity. Two of the most important studies of drug dealing in "inner-city" contexts that address cultural production and identity formation are Elijah Anderson's account of the "moral lives" of young people in Philadelphia, *Code of the Street: Decency, Violence, and the Moral Life of the Inner City* (New York: W.W. Norton, 1999), and Philippe Bourgois' *In Search of Respect: Selling Crack in El Barrio* (Cambridge: Cambridge University Press, 1996). Both focus on what we might call a "culture of threatened masculinity" among U.S. minority communities. Within what Bourgois terms "inner-city street culture," drug dealing is a principal means for Puerto Rican men in New York to achieve social dignity (8). Thus, the "search for respect" often ends with the only option consistently available to them: entry into the drug trade. Though it would frequently come available for periods of time, the feminized world of legitimate low-wage service work was too often an affront to the "culture of the street" sensibilities of the Puerto Rican men. According to Bourgois, the drug trade, as a structural element of street culture, is one of the only and certainly the most critical means for Puerto Rican men (and in some cases women) to reconstitute their senses of *respeto*. Anderson's *Code of the Streets* describes the emergence of a remarkably similar cultural code along with an emphasis on "respect" and "dignity" among African Americans in a Philadelphia ghetto. His book takes shape around a distinction between "decent" and "street" social typologies. According to

Anderson, the categorical split between the two reflects, in the designee, varying degrees of "distance from the rest of America," or degrees of "alienation" among African Americans from both the cultural mores and structural opportunities associated with abstracted imaginings of the "mainstream" (33).

21. Ze'ev Chafets, "The Tragedy of Detroit," *New York Times Magazine*, July 29, 1990, http://query.nytimes.com/gst/fullpage.html?res=9C0CEFDD1E38F93AA15 754C0A966958260&sec=&spon=&pagewanted=8.

22. The expansive literature on childhood and subjectivity is informative here. See, for example, Sharon Stephens, *Children and the Politics of Culture* (Princeton, NJ: Princeton University Press, 1995); Tracey Skelten, *Cool Places: Geographies of Youth Cultures* (New York: Routledge, 1998); Stuart Hall, *Resistance through Rituals: Youth Subcultures in Post-War Britain* (New York: Routledge, 1990); Andy Bennett, *After Subculture: Critical Studies in Contemporary Youth Culture* (New York: Palgrave Macmillan, 2004); Dick Hebdige, *Subculture: The Meaning of Style* (London: Methuen, 1979); Gill Valentine, *Public Space and the Culture of Childhood* (Burlington, VT: Ashgate Press, 2004). Of particular importance are also a range of ideas growing out of transnational anthropology and critiques of orthodox understandings of the relationship between "center" and "periphery" in global politics, from which ideas about hybrid subjectivities are emerging. See, for example, Homi K. Bhabha, "Life at the Border: Hybrid Identities of the Present," *New Perspectives Quarterly* (Winter 1997): 31; Homi K. Bhabha, *The Location of Culture* (New York: Routledge, 1994); Arjun Appadurai, "Disjuncture and Difference in the Global Cultural Economy," *Public Culture* 2, no. 2 (1990): 1–24; Roger Rouse, "Thinking through Transnationalism," *Public Culture* 7, no. 2 (1995): 353–402.

23. My emphasis here is informed by the work of Henri Lefebvre, who pursues "an approach which would analyze not things in space, but space itself, with a view to uncovering the social relationships embedded in it." He writes that "the ideologically dominant tendency divides space up into parts and parcels in accordance with the social division of labor. . . . It bases its image of the forces occupying space on the idea that space is a passive receptacle. Thus, instead of uncovering the social relationships that are latent in spaces . . . we fall into the trap of treating space as space 'in itself,' as space as such." Henri Lefebvre, *The Production of Social Space* (Oxford: Blackwell, 1991), 416. Lefebvre's work is particularly evocative around questions about the relationship between space and subjectivity and identity formation: "Nothing and no one can avoid trial by space—an ordeal which is the modern world's answer to the judgment of God or the classical conception of fate. It is in space, on a worldwide scale, that each idea of 'value' acquires or loses its distinctiveness through confrontation with the other values and ideas that it encounters there. Moreover—and more importantly—groups, classes or fractions of classes cannot constitute themselves, or recognize one another, as 'subjects' unless they generate (or produce) a space" (416). Amid their many juridical trials, this is indeed

the struggle with which young people in the drug trade are most preoccupied: the making of space that is their own and that will effectively constitute them.

24. Of course, this had a lot to do with my interest in him as well—but more on that later.

25. Regular curfew hours in Detroit are generally between 10:00 P.M. on Friday and 6:00 A.M. on Saturday for fifteen-year-olds, and between 11:00 P.M. on Friday and 6:00 A.M. on Saturday for sixteen-year-olds. Minors age fifteen and younger also need to be indoors between 8:00 P.M. on Sunday and 6:00 A.M. on Monday, and minors ages sixteen and seventeen need to be indoors between 9:00 P.M. on Sunday and 6:00 A.M. on Monday.

26. The detention facility is a particularly rich space for narrative construction about selves and the city—where the city and its fledgling citizens come into contact with one another. It was in the nature of the space, one of relatively few where young people from socially isolated neighborhoods would congregate and mix together, that the articulation of identities and ways of being were especially important. I explore this further in part III.

Chapter 2: Detroit Revisited, Revisionist History

1. Desolate discussions of Detroit, elevating its difficulties to nearly mythological status, probably culminated with the publication of Ze'ev Chafets's wildly popular *Devil's Night: And Other True Tales of Detroit* (New York: Random House, 1991). This entertaining, if sometimes sensational, book is organized around metaphoric descriptions of the macabre pre-Halloween spectacle of hundreds of abandoned buildings simultaneously burning to the ground—an annual ordeal in the city through the 1990s. In an excerpt of his book published in the *New York Times Magazine* ("The Tragedy of Detroit," July 29, 1990,), Chafets famously designated Detroit a "third world city," a phrase that was seized by the popular press and television journalists, who produced a spate of startling exposés and mournful eulogies detailing Detroit's struggles. But more recent and more scholarly work has also positioned Detroit as something of an emblem of contemporary urban malaise. Thomas Sugrue, in his enlightening *Origins of the Urban Crisis: Race and Inequality in Postwar Detroit* (Princeton, NJ: Princeton University Press, 1996), offers a sustained meditation on the long-standing antecedents to current social difficulties in Detroit and presents the city as an instructive case for those wanting to understand other disenfranchised urban centers in the United States.

2. For an examination of labor politics in the African American community in postwar Detroit, see Heather Ann Thompson, *Whose Detroit? Politics, Labor, and Race in a Modern American City* (Ithaca, NY: Cornell University Press, 2001).

3. Chafets, *Devil's Night*, 162.

4. Bill McGraw, *The Quotations of Mayor Coleman A. Young* (Detroit: Wayne State University Press, 2004).

5. U.S. Census Bureau, 2000, http://www.census.gov/.

6. U.S. Census Bureau, http://www.census.gov/PressRelease/www/releases/
archives/income_wealth/007419.html; Robyn Meredith, "Five Days in 1967 Still
Shake Detroit," *New York Times*, July 23, 1997, http://query.nytimes.com/gst/fullpage
.html?res=9F06E5DE113BF930A15754C0A961958260.

7. See Jane Jacobs, *The Death and Life of Great American Cities* (New York: Random House, 1961).

8. There have been numerous studies examining the significance of small businesses in this regard, though they have tended to mirror Jane Jacobs's emphasis on
social harmony. See, for example, Jennifer Lee, *Civility in the City: Blacks, Jews, and
Koreans in Urban America* (Cambridge, MA: Harvard University Press, 2002);
Mitchell Duneier, *Slim's Table: Race, Respectability, and Masculinity* (Chicago: University of Chicago Press, 1992).

9. I am not, however, supposing that young African Americans are involved in
drug dealing because they are excluded from the small business community (though
there might be some truth to this). There are certainly lots of members of the Arab,
Chaldean, Mexican American, and Albanian American communities in the drug trade.
In fact, they are running drugs through their own small businesses in some cases.

Chapter 3: Renewal, Relocation, and Riot

1. In 1920, the social scientist Forrester Washington conducted a broad survey of
conditions in the black community in Detroit. He found that Detroit's black population—which had just a few years prior been almost entirely confined to a concentrated area covering several city blocks and centered around the Old Saint Antoine
Street district, which runs north and south just to the east of downtown—had, in only
a few years, expanded to cover nearly sixty city blocks. By 1920, the area of most
concentrated black residence extended all the way down to the river, eastward to the
historic Elmwood Cemetery, and to Waterloo Street to the north. While this represents an enormous and rapid geographic expansion, it is all the more striking in light
of the fact that the density of the black community increased during this period as
well. While residential configurations of blacks and whites on the East Side of Detroit reflected broad patterns of segregation that would continue to ossify in later
years, residential patterns also prefigured patterns of integration that would characterize the Kercheval area as late as 1970. Olivier Zunz, *The Changing Face of
Inequality: Urbanization, Industrial Development, and Immigrants in Detroit, 1880–
1920* (Chicago: University of Chicago Press, 1982).

2. As Thomas J. Sugrue notes, "During the Great Migration, the owners of old
hotels and once-grand nineteenth-century row houses chopped up large rooms and
converted them into small apartments and boarding houses, over a quarter of them
without modern amenities like plumbing and full kitchen facilities" (*Origins of the
Urban Crisis: Race and Inequality in Postwar Detroit* [Princeton, NJ: Princeton Uni-

versity Press, 1996], 37). According to Forrester Washington, 25 percent of the homes that he and other members of his surveying team visited in 1920 had only outside toilets, and many others had open toilets situated in bedrooms or even kitchens. Many of the homes had no insulation and were constantly wet. Fire hazards abounded in the area.

3. Sugrue, *Origins of the Urban Crisis*, 43.

4. Taking account of the ages and conditions of each of the neighborhoods' buildings as well as the degree of social homogeneity in each neighborhood, the maps divided all areas of the Detroit metro region into four categories of lending priority: A (green) through D (red). Any African American presence in a neighborhood would ensure a rating of D and would galvanize white resistance to the entry of blacks into previously white neighborhoods. Moreover, under the redlining policies of the federal government, it became impossible to establish housing projects or residential developments targeting the housing needs of black residents of the city.

5. In its 1948 decision in *Shelley v. Kramer* regarding restrictive covenants in Saint Louis, Missouri, the U.S. Supreme Court acknowledged that there was no federal prohibition against including such covenants in property deeds, but ruled that no state or federal court could enforce them. In any case, African Americans faced other challenges in finding housing throughout Detroit. Sugrue (*Origins of the Urban Crisis*, 46) reports on an Urban League study that found white investors believed "that to make mortgages (to blacks) would incur the hostility and wrath of their white depositors," and "court the great disfavor of other investors, realtors, and builders." Fearing a backlash against their businesses within the white community, moreover, Detroit Real Estate Board Brokers "were especially sensitive to the impact of accusations of 'block-busting' on their business." Any broker found in violation of the encoded imperative not to sell properties to blacks in white areas would be denied access to the listing services and business benefits of Board membership.

6. In *Arc of Justice* (New York: Henry Holt, 2004), Kevin Boyle has crafted an engaging narrative documenting the efforts of Dr. Ossian Sweet, an African American physician, to move into a white Detroit neighborhood in 1925.

7. Sugrue, *Origins of the Urban Crisis*, 195.

8. Even in cases where there is not pronounced displacement of the African American community, as there was with many developments undertaken in the name of urban renewal, the unwavering focus among city leaders on large-scale, flashy development projects has, at the very least, drawn attention away from the plight of black neighborhoods.

9. Indeed, only with the establishment of Empowerment Zones under Clinton administration policy (designed to flood impoverished neighborhoods with capital and entrepreneurial incentives) have massive (re)development efforts taken an explicit, if not necessarily primary, interest in the condition and apparent health of specific neighborhoods and their residents.

10. See, for example, June Manning Thomas, *Redevelopment and Race: Planning a Finer City in Postwar Detroit* (Baltimore: Johns Hopkins University Press, 1997).

11. One striking example can be seen in a youth theater project. For more about this, see Charles Bright, "'It Was as If We Were Never There': Recovering Detroit's Past for History and Theater," *Journal of American History* 88, no. 4 (2002): 1440–45.

12. With assistance from organizations such as the Booker T. Washington Business Association, which was established in 1930 to provide institutional support to black business owners and continues to be an influential organization in the city, black entrepreneurial activity thrived in certain quarters of Detroit.

13. Wilfred Little worked in a department store there in the 1940s. "Along Hastings, that was the most active of the streets, because there was so much going on over there, everything from A to Z, which created a lot of activity. . . . At night it was a whole different population than there was in the daytime. . . . They had a lot of prostitution. . . . But in the daytime it was the grocery stores and household furnishings stores, [and] the cleaners." Cited in Elaine Latzman Moon, *Untold Tales, Unsung Heroes: An Oral History of Detroit's African American Community, 1918–1967* (Detroit: Wayne State University Press, 1994), 273–78.

14. Sugrue, *Origins of the Urban Crisis*, 47.

15. Joe T. Darden, Richard Child Hill, June Thomas, and Richard Thomas, *Detroit, Race and Uneven Development* (Philadelphia: Temple University Press, 1987).

16. For more on the difficulty of developing resistance efforts in the face of urban renewal delays, see Darden et al., *Detroit*, 173–74; Sidney Fine, *Violence in the Model City: The Cavanagh Administration, Race Relations, and the Detroit Riot of 1967* (Ann Arbor: University of Michigan Press, 1989), 62–63.

17. Eleanor Wolfe and Charles Lebeaux were contracted by the state to study the impacts of relocation on individuals and communities in the wake of urban renewal in Detroit. Their interviews with relocated former residents of the Elmwood community, conducted between two and three years after relocation, reveal the ways in which renewal projects can exact a lasting circumstantial and emotional tax on the affected residents. While one-quarter of the residents whom they interviewed felt "somewhat positive" about urban renewal generally, 30 percent felt "some resentment," and another 13 percent felt "very bitter" or "angry" about urban renewal in the city. When asked to recall their feelings at learning that they would have to move, over 70 percent of those interviewed said that, overall, they felt badly. And while half of the relocatees could name something positive about moving to a new neighborhood, these sentiments were usually oriented around the acquisition of superior lodging or other minor circumstantial improvements, such as cleaner yards, brighter streets, and so on. Expressions of loss were more frequently oriented around more intractable issues of "emotional disruption." Appraising the impact of relocation on their lives, former residents of Elmwood said things such as: "I lost my dream"; "I can't never have my own place again"; and "It's just the neighborhood. It

felt like home. That's the part I'm missing the most. Now it feels like I have no home." In Wolfe and Lebeaux's summation, "Seventy-seven percent referred at least once, and usually more often, to the loss of especially valued personal friendships and neighborhood relationships." Eleanor Wolfe and Charles Lebeaux, *Studies in Change and Renewal in an Urban Community* (Detroit: Wayne State University, 1965), 425–26.

18. Cited in Wolfe and Lebeaux, *Studies in Change*, 448, 468.

19. In 1966, while 65 percent of the population of Detroit was black, only 38 percent of the businesses were black owned. See B.J. Widick, *Detroit: City of Race and Class Violence* (Detroit: Wayne State University Press, 1989), 195.

20. Cited in Fine, *Violence in the Model City*, 160.

21. Ibid., 291.

22. Rita Griffin, "Soul Brother Signs Worked—For a While," *Michigan Chronicle*, July 29, 1967, 1A.

23. Fine, *Violence in the Model City*, 294.

24. Barbara Stanton, "An Orgy of Pillage Erupts Behind Fires and Violence," *Detroit Free Press*, July 25, 1967, 1A.

25. Recently, for example, John Hartigan has convincingly demonstrated how perceptions of the significance of race to the events of 1967 are locally and culturally contingent. He notes that "in the immediate aftermath, experts on civil disorders expressed opinions that the 'cause' of the riot was based more in the problem of poverty than in racial antagonism and conflict" (*Racial Situations: Class Predicaments of Whiteness in Detroit* [Princeton, NJ: Princeton University Press, 1999], 50). The circumstances that led to deadly rioting in Detroit in 1967 were hardly exclusive to that city and the peculiar state of race relations there; there were more than forty significant eruptions in other U.S. urban areas in the same year, most notably in Newark, Cincinnati, and Milwaukee, all born of a complex intertwining of racial tension along with the multiple and conflating stresses of economic disenfranchisement. Race relations in Detroit were also widely seen as much better than in many other large urban centers, particularly those where violence erupted in 1967. The intervention of the United Auto Workers, the Detroit Urban League, and the Detroit branch of the National Association for the Advancement of Colored People (NAACP) had provided the African American population with a soothing integrationist voice in public discourse that had tamed tensions over the course of the radical demographic changes in Detroit in the postwar era (Fine, *Violence in the Model City*). Heather Ann Thompson's book *Whose Detroit? Politics, Labor, and Race in a Modern American City* (Ithaca, NY: Cornell University Press, 2001) addresses the uncertain nature of the riots.

26. The African American Unity Movement, which had been associated with a violent outburst on Kercheval in 1966 that garnered national attention, had become a significant presence in the city. But the African American Unity Movement was only on the periphery of a much larger constellation of African American and black na-

tionalist organizations that emerged in the early 1960s, and that defined themselves against what they saw as the compromised politics of the NAACP, the United Auto Workers, and the Detroit Urban League. For example, the reverend Albert Cleage Jr., a young middle-class pastor on Detroit's West Side, developed an unlikely and stridently black nationalist agenda and became an articulate voice in front of the movement. Cleage was instrumental in organizing the Group of Advanced Leadership, which encouraged gun ownership in the black community. The New Student Movement, which was founded at Yale University, opened a chapter in Detroit in 1962, and worked to organize adolescents and young people, particularly on the lower East Side. UHURU (Swahili for "Freedom Now") was formed in 1963 by a group of students from Wayne State University and shared the militant orientation of the New Student Movement. Probably the most efficacious grassroots civil rights organizations in the city were the West Central Organization, which claimed to represent 60,000 people, mostly on the lower West Side, and the Detroit Council for Human Rights, which was instrumental in organizing the Walk to Freedom down Woodward, led by Martin Luther King Jr. and attended by 125,000 people in 1963 (Fine, *Violence in the Model City*).

27. Fine, *Violence in the Model City*, 99–104. It should hardly be surprising that African Americans were sorely underrepresented on the police force. While the hiring practices of the police department were discriminatory, according to federal district court evaluations, the revulsion between African Americans and the police department was mutual. For many in the black community, joining the police department was tantamount to an act of community betrayal. Out of 457 hirings between 1962 and 1963, a mere 19 were black. And even after more concerted, if still only halfhearted, efforts to recruit more blacks to the police force were instituted under the Cavanagh administration, the numbers hardly improved. In 1964 and 1965, when over 65 percent of the city's population was black, only 22 out of 314 new recruits to the department were African American (ibid., 104).

28. Lawrence P. Doss, "Tens Years Later: A Decade of Progress," *Michigan Chronicle*, July 23, 1977, 5A.

29. Lisa Pollak, "Rally to Recall Riot, Fight Despair," *Detroit Free Press*, August 1, 1992, 12B.

30. In late 1999, when there were 222 grocery stores in the city, only one was black owned. Oralander Brand-Williams, "Arab Shop Owners Open Job Doors to Young Blacks," *Detroit News*, August 13, 1999, 1A.

31. The Detroit metro area has been a primary destination for immigrants coming from the Middle East since the early 1940s. Estimates of the Arab population in the area range from one hundred thousand to three hundred thousand. The community of Dearborn, which borders Detroit on the city's West Side and is home to the Ford River Rouge plant, is now home to the largest Arab American community outside the Middle East.

32. The great disparity in small business entrepreneurialism between African

Americans and both whites and a host of immigrant groups cannot be explained solely through the social engineering agendas underlying, or embedded within, urban renewal projects. Indeed, the relative scarcity of blacks who are self-employed in small business has become the subject of considerable scholarship. While most recent work is concerned with the quality and breadth of African American entrepreneurial activity in the wake of the general shift to a service economy, some of these studies are relevant to circumstances in postwar Detroit. Roger Waldinger, *Still the Promised City? New Immigrants and African Americans in Postindustrial New York* (Cambridge, MA: Harvard University Press, 1996), formulates a theory of ethnic hiring queues that emphasizes the roles of social and familial networks in hiring practices among small business owners. He suggests that ethnic groups establish niches in the labor market where, though not free from racial and ethnic contestation, their social and familial networks will ensure a steady supply of affordable labor.

33. While doing fieldwork in southeast Detroit, I met an elderly gentleman at a local community center who had been a small business owner in the neighborhood between the 1950s and 1970s. Even though he was able to sustain his food distribution business by exploiting connections in local black churches, he faced all kinds of difficulties in finding funds to build his business. "So I had to cut back. And to keep from cutting back too much, I had to do business with a small loan company with high interest rates, interest on unpaid balance, like you pay on your credit card now. You get in a situation like that, and you're stuck with it for two years, and as fast as your profits come in, they going out. Now two or three of the white boys who I used to work with, all Jew boys, they went out and they made enough money, and while I'm out there struggling trying to get my merchandise in the chain stores, each one of them done opened up a packinghouse down on Eastern Market there. We was the same, hustling out there in the streets; they're white, doing business in our black neighborhood, [and] made enough money to open up their own packinghouse. And I can't borrow enough money to do business within my own neighborhood."

34. Associated Press, "Tensions High between Arab Store Owners, Black Patrons after Beating," May 21, 1999; Robyn Meredith, "Black Man's Death Raises Racial Tensions in Detroit," *New York Times*, May 19, 1999, http://query.nytimes.com/gst/fullpage.html?res=9A05E0DB133EF93AA25756C0A96F958260.

35. In August 2001, a campaign waged by the outspoken African American minister Horace Sheffield asked blacks throughout the city of Detroit to curtail their purchase of gasoline from Arab-owned gas stations. At the outset of Sheffield's campaign (called the B-Gas campaign), only ten of the city's approximately fourteen thousand gas stations were owned by blacks. Lolita Standifer, "Campaign Supports Black-Owned Businesses," *Michigan Chronicle*, August 8–14, 2001, 1A.

36. These categories have long had considerable purchase in urban anthropology, from Ulf Hannerz's *Soulside: Inquiries into Ghetto Culture and Community* (New York: Columbia University Press, 1969), to Elijah Anderson's *Code of the Street: De-*

cency, Violence, and the Moral Life of the Inner City (New York: W.W Norton, 1999),
to Mitchell Duneier's *Sidewalk* (New York: Farrar, Straus and Giroux, 2000).

Chapter 4: Called by a Holy Name

1. Since the mid-1980s, the lower East Side of Detroit has been the seat of a
widely publicized campaign to ban street billboards advertising liquor, called the
Coalition against Billboards Advertising Alcohol and Tobacco. Spearheaded by media-
savvy city councillor Tinsley-Talabi, the campaign has made effective use of local
grassroots organizations, especially Mack Alive, and has received lots of attention in
the local press. See http://www.drugstrategies.org.

2. See Thomas J. Sugrue, *Origins of the Urban Crisis: Race and Inequality in Post-
war Detroit* (Princeton, NJ: Princeton University Press, 1996); Reynolds Farley,
Sheldon Danziger, and Harry J. Holzer, *Detroit Divided* (New York: Russell Sage
Foundation, 2000).

3. The counterrallying residents, of course, were inaccurate in their repeated assertions that all the Mack Alive protesters were from the *east* side of the Mack Avenue bridge (spanning the Chrysler plant). Many of the Mack Alive protesters,
including Tinsley-Talabi, who was particularly vilified by Nafso and James, live on
the west side of the bridge. But I would argue that it is in part *for* their inaccuracy
that these assertions are so meaningful. For in this case, the continual invocation, by
the counterrallying residents, of the Chrysler plant as the geographic divide between
themselves and those whose interests lie with Mack Alive (those "on the other side
of the bridge") signifies a presumed association between the two that is independent
of geographic proximity. For the counterrallying residents, the Chrysler plant symbolizes the geographic *and* moral distinction between themselves and those whose
interests lie with Mack Alive; the interests of Chrysler, Mack Alive, and the city in
the lower East Side become deeply conflated.

4. Fears of residents living in the neighborhoods proximate to the proposed liquor
store are exacerbated by the emergence of housing developments that have been going up south of Jefferson Avenue, along the river, and in small pockets of green
ghetto near Indian Village. At the time of the protest, one townhouse development,
called English Village, was selling new condominiums in one of the most devastated-
looking neighborhoods in the city, at the corner of St. Paul and Crane. They were
market-price condos with an asking price of nearly $200,000.

5. In an article on community development, Wayne State University professor
and former city councillor Mel Ravitz pays particular attention to the Jefferson
Avenue Chrysler plant, and the trouble and suspicion that it engendered among
residents of city government and corporate agendas in the city ("Community Development: Salvation or Suicide," *Social Policy* 19, no. 2 [1988]: 17–22). Even the Empowerment Zones, it is worth noting, have been characterized by some acrimony and
distrust between those who are administering the program and residents of the

neighborhoods within the Empowerment Zone boundaries. This is not even to mention the more than coincidental alignment of the Empowerment Zones with influential industrial and business interests. That the geographic parameters of the Empowerment Zones include the Chrysler plant betrays some of the limitations of the program's commitment to neighborhood revitalization and maintenance. The Empowerment Zones, it might be argued, are as much about big business as they are about the microscopic struggles undertaken by neighborhood residents and community members. The specific inclusion of the Chrysler plant within the Empowerment Zone, at the expense of the surrounding residential and small business neighborhoods, seems especially egregious when one looks at the surrounding neighborhoods—those lying outside of the Empowerment Zone—where big businesses have not had a drawing power but where there is still a clear need for intervention.

6. Patricia Edmonds, "City Details Plans to Move Neighbors of Chrysler Plant," *Detroit Free Press*, August 16, 1986, 3A.

7. Jeannie Wylie, *Poletown: Community Betrayed* (Champaign-Urbana: University of Illinois Press, 1989).

8. David Ashenfelter, "Mayor Keeps Tight Lid on Public Information," *Detroit Free Press*, July 17, 1991, 1A.

9. Betsey Hansel, "Jefferson Plant Neighbors Complain of Secrecy," *Detroit Free Press*, August 21, 1986, 3A.

10. "About 350 people whose homes may be confiscated for renovation of the Jefferson Avenue Chrysler plant complained Wednesday that the city is keeping them in the dark about its plans while it is taking steps to evict them. . . . Rowana Massey . . . asked whether residents will be 'forced to sell . . . because private funders are sneaking up . . . to build condominiums so other people can live where we once lived? Why can't we lease our land so we can have something come in at the end of the month?' Parks said, 'There is no official agreement between the city and Chrysler.' 'If there is no agreement, why are people going through people's homes measuring?' responded Darann Johnson, 43, of Hillger. Parks replied, 'We are anticipating there will be some agreement.' Marie Wrickeson, 66, who has leased a house on Hillger for more than 30 years, said an assessor told her, 'The city is going to take your house whether you like it or not,' but she kept him out all the same. Many residents said they were resigned to the move, but they wanted to know the city's plans and be assured of a fair price for their property." Edmonds, "City Details Plans."

11. Nancy Ann Jeffrey, "Chrysler Plant Construction Rattles Suffering Residents," *Detroit Free Press*, September 27, 1990, 1B; Robert Musial, "Neighbors of Chrysler Protest Noise Wall," *Detroit Free Press*, November 13, 1990, 1B; Ginger Pullen, "Neighbors Say Street Has Lost Its Charm," *Detroit Free Press*, July 22, 1994.

12. For counterrallying residents from the west side of the Chrysler plant, Mack Alive thus represents the increasingly blurry boundaries of governmental bodies. Social theoretical work on the nature of states draws attention to this sort of categori-

cal blurring: Timothy Mitchell, "The Limits of the State: Beyond Statist Approaches and Their Critics," *American Political Science Review* 85 (1991): 77–96; Bob Jessop, *State Theory: Putting the Capitalist State in Its Place* (University Park: Pennsylvania State University Press, 1990).

One of the more interesting means through which states define their boundaries is through invocations of "community." Bolstered by a range of social and scholarly movements, including emphases on new social movements, identity politics, and cultural pluralism, the salience of community, as a notion that is usually counterposed against the state, has become especially pronounced in both local political activism and a wide range of activist scholarship; see, for example, Marie Weil and D. Gambel, "Community Practice Models," 577–94, in *Encyclopedia of Social Work*, ed. R.L. Edwards (Washington, DC: NASW Press, 1995). Both scholarly and colloquial invocations of community are, however (and obviously), rife with political significance. Whatever its particular connotations—shared values, traditions, skin color, or place of employment—community is a political construct and cannot be categorically distinguished from the state or state apparatuses. But what makes invocations of community particularly evocative is that they explicitly deny their own politics; they actively eschew their connections to the state. Hence, where Phillip Abrams ("Notes on the Difficulty of Studying the State," *Journal of Historical Sociology* 1, no. 1 [1988]: 58–89) has suggested that the state may hide actual political practice, it also makes sense to look at how community may hide the state.

13. Another line of rhetoric that surfaced during the speeches delivered by Mack Alive participants, but that I don't address here, drew parallels between crack cocaine and liquor. This, of course, draws a congruent parallel between Nafso and drug dealers. One speaker said, "There is a value that we place on lives. How much will a man give for his life? Surely not a bottle of liquor. Surely not an ounce of crack cocaine." And earlier in the day, Tinsley-Talabi had said, "Crack comes in a lot of forms, and what they want to sell is liquid crack. And we don't need any more crack in this community. Liquid crack, you gotta get it out of our community."

Chapter 5: Families and Fortunes, Spots and Homes

1. Some of this may be residually related to the demolition of enormous public housing projects, such as Harmon Gardens and the Jefferson Towers, in Detroit, after they had become overrun with drug-dealing activity. Jodi Wilgoren, "In Detroit, Abandoned Buildings Fall, Nothing Likely to Replace Them," *Grand Rapids Press*, July 7, 2002, 16A.

2. Homi K. Bhabha's discussion of "third spaces" (*The Location of Culture* [New York: Routledge, 1994]) where multiple cultural dimensions interact was particularly helpful to me in conceptualizing the nature of drug-dealing houses in Detroit.

3. Throughout the next three decades, Mobile and Detroit would become points at the ends of a shifting lever, as Ruby and members of her family would continu-

ously travel between them. For Ruby's family, each place, the South and the North, inflects the meanings and circumscribes the possibilities and liabilities of the other. Each has become, in different ways and at different times, a seemingly paradisiacal promised land and a refuge of last resort. In general, following the period of most frequent northerly movement of blacks in the United States, ending in the mid-1970s, there has continued to be a significant residual flow between Detroit and many Southern communities. Not only are there established patterns of return migration, especially among African American women, but through the end of the last century, long after myths of a promised land at the end of a free ride on a freight train had been dispelled, blacks have continued to come up to Detroit, often moving in with family members and seeking employment or business and entrepreneurial opportunities.

4. Over the course of Dude's incarceration, I continued to spend time with Ruby, eventually conducting several long interviews with her in her house in northeast Detroit, during which time we talked about some of the milestones in her life and her history in Detroit. Since she didn't have a car, I would often take her grocery shopping and run other errands for the household or for things related to Dude.

5. While her moving in with Booker obviously reflects Ruby's effort to hang on to both memories and a physical index of her daughter, it might signal other things as well: a move away from the drug trade, and a related move toward an imagined residential stability and domestic continuity. It is clear that for Ruby, the loss of Evie becomes wrapped up with and around her exhaustion with Marvin's involvement in drug dealing. As she describes it, her decision to leave Marvin seems to emerge from a blurred confluence of Evie's death and Marvin's continued dealing out of the house on Piper. And her move in with Booker reflects not only her desire to inhabit the space where her daughter died but to inhabit a stable space, where memories and expressions of family are not intruded on by the mercenary motivations and violence of the drug trade. It is of course a cruel but instructive irony that it was the city's demolition crews that led to Ruby's subsequent abandonment of the place where Evie last lived.

6. Affie is a quantity of dope (crack) that is equivalent to a kilo and at this writing has a street value of around $7,000.

7. Ruby's continual movement away from the drug trade, her practiced conviction that the infiltration of drug dealing into her house signaled its end as a home, stands in great contrast to the cultivation of household space undertaken by her children. In both Felicity's and May's cases, the distinction between spots and houses seems important and, as with many such distinctions, both clear and unresolved at the same time. According to Felicity, the distinction seems to hinge on whether one lives where they are working. A spot, according to her formulation, is a space devoted solely to selling drugs, while a house may be a place where customers come to buy drugs, but it is also where people are residing, where a household (with attendant familial connotations) has been established. For May, the distinction turns on

a slightly different fulcrum. For her, a spot is someplace where "nics" or "dime rocks" are sold; someplace, then, with a particular threshold of active customer foot traffic, especially among poor crack addicts, who would typically not have money to buy more than a couple of rocks at a time. Thus, even though May and her boyfriend were moving drugs though the house, and even though there was a modicum of small-time dealing around it, the house on Van Dyke was not a spot because there wasn't a steady stream of customers there. And here Felicity's and May's assessments converge. Spots, in both of their estimations, are public spaces, and houses are not. But the categories, then, become slippery. For Felicity, the devoted house on Van Dyke becomes a family space, full of friends and relatives. Unlike Ruby, however, neither imagines family household spaces to be incompatible with drug dealing. For both, the relationship between residential habitation, household formation, and residential drug dealing is much more fluid.

8. As for so many other young dope dealers in Detroit, family becomes, as a matter of both practical arrangement and meaning, inextricably tied to the drug trade for Dude. But for all his acknowledged indebtedness to members of his family and people living in the "Parkview neighborhood" who are part of the "family" of dealers in the area, Dude was nevertheless insistent about his independence in the dope game and his potential to provide for himself through it.

Chapter 6: The Thickness of Blood

1. One of the programs offered through intensive probation in Wayne County is a visit to the county morgue, where juveniles are exposed to the performance of an autopsy.

2. Ruby's prescription drug dealing became an important source of supplemental income. While she was reluctant to discuss this with me, she was always insistent that this was categorically different than selling illegal narcotics, as members of her family were doing.

3. Included within the estimated project expenditures was over half a million dollars earmarked for residential relocation costs. Among other expenditures detailed in development plan records, only the costs associated with buying the real estate itself, an obviously related expense, approaches this amount. Source documents acquired from the Detroit Planning and Development Department.

4. John Hartigan, "Green Ghettos and the White Underclass," *Social Research* 64 (Summer 1997): 339–65.

5. The house is owned by one of the few men from the neighborhood who has managed to parlay his involvement in the dope game into successful participation in legitimate business ventures. Its titleholder owns several houses in the area and a dry-cleaning store as well, and is particularly accommodating of the efforts of younger dope hustlers to establish dope spots.

6. When he was still locked up, I had asked Dude about the spreading popular-

ity of ecstasy (MDMA) among black kids in southeast Detroit (something that I had seen occur with remarkable rapidity and seeming social significance in other neighborhoods), and he said that he hadn't seen any of it. But now, only several months later, it seemed ubiquitous to Dude, and had become an important part of the daily life of both the men and women, girls and boys, who were hanging out and working on Pleasant.

7. This, of course, hardly sounded like an effective modeling of wraparound services to me. As she explained it to me, Dude's treatment would only be meted out under residential conditions established by the treatment team: that Dude stay with his mother. But this is treatment that does not acknowledge any responsibility for the obvious and real difficulty (and difficulty at the heart of many other problems for young people in Detroit), in this or surely many other cases, involved in getting clients to stay where the treatment team would like them to stay.

8. With his decision to lay low in the house on Pleasant, taking advantage of its institutional invisibility and thus safety from the wrapping fingers of the juvenile justice system and other state institutions, Dude elicits a tension between public and private household space. While Ruby's house on the northeast side is where a number of Dude's close biological relatives live and is the official residence of both his guardian and himself, it is also (*and therefore*) the site around which Dude and members of his family are most vulnerable to state intrusion and sanction. For Dude, Forrester's Christmas morning apprehension by the police, after opening presents at Ruby's house, made this unequivocally clear. But sites of heavy drug-dealing traffic, while they are public spaces of a sort, are for obvious reasons off institutional maps. Even when they are put onto institutional maps—when they become the frequent targets of police or negative community attention—they are usually promptly shut down. While Ruby's house may in some ways be the most domestic of the households through which Dude was traveling (in its association with family co-habitation and the explicit exclusion of drug-dealing activity), it is also the least "private." And isn't privacy critical to making domestic space what it is?

9. Pam Belluck, "Detroit Police Cast Wide Net over Homicide 'Witnesses,'" *New York Times*, April 11, 2001, http://query.nytimes.com/gst/fullpage.html?res=9C03E1 D71631F932A25757C0A9679C8B63&sec=&spon=&pagewanted=all.

Chapter 7: Playgrounds and Punishment

1. There has been considerable work done on the constructions of *time* in the production and reproduction of subjectivity, most influentially in Michel Foucault, *Discipline and Punish: The Birth of the Prison*, trans. Alan Sheridan (New York: Vintage Books, 1977); Michel Foucault, *Power/Knowledge: Selected Interviews and Other Writings, 1972–1977*, ed. and trans. Colin Gordon (New York: Pantheon Books, 1980); Michel Foucault, "Governmentality," in *The Foucault Effect: Studies in Governmentality*, ed. Graham Burchell, Colin Gordon, and Peter Miller (Chicago:

University of Chicago Press, 1991); Katherine Verdery, *What Was Socialism, and What Comes Next?* (Princeton, NJ: Princeton University Press, 1996).

2. In his effort to explain how "total institutions" such as prisons suspend the identities of their charges, making them more pliable for carceral administrators, Erving Goffman writes: "The full meaning for the inmate of being 'in' or 'on the outside' does not exist apart from the special meaning to him of 'getting out' or 'getting on the outside.' In this sense, total institutions do not really look for cultural victory. They create and sustain a particular kind of tension between the home world and the institutional world and use this persistent tension as strategic leverage in the management of men" (*Asylums: Essays on the Social Situation of Mental Patients and Other Inmates* [Chicago: Aldine, 1961], 13).

I am less interested here in the managerial efficacy of the administrative strategies employed by the keepers of juveniles than the nature of the tension between *outside* and *inside* moralities and discourses for young people in Detroit, especially as they pertain to questions about the dimensions of and distinctions between childhood and adulthood.

3. The decline of the crack cocaine epidemic has also been significant in shaping the relationship between drug dealing and social understandings of childhood. Images of the "crack fiend" have become potent symbols of the crisis within struggling urban communities, and the attendant social stigma has compelled most young people to avoid using the drug. Indeed, one of the features that most distinguishes the contemporary drug trade from its earlier forms is that crack and heroin dealers working on the street today categorically avoid using or abusing most of the drugs that they sell. Of hundreds of youths, I met only one or two young black men who had both sold and used crack or heroin. This prevailing tendency in Detroit is borne out in studies of the drug trade in other cities. See, for example, J. Fagan, "Drug Selling and Licit Income in Distressed Neighborhoods: The Economic Lives of Street-Level Drug Users and Dealers," in *Drugs, Crime, and Social Isolation: Barriers to Urban Opportunity*, ed. Adele V. Harrell and George E. Peterson (Washington, DC: Urban Institute Press, 1992); Bruce Jacobs, *Dealing Crack: The Social World of Streetcorner Selling* (Boston: Northeastern University Press, 1999). But as some dealers have informed me, "Everyone has a relative on crack in Detroit." And these family members, consistently from the dealers' parents' or grandparents' generations, contribute to the construction of a generational rift drawn by crack cocaine.

4. The semiotic significance of this is relatively plain: these are inscribed connections to the outside world, to places around which the identities of the kids at the facility are formed. And it is not insignificant that these inscriptions are made on facility property. For kids who must always wear the phrase "Property of the Wayne County Juvenile Detention Facility" stenciled on their backs, such inscriptions, on file folders, lunch trays, and paper cups, are a means of literally remarking on and reappropriating their physical surroundings.

5. While Rodney's movement of our conversation from his case, to his ambiva-

lence about hustling drugs, to theology seemed at the time more manic than thematic, his shifting concerns about drug dealing, mortality, eternity, and his uncertainty about his future in the justice system appear to hang together in the same tilted balance. Concerns with a punitive God, informing ambivalence about continued participation in drug dealing, would arise over and over in my discussions with young people in the juvenile detention facility. And my sense is that this tendency toward contrite reflection is provoked not only by the fear of punishment and the hopes of detained kids that they might earn at least a measure of karmic reprieve through promises to lead a better life. Rather, much of the provocation for the moral rumination that happens in the juvenile detention facility revolves precisely around questions about the relationship between and parameters of adulthood and childhood. Detained young people wonder if they are good in the eyes of God and, in the same breath and with a sense for their mutual dependence, if they are children in the eyes of the court.

Chapter 8: Across the Street

1. Pickett was a black rodeo star who lived from 1870 until 1932 and performed in the "101 Wild Ranch Show" with Buffalo Bill and others.

2. Interestingly, the kids often turned the "threat" of movement across the street back onto the staff people. When older inmates were especially fed up with staff at the Wayne County Juvenile Detention Facility, they would frequently plot to be moved across the street, where, it was perceived, they would be "left alone."

3. The so-called punk prison was a correctional facility designed to detain minors sentenced as adults until they turned twenty, at which point they would be transferred to a regular adult correctional facility. The pet project of former governor Engler, the punk prison was meant to house an anticipated wave of young "superpredators." The facility was closed in 2005, when these young criminals never materialized.

4. Circumstances where young people face both adult and juvenile charges at the same time were not especially rare on Pickett. Rodney is another example.

5. The institutional response to Dude's acting out was typical. That is, such behavior was generally not seen as potentially treatable or understandable in any case—in a young person suffering extraordinary anxiety and despair about his circumstances and what the future might hold. Rather, it was simply taken as misbehavior. There was virtually no effort made to get Dude a counselor or social worker, even though isolation was clearly only exacerbating his frustration and increasing the likelihood that there would be eruptions of violence on the unit. While Dude was in isolation on Pickett, I talked with another staff person about getting him mental health treatment. She said that she had been trying to get someone to come talk to Dude for several days. "I could see for a couple of days that he has been about to snap. I mean, he's been getting into it with kids on the unit, and he's throwing stuff

around—the boy needs help! I like Dude, I really do. And you know, if he likes you, he'll really talk to you. Course, if he doesn't like you, then you better watch out! I'm tellin' you, the mental health people don't give a shit. They only want people on their unit that's taking drugs or that's easy for them to deal with. But instead of taking the kids who need to go, and believe me, there are plenty of kids on each unit who are having a lot of trouble and could really use the help, they take the level 4s only—the best-behaved kids. What kind of bullshit is that?! They only want to take the kids that it's going to be easy for them to deal with?"

6. In an institutional context where childhood is equated with the impossibility of intent, drug dealing is thought about as a means to be both a child and behave with intention. The dope game is an institution where, in any case, the distinctions between childhood and adulthood are fluid instead of contradictory.

Chapter 9: Neighborhood Watching

1. For an interesting, if not especially theoretically enlightening, engagement with mapping, see Harriot Beazley, "Street Boys in Yogyakarta: Social and Spatial Exclusion in the Public Spaces of the City," in *A Companion to the City*, ed. Gary Bridge and Sophie Watson (Oxford: Blackwell, 2000).

2. It was clear from the conversations that he and I were having in the detention facility that the dimensions of Rodney's neighborhood were inextricably linked to various sorts of drug-dealing activity there. The spaces people were inhabiting, and the particular combinations of people inhabiting particular spaces, in other words, were for Rodney first and foremost referenced and understood in relation to one another through their importance to the neighborhood drug trade.

3. The de Certeauean walk that Dexter Boys take, the elementary form of their everyday experience, and the conditions of their subjectivity and collective identity are characterized by these transgressive possibilities. In the last decade or so, such cross-cultural "routes" have become an explicit interest of anthropologists. See, for example, James Clifford, *Routes: Travel and Translation in the Late Twentieth Century* (Cambridge, MA: Harvard University Press, 1997).

4. The vaguely sociological nature of the introduction to the neighborhood that Rodney had given me suggested an almost neat taxonomy. There seemed to be a kind of mechanical simplicity or order to the configuration of the various drug markets in the area. As Rodney described it to me, and as it seemed as he was chaperoning me from small side streets out to the corners on Dexter, the neighborhood space where the Dexter Boys circulated was a relatively insulated world unto itself. But for the Dexter Boys, the neighborhood is both bounded and permeable. They have strong sentimental relationships to it, but as both a "home" and a market space. Their dreams for it, then, do not only have to do with a thuggish "claiming" of it; this is not about gang territory. Their sentiments about the market value of the Dexter neighborhood draw much more significantly on the history of retail space in

the area, and their own potentials to participate in the legitimate retail business community.

5. The shirt, which still hangs in my closet, is gray and white, half silk and half polyester. It's sewn from a print fabric on which is written the phrase "It's not where you're from, it's what you Roc," in a sort of pseudogothic font. Though Rodney did not look at it too closely, the shirt alone amounts to a cultural critic's field day. On one level, the phrase adorning the shirt is an obvious reference to the countless stories told by members of the black community who have "done good" and "made it out of the hood" to those aspiring to do the same, whom, it is presumed, include most blacks living in poor neighborhoods in cities such as Detroit. But in this case, its inscription on and reference to clothing sends a slightly altered message: it is now an evocation of possible liberation through consumption, the magical semiotic potency of clothing in the mythologized struggle of young African Americans to overcome the gravity of their surroundings and places of origin. None of this is even to mention the great irony of my wearing the shirt in the company of Rodney and his friends from Dexter. Indeed, the shirt articulates with eerie pithiness Rodney's precise hopes for the semiotic significance of the clothing for me and my potential legitimacy on Dexter—exactly the sort of neighborhood that the clothing, on one level, imagines its wearer coming from. Of course, it is widely known that the most voracious, consistent, and solvent consumers of hip-hop cultural material are white suburban young people, many of whom may fantasize about achieving a sense of belonging in the "gritty," urban neighborhoods about which so many hip-hop artists rap. The message on the clothing may also be read as targeted precisely toward them. In its formulation of these two antithetical audiences, the Rocawear shirt both dismisses and romanticizes the quintessential urban ghetto.

6. The Detroit police headquarters is located at 1300 Beaubien.

7. For the Dexter Boys, most legitimate means of making money are preferable to slinging drugs, even if they involve submissions to various sorts of cultural "disrespect," like meniality, having to answer to a hierarchy, and so on. This becomes particularly clear through talk about the distinction between "legal" and "illegal" money. For those working in the drug trade, any hopes of accumulating assets is dependent on a transformation of cash—it's *laundering* in the common fiscal parlance; illegal money is simply not worth as much as legal money. Any work that can provide a steady flow of legal money is therefore especially valuable.

Chapter 10: Of Hot Dogs and Heroin

1. Michel Foucault introduces the idea of a micro-physics of power (*Discipline and Punish: The Birth of the Prison*, trans. Alan Sheridan [New York: Vintage Books, 1977]) to demonstrate how forces of political and disciplinary power play on physical bodies.

2. Some estimates put the total number of Albanians residing in the metro area

at around sixty thousand. Detroit is the second-largest Albanian community in the United States, after New York City. Kenneth Walters cited in Wayne State University, "First in the USA: Albanian Language Instruction Comes to WSU," press release, February 17, 2003.

3. Bloomfield Hills and Farmington Hills are both wealthy, predominantly white suburbs of Detroit.

4. It is a walk, in this case, that is mapped by ecstasy. As a white, adolescent drug, ecstasy is the subject of news reports about suburban kids feeling constrained by the institutional roteness of their leisure-class privilege. But as the Dexter Boys say, "It's hit the city." Most of the neighborhood drug dealers have tried it, some take it regularly, and for kids on Dexter it promises an embodied chemical and semiotic transportation to the privileged sectors of U.S. society—to Bloomfield, to Farmington Hills.

Chapter 11: Being Seen

1. James Baldwin, *The Fire Next Time* (1963; repr., New York: Vintage Press, 1991), 2.

2. But such displays are also, of course, a kind of self-conscious parody of the accumulation of wealth itself.

Index

Abrams, Phillip, 298n12
Admiral Theater building, 61, 65, 66–67, 73–74
Adult Community Movement for Equality, 51
African American Unity Movement, 51, 293–94n26
Albanian Americans
  and Coney Island restaurants, 41–42, 208, 223–24, 230, 231, 232–33, 234–37, 254
  Detroit-area population, 305–6n2
  and drug trade, 236–37, 290n9
Anderson, Elijah, 287n20
Anthony, Wendell, 57
Arab Americans
  African American–Arab American relations, 57, 295n35
  Dearborn community, 41, 294n31
  Detroit-area population, 294n31
  and drug trade, 127, 290n9
  small businesses, 41, 56, 57, 205–6, 295n35
Archer, Dennis, 79, 80
automobile industry, 14–15, 46, 53

Bachelard, Gaston, 77, 82
Baldwin, James, 260
Baltimore's urban renewal projects, 285n2
Barthes, Roland, 195
Bennet, Karen, 55
Bhabha, Homi, 23, 298n2
"blockbusting," 45–46, 291n5
"Blood" influenced gang culture, 103–4

Booker T. Washington Business Association, 292n12
Bourgois, Philippe, 287n20
Boyle, Kevin, 291n6
"Branford," 176–79
Brown, Jake, 51–52

Canadians in Detroit, 43
Carroll, Lewis, 223
"Cedric," 179–81, 182–83
Chafets, Ze'ev, 289n1
Chaldean Americans
  and drug trade, 127
  and riots of summer 1967, 52–53
  small businesses, 4–5, 41, 52–53, 56, 57, 127
Chalmers Motor Corporation, 69
Chicago youth gangs and drug trade, 286n16
Chrysler Corporation, 68–70. See also Jefferson Avenue Chrysler Plant
churches, black, 4, 41
Civil Rights Commission, Community Relations Division, 54
civil rights movement in Detroit, 4, 50–56, 293–94n26
Cleage, Albert, Jr., 293–94n26
Coalition against Billboards Advertising Alcohol and Tobacco, 296n1
Cobo Hall, 46
Comerica Park, 46
Commission on Community Relations, 51
Compuware, 37

Coney Island restaurants
    "A-Eagles" chain, 234
    Albanian American owners, 208, 223–24,
        230, 231, 232–33, 234–37, 254
    Dexter and Providence location, 207–8,
        213–15, 218–19, 222, 223–57
    and drug trade, 224, 227–28, 229–32,
        237–55
    shooting at, 218–20, 235–36
    spatial politics/interior configurations,
        213–14, 224–26, 254–55
Conyers, John, 54
court-appointed lawyers, 170, 178, 181, 185,
    188
crack cocaine
    decline of epidemic, 302n3
    parallels drawn between liquor and, 298n13
    selling, 125, 165
"Crip" influenced gang culture, 103–4
Culpepper, Otis, 180, 182
"culture of the street," 23, 287n20
curfews, 26, 289n25

de Certeau, Michel, 195
Detroit 300 Committee (tercentennial commit-
    tee), 33–35, 36–37, 40
Detroit City Council, 72, 79
Detroit city government
    black representation (and Young's mayor-
        ship), 36
    and the school takeover (1999–2005),
        18–19
Detroit Council for Human Rights,
    293–94n26
Detroit Economic Club, 14
Detroit Free Press, 1, 18, 53, 54–55, 70
Detroit Medical Center, 48, 50, 55
"Detroit Plan" (1949), 48
Detroit Police Department, 54
Detroit Real Estate Board, 45, 291n5
Detroit Urban League, 293nn25–26
Detroit's history, 19
    and African American identity, 19, 35,
        36–37
    marking of 2001 tercentennial, 33–35,
        36–37
    postwar era, 15, 19, 34–35, 43, 48–50
    prewar black migration, 44, 290nn1–2
    World War II–era, 34
Detroit's national reputation
    as America's only "third-world city," 23,
        289n1

as emblematic of postindustrial urban
    tragedy, 23, 289n1
as "The Most Dangerous City in America,"
    16
Dexter neighborhood and Dexter Boys, 1–2,
    4–5, 207–8, 212–22, 223–57, 272–84
    identification with neighborhood, 202–3,
        217–18, 252–54, 281–83, 304n2, 304n4
    Party Time liquor store/grocery store, 207
    Rodney and neighborhood drug trade, 202,
        205–15, 220–22, 227–28, 256–57,
        304n2, 304n4, 305n7
    Rodney and the shooting at the Goal Post,
        257, 259–60, 262–63, 265, 268–69
    Rodney and the Wadsworth house, 197–99,
        203–4, 269–71
    Rodney's murder, 274–84
    and suburb/city divide, 217–18, 252–54,
        306n4
    talk about jobs/work, 221–22, 305n7
    and transgressive cross-cultural movement,
        203, 254–55, 304nn3–4
    See also Coney Island restaurants; Goal Post
        strip club; "Rodney"
Doss, Lawrence, 54
drug trade (street drug trade)
    and adolescent girls, 91, 100–101
    arrests per year, 286n17
    and childhood/adulthood, 155–56, 302n3,
        302n5, 304n6
    Coney Island restaurant on Dexter, 224,
        227–28, 229–32, 237–55
    conversations with Dude during his proba-
        tion, 121–22, 123–31, 132–34, 136–41
    conversations with Dude's adopted mother,
        Ruby, 83–94, 102–3, 105–7, 111–21,
        134–38, 299n4
    conversations with Rodney, 9, 11–13, 25–27,
        158–72
    crack cocaine, 125, 165, 298n13, 302n3
    creation of social spaces and identities,
        13–14, 23, 24, 75, 82, 155–56, 217–18,
        261–62, 288n23
    and Detroit public schools, 17
    distinction between "legal" and "illegal"
        money, 305n7
    distinctions between "homes" and "spots,"
        81, 101, 102, 117, 299–300n7
    domestic/commercial spaces, 82
    drug use by dealers, 302n3
    Dude's family, 28, 82–110, 111–44, 300n8
    Dude's household on Pleasant Street,

121–25, 131–34, 136, 139, 142–44, 300n5, 301n8

and Ecstasy (MDMA), 133, 142, 236, 251–53, 300–301n6, 306n4

and emblems of marginalized black underclass, 22–23, 287n20

and families/family dynamics, 21–22, 28, 82–110, 111–44

and gangs, 20–21, 103–5, 180, 242, 286n16

"getting ghost" metaphor, 2–3

and guns/weapons, 89, 101, 117

and house raids, 97–99, 102–3, 134–35, 301n8

household spaces (selling drugs out of houses), 81–82, 88–90, 92, 93, 96–99, 100–101, 102, 106, 109, 116–18, 255, 298n2, 299n5, 299n7, 301n8

the Kercheval-Pennsylvania neighborhood, 120–21, 122–27

and life expectancy, 27

and liquor stores, 16, 126–31

moral/religious ruminations, 11–13, 171, 188–90, 193, 302–3n5

pervasiveness in interior city, 21

and the police, 117–18, 126, 129–30, 134–35, 144, 233, 238–39, 244, 246–47, 249–50, 251–52

prescription drugs, 115, 300n2

Rodney and Dexter Boys, 202, 205–15, 220–22, 227–28, 256–57, 304n2, 304n4, 305n7

Ruby's reasons for moving away from lower East Side, 84–85, 102–3, 105–6, 118

and suburb/city spatial divisions, 217–18

trajectories of distribution and exchange, 21, 155–56

and urban renewal/demolition of abandoned houses, 80–81, 298n1

and visibility/invisibility, 261–62

white customers, 227–28, 239–40, 248–49

"Dude"

acting out and enforced "isolation," 186–87, 303–4n5

and adult time/juvenile time, 183–84, 189, 191–93

conversations while on probation, 121–22, 123–31, 132–34, 136–41

conversations within the detention facility, 9–10, 27–29, 95–99, 103–5, 107–10

court hearings/trial, 183–86, 187–93

describing a house raid, 97–99

on drug selling and indebtedness to family, 108–10, 300n8

drug treatment and wraparound services, 139, 301n7

enrolling in school, 137–38

family dynamics and drug trade, 28, 82–110, 111–44, 300n8

and gang culture, 103–5

in mental health unit, 141–44, 147–48, 149–53

moral ruminations, 188–90, 193

in prison, 194

on probation from detention facility, 107–10, 111–15, 121–22, 136–41

probation violations, 137–40

reputation at detention facility, 94–95

skepticism about the criminal justice system, 96

and Walker's accidental death, 141–44, 147–49, 183–86, 187–93

East Side. *See* lower East Side

East Side Medical Clinic, 121

Eastpointe suburb, 251

Ecstasy (MDMA), 133, 142, 236, 251–53, 300–301n6, 306n4

Ellison, Ralph, 258, 261

Elmwood Park urban renewal area, 48–49, 50, 292n17

Empowerment Zones, 291n9, 296–97n5

Engler, John, 175–76, 303n3

families

conversations with Dude's adopted mother, Ruby, 83–94, 102–3, 105–7, 111–21, 134–38, 299n4

and drug trade, 21–22, 28, 82–110, 111–44

Dude's family, 28, 82–110, 111–44, 300n8

selling drugs out of houses, 81–82, 88–90, 92, 93, 96–99, 100–101, 102, 106, 109, 116–18, 298n2, 299n5, 299n7, 301n8

violence/abuse of children, 91

Federal Home Loan Bank board, 45

Finch, Mary, 61–62

Fine, Sidney, 52, 53

Ford, 34

Ford Field, 46

Foucault, Michel, 145, 225, 305n1

Frank Murphy Hall of Justice, 168, 175

Franks, Samuel, 119–20

"Fredrick," 181–83

freeway development, 47–48

gangs
  "Blood"/"Crip" influenced gang culture,
    103–4
  Chicago, 286n16
  and drug trade, 20–21, 103–5
  Dude and lower East Side, 103–5
  recent trends in youth gang membership, 21,
    286n16
  "YBI," 20–21, 180, 242
Gangster Disciples, 103
gas stations, 41, 57, 205–6, 295n35
General Motors, 34, 37, 69–70
geography of Detroit, 19–20, 35–36, 37–39,
    263–64. *See also* neighborhoods of Detroit
"getting ghost," 2–3
Goal Post strip club, 215–16, 257
  shooting at, 257, 259–60, 262–63, 265,
    268–69
Goffman, Erving, 302n2
Great Migration, 44, 290nn1–2
Great Society Programs, 55
"green ghetto," 123
Grosse Pointe suburb, 38, 119
Group of Advanced Leadership, 293–94n26
gun violence, 24, 95–96, 179, 209
  and drug trade, 89, 101, 117
  Dude and Walker's accidental death,
    141–44, 147–49, 183–86, 187–93
  and gangs, 105
  Rodney's gunshot wound in Jackson, 265–67
  Rodney's murder in Dexter neighborhood,
    274–84
  See also Goal Post strip club

Harlem Renaissance, 44
Hartigan, John, 293n25
Hastings Street neighborhood
  freeway development/urban renewal, 47
  small businesses, 47, 49–50, 292nn12–13
Henry Ford Hospital, 219
Hill, Gil, 79
Home Owners' Loan Corporation, 45
house raids, 97–99, 102–3, 134–35, 301n8
houses and drug trade
  distinctions between "homes" and "spots,"
    81, 101, 102, 117, 299–300n7
  house raids, 97–99, 102–3, 134–35,
    301n8
  selling drugs out of houses, 81–82, 88–90,
    92, 93, 96–99, 100–101, 102, 106, 109,
    116–18, 255, 298n2, 299n5, 299n7,
    301n8

urban renewal and "teardown policies,"
    80–81, 298n1
Huizinga, Johan, 145

identities of young drug dealers
  and childhood/adulthood, 155–56, 302n3,
    302n5, 304n6
  creation of, 13–14, 23, 24, 75, 82, 155–56,
    217–18, 261–62, 288n23
  identification with the "dope game," 155–56
  and suburb/city spatial divisions, 217–18
  visibility/invisibility, 261–62
Indian Village, 14, 38, 122–23, 296n4
Iraqi Americans. *See* Chaldean Americans

Jackrabbit's liquor store, 126–31
Jacobs, Jane, 41
"Jarhead," 116–17, 135
Jefferson Avenue Chrysler plant, 60, 63–64,
    67–70, 296n3, 296n5, 297n10
Jeffries, Edward, 48
Joe Louis Arena, 46
Johnson, Pres. Lyndon, 55
Jones, Milton "Butch," 20–21
"Justin," 179–81
juvenile detention facility (Wayne County
    Juvenile Detention Facility), 9–13
  adult time/juvenile time, 154–55, 174–79,
    183–84, 189, 190–93, 303n4
  and "aftercare" programs, 17
  author's conversations with Dude, 9–10,
    27–29, 95–99, 103–5, 107–10, 183–93
  author's conversations with Rodney, 9,
    11–13, 25–27, 158–72, 179–80, 182
  Branford's case, 176–79
  Cedric and Justin, 179–81, 182–83
  charter school classrooms, 157
  and court-appointed lawyers, 170, 178, 181,
    185, 188
  decisions made for/about the incarcerated
    youth, 153–54
  distinctions between childhood and adult-
    hood, 154–56, 302n2, 302n5, 304n6
  Dude's enforced "isolation," 186–87,
    303–4n5
  Fredrick, 181–83
  individual cell units, 162–63, 173–74
  inmate newsletter, 161–62
  inmates' cynicism about criminal justice
    system, 10, 158–59, 161–62, 183
  inmates' emergent identities, 154–56,
    289n26, 302n2

inmates' identification with "dope game,"
    155–56
inmates on "Bill Pickett" unit, 174–83
and intentions/capacity for intent, 190,
    192–93, 304n6
and "level system," 174
mandatory "reflection" periods, 161, 169
mental health services, 141–44, 147–48,
    149–53, 303–4n5
move to the new building, 173–76
and original juvenile jail building (the old
    youth home), 156–58, 173, 175
passage of time in, 153–56
proximity to adult county jail across the
    street, 173–74, 175, 303n2
volunteer chaplain, 11–13, 25–26
"Juwan," 4–9

Karim, Talib, 55
Keep the Vote, No Takeover Coalition, 18–19
Kercheval and Pennsylvania neighborhood,
    38–39, 43
    citizens' district council, 119–20
    and the "green ghetto," 122–23
    Jackrabbit's liquor store, 126–29
    and riots of summer 1967, 50, 51, 53, 55
    and street drug trade, 120–21, 122–27
    transformation into exclusively black
        neighborhood, 43
    urban development and housing
        demolition/residential relocation,
        118–21, 300n3
    World War II–era, 43
Kilpatrick, Caroline, 79
Kilpatrick, Kwame, 79–81
King, Martin Luther, Jr., 293–94n26

Lamont Gardens, 181–82
Lebeaux, Charles, 292n17
Lefebvre, Henri, 288n23
Levy, Burton, 54
Lincoln Hall of Juvenile Justice, 156
liquor stores, 4–5, 41, 127
    at corner of Mack and Bewick, 59, 62
    at corner of Pingree and Linwood, 4–5
    glass partitions, 127–28
    Iraqi Chaldean owners, 4–5, 41, 127
    Jackrabbit's, 126–29
    and Mack Alive protests, 60–61, 62, 298n13
    spatial tensions, 127–29
    and street drug trade, 61, 126–31
    See also Mack Alive demonstrations

Little, Wilfred, 292n13
Lodge and Ford freeways, 47–48
Lomax Temple A.M.E. Zion Church, 55
Lou's Motor City Marketplace, 60, 61. See also
    Mack Alive demonstrations
lower East Side
    campaign to ban billboards advertising
        liquor, 296n1
    and civil rights movement/black nationalist
        politicization, 293–94n26
    gang culture, 103–5
    and the "green ghetto," 123
    impact of freeway development, 47
    postwar urban renewal projects, 48–49
    and Woodward Avenue, 37–38
    See also Mack Alive demonstrations

Mack Alive demonstrations, 59–75
    and Admiral Theater building site, 61, 65,
        66–67, 73–74
    campaign to ban billboards advertising
        liquor, 296n1
    counterrallying residents, 65–74, 296n3,
        297n12
    drawing parallels between crack cocaine and
        liquor, 298n13
    and history of hostilities between
        middle-class/poorer blacks, 64,
        67–68, 296n3
    influential membership, 59–60
    invocations of belonging and "community,"
        71–74, 297–98n12
    and Jefferson Avenue Chrysler plant,
        60, 63–64, 67–70, 296n3, 296n5,
        297n10
    leaders' speeches, 70–73, 298n13
    Nafso's proposed neighborhood grocery
        store, 60–74
    public opinion of nonblack businesses
        selling liquor, 60–61, 62
    street demonstrations/rally, 61–74
    suspicions surrounding neighborhood gentri-
        fication/control of neighborhood property,
        67–71, 296nn3–5, 297n10
marginalization and black underclass, 22–23,
    287nn19–20
Maxey Boys' Training School, 177
mental health services, 141–44, 147–48,
    149–53, 303–4n5
Mexican Americans, 290n9
Michigan Chronicle, 52, 54
Michigan Family Independence Agency, 178

migration patterns between American South
    and Detroit, 85–88, 100, 298–99n3
    prewar Great Migration, 44, 290nn1–2
    return migration, 88, 100, 298–99n3
Miller, Arthur, 1
Moore, Helen, 18–19
moral ruminations
    Dude's, 188–90, 193
    Rodney's, 11–13, 171, 302–3n5
Mt. Elliot Cemetery, 38

Nafso, Lou, 60–71, 74. See also Mack Alive
    demonstrations
National Association for the Advancement of
    Colored People (NAACP), Detroit chap-
    ter, 54, 293nn25–26
    and African American–Arab American
        relations, 57
    and riots of summer 1967, 293n25
National League of Cities, 79
Native Americans in Detroit, 39
neighborhoods of Detroit
    architecture, 43
    and freeway development, 47–48
    geographic dispersion of middle-class blacks,
        45–46
    Hastings Street and black-owned
        businesses (1940s–1950s), 47, 49–50,
        292nn12–13
    and housing demolition programs, 80–81,
        118–21, 298n1
    housing discrimination/discriminatory racial
        covenants, 45, 291nn4–5
    Kercheval and Pennsylvania neighborhood,
        38–39, 43
    Mack Alive protests and suspicions sur-
        rounding control of neighborhood prop-
        erty, 67–71, 296nn3–5, 297n10
    and new housing developments and town-
        houses, 296n4
    original black community and prewar migra-
        tion, 44, 290nn1–2
    "Paradise Valley," 44, 47, 48
    and Poletown plant construction, 69–70
    population growth and housing shortage
        (1940s), 44–45, 290n2
    postwar housing boom, 43
    postwar slum clearance, 48–50, 292n17
    prewar residential distribution/population
        density, 44, 290n1
    urban renewal and impact on, 46–50,
        80–81, 291nn8–9, 292n17

and white flight, 45
    Woodward Avenue and East Side/West Side,
        37–38
    See also Dexter neighborhood and Dexter
        Boys; Mack Alive demonstrations; small
        businesses (neighborhood retail stores)
New Bethel Baptist Church, 4, 7
New Detroit Inc., 54
New Student Movement, Detroit chapter,
    293–94n26
Nietzsche, Friedrich, 1
Northwestern High School (West Side), 16

Oakland-Hastings Freeway (Chrysler Freeway),
    47
Old Saint Antoine Street district, 290n1
Osborne High School (northeast Detroit), 16,
    106–7, 137–38

"Paradise Valley" neighborhood, 44, 47, 48
Patterson, Orlando, 286n18
Perry, Carl, 52
Pitts, Grover, 62–63, 64–65
Pittsburgh's urban renewal projects, 15
"Playboys" (gang), 103
Poletown plant (General Motors), 69–70
police, Detroit
    black representation, 36, 294n27
    Dude's fascination with, 96–97
    house raids, 97–99, 102–3, 134–35,
        301n8
    insurance fraud by, 96–97
    and riots of summer 1967, 50–51, 52,
        53–54, 294n27
    and street drug trade, 117–18, 126, 129–30,
        134–35, 144, 233, 238–39, 244, 246–47,
        249–50, 251–52
Polish community, 43
Porter, Kalvin, 57
postwar Detroit, 15, 19, 34–35, 43, 48–50
poverty, 39–40
    abandoned buildings and urban dilapidation,
        39–40
    and divisions within black community, 22,
        64, 67–68, 287n19, 296n3
    and riots of summer 1967, 53
prescription drugs, 115, 300n2
prison system and black population
    discussions within juvenile detention facility,
        10, 158–59, 161–62, 183
    statistics, 158
"punk prison," 175–76, 303n3

Ravitz, Mel, 296n5
redlining polices, 291n4
Renaissance Center, 33, 34–35, 37
"Residential Security Maps," 45, 291n4
"restrictive covenants," 45, 291n5
riots of summer 1967, 1–2, 36, 50–56
   and black-owned small businesses, 50–53,
     55–56
   and businesses owned by nonblacks, 52–53
   and civil rights movement/black nationalist
     politicization, 50–56, 293–94n26
   and Detroit police, 50–51, 52, 53–54,
     294n27
   and drinking club ("blind pig") at corner of
     Twelfth and Clairmount, 50–51
   and Kercheval-Pennsylvania neighborhood,
     50, 51, 53, 55
   legacy of, 54–56
   looting and property destruction, 51–53
   role of poverty/economic hardship, 53
   role of race/race relations, 53–56,
     293nn25–26
River Rouge plant (Ford), 34, 263, 294n31
Rockind, Neil, 180
"Rodney"
   conversations within the detention facility,
     9, 11–13, 25–27, 158–72, 179–80,
     182
   court appearance and charges, 170–72
   on Detroit dope game, 164–65
   and the Dexter Boys, 166–67, 202–3, 206,
     207–8, 212–22, 224, 226–57, 272–84,
     304nn3–4
   and Dexter neighborhood drug trade, 202,
     205–15, 220–22, 227–28, 256–57,
     304n2, 304n4, 305n7
   GED studies, 212
   girlfriend's abortion, 271–72
   gun death/murder, 274–84
   gunshot wound in Jackson, 265–67
   hiding out/laying low at Dearborn motel,
     258–60, 262
   high school experiences, 16
   house on Seven Mile Road, 255–57
   leaving Detroit for Jackson, Michigan,
     263–65
   moral ruminations on drug dealing, 11–13,
     171, 302–3n5
   mother's conversations with author,
     197–201, 203–4
   plans for reclamation of Wadsworth house,
     269–71

   plans for selling drugs in Jackson, 264–65
   pretrial hearing, 267–69
   and shooting at the Goal Post, 257, 259–60,
     262–63, 265, 268–69
   and Wadsworth house (Dexter neighbor-
     hood), 197–99, 203–4, 269–71
   See also Dexter neighborhood
Romulus (Michigan community), 263
"Ruby" (Dude's adopted mother)
   conversations with, 83–94, 102–3, 105–7,
     111–21, 134–38, 299n4
   and death of daughter, Evie, 92–94,
     299n5
   and death of her husband, Marvin, 84, 116
   on the drug dealer called "Jarhead," 116–17,
     135
   and Dude's murder charge/court hearings,
     187
   entry into selling drugs out of houses,
     88–89
   family/early life and travel between Mobile
     and Detroit, 85–88, 298–99n3
   house of, 82–84, 113, 134–35, 301n8
   and imprisoned son, Elvin, 84, 135–36
   prescription drug dealing, 115, 300n2
   reasons for moving away from lower East
     Side, 84–85, 102–3, 105–6, 118
   worries about Dude's release on probation,
     110–15, 121–22, 136–37

Saint Antoine YMCA, 47
schools (Detroit Public Schools), 16–19
   city leadership assuming control ("school-
     takeover law"), 18–19
   exemplary magnet schools, 285n7
   financial problems/budget shortfalls, 17
   performance and graduation rates, 17
   racial makeup, 18, 286n10
   and relationship between African American
     community and city of Detroit, 17–18
   school integration busing policies, 286n10
   and the street drug trade, 17
   and urban renewal/revitalization projects, 18,
     286n11
segregation and Detroit
   prewar lower East Side, 44
   racial makeup of public schools, 18,
     286n10
   suburb/city divide, 19–20, 35–36
Sheffield, Horace, 295n35
Shelley v. Kramer (1948), 291n5
Shrine of the Black Madonna, 4

small businesses (neighborhood retail stores), 40–42, 56–58
  African Americans' exclusion from legitimate retail activity, 42, 49–50, 56–57, 290n9, 294n30, 294n32, 295n33
  and Albanian Americans, 41–42, 234
  Arab Americans, 41, 56, 57, 205–6, 295n35
  banks and discriminatory lending practices, 56–57, 295n33
  black-owned businesses (by late 1960s), 50, 293n19
  black-owned businesses/entrepreneurial activity (late 1940s and early 1950s), 47, 49–50, 292nn12–13
  Chaldean Americans, 4–5, 41, 56, 57, 127
  Coney Island restaurant on Dexter and Providence, 207–8, 213–15, 218–19, 225–57
  and drug trade, 42, 127, 290n9
  ethnic/racial distribution of commercial space in black neighborhoods, 41–42, 56–57, 225, 294n30
  gas stations, 41, 57, 205–6, 295n35
  glass curtains/partitions, 127–28, 213–14, 224–25
  Hastings Street neighborhood, 47, 49–50, 292nn12–13
  Jewish-owned, 52–53
  Kercheval neighborhood, 39, 50, 53, 55
  liquor stores, 4–5, 41, 127
  and "micro-physics" of power, 225, 305n1
  Middle Eastern immigrants, 41, 56–57, 294n31
  and postwar urban renewal programs, 49–50
  and riots of summer 1967, 50–53, 55–56
  and scholarship on African American entrepreneurial activity, 294–95n32
  spatial politics/interior physical configurations, 213–14, 224–26
  as unique public spaces/centers of social tensions, 40–41, 56–58, 74, 128–29, 224–26
  See also Mack Alive demonstrations
sociological divisions within black community
  cultural marginalization, 22–23, 287nn19–20
  poor and middle class, 22, 64, 67–68, 287n19, 296n3
Southeastern High School, 106
spatial tensions
  Coney Island restaurants, 213–14, 224–26, 254–55

and Detroit's racial identity/history, 19–20, 36–37
domestic (residential) spaces/commercial spaces, 82
glass curtains/partitions, 127–28, 213–14, 224–25
and liquor stores, 127–29
maps and cities, 201–2
and "micro-physics" of power, 225, 305n1
neighborhood retail stores, 41, 56–58, 74, 128–29, 213–14, 224–26
and social disenfranchisement, 19–20
suburb/city divide, 19–20, 35–36, 217–18, 252–54
"spots," distinctions between homes and, 81, 101, 102, 117, 299–300n7
St. Clare Episcopal Church, 206
Sterling Heights suburb, 234
suburb/city divide, 19–20, 35–36
  and automobile industry/jobs, 46, 53
  "blockbusting" and white flight to suburbs, 45–46, 291n5
  for Dexter Boys, 217–18, 252–54, 306n4
  and Ecstasy, 306n4
  "edge cities," 35–36
  and spatial tensions, 19–20, 35–36, 217–18, 252–54
  and urban revitalization projects, 37
  and Young's mayoralty, 36
Sugrue, Thomas J., 289n1, 290n2, 291n5
Sweet, Ossian, 291n6

tercentennial committee (Detroit 300 Committee), 33–35, 36–37, 40
Thirty-sixth District Court, 175, 184, 185
Tinsley, Artena, 59–60, 68
Tinsley, Daisy, 88
Tinsley-Talabi, Alberta
  campaign to ban billboards advertising liquor, 296n1
  drawing parallels between crack cocaine and liquor, 298n13
  and Mack Alive, 59–61, 68, 71–73, 296n1, 296n3
  residence in East Side neighborhood, 39, 123

UHURU ("Freedom Now"), 293–94n26
United Auto Workers, 34, 293nn25–26
urban renewal and revitalization projects in Detroit, 15–16, 46–50
  and black-owned small businesses, 49–50

celebrations marking 2001 tercentennial,
      33–35, 36–37, 40
and central business district, 46–47
efforts of 1970s and 1980s, 33
freeway development, 47–48
and housing crisis, 48
housing demolition programs, 80–81,
      118–21, 298n1
and impact of relocation on individuals and
      communities, 49, 292n17
impact on African American
      community/black neighborhoods, 46–50,
      80–81, 291nn8–9, 292n17, 298n1
lower East Side, 47, 48–49
postwar era modernist projects, 15,
      285n3
postwar residential renewal plans (slum
      clearance), 48–50, 292n17
programs of 1940s, 47–50
and public school system, 18, 286n11
recent construction projects, 37, 46–47
"Renaissance Center," 33, 34–35, 37
and "shareholder citizens," 15–16
and suburbs/white suburban population, 37
West Side, 47–48

Venkatesh, Sudhir, 286n16, 287n20
violence. See gun violence
Virginia Park newsletter, 6
visibility/invisibility for young black men, 258,
      260–61

Waldinger, Roger, 294–95n32
Walk to Freedom (1963), 293–94n26
Washington, Forrester, 290nn1–2
Wayne County Community College, 208, 221
Wayne County Jail, 173
Wayne County Juvenile Detention Facility. See
      juvenile detention facility (Wayne County
      Juvenile Detention Facility)
West Central Organization, 293–94n26
West Side
      grassroots civil rights movement, 293–94n26
      impact of freeway development, 47–48
      and Woodward Avenue, 37–38
Wideman, John Edgar, 145
Willow Run assembly plant, 34
Wilson, William Julius, 287n19
Wolfe, Eleanor, 292n17
Woodward Avenue, 37–38
World War II–era Detroit
      black population and residential patterns,
            44, 290n1
      postwar, 15, 19, 34–35, 43, 48–50
      war assembly efforts, 34
wraparound services, 139, 301n7
Wyche, Evelyn, 62–63, 71

Young, Coleman, 36, 37, 54, 70
Young Boys Incorporated (YBI), 20–21, 180, 242
youth home. See juvenile detention facility
      (Wayne County Juvenile Detention
      Facility)